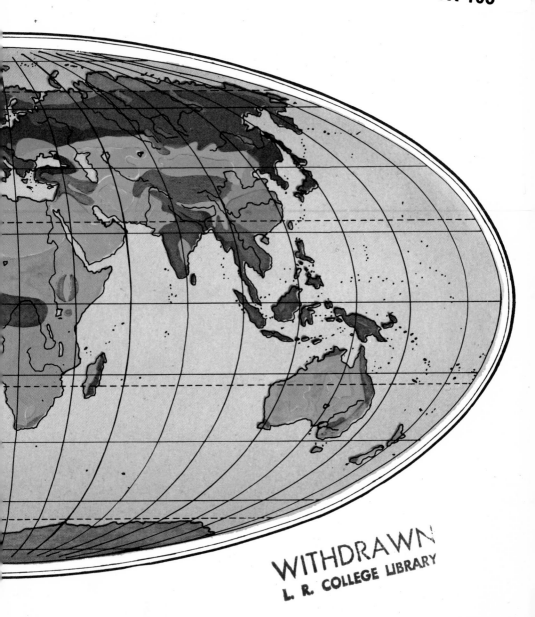

Vegetation, as the sole means of converting solar energy, minerals and moisture into forms sustaining animal life, determines the basic patterns of the natural and the human environment.

The hundreds of distinguishable vegetation types are here compressed into a dozen broad groups, half forest, half composed of lower or sparser plants.

With many detailed exceptions these groups are distributed mainly in zonal belts, as shown on this outline map, and as described in Chapter 4.

THE
ENVIRONMENTAL REVOLUTION

also by Max Nicholson

THE SYSTEM

The Misgovernment of Modern Britain

"What oft was thought but ne'er so well expressed—and then some. . . . His prescriptions include more professionalism and more decentralization. These needs are practically worldwide, but Mr. Nicholson is usefully specific. He is also impassioned, sensible, and drolly realistic."

The New Yorker

"An important book that examines the gray hairs on contemporary England's head."

Publishers' Weekly

"A valid contribution to a continuing debate."

Library Journal

"Nicholson has written a witty, incisive, and devastating attack on the whole English society and power-structure. He has shattered many myths of some of the world's cherished institutions and, at the same time, demolished some of England's dearly held delusions."

The Houston Post

"Something of a surprise; sometimes eccentric, always provocative, and never dull."

The Observer

"Trail-blazing and controversial."

"Brings to it a training in economics and ecology, a lively and idiosyncratic sense of history, a strong and original intellect, a gift for invective and experience in public administration."

The Times (London)

MAX NICHOLSON

THE ENVIRONMENTAL REVOLUTION

A Guide for the New Masters of the World

McGRAW-HILL BOOK COMPANY

NEW YORK   ST. LOUIS   SAN FRANCISCO

DUSSELDORF   MEXICO   PANAMA

333.72
N51e
83492
June 1973

Library of Congress Catalog Card Number: 74-108612

46486

Printed in Great Britain by C. Tinling & Co., Ltd., Prescot, Lancashire

FOREWORD

Awareness of the decisive importance and of the disturbing vulnerability of man's natural environment is bursting upon most alert and public-spirited people. The pride of having reached the moon is cancelled out by the humiliation of having gone so far towards making a slum of our own native planet. Quite suddenly the long struggle of a small minority to secure conservation of nature has been overtaken by a broad wave of awakening mass opinion reacting against the conventional maltreatment and degradation of the environment which man finds he needs as much as any other living creature. Old values, habits of thought and established practices are being challenged all over the world. New studies are being made, fresh conclusions confirmed, and pioneering institutions, laws, programs and policies are being devised in plenty. It is no longer premature to regard all this as adding up to a revolution in human affairs, for which the obvious descriptive label is the term, once so infrequent and now becoming so universal, "environmental".

Chance seems often to determine whether some tangle of problems and actions acquires an accepted identity and a familiar name, giving it an explanatory literature and a secure place in the minds of informed people, or whether it stays shapeless, neglected and unidentified in limbo. Some problems, such as the consequences of epidemic disease, or outbreaks of violence or economic breakdowns brusquely seize a place on everyone's agenda; others are added only through the pertinacity of people who are convinced of their seriousness and insist upon everyone taking notice of them. But others, of equal intrinsic importance, fail to win effective protagonists and smoulder away like a fire under peat, or in a burning tip.

Until very recently the conservation of nature and the natural environment undoubtedly fell within the third group in almost all countries. Lately it has pretty well established a place in the second, and with such newsworthy events as the wreck of the *Torrey Canyon*, the oil leak off Santa Barbara and mass poisoning of fish in the Rhine it is enabled to take full advantage of a surprisingly widespread public anxiety and to gain a foothold in the first class.

Well-worn subjects have long been examined from every standpoint and somehow fitted into a context of common knowledge and a relationship to the issues and alignments around which public affairs revolve. New items on the agenda, however, are greeted with resentment, scepticism or sheer bewilderment. I recall, for instance, soon after Mussolini's March on Rome being asked by a puzzled businessman who were these Frascati who were shaking things up in Italy. Even Fascism once had to be explained.

Revolutions, unfortunately, have a way of overtaking the revolutionaries, defeating their attempts to understand or control what is going on, and baffling or alienating those at the receiving end. If our environmental revolution is to prove less of a shambles than most we must correctly marshal the events and forces leading up to the present situation, evaluate the weaknesses, the mistakes and the progress which has been made, and find a sound and acceptable basis for judging where we go from here. That, roughly is what this book is about.

To me, having by chance been somewhat centrally involved in this environmental revolution, the most exciting part of it is its extraordinary dynamism. As in all the best revolutions this manifestly far outruns all the measurable input of human effort; presumably some deep and powerful current of man's subconscious has been tapped with spectacular results. I feel sure that this evident but unaccountable and mysterious element will result in the environmental revolution having much greater, more enduring and more surprising consequences than can yet be clearly foreseen. It is unwise to judge the capability of a firearm simply by measuring the thickness of its trigger.

Through my involvement at so many points I have had the good fortune to be able to learn a great deal from a great many specialists and generalists in many countries and about many matters. There are perhaps few human activities in which it is so easy to meet dedicated and gifted people ready to share their knowledge and experience freely and talented in communicating its essentials. When I reflect on what this book owes, and what I myself owe to so much help from so many I find it sobering to face the total impossibility of beginning to do justice to such indebtedness, and to question whether I have even put such generously lavished resources to anywhere near as good use as I should have done. At least I would claim that I have tried to do justice to the efforts that have been made, and to ensure that they are effectively followed up. I hope that all who have helped, instructed and informed me in any way will take this expression of gratitude as addressed to them personally. In W. H. Auden's words: "the powers that we create with are not ours."

In the circumstances I will add only a very brief list of specific acknowledgments and thanks. My vision of accompanying the text with groups of pictures which would independently of words unfold something of the story of man and nature and the moulding of landscape could not have been given any substance without the talented and enthusiastic efforts of my colleague in Land Use Consultants, Chris Glaister, who designed the graphics, ably assisted in the case of the end-papers, the Seven Circuits and the jacket design by Anne Colsell.

The mere assembly for selection of so many varied pictures was a heavy task, in which we were generously assisted by Dr F. Vollmar, Secretary-General of the World Wildlife Fund, Mr B. F. Grimes, Peter Wakely and other colleagues at the Nature Conservancy, Fred Packard of the U.S. National Parks Service, Dr J.K.S. St Joseph of Cambridge University and others.

I am indebted to Dr David Daiches for the permission to quote his verse on page 144.

Foreword

Any reader who may be concerned to find minor divergencies in the text from conventional English spelling is invited to refer to The Spelling of English on page 349 for an explanation.

CONTENTS

	Introduction	13
1	The Approach Stated	15
2	Man's Use of the Earth	33
3	The Earth and Its Living Patterns	48
4	Seven Circuits Round the Earth	69
5	The Marks of Man	104
6	The Road to Conservation	132
7	The British Story	141
8	The American Story	162
9	Towards Worldwide Action	188
10	Where We Stand Now	239
11	The Way Ahead	263
	Conclusion	280
	Annex 1 The Vegetation Cover of the Earth	288
	Annex 2 Chart of Human Impacts on the Countryside	308
	Annex 3 Flow Chart of Conservation Processes	336
	Notes on Sources	339
	The Spelling of English	349
	Index	353

A*

ILLUSTRATION SECTIONS

		following page
A	Man's Impact	64
B	The Natural Environment	128
C	The Emergence of Landscape	192
D	The World of Conservation	256

MAPS

Front Endpaper   World Vegetation

Back Endpaper   The Distribution of Man and his impacts on the Environment

CIRCUITS

One   Inverness/Aleutians/Labrador/Ireland

Two   Shannon/Vladivostok/San Francisco/Portugal

Three   Tagus/Himalaya/Hawaii/Mauritania

Four   West Africa/Arabia/Vietnam/Galapagos/Amazon

Five   Lambarene/Aldabra/Java/Rio de Janeiro/South-West Africa

Six   Walvis Bay/Madagascar/South Australia/Valparaiso/Tristan da Cunha

Seven   Cape of Good Hope/Tasmania/Tierra del Fuego/Cape Crozier/South Pole

PICTURE SOURCES

Aerofilms Ltd.	A.10, A.19, A.20, A.22, C.10, C.11
Anpfoto	D.14
Architectural Review	C.14
Aviaphoto	C.16
Bayrischer Flugbinst	C.17
Professor F. Bourlière	B.12
British Museum	A.8
British Museum of Natural History (Maurice Wilson)	A.1, A.2, A.4, A.5
Country Life	C.12, C.15
Director in Aerial Photography, University of Cambridge (photos: J. K. St. Joseph)	A.9, B.6, B.7, C.1, C.2, C.5, C.6, D.3, D.10
Esso Petroleum Co. Ltd.	D.8, D.9
Forestry Commission	D.6
Government Printing Office of the Netherlands	D.15
Eric Hosking	B.8, B.15
International Press Service	A.17
A. F. Kersting	C.13
Musée de l'Homme	A.3
N.A.S.A.	B.1
Nature Conservancy	B.10
Mrs. C. S. Orwin and the Clarendon Press	C.10
Paul Popper	A.13, A.16, D.1
Solarfilma S.F.	B.2
Dr D. Stoddart	B.9
Syndication International	A.18

INTRODUCTION

I⊤ has been aptly said that one thing in the world is invincible—an idea whose time has come. Such an idea, in these days, is the care of man's environment, or, in a word, conservation. Until very lately this idea was present only in a primitive form in the minds of a small and relatively uninfluential minority. Only through opening up by a great diversity of recent work on different relevant aspects have we suddenly emerged at a commanding viewpoint from which we can begin to see conservation in broad perspective, and to appreciate its true significance for man's way ahead.

As nature is man's ancestral home and nurse, and as landscape is his modern mirror, the achievement of a fresh recognition by mankind of the potential for the renewal and for the healing of a sick society through creative intimacy with the natural environment could bring a transformation of the kind and scale which our degenerate and self-disgusted, materialist, power-drunk and sex-crazed civilisation needs. The lesson is plain that without some immensely greater and more enduring inspiration and support than everyday affluence and hollow success any human civilisation must totter. A civilisation which through its own intellectual advances has gone far to cripple supernatural religion as a living force has probably no option but to return in some form to the wilderness from which religion itself sprang.

Already after a few decades the brief authority, prestige and dominance of the man-made wilderness of the great cities is collapsing. At every opportunity for a holiday respite the law-abiding millions flee from megalopolis in a usually vain quest for refreshment from nature in some form—the sea, the mountains, the forests or the snows. At every occasion sanctioned by political differences the lawless try to burn or break down megalopolis in an orgy of senseless destruction. The vote of no confidence in the vainglorious religions of big capitalism and big Marxism is too clear to be any longer denied.

What then remains? Some of the fugitives, in disturbingly increasing numbers, turn to drugs for the escape route and for the transcendental release which neither revealed religion nor the grandiose ostensible alternatives of the affluent or the marxist society can any longer plausibly offer them. But, setting aside all moral considerations, there is evidently no future in a society so spiritually and intellectually insolvent that many of its most sensitive citizens can see no satisfaction for themselves except in chemically induced insensibility.

To have allowed matters to reach this stage before beginning to face the fact that religious and political guides have failed in their stewardship is an appalling revelation of stupidity in the highest circles in every country. Repressive measures against freedom of opinion and speech are widely and justly condemned in nations which themselves are increasingly compelled to resort to police repression of highly objectionable kinds in order to try to dam back the flood of drug-taking, of crimes and misdemeanors, and of racial and sectional demonstrations which are the manifest and inevitable result of their misdirection of human resources, and their wilful failure to heed the many repeated warnings given them by independent men and women of greater foresight and imagination.

It may be that the rot has already gone too far. Human numbers and material demands may be destined hopelessly to outrun the most that ingenuity can now achieve towards restoring the equilibrium through the sensitive and healing use of the natural environment, to enable man to make the great re-adjustment now required of him, from materialism to quality of living, and to fulfilment of the potentialities of each and all. Yet the fact that so many who have plainly lost confidence in the releases offered them by material progress, by religion and even by drugs are turning in ever increasing numbers towards what they see as wilderness in nature must mean something. This is the choice of wildernesses which all must make. The true wilderness evidently has something to offer beyond and above all other satisfactions to many members of today's sick society.

To reflect upon all that has been lost in the course of recent changes in ways of living, to examine the possibilities of making good such losses at least in part, if necessary by substitutes, and to define the requirements for a fresh approach to harmony between man and nature in realistic and practical terms—these are the broad problems which have to be resolved if the great advances in civilisation are not to be offset, and perhaps even undermined and nullified, by a widening gulf between basic human needs and dangerously unnatural and unsatisfying ways of living. Harmony between man and nature is no longer a mystical and abstract but a practical and pressing matter. To demonstrate its scale and character, and to show how it may be successfully tackled, will be the objective of this book.

THE APPROACH STATED

THE environmental revolution, amid which we live, has a double face. It can be seen as a man-made change, sudden and worldwide, in our natural environment. It can equally be regarded in the light of a transformation in our attitude to that environment.

By going so far as he now has towards taking over the earth from nature man has made it inevitable, not only that he should manage nature, but also that he should henceforth learn to manage himself as a part of nature.

This shift of power, and of its corresponding responsibilities has, like others before it, taken almost everyone unawares. It is still common, almost universal, to speak as if man's main environmental problem were to bend nature to his will by the use of bigger and better technology. Few appreciate that our only practical choice is between continuing to permit nature to function unhampered, and adopting an exacting man-nature partnership on quite new lines, using nature's processes and resources so far as possible to serve man's varied needs.

Having rejected the first of these choices we have, whether we know it or not, whether we like it or not, opted for the second. That is the only way we can go from here. The apparent alternative of continuing to live on this planet with our present utter disregard for the limitations and requirements which nature sets for us is simply not a course which can be pursued much longer without disastrous consequences.

Man has emerged from an animal to a human state largely through an age-long, often unspoken, dialogue and a running struggle with his natural environment. That environment cannot be regarded as just an external framework, still less as the mere backdrop of city imaginations. Its pressures and its challenges have become built into man's bodily and emotional make-up.

Unfortunately much of that inheritance has temporarily become rigidly bound in tradition and habit. Just at the time when a great effort of imagination and adjustment is called for, human minds are widely enslaved to influences tending to close them. We have to make a break-through.

It is my intention in this book to present with some detachment, but not without occasional forthright comment, a picture of the emerging relationship between modern man and nature arising from successive human experiences and advances, and from recognition of failures and misdeeds. It cannot be an easy book, since it recognises that all of us are caught up in attitudes and beliefs which are no longer tenable, and which we must find means to unlearn and to replace by a new approach as soon as possible.

Politicians, administrators, economists and journalists are accustomed to using timescales of only a few years, and to dealing with policies and programs on the assumption that events will occur but that people at all levels will remain unchanged. Ecologists and conservationists think in terms of much more extended timescales, often extending over centuries, and the recent telescoping into decades of changes which would formerly have taken centuries does not therefore bewilder them, as it is apt to bewilder the stock products of modern education and training.

Being accustomed to listen less to the words than to the music of evolutionary change, conservationists understand that actions which would never be taken by certain types of institution imbued with a certain mentality will quite readily be taken by such institutions following a change in outlook and values which may appear impossible but has in fact frequently been brought about or matched. We know that this is so, because we have achieved and experienced it, but we nevertheless understand that to many who have not done so, or who are blinkered by other preconceptions, our thoughts and conclusions may appear incomprehensible or wrong-headed. They cannot adapt themselves to changing means towards changing ends within a changing environment.

Such a book as this therefore starts with the handicap of having to surmount large obstacles of attitude and mental equipment in order that readers unfamiliar with its subject and alien to its approach may be able to put themselves in a position to take in and evaluate its message. A Scots teacher in Glasgow, puzzled by apparent stupidity in a class, found its explanation in the discovery that the word "tree" conveyed nothing to a number of the pupils because they had never seen one, or rather never taken any notice of one. At a much higher level of experience and information there are equally fearsome deficiencies of which those who suffer from them are often gaily ignorant.

Even among trained and experienced students of the natural environment the speed and scale of recent advances in knowledge, and of consequential changes in outlook renders the task of keeping abreast extremely exacting. Being exposed to these advances and changes continuously through many channels in many countries I am keenly aware of the handicaps suffered by many whose eyes have had to be more narrowly focussed.

No amount of awareness, however can dispose of the inherent difficulty of bridging the gap. I have done my best to help, but the reader also needs to be constantly on guard against being misled by preconceptions and habits of thought which are now identifiable as barriers to understanding of the problem of man's relation to his environment. It is hoped that the carefully selected and arranged visual sections will help to complement the text in conveying something of the basic approach, and of its relationship to what everybody sees but few begin to understand. Unless we can make the effort to look at nature and at ourselves with new eyes there is no hope for us on this earth.

The way we must go is shown somewhat dimly by the record of man's social evolution and of his impacts on the land, and by the working processes of nature as we are at last learning to know them on a worldwide scale. More concretely, the recent history of man's efforts to conserve natural resources and to ensure wise use of land provides us with a series of empirical demonstrations of methods capable of giving predictable results.

In discussing such matters, however, each of us is limited and biased by his personal tastes, education and experiences.

We sometimes sincerely believe we see "nature", but we merely delude ourselves. When we resolutely cast off and leave behind the identifiable works and impacts of civilisation and attempt serenely to contemplate what we think is virgin wilderness, what we see and feel is still largely something that we have brought with us in our own minds. Our spontaneous attitudes, our conventional assumptions, our blind incapacity to perceive the unsuspected or the mentally inconvenient, our psychological longing for particular kinds of satisfaction, reassurance or compensation, forbid us to see the "true" face of nature. At best we are permitted to half-see it in fragments, blended and colored with a good deal which is not in it, but is injected unconsciously by ourselves and then reflected back to us as if it had some independent existence.

Any presentation of the subject therefore must contain a large subjective element, which will differ widely according to the particular background of the author. If this background is left entirely to the reader's imagination he is liable to be confused or misled, in so far as it differs from his own. To mitigate this tendency, and to enable allowance to be made for inevitable bias, it seems advisable first to outline briefly the personal experiences and outlook underlying this book.

Any acquaintance with naturalists brings out the differences between those who started young and those who took up the pursuit at later stages in life. As William Wordsworth showed in some of his best-known poems, if nature happens to become a dominant preoccupation during early childhood its imprint can prove particularly vivid, moving and enduring throughout life. So it has been in my own case. A Sparrowhawk seizing and making away with a favorite yellow chicken about the age of four, and other such early vivid experiences no doubt prepared the way for a visit on which I was taken at the age of seven to the Bird Gallery of the Natural History Museum in London. There I saw superbly realistic habitat displays of British birds at the nest—Golden Eagles and Green Woodpeckers, Partridges and Common Terns, Chaffinches and Dotterels. I was captivated and carried away by them.

How to find these fascinating creatures in the wild and to learn their secrets became my strongest desire. Without anyone knowledgeable to guide or help me I started to seek them out, and found enough to whet my curiosity further. Gilbert White's *Natural History of Selborne* was given me, and taking it as a model I began to observe and to record in field notes in the same style, although it was a century and a quarter old at the time.

Wherever I went birds were my first interest, but plants, mammals, butterflies and other creatures shared part of the attraction. Scenery too, such as woods, hills, streamsides and above all the sea-coast excited wonder and eagerness for more. The places themselves came to yield keen pleasure, which would be crowned by the sight of a new bird, or of something new about one already met. Movement in utter silence was a perennial thrill, especially on a bicycle along narrow paths through the countryside. Having the chance to explore a wide range of different kinds of country, with always the joy of exploration to offset the pangs of separation from earlier favorite haunts, I necessarily acquired a hunter's or nomad's attitude, ever ready to shift to strange and unknown environments, and to extract from each all that it had to offer me. This tension between passionate attachment and inquisitive non-attachment was a strongly formative influence.

In these early days there was a special magic in visible change—a sudden fall of snow, a swirl of mist, an overnight sheet of white hoarfrost on the grass, the shapes of great clouds passing across with their shadows, the buds and catkins and new foliage of spring and the eagerly expected but ever surprising return of the swallow and the cuckoo. Such signs of the dynamic and dramatic workings of nature were an unfailing counterpoise to taking it for granted, or looking on it as a picture gallery or museum. It was challengingly alive, and it demanded awareness, alertness and skill in its exploration and penetration, for example by moving unheard, and so far as possible unseen, through woodland paths, by picking the best ways over rough or wet terrain, and by divining where particular animals or plants might be found. Its signs had to be mastered, and above all the calls and songs of the birds, so full of information and so unfailingly pleasure-giving.

At this time also the scale of perceived environment and the theaters of action were often very small. A chalkpit or sandpit, a little pond, a gorse thicket or the bend of a stream became a world in themselves, where time stood still, and there was no thought of pressing on elsewhere or scanning the far horizon in search of something fresh. The drive to pass on restlessly from one stimulus to the next hardly existed. A sense of being new to it all, and of passionately wanting to absorb it, to avoid distracting or disturbing it from revealing itself as it was, was paramount. Selectivity was guided by the need to avoid sources of human disturbance and to seek out the most promising and compact theaters in which some fascinating aspect of nature might be found on display.

Essentially this was an escapist activity, to be practised alone, or at most with one or two companions ready to accept the same code of unobtrusiveness for the time being. It was also closely linked with the outdoors, and brought with it no desire to keep animal pets in the house or garden, or to destroy or collect, except for a token collection of birds' eggs, feathers and certain insects, serving mainly as souvenirs of transient experiences. It certainly stimulated a thirst for knowledge, but only in relation to nature as it could be seen in the field.

Not until I was myself an adult did I ever find opportunities of going out with naturalists whose knowledge and skills were greater than my own. This was never felt as a deprivation, since it hardly occurred to me in boyhood that learning about nature could be anything but a first-hand task, the pleasure and rewards of which came from tackling it in the light of personal appreciation. Any suggestion that it ought to be done in any particular way, or that targets and programs should be set by anything other than personal response to the more interesting of the near-by environments, or that it should be linked with school subjects, would not have been at all congenial. Occasional difficulties and frustrations through lack of advice and equipment were a small price to pay for freedom from ham-handed and unperceptive adult interference, conflicting with the more rewarding guidance to be gained directly from nature. A sense of wariness and unwillingness to take on trust anything which could not be satisfyingly demonstrated grew deeper with time, and gradually extended itself from the sphere of nature to human affairs generally.

An exception of great importance, however, was the influence of certain authors whose writings showed them as kindred spirits in their approach to nature. Lines which I came across in poetry had sometimes a peculiar power to express my situation. For example, a poem of Longfellow's in which the dilettante Spanish Count Arnaldos sought by questioning a seasoned mariner to grasp at second-hand the significance of sea-faring, and was dismissed with the telling rejoinder;

> "Wouldst thou", so the helmsman answered,
> "Learn the secrets of the sea?
> Only those who brave its dangers
> Comprehend its mystery!"

After Gilbert White it was above all W. H. Hudson who inspired and moulded my thoughts on nature from the age of twelve for nearly a decade.

Little by little the degree to which human interference had changed habitats away from the natural, depressed some species and multiplied others, and in innumerable ways rendered almost indecipherable in Britain the spontaneous processes and rich manifestations of life undisturbed by mankind, became more and more obtrusive and irksome to me. Such feelings generated a keen desire to come face to face with nature in lands which had not been exposed to the blight of exploitation or settlement. The first serious opportunities to present themselves were on Oxford University expeditions to Greenland and to the Amazonian forest near its northern fringe in British Guiana, or Guyana as it has since become. Here, first on the edge of the ice-cap and then in the ageless unbelievably mature and unending realms of tropical forest trees, it was possible by an effort of the imagination to gain some insight into nature, untouched or almost untouched by man. Or perhaps rather to see the puniness in comparison to nature of the influences of man, as in the long deserted habitations of Erik the Red's Viking settlers recently re-emerged from under the icecap, or the small forest clearings made by passing travellers or timber cutters along the Guyana rivers.

Strongly predisposed as I was in favor of nature as against the assaults and dominance of mankind, it came as a surprise to me to find that once beyond the bounds of past or present human influence something very important was subtly missing. Unsullied nature was no less majestic, fascinating and varied than I had confidently assumed, but it was uncompromisingly impersonal, mindless and somewhat chilling.

Scientifically it offered immense opportunities, and as a theater for adventure and escape from the pressures and distractions of the world it was perfect. But to try to give oneself to it and to become immersed in its atmosphere and its ways was to sacrifice more with a prospect of gaining less than I had expected.

Perhaps, like outer space and the depths of the ocean or of Antarctica, the earth's surviving wildernesses held secrets which could add to the dimensions of the spirit and of the mind. Certainly places could be found where the sheer scale and majesty of mountains or coastline, the power of a great waterfall, or the silence and vastness of a desert commanded surrender and gave a serene ecstasy. But it did not appear that their gifts could be continuously enjoyed and absorbed like those of tamed nature in lands where man had exerted his sway.

It is obvious that nature can be impoverished and mutilated by man, and equally that through talented landscaping, considerate and sympathetic land use and careful management it can be transformed into something more congenial and attractive to many than its primitive state. The ideal of the paradise garden is the extreme example here. Yet to a purist both these types of treatment are in principle equally unpalatable, in that they replace the spontaneous natural community with a transformed substitute, or an artefact.

From the specialist standpoint of an ecologist or an ethologist it may be essential to success to find a study area which has not been tampered with or in any way disturbed. The superiority of wilderness in such situations is self-evident. The needs of those who feel an overwhelming urge to get away from all other human beings and their traces in order to be temporarily undisturbed and relaxed in some solitary spiritual or intellectual adventure are also clear, although it is uncertain how great the future demand for that will be. Meeting a mass demand for undisturbed wilderness would certainly present problems.

In all such instances nature is treated as an inanimate object, a quarry for useful or inspiring material, a springboard for human virtuosity, a stimulus to evoke deeper feelings or to summon up thoughts otherwise inexpressible. But what of the concept of wresting directly out of nature some fundamental grasp of its buried essence? Is it possible to enrich and transmute the stale human world by permeating it with some hitherto latent and wordless wisdom and harmony? Is there something yet to be discovered which, when mastered and interpreted, might supplement and balance what mankind has learnt by other means, and correct stresses and deficiencies which inhibit social evolution? Such a dream had vaguely inspired my early travels to remote wild places. Would nature now reward the dedicated pilgrim by enabling him perhaps in some fuller measure to "comprehend its mystery"? Nature, on close approach, gave no such encouragement, and under other pressures I let pass opportunities of pursuing it further, but the question stays in mind.

On growing up, every person who has earlier become deeply absorbed in any aspect of nature has the dilemma of reconciling it with some mundane career which may either be irrelevant to it, and permit it to be pursued further only in leisure time, or may somehow utilise that bent and experience, but not necessarily in the most satisfying way. Only very recently have ecology and field studies, and activities in conservation and care of wildlife, grown to a point where they create a number of paid posts closely akin to the interests of keen amateur naturalists. Even so, through failure to acquire beforehand the required type of education and training, many of those who would personally be best attuned and most keen are disqualified from such posts.

Largely owing to my study of W. H. Hudson as a master I was equipped at this stage to maintain myself simply by writing about nature. That enabled me to continue with virtually full-time self-directed field work for a period which proved of the utmost value. At this stage also I found that writing about nature was no tiresome chore but in itself a stimulus and a key to greater insights and clarity of appreciation. Nature's close presence even seemed to influence refreshingly the choice and ordering of words, and to offset stale literary conventions. The questions framed by nature were all the better for being deciphered and expressed in exact terms which could be held more readily in the mind's eye, and critically re-examined after further looking. I wrote in quick sucession half-a-dozen books, all on different aspects—*Birds in England* (1926), *How Birds Live* (1927), *The Study of Birds* and the *Report on the British Birds Census of Heronries* (1929), *Gilbert White's Natural History of Selborne* (edited) (1930) and *The Art of Bird-Watching* (1931), besides quite a number of articles and scientific papers.

A choice, however, presented itself to me during this period between such comparatively independent and isolated activity and switching to a new approach. The time proved to be ripe for reshaping the form and character of field ornithological activities in Britain. Largely through chance contacts at Oxford I found myself enrolled in a vigorous group effort which from 1927 onwards took institutional form successively in the Oxford Bird Census, the Edward Grey Institute of Field Ornithology and the British Trust for Ornithology. A comprehensive program for advancement of knowledge and co-ordination of field studies through carefully planned and organised national inquiries now became the order of the day.

With surprisingly little serious friction or counter-drift the new approach prevailed during the 1930's, but it involved a great deal of committee work, drafting, applications for grants, editing of reports and other occupations which were as new and as little congenial to me as to most of the others. A great stride forward was achieved through a new winning combination of full-time professionals and keen organised amateurs. There was however a price to be paid, above all by me, and that price was increasing estrangement and remoteness from the intimate and dedicated relation to nature enjoyed during earlier years.

Time was now denied me to pursue rewarding lines of field study long enough to continue as an effective contributor to the sum of ornithological knowledge. Forty years ago I regarded such projects as ornithological transects of the North Atlantic as a means of filling in otherwise empty and boring interludes on the way to more intensive field work in Greenland or in South America. Gradually such opportunities became the best available, as I was thrust back into the role, to me much less rewarding, of an occasional birdwatcher. The one partial compensation was a growth of opportunities for travel, even though the resulting glimpses were fleeting and frustrating.

During World War II it was often a case of snatching opportunities for seeking out some of the local birds while grounded on some airfield in Labrador, Newfoundland or North Africa, or in some odd half-hour break at Cairo, Quebec, Yalta or Potsdam. Such episodes were precious and eagerly pursued, but the whole quality of the experience of nature was inevitably of a lower order than before. Yet it was this kind of experience that so many new recruits to the naturalist ranks were so keenly enjoying, and it was not to be despised. As a foil to other duties it brought refreshment and in some measure revived neglected faculties.

Partly through more frequent long-distance air travel at lesser altitudes than normal the broad zones of desert and forest, and the larger landforms now presented to me a challenge to interpretation distinct from the more intimate study areas of earlier days. The personal influence in the field of such great synoptic ecologists as A. G. Tansley and W. H. Pearsall later reinforced this shift of interest from the micro to the macro scale. Mountains and moorlands, forests, and wetlands came to loom larger in my mind's eye than clusters of individual territories of small birds, or detailed scrutiny of a few tens of acres.

In this there was loss as well as gain, but as a basis for more awareness of international problems and responsibilities, and for the comparative review of issues of conservation management and administration, such a shift of viewpoint had merits. It demonstrated the long-term and

gross effects of varying local factors and trends, and the differing significance of apparently similar habitats in different settings and contexts.
It compelled reconciliation between the highly personal experience of
nature encountered at leisure in compact areas and the impersonal
message of vast natural communities and habitats seen from a height
as realms of living creatures. This new strategic insight was no less valid
or less essential to interpreting nature than the earlier tactical insights.
It was complementary.

The ending of World War II, instead of fulfilling my hopes of being
able to revert, at least for some periods, to the pursuit of bird studies
in the field, confronted me with urgent challenges to harness my
experience and energies for the firm construction of institutional props
to strengthen and broaden the still narrow and precarious base of the
natural history and conservation movements. First as postwar chairman
of the British Trust for Ornithology, it fell to my lot to build up an
efficient organisation for ensuring the future expansion of field ornithology in Britain on scientific and co-operative lines, making full
provision for diversity and decentralisation throughout the land, and
enabling the growing corps of professionals to work in harmony with
the amateurs by a realistic division of function. The bringing on of a
new generation, and of recent senior recruits, to share in these responsibilities was an important part of the task. The need for it was tragically
underlined when, as a result of a succession of deaths among ornithological leaders, I had also to take over and reconstitute a directing
editorial team for *British Birds*, the monthly journal round which so
much of the new movement in field ornithology in Britain had been
developed.

In terms of ornithology as a separate world this was to prove for me
a culminating phase. The new approach here could now continue its
impetus without much difficulty, while the urgent and pitiful demands
of long-neglected nature conservation claimed priority. It was initially
through being drafted, as World War II ended, onto the official Wild
Life Conservation Special Committee which was to plan the Nature
Conservancy that I became irrevocably involved in these exacting and
often agonising activities. Part of the work of this Committee, so
admirably manned with gifted and far-seeing ecologists, was to make
field visits to sites which might require scientific conservation, and to
find out what was still on them and what needed to be done to safeguard their future. Although twenty years earlier, while running the
Oxford Bird Census, I had promoted sporadic concerted efforts by
entomologists, animal ecologists, botanists and others in aid of the
ornithological program, the initiative had been premature. It was only

now that naturalists from different specialisms found themselves compelled together to examine specific areas in the round and to try to agree what to do about them. The discipline was salutary, and the influence of such a profound intelligence and far-reaching sympathy as A. G. Tansley's brought home the parochialism and narrowness of most individual and even corporate concern with nature.

We could not see or understand nature, still less begin to conserve nature, without mastering these petty limitations, and learning at least to be sympathetically acquainted with many aspects and interests other than our own. In practice this often meant setting aside the pursuit of problems which were of keenest personal interest, and which exercised highly trained faculties, in order to become a somewhat clumsy and fumbling learner in neighboring fields. Humility and realism were thrust upon us. It was sometimes a trial and a frustration, but it was essential if we were to face nature with an outlook sufficiently broad and deep to be even potentially capable of reaching towards harmony between nature and man, and meanwhile of preventing the wholesale destruction of man's natural inheritance. To many simple-minded people the problem was merely one of harassing and defeating successive interferences and designs for destruction. Given success here the rest would take care of itself. Others naïvely assumed that existing ecologists, once entrusted with the care of some natural area, would instantly receive from on high the necessary inspiration to see and do exactly what was required.

The countless activities in these fields which the 1950's and 1960's brought to us who were concerned with them are outlined in a later chapter. On a personal plane, and keeping to the story of challenge and response in terms of nature itself, an entirely new perspective now emerged for me. It was one thing to pass silently and slowly alone through some quiet reedbed or glade with field-glasses and notebook, finding out what went on among a selected few of its more conspicuous inhabitants. It was quite another proposition to go in with a diverse team of specialists to some large natural area and to assess the total ecological situation and trends, to diagnose past or current deviations from ecological health, and form a collective view on a possible course of intervention, or on the merits and demerits of non-intervention as a prescription for future management. The very word management as applied to nature was strange and unpalatable, smacking of a contradiction in terms. But the ecologically crippled and maimed communities of plants and animals which confronted us on many even of the best surviving areas for nature conservation in Britain left room for no honest alternative, if the best possible was to be done for the future. We

25

desired a paradise to care for, but what we found called rather for the improvisation of a field hospital.

On many of the problems which arose I have written fully in the Annual Reports of the Nature Conservancy up to 1964, and in *Britain's Nature Reserves*. Comparison of these with our group conclusions beforehand in the Wild Life Special Committee's Report (published as Cmd 7122 in 1947) reveals plainly the influence of growing practical experience upon the clearly formulated and, as it proved, remarkably far-seeing ecological and administrative approach with which we had started the task. My role in these years was rather as an eager interpreter and executant of the ideas and vision of others than as a shaper of fundamental aims.

For the current purpose the essential point appears to be that the task of mobilising and directing the first major effort towards conscious and continuous science-based management of a wide variety of natural areas happened to fall to one whose outlook had been shaped first by a drive towards identification with nature as against the world of man, and later by a series of experiences of human social and economic problems at the levels both of research and of large scale administration. Such an unusual blending of backgrounds was largely responsible for the fact that the Nature Conservancy grew up with a deep and all-pervading commitment to the fuller understanding and more sympathetic conservation of nature as a professional task. At the same time, despite being an official organisation, it was ready and equipped to take the initiative, and wherever necessary to enter the fray. It was thus by no means disposed to accept a role second to any where the effective fulfilment and vindication of its responsibilities for the future were at stake. Humility was called for in face of the unsolved problems of ecology, but not in face of the pretensions of an ill-trained bureaucracy. If a project which had not been correctly considered by a sponsoring government department came to public inquiry the faults were openly stated and appropriate criticisms made. To some observers this blend looked odd and even shocking, but it worked in practice, and it has greatly influenced the diagnosis and ideas of the nature and future of conservation presented in this book. He who wills the end must will the means. The development of the means in itself serves as a check upon and a spelling out of the end, and of all its implications. It is pointless to express aspirations and to make demands implying that conservation should be accorded the highest priority in human affairs without being able to show that the task is administratively practicable and politically sustainable within the general context of human needs and ways of life.

To demonstrate how a new fundamental ecological approach could be made effective through a concrete program and technique of conservation, and how it could establish a firm place in one country's institutions and way of life was the main task of the 1950's. It involved not merely the rapid build-up of the Nature Conservancy, but the redeployment and transformation of an initially feeble and divided British voluntary movement into a strong concerted and confident effort through many channels. All this, from a world standpoint, had been left disastrously late.

With ever-increasing urgency the threat to nature in the recently more active regions of development all over the world demanded a practical response. In many of these countries appreciation of the dangers and a desire to do anything about them were confined to the barest handful of men and women, without funds, organisation, manpower or experience. Many of them did wonders within these limits, but the results were pitifully insufficient. It grew more and more indefensible to devote so much effort to conservation in a country with so little of the truly primitive left to conserve and with such a relative abundance of resources for the task, when such immense and irreversible setbacks to the primitive were occurring in so many other parts of the earth.

The first step was to consolidate the complex of conservation bodies in Britain, to harmonise their efforts and to draw in as many lively recruits as possible to safeguard the foreseeable future. As this stage was adequately achieved in the early sixties a series of new tasks presented themselves.

On a worldwide basis it was essential first to take the measure of the intricate and fast-moving new problems of nature conservation, and of the strengths and weaknesses of the resources for tackling them. Almost simultaneously emergency steps had to be taken to improve and systematise the gathering of reliable up-to-date information about specific problems demanding action, to create a more efficient organisation for raising funds and routing them to where they were most needed, and at the same time to feed more and better news about the struggle to general worldwide media of communication.

Simultaneously a new large effort was demanded in Britain to break down the barriers between different interests in what came to be conveniently lumped together as "the countryside", and to bring together a far more broadly based, tolerant and constructive alliance able to approach these great problems with greater strength, confidence and capabilities for practical achievement on acceptable lines. The care and use of the natural environment as a whole emerged as a

27

first-class national interest, embracing but far transcending nature conservation, which so few years before had itself loomed so large as a challenge to effort. The demands of this new and even broader approach led beyond conservation into the neglected fields of large-scale landscape improvement and land use. The want of imagination, of information and of the appropriate organisation to call these functions into full activity now emerged as the key problem to be solved if progress was to be made towards an environmentally literate and responsible society.

While following along that path at home my simultaneous efforts internationally became focussed, largely by chance, on responding to a challenge which, although highly inconvenient, appeared equally irresistible. The crippled and fragmented state of biology, the feebleness of ecology, and the all but universal failure of biologists to recognise the need for conservation and to do something about it had long ranked among the greatest obstacles to getting conservation taken seriously, especially in governmental quarters in many parts of the world. When the International Geophysical Year goaded a number of biologists into some compensatory action, and when it proved that this could only take the form of a basically ecological world program, I could not refuse the request to undertake the task of building into it a suitable conservation element by becoming convener of the section for conservation of terrestrial communities in the International Biological Program.

This challenge was the more compelling since it was becoming clear that the dawn of the computer age and the new potential for storing, retrieving and analysing very large amounts of varied international data offered a tool for breaking out of narrowly bounded horizons within which ecology had hitherto become accustomed to try to function. Such a new tool would allow ecology to fulfil its true universal and open-ended role. Seeing this early, and equipped with the necessary experience of large-scale organisation, I felt bound, despite the miserable inadequacy of available resources, to try to seize the opportunity for opening this broader road to the development of ecological science and its application in conservation and land use.

Whether that effort will succeed it is still too early to say, but it is already well launched and is gathering a promising momentum. If it does succeed science may well gain as commanding a position in the further evolution of land use and land management as it has recently acquired in relation to agriculture and medicine. These steps to equip the relevant sciences with the apparatus, the techniques, the communications and not least the confidence and understanding to make an enlightened scientific attitude prevail in decisions affecting the use and care of land hold a potential which can scarcely be over-estimated. But will it be realised, and will it be properly used? These are still open questions.

Whatever may be the answers, that is where I now stand. The diverse experiences here briefly outlined provide the foundations for the views expressed in this book. Not many people can have undergone so many different transformations of role in relation to nature, beginning from a solitary unguided early personal passion, and passing through individual and organised field studies, administration of voluntary efforts, writing and editing on the subject, and serving on formative official and unofficial investigating bodies. Then, as a chief executive and co-ordinator of a large-scale official program, charged with devising techniques and plans of management and of far-ranging expansion of research. Finally, as an organiser and co-ordinator of a world-wide international program, as a pioneer of liaison with many related but formerly uninterested or hostile groups at national level, and as a promoter of fresh inter-professional effort extending through land use to landscaping and resource planning. It seems unnecessary here to enlarge upon other experience, especially in government and in the social sciences, which has only indirectly contributed to the formation of the views expressed in this book. Whether such an experience brings release from sectional bias, and whether it forms a story of progress or of degeneration, are matters which the reader can best judge. Given a free choice I would in many ways have preferred to continue where I began, but a man is not free in a world so cluttered with arrears of unfinished business the cost of further neglecting which is so plainly intolerable. To live during the technological revolution and the population explosion is to be a conscript, forced to sweep the streets of a slum civilisation.

Many of those who now and in future turn towards nature will find themselves inevitably absorbing a great deal of highly processed information and impressions from others. Try as they will a genuinely first-hand experience will rarely be attainable. Much will be spoon-fed to them, whether they like it or not, and many incidents which formed an everyday part of the lives of their forerunners will become unknown or forgotten among them. It is useless to seek to turn the clock back, or to neglect providing the facilities which our times make possible to offer new kinds of experience, even though those who have known older kinds may suspect that the change may be at least sometimes or partly for the worse. Not only will those who in future turn to nature find different experiences from their fore-runners; they will themselves bring to it quite new attitudes and perceptions, the evolution of which they may find it hard to understand. For example, no one who has looked closely at the moon, even by proxy, will ever again see the earth with the same eyes as before. No one who has been initiated in the study of biological productivity will later fail to perceive in natural communities something of the busy dynamism which they clothe. On the other hand no one who has learnt about nature almost entirely in a school class can ever regard it with a personal wonder and affection similar to that acquired from growing up with it in the woods and fields.

That is why I have prefaced the following review of problems and challenges by a personal account of the shaping of my individual standpoint in special conditions which are not widely shared and can probably never recur.

On the basis of these varied experiences it seems to me that the time has come to seek a new approach, more comprehensive, more closely linked to known facts, better integrated and above all more definitely aimed at promoting fuller harmony between man and nature.

In its human aspect such an approach involves working over the known stages of social evolution from the animal to the human plane of man's existence, and reviewing at each stage the growth of awareness of nature, the type and scale of relations implied between man and nature, and the kinds and results of man's impacts upon nature, first unconscious and later increasingly realised and deliberate.

In its natural aspect it involves a fresh look at ecology, the study of living organisms in relation to their environment and to one another, and biogeography, which deals with the distribution of all forms of life on the earth, in order to find a sufficiently simple and true working basis for understanding not only the wealth of nature but the conditions of its healthy continuance as a functioning system, in which man himself is included.

In both the human and the natural aspects very recent advances in knowledge, and above all in the interpretation and analysis of knowledge, make possible the proposal of new lines of synoptic treatment and new stages of synthesis which would have been unattainable even a few years ago. Nevertheless, the very newness of much of this information and appraisal makes any attempt at this early stage to handle it on a comprehensive global scale run the risk of proving over-ambitious. This book can at best claim to be a very rough provisional sketch to help in defining and to stimulate the elaboration of a more considered and detailed system at the next stage.

A valid new approach ought to fulfil at least four conditions. It must be based on a sound appreciation of future intellectual requirements, and of the shortcomings of existing approaches in relation to these. It must be capable of sorting out, within existing approaches, the obsolete or faulty elements, which need to be utterly discarded and unlearnt, from the sound elements of enduring value which need to be restated and reintegrated. It must be able to formulate the main new elements to be blended with those retained from earlier approaches, and to show how and where they should be injected, in order to make the new approach comprehensible and viable. And finally it must not hesitate to offer the necessary destructive as well as constructive criticism, in order to carry the point that drastic change is needed, that it is needed now, and that it should be on the general lines indicated. I hasten to add my apologies to the reader that the chapters which follow fail in so many ways fully to live up to this exacting specification.

As a very rough initial guide the reader may care to have in mind the following clues to the difference between the approach here offered and its predecessors. In its human aspect it seeks to supersede classical and theological Western assumptions about man and to substitute an interpretation derived from present knowledge of social evolution of the various stocks and cultures and the traceable steps by which what we term civilisation has been achieved, using archaeological, anthropological and historical sources in a freer blend.

In its natural aspect, in relation to life on the earth, it makes use of what have been termed the genetic approach based on causal environmental factors such as geology and climate, the landscape approach based on observable units sharing common factors such as types of soil or vegetation, and the newer parametric approach based upon selecting, mapping and measuring a selected range of attributes using multi-factorial analysis as a tool for correlating the characteristics and potential of an infinite number of sites. Above the plane of inventory-making, modern ecological techniques such as measurement of biomass and of biological productivity (primary in respect of vegetation and secondary in respect of animal population), allow us to begin thinking in terms of models and systems analysis for natural processes. Since this is not a technical work I confine myself here to lightly sketching in this natural aspect. Beyond indicating that it exists and what its relevance may be the emphasis is chiefly upon assisting the reader to appreciate and develop what may be termed the ecological eye.

On such a summary basis the main detailed task of the book is to spell out the evolution and developing practice of the two distinct but closely linked and converging types of human conscious intervention in the environment. The first, which may be called landscape and land use, is concerned with visual, spatial and physical aspects expressed in planning, design and management of the land generally, as well as of particular sites. The second, which may be called conservation (see

31

definitions on pp. 396–7) is concerned with human restraint in utilising natural or semi-natural areas and with the methods of so managing or rehabilitating land as to permit beneficial natural processes to operate to the fullest extent compatible with whatever justifiable human demands may need to be satisfied on it.

The visual sections and the maps forming the end-papers are designed to assist the reader in getting the message.

In the latter part of the book will be found some discussion of the implications and comment on controversial issues, and an attempt to put forward some ideas concerning where we go from here. While every effort has been made to keep the book intelligible to readers who lack previous knowledge of the subject it is assumed that any who are seriously interested in following it up will also read some appropriate works among those cited in the note on sources. Given a field so wide, so complex and so much affected by fast-moving advances in knowledge, and rapid, often adverse developments on the ground, no one book can do more than help to focus and interpret much that is more fully treated in others, and in many journals and papers of a more specialised character.

MAN'S USE OF THE EARTH

MAN'S impact on his environment goes back far beyond the beginning of history. As human numbers increased, people colonised new lands so that a larger and larger area was affected. Before reviewing the earth, its vegetation and its animal life, it is important to consider the emergence and growth of human demands and impacts. It is relevant also to indicate something of the evolution of beliefs, attitudes, policies and practices arising from those demands and impacts, from as far back as our knowledge extends to the present time. Without such historical background, however sketchy, the complex environmental problems now facing us cannot be understood.

Recent discoveries have produced significant evidence of a very long period of co-existence and competition between rival species of early hominid, ending only relatively recently in the elimination of all except the ruthless and cunning form *Homo sapiens*, to which the author and his readers belong. This knockout victory over his simpler cousins left all the other species on the planet defenceless in face of the most formidable breed of the most formidable animal ever to tread the earth.

According to present knowledge man's earliest ancestors were forest-dwellers whose evolution gradually led them out into the savanna and the open plains. With this change of habitat would be associated some change of diet, since food-gathering would no longer be confined to wild fruits and vegetable sources, while dead meat, fishes and large insects would be picked up often enough to substitute an omnivorous for a vegetarian pattern. Such a more diversified, opportunist existence would lend enhanced survival value to cunning, learning and mobility, and would inevitably lead to conflicts with other scavenging and eventually predatory animals with rival claims to prey. Thus killing and being killed or injured would become a normal contingency of living, with all the far-reaching evolutionary consequences involved—physical, psychological and social.

Starting probably with crudely concerted drives by families or small tribes working together, the threshold of an identifiable hunting pattern would eventually be crossed. Use of convenient topography such as

B

precipices, torrents and morasses would lead to the contrivance of rich harvests of game, which however could not be too often repeated at the same spot without depletion of stocks or adoption of successful evasive expedients by the quarry. Intermittent hunger and primitive mental processes would thus lead naturally to the adoption of such artefacts as stone tools or weapons, the artificial construction of such aids to hunting as stone barriers or dug pitfalls, and the improvement of cave or other troglodyte shelters, supplemented by rough structures made with branches, leaves and treestumps, to serve as more secure resting-places and bases in otherwise open country.

Throughout such protracted early stages of evolution the natural environment would continue virtually unaffected by human influences. On the other hand the influence of that environment on early man would be immense. It would amount to the direct opposite of the situation today, in terms of conscious experience. Man would feel himself not the lord of creation but its naked slave and butt. The shift, however gradual, from a close perpetually covered forest habitat to the open plains; the accompanying change from a vegetarian to an omnivorous diet; the resulting compulsion to participate in the game of killing and being killed; the enhanced pressures and opportunities for exploiting artefacts and for developing group mobility over distances; the need for seeking or making cover and shelter rather than being able to take it for granted—all these would demand a rapid physical, psychological and social evolution, without which the breakthrough away from the dark forest would be doomed to eventual failure.

While numbers remained small and localised early pressures through food gathering and primitive hunting and fishing can have made no appreciable impact on the environment. The emergence of added demands for clothing, shelter and tools appears significant only as the first clear indication of the eventually insatiable demands which man was destined to make upon natural resources.

Early gathering of food and of materials for clothing, shelter and eventually tool-making put a survival value on capacities for observation, identification, testing and experiment, memory of sites and routes, awareness of ecosystems and of seasons, exploration and powers to communicate and co-operate, all ante-dating coherent speech and of course reading and writing. Outstanding significance must be accorded to the emergence of capabilities, independent of words, for recognising and relating broad visible configurations of stars, of weather and of vegetation. Such word-free perceptions of recurrent or related forms are among the springs of scientific discovery and of aesthetic creation to this day. Unfortunately the inevitable near-monopoly of cultural trans-

34

mission acquired by those who write has enabled them greatly to exaggerate and distort the creative role of writing in social evolution, and to depreciate the resources of knowledge, perception and wisdom developed by man long before writing was invented.

At present, unfortunately, our knowledge of our remote ancestors, although lately much improved by the splendid efforts of such investigators as the Leakeys in East Africa, is inevitably limited to handfuls of tangible remains which tell us next to nothing about their aspirations, emotions and mental equipment. From such far later relics as the talented cave pictures of Altamira, Lascaux and the Saharan crags we obtain some insight into the profound emotional bond between hunters and hunted, and the insatiable yearnings which lent motive force to the evolution of primitive religion and art. It was again the natural environment which afforded the stimulus and the subject-matter for these transcendental emotions, long before the human figure and human activities or ideas emerged as a rival area of interest.

Hunting in particular took men into the wilderness, and exposed them to the wonders, mysteries and dreads of the closed forest from which they had originally broken out. The uncertainty and arbitrariness of its yield aroused a vivid sense of good and bad fortune, and of the possibility of supernatural powers swaying it, perhaps arbitrarily or perhaps in vindication of a sense of guilt or righteousness becoming uncomfortably perceptible in the consciousness of the early human society. From storms and natural catastrophes, sacred beasts, trees, groves and mountains, and tabus linked with hunting and exploration, it was an easy step to imagine quasi-human or godlike beings lurking invisibly in the background. Thus may have been initiated the transference of faith and reverence from the natural to the specifically human realms of religion and philosophy.

Even when man became capable of leaving some mark on his environment that mark long remained insignificant, owing to the fewness of his numbers, his localised distribution and the feebleness of his technology. Considering the impressive traces imprinted by fairly modest concentrations of elephants and hippopotamuses on their haunts in Africa, and the widespread and drastic mark left on many parts of Britain even by rabbits (before myxomatosis hit them) the impact of man upon nature must for many thousands of years have appeared insignificant even among biotic influences. Incapable of colonising the earth's major deserts, ice-caps, mountain ranges, seas or unbroken forests, early men were largely confined to open plains, steppes and savannas and to river banks, accessible coastlines of seas and lakes, and certain types of wetland and valley. Such habitats were in any case liable from time to time to be much more drastically changed by natural disasters such as floods, earth movements and marine transgression than by man. Indeed it is partly owing to this circumstance that the petty traces left behind by early man have been preserved under covering deposits and can be dated by modern science. As we have lately become aware, there was a significant coincidence in time between some of the more dramatic geomorphological and climatic changes of geologically recent ages and certain vital stages in man's prehistoric evolution and distribution.

Multiplier effects sufficient to begin affecting ecosystems were first developed by men with the deliberate use of fire as a means of clearing forests.

With the attainment of capacity to use and to create fire the mischief-making capability of the species, and its tendency to embark upon the use of destructive instruments without understanding the necessary restraints, became manifest.

Fire brought three kinds of effect which were quite new in comparison with earlier impacts on the natural environment with the exception of major sudden natural catastrophes such as earthquakes and volcanic eruptions. It was, at least in some cases, widespread, affecting sizeable areas of forest or grassland. It was inherently a repetitive process, able to hit the same areas at fairly frequent intervals. It was also highly selective, exterminating locally some species and communities while indirectly encouraging others gifted with rapid powers of recovery or an inbuilt fire resistance.

For these and other reasons command and use of fire must be rated as the first advance in human technology which struck the natural environment hard wherever it was practised. It remains to this day the only case in which the capacity of modern man to inflict large-scale damage upon the natural environment is matched by that of pre-technical man. It was however mainly confined to tropical, sub-tropical and temperate forests and grasslands, excluding humid forests but including certain wetlands. Deserts and semi-deserts, what we used to call rainforests, most mountain ranges, most boreal and subarctic forests, tundra and many less widespread habitats remained relatively immune.

While no doubt to some extent fire was employed as a tool for assisting hunting success this could not be repeated often. The main incentive for its use was as a rapid means of clearing forest and stimulating growth of plants suitable for grazing and browsing. It was therefore a favorite tool, first of man as pastoralist and then of man as agriculturalist. It acquired significance largely with the discovery and advance of

36

techniques for domesticating livestock, together with animals valuable in managing them, notably the dog and the horse, followed by the development of methods of growing and improving crops of food plants and raw materials.

Activity in finding, identifying and testing wild species for such purposes must have been prolonged and intense, as is shown by the very high proportion of all currently exploited species which were already familiar and widely used in neolithic times, more than 7,000 years ago. The great value of these discoveries was that they opened potentialities for massive quantitative increases in the supply of food and raw materials for mankind, and thus for a multiplication of human numbers and division of labour. They also, however increased human energy requirements beyond the capacity of aggregate muscle-power, and thus demanded a build up of draught and transport animals, and of systems of irrigation and waterpower.

The stage was accordingly set for a rise of concentrations of human population involving for the first time a substantial take-over of land from natural to artificial forms of productive use. We know that this takeover began in such areas as the Anatolian uplands, with the adjoining Fertile Crescent of south-west Asia, parts of the great river valleys of the Far East, the lower Nile Valley and later in parts of Central and western South America. It soon gave rise to very extensive modification of the natural environment.

Important as were the direct repercussions of these advances their indirect repercussions were equally so. The need for tending flocks, and still more for growing crops demanded a more highly organised and also often a permanently settled pattern of living. Although in areas of precarious climatic suitability nomadism maintained itself, as it still does, wherever practicable settlement was preferred.

This stage of human existence in settled communities vastly altered the relationship between man and the natural environment. First it created a more or less continuously occupied site, or cluster of sites, on which arose structures for shelter and living, middens of refuse such as shells and bones, crude workplaces and primitive latrines, and stockades or other peripheral barriers against animal or human raiders. Such sites formed the first nuclei for the growth and spread of pollution, disease and erosion, and the first regular targets for the incipient art of warfare, which itself has so greatly contributed to injuring the natural environment, and to distracting human effort from the task of growing in harmony with it.

Around such sites, and among them, were created herds of domestic animals and plots sown with primitive crops of useful plants, involving

37

the disturbance or replacement of natural ecosystems by modified or impoverished plant and animal communities. Elimination of dangerous animals, clearance of forest, and removal or partial treatment of obstacles to movement extended the radius of human impact. From the earliest days an assured source of potable water was essential to a settlement. The need to cope with fluctuations of drought and flood, and to secure convenience of availability and transport must not only have led to much primitive consideration and argument regarding site selection, but also have triggered off a good deal of inventive effort. Man's perennial need for water, and the perennial mystery of water's ways, must be assumed to have been one of the most important focal areas of the application of early man's newfound mental powers. It also provided, as we now know, a main basis for the subsequent rapid and intensive development towards cities and organised states associated with the hydraulic civilisations.

Settlement and the development of a primitive economy dictated a new pattern of distribution of human population in terms of early technology. Gradual increases were easiest and best assured either in the areas of origin of wild plants cultivated for food, or in areas of good rainfall and favorable opportunities for clearance and tillage. As the most suitable food plants became better disseminated, and methods of husbandry better understood, it became apparent that the valleys of certain great rivers such as the Nile, Tigris and Euphrates, and the Indus could sustain relatively large populations given sufficient knowledge of their seasonal water regimes, and a capacity to divert part of the flood for irrigating crops. The necessary calculations, techniques and regulations gave rise more than five thousand years ago to the arts and sciences of writing, of mathematics, of engineering and construction and of administration, which grew up together in Mesopotamia, the Nile Valley, the Indus Valley and along the Yellow River in China. Sustenance and government of mass populations had arrived.

One of the first problems confronting the early river civilisations was management of the environment. Our knowledge of how they fared at it is scanty, but they undoubtedly made serious mistakes, although apparently not so grave as in themselves to undermine the communities concerned. Of their areas of operation the Nile and the Yellow River continue to perform similar roles for populations not even now sufficiently richer or denser to contrast unduly with results achieved in very early times. Only, perhaps, in Mesopotamia are there indications that erosion and other misuse of the land may have contributed towards rendering beneficial use of certain community sites impossible. Not so much directly as by encouraging excess growth and concentration of population over wide surrounding areas, which became deforested, overgrazed or overcropped and eroded, did the new cities and states become an instrument for severely degrading their natural environment.

As settled communities developed and reached out their claims to land use it became inevitable that conflicts between them should also develop, becoming less sporadic or random and more chronic, violent, tense and systematic. In this situation embryonic states of warfare must quickly have led to three revolutionary new requirements; for looking ahead beyond the immediate present, for a process of rapid and effective decision-making on behalf of the community; and for securing authoritative personal leadership to carry out decisions and to safeguard the interests and survival of the community in emergency.

Reinforced and underpinned by the economic potential of pastoralism, agriculture and the winning of minerals, this early political evolution must be regarded as a moment of breakthrough from the situation of man as essentially one among the animals benefiting from the natural ecosystems, to his present role of dominating, exploiting and where necessary replacing them. It had by this time become possible to undertake purposeful collective action on a locally significant scale to modify the environment. Such grand examples as the Pyramids, Stonehenge, Easter Island and others show how much could be achieved by the skilful and ruthless concentration of manpower. No doubt many smaller demonstrations of this were undertaken with less enduring results in earlier periods. The sheer bigness and uninhibited ambition of such megalithic exercises suggest a tremendous emotional drive to repudiate the tradition of man's helpless subordination to nature, and to substitute a crude full-blooded and enduring demonstration of human superiority and power.

This propaganda was confronted with two immense obstacles—the inconvenient and undeniable fact that even the most powerful men must die, and the overriding and awesome destructive forces of nature exhibited in great storms, floods, volcanic eruptions, landslides, and earthquakes, beyond the powers of men to anticipate or to counter. It was doubtless the need for rationalising and ritualising these contradictions to man's mounting self-confidence which fostered the growth of religion, and the emergence of priesthoods. With these early history, medicine, mathematics, astronomy and magic were often intimately connected.

Through the conception of invisible gods, to whom man stood in a remote and precarious relation, it became possible to explain away the apparent and true natural limitations upon man's powers over

39

nature, and to substitute for the painful man/nature dialogue a new triangular communication between man, god and nature, in which priests and leaders with priestly functions exercised a mediating role.

Another equally serious indirect effect of the rise of cities was their role in promoting warfare to higher levels of destructiveness, partly by internecine quarrels but perhaps more by the tempting target which they offered to raiding troops and hosts. For the growth of larger settlements had created the beginnings of the vast contrasts and inequalities which have ever since characterised the varying levels of human development, and which have enabled favored groups and peoples to enjoy conspicuously higher standards of life, greater power and more mobility and range of choice than the rest.

Safeguarded by Sinai and the Sahara, and by the continued primitiveness of human cultures in the earlier nurseries of mankind in eastern and southern Africa, the great early Egyptian civilisation was able to survive for a remarkably long period. The corresponding civilisations in south-western Asia were less fortunate, especially those based in the area of modern Iran, Iraq, and Turkey. In addition to common difficulties and hazards they found themselves threatened by a new rival and opposite type of culture which had spread throughout the broad steppe zone of central Asia and South East Europe between the Altai mountains and the delta of the Danube. After discovering the vast potential of this zone for breeding cattle and horses the neighboring peasant and hunting tribes boldly uprooted themselves, abandoned their fixed settlements and crops, adopted a horseback and tented life, bringing their women, children and bulkier possessions after them in oxcarts. By exploiting their new mobility as well-equipped nomads they soon created a homogeneous culture of vast extent and formidable energy. Their authoritarian but flexible social system and their massive forces of horseborne archers, practised and skilful, proved more than a match for the more sedentary and rigid major states of the settled richer regions to the south.

For reasons not yet fully understood, probably partly related to climatic change in Central Asia and partly to this social and technological revolution, there occurred roughly three thousand years ago a series of explosive population movements over large parts of Asia and eastern Europe. Its indirect repercussions may arguably be said not even yet to have fully worked themselves through. Although three thousand years may appear a long time in human history it represents much less than one per cent of the period of man's evolution on earth. There is no reason to regard what we call historical times as any more normal or typical of what is to come than the totally different pattern which prevailed earlier.

From the standpoint of relations between man and nature this outbreak of major long-distance population movements is particularly significant since it ended the era of purely localised impacts on each natural environment by human groups who had long been acclimatised to it and grown experienced in its limitations. Henceforth the arbitrary decisions and actions of great intruders, of absentee rulers far away from the scene, began to play the ever-increasing role which they have since maintained in overriding or over-persuading people on the spot to adopt practices and programs which, left to themselves, they would have refrained from. In few traceable cases have these imposed or infiltrated practices proved favorable to conservation, and in many they have ignored it, often with very bad results.

In those early days of the historical period it is already possible to trace a deepening division of mankind into three contrasting elements, empire-builders, nomads and simpler peoples, which are still conspicuous to this day. In a belt of favored land then extending from the Aegean and the Nile (with considerable interruptions) to India and China, advanced technology and intensive settlement had lifted large localised populations to the level of organised states and empires using division of labor and exerting widespread influence, but for that very reason frequently colliding and suffering severe instability. Neighboring this belt were temporarily less developed regions, inhabited by restless and resourceful peoples, uncommitted to the ways of the earlier advanced cultures. The settled peoples proved very easily challenged by the nomads, once these were given the necessary tools to confer on them greatly improved mobility and power of rapid concentration at a distance.

The first of these tools was the rearing of horses, cattle and sheep in large numbers on the Euro-Asian steppelands, which triggered off the upheavals already mentioned. The second was the domestication and breeding of camels, supplemented by horses and the consequential stimulation of the desert cultures of Arabia and North Africa, which was to come to a head in the great Arab conquests of the 7th and 8th centuries AD. The third was the development of shipping and navigation leading in Greek and Roman times to the partial, and in recent times the almost complete substitution of seapower for landpower as an ultimate instrument of domination. In contrast to the very latest advances of rail, road and air transport and of airborne strike forces, those early developments of mobility arose among and favored the expansion of peoples hitherto outside the ranks of the leading states and

B*

empires of their times. These empires accordingly found their previously strong positions rendered untenable, by the "hordes of barbarians" who over some three thousand years overcame all the earlier empires from the Hittites to the Romans, Byzantines and Hindus, leaving only China and Egypt intact.

In broad historical terms the English, Dutch, Portuguese and Spaniards rank with the Persians, Scythians, Mongols, Arabs, and others in this new wave of expanding and aggressive cultures. One common effect which it had was enormously to widen and gravely to intensify the impact of man upon natural environments. The mistakes and the desert-making activities of some of the earlier settled cultures, although serious, were at least much more localised. They were partly offset by the interest of these cultures in and care for water yields, crops and pasturage, as exemplified by their reservoirs, aqueducts and wells, their hillside terraces and their irrigation schemes.

The third more primitive and passive great element in mankind, which is only now shrinking rapidly under the influence of technical and economic development, is formed by the innumerable tribes in Africa, Asia, South and Central America and the Pacific which never entered the major technological, economic and political race, retaining cultural patterns more akin to that of mankind before the rise of states and empires. Inevitably and increasingly in course of time the lands of such peoples have become a theater for activities inspired from the more advanced and restless westernised cultures. In many cases these activities are, judged from a conservation standpoint, more destructive than the traditional practices which they brusquely supersede.

The new dynamic, mobile, innovating civilisations which have become paramount during the past three thousand years, at the expense of both the more primitive cultures and of the early sedentary civilisations, have unfortunately been inclined to extend to their treatment of nature the aggression, arrogance and impatience which has so often characterised their relations with their fellow-men. As heirs to these newer cultures we have to face and resolve this problem, which is both objective and subjective.

It took the newer civilisations some two thousand years to establish between them a loose hegemony over virtually the entire then known world except China. After a pause of some seven hundred years there began, with the age of the fifteenth-century navigators, a systematic extension of this hegemony to all the hitherto unexplored parts of the planet, which, on its virtual completion in the twentieth century, has now been further extended into outer space.

At this point we are concerned with that part of the background consisting of the development of human attitudes and actions; at a later stage the record of successive impacts on and modifications of the natural environment resulting from these actions will also need to be reviewed.

Until modern times major influences exerted by man on the environment were almost all direct and concrete, such as burning and cutting forests, converting land to grazing areas or crop-growing, diverting streams and so forth. Indirect, unintended and unrecognised interferences were relatively insignificant. When occasional local conflicts gradually developed into organised warfare as a general and recurrent expression of many cultures, defence became the first dominant human activity with strong incidental rather than direct effects upon land use.

Perhaps the most serious impact of defence has been through a tendency to select islands, peninsulas, crags and other readily defensible points which man would find unattractive for production and other purposes, and which are often the base of special ecosystems and the habitat of rare species. The concentration in such areas of forces of able-bodied men, with little to occupy them except beating up the wild life, has been a threat to conservation from early times right up to the present day. Compensating benefits have been few, although as competition for land and disturbing uses become more frequent the virtual sterilisation of certain areas in the interests of secrecy or military training have sometimes brought limited side benefits.

The other main indirect influence going back to early times is recreation. There is room for argument over the precise stage at which the necessity for hunting as a condition of being able to eat first became qualified by an element of hunting for sport, but there are indications pointing to some fairly early date. No doubt proven risks of over-cropping local game and causing local exterminations gave impetus long ago to increasingly sophisticated and drastic regulation of hunting activities. While among certain peoples such as the Eskimos and the American Indians the function of hunting seems to have fallen to the most suitable and skilful males, in many other cultures it became partly or wholly reserved to the higher social groups, and especially to royalty, wherever the scarcest and most desirable game were concerned. In Christian Europe, where scarcity arose early, the promulgation of extremely detailed and rigorously enforced controls of hunting antedated by at least a century similarly detailed attention to the conduct of such basic social institutions as local government or marriage. In England recreation as an officially recognised form of land use in the shape of royal forests is already more than a thousand years old.

The first widespread and profound impact of recreation on the land

43

in Britain was, however, during the late 17th and 18th centuries, with the rise of the sporting estate and of a large wealthy group of land-owning families who combined development of agriculture, forestry and at times of local industry with the systematic use of their lands for enjoyment and outdoor sports. Not wholly content with this outlet a minority of these privileged persons indulged in what we now know as tourism, identifying and indeed creating the first health and seaside resorts, cultural shrines, and beauty spots, where miniature but often elegant facilities grew up for them. It proved possible and attractive for the leaders of growing affluent classes to follow in their footsteps, and in those of such poets as Wordsworth, Shelley and Byron.

The rapid growth of improved communications, and the period of peace after Waterloo set in hand an expansion of tourism which continues to escalate with no sign of slackening. The great importance of this movement lies in its direct and intense relationship to appreciation of the natural environment, and in the emergence for the first time of a large human group interested in that environment for its own sake, and not merely as a site or quarry for exploitation to satisfy some other requirement. Unfortunately most of the potential benefit has so far been missed, owing to the concentration of so much of the resulting revenue in the hands of ignorant and uninterested commercial or local government bodies, and to the sluggishness of educationists in recognising its vast educational potential.

In very recent times a number of other strong and pervasive indirect influences have begun to play a part in relation to the natural environment. On the positive side the world conservation movement, lately forged from a blending of the interests of naturalists, scientists, country-lovers, specialists in natural resources and a large sentimentally inclined public, now contrives with some difficulty to keep most of the earth under review, and to intervene with increasing effectiveness at a number, still far too small, of threatened points.

Fairly closely related to this is the growth of regional and land planning, linked with the development and economic plans which are rapidly becoming common form among governments. The researchers, designers and executive officers for such plans vary from country to country in their background and training, their priorities and emphases, and their interest in conservation of the environment. But the trend, although disappointingly slow and patchy, is towards embodying and implementing conservation objectives in the course of such plans, or at least of discouraging projects plainly incompatible with such objectives.

Negative influences are, however, growing at an even greater rate. Among these are the enormously expanding demands upon land for many purposes, the rapid spread and widespread penetration of permanent or temporary human occupancy to innumerable hitherto uninhabited places, and the growing range, intensity and scale of such accompanying nuisances as pollution of air, water and soil, noise, disturbance and erosion.

In considering the impact of modern man upon the land we must always bear in mind, in addition to his growing requirements and ambitions, his vastly expanding capabilities which have recently enabled him to achieve a breakthrough so complex that eight distinct thrusts are identifiable in it.

Of these the most spectacular confer fresh types of mobility—on the land surface through all kinds of wheeled and tracked mechanical vehicles from landrovers or jeeps to snocats and amphibians; on the water surface from hydrofoils and hovercraft to monster tankers and aircraft carriers; under the water from long-range fast nuclear submarines to bathyspheres and submerged dwellings accommodating subaqua explorers; in the air through fixed-wing and VTOL to almost wingless aircraft, helicopters, gliders and individual backpack propulsion units; and beyond the stratosphere through a series of rocket-driven spacecraft and space platforms. This immense and fast-developing range of new vehicles, accompanied by new forms of protective equipment or clothing and controlled internal environments, now gives almost unlimited access to the many hitherto impenetrable regions of the earth and its neighbouring planets. Only the deeper waters continue for the time being inaccessible to man.

Armed with these new capacities man is confronted with the problem of using them not only economically and efficiently but wisely and with restraint. Yet these are not all. Added to these five main types of mobility for man and his belongings is a sixth of a more tactile and indirect nature—the capacity through powered drills, boring and tunnelling equipment and controlled explosions, conventional or nuclear, to probe deep into the earth's mantle and even beneath its outer crust, and to bring about major changes in its geographic forms through canals, dams, drainage and removal of rock and soil. A complementary new capacity for managing and modifying the earth's surface is through chemical additives to soil and water.

Finally, the most comprehensive and pervasive of these eight new human capabilities is that for systematically exploring and surveying every aspect of the environment and for constructing intellectual models, assembling, processing and using complex data, and for the first time enabling the human mind to grasp and consciously influence the interplay of countless factors which go to make nature tick.

Such, in highly condensed form, is the picture of man's cumulative efforts to date as they bear upon the natural environment. In this record certain points have emerged which should be emphasised as of special importance to our subject.

No other animal species to our knowledge has ever made such immense and hasty shifts of habitat within a very brief period, looked at against the scale of evolution, as man has from the forest to the plains and from the open plains to urban living. There is a very strong presumption that this precipitate double switch must have created gross maladjustments, especially psychologically and socially, which a more leisurely evolution might have avoided. Thus posed, the problem is to use man's resourcefulness at social evolution to buffer for an indefinite period the harmful psychological and social impacts upon him of his sudden breakthrough as the dominant animal species on earth. Assuming that any curbing of man's adventurousness is undesirable and impracticable the requirement appears to be to develop some kind of environmental and social base for balancing and refreshing him to mitigate the distortions and stresses otherwise inherent in his strained and exposed situation.

Man has suddenly emerged from the period of intense struggle against stronger adverse forces, through which his outlook and makeup have been moulded, to a position of immense power and responsibility for which his background has done little to fit him. Some of the most prominent inclinations which he has developed to an extreme degree, such as philoprogenitiveness and addiction to large scale warfare, are in conspicuous conflict at present with the elementary requirements for human survival. Others such as obsession with material development and a blind eye for the environment are less dramatic but may well be equally detrimental.

A further point of great importance is the series of shifts of the main social evolutionary initiative from one part of mankind to another. From the earliest primitive groups which emerged from forest living this initiative passed to omnivorous food-gatherers, hunters, domesticators of animals, farmers, irrigators, and thence to hierarchical chiefs, priests and kings, with their growing corps of administrators and advisers until irruptions of less sophisticated cavalryman, and traders commanding economic resources, ports and shipping took over the leading role.

It is now a commonplace that we are currently experiencing another of these decisive shifts of initiative and power, in which the technocrat is progressively, although gropingly and hesitantly, stepping into the shoes of earlier ruling types. This replacement is essential and indeed badly overdue. Even in relation to environmental management alone the capability of a classically educated group of administrators and politicians for handling the new forces and tools here outlined is little better than that of a band of apes faced with the task of devising an agricultural system.

The problem of educating new technocratic masters in the full breadth and depth of these issues is nevertheless acute, since the narrowness and inadequacy of their existing education is currently so serious as to create something near a deadlock in the process of changeover. Technologists of broader and deeper formation, with complex and well-balanced professional training, will alone be capable of successfully handling the immense problems of adaptation now facing us, and of using wisely the concentrations of power which will inevitably for good or ill be thrust into their hands. As a counterpoise, means must simultaneously be found for enabling a larger fraction of the citizens to learn and digest the main outlines of these problems of adaptation, and to exercise a sufficient check and supervision over the policies and actions of authorities concerned with government in its various aspects.

It will not be possible to harmonize human development with the natural environment on the necessary grand scale until those in charge, the politicians, administrators, managers, technologists and others are educated afresh so that they learn to see problems as a whole. At present their education has taught them to think about the environment only spasmodically and in unrelated compartments. Indeed modern man has been artificially conditioned not to see his environment as a whole.

But the great tool which should enable us to overcome the piecemeal approach most rapidly is the computer. With its need for careful programming it should ensure that questions are fully thought out and comprehensively related to the activities they purport to handle. This in turn should eliminate many of the omissions, ambiguities and inconsistencies which have hitherto got by, and provide a more adequate flow of statistics and information.

Reinforcing this discipline of the computer is the revitalising influence of television, the film and the other pictorial mass media. These media are far better able than the older entirely verbalised channels to help mankind to perceive and understand how nature functions. They carry no literary and rhetorical traditions, no ancient dogma and no strong but unfounded assumptions and they can therefore permit the public to see for themselves without the interposition of false or confusing noises into the messages direct from nature.

THE EARTH AND ITS LIVING PATTERNS

So far relations between man and the natural environment have been looked at mainly from the standpoint of man. It is time now to consider the other side, by looking at the environment itself on a world scale. This chapter will deal with the global aspects, while the following chapter will attempt, very selectively, to indicate how the many diverse features of the natural and man-made environment are deployed over the different regions of the earth.

On a cosmic plane the earth is an imperfect sphere of solid mineral mass, not unlike the much smaller moon. The distinctions which enable the earth to be a home of life are relatively fine. Even its crust is alive in a sense, still shaken by seismic and volcanic forces, and continually vibrating, even away from the oceans, to the impact of the waves upon distant coasts. The emerging dry land of continents and islands is in places dominated by rock masses so recently uplifted that their destined erosion is still in full swing, aided by avalanches, landslides, glaciers and torrents. The periodicity of the earth's spinning motion, and its seasonal tilt in relation to the sun, give rise to a global circulation of air and water in various forms, so complex that its prediction, and still more its control, elude even computer-assisted meteorological resources so far. There is some recognisable affinity between the seemingly spontaneous and sudden outbursts with which the weather confronts us and the infinitely variable behavior of living things. These, headed by man, can however only exist within certain given limits. Indeed the vast majority can function most efficiently and conveniently only between temperatures of about 10° to 23° C. Rocks and their derived soils; water, saline or fresh, and its derived moisture, snow or ice; air, and solar radiation provide the basis of all life on earth in its infinite variety.

From a spaceship the earth contrasts most strikingly with other known planets in being mainly clothed by the water of oceans and seas. These cover about 139 millions of its estimated area of nearly 197 million square miles, or about 70·6 per cent. The residue of land is about 29·4 per cent, or nearly 58 million square miles of land. The split between liquid and solid *surfaces* differs, however, owing to the extent of frozen seas to be added to the land, reducing the liquid surface to approximately two-thirds and increasing the solid to one-third.

In considering the use of land, it is more appropriate to deduct from the total land surface at least the 6 million square miles (10.4 per cent of it) which are permanently covered with ice, often to a great depth. A similar, although less simply measurable and possibly usable area lies within major deserts, to which the Sahara contributes just over half. The extent of these massive subtractions may be visualised from the comparisons that the glaciated tract is more than twice as large as the Australian continent, while the total desert zone matches China and India combined.

Beyond this almost unusable fifth of the earth's land surface is a further huge area, mainly mountainous or rocky, which carries no soil or vegetation, and is thus incapable of continuously sustaining living creatures. We are not yet in a position to estimate its extent, but it doubtless much exceeds the 6 million square miles at above 6,000 feet altitude, and is thus at least of the same order of magnitude as the ice-caps and the deserts.

Other fractions of the surface which cannot yet be accurately quantified, but must be deducted from the potential habitable area, are the tracts submerged under inland waters, both fresh and saline, both static and flowing as rivers. An estimate for this group of about 2 million square miles appears reasonable. Even the relatively few lakes internationally well-known for their size represent a total of some 400,000 square miles, and this must be greatly exceeded by the aggregate of less extensive inland waters, both natural and artificial, which are especially numerous in Northern Asia and Europe and in North America. In total also the great rivers of the world cover a substantial area. More than fifty of them, including four tributaries of the Amazon, are over 1,000 miles long. The delta of the Ganges-Brahmaputra alone is rather larger than Scotland, with much water surface mingling among the tracts of land. Admittedly the land here, so far as it goes, is fertile and productive. Land subject to frequent or occasional but deep and destructive flooding is however to be included as a useful asset only with reserve. Further allowance must be made for substantial areas of infertile land, including those whose only available resources of water are of low quality.

After making deductions on such grounds for barren or largely unusable tracts equivalent to almost one-third of the earth's land surface, which itself forms well under one-third of the whole, we are left with the residue which alone can carry a permanent standing crop of some kind of vegetation, whether forest, scrubland, savanna, steppe, grassland or farmland. It is within this final one-fifth residue of less than 40 million square miles that acute competition arises among the 3,500 million human inhabitants currently on the planet, and as between them and its non-human living creatures.

This biologically productive residue of some 40 million square miles may first be broken down into three blocks. The first of these consists of those areas which in the present state of technological development remain virtually untouched by man owing to technical limitations or, in certain cases partly also to geographic inaccessibility. These include the northern tundra of North America and Asia (plus a smaller strip in northern Europe); the more extensive northern coniferous forests adjoining the tundra, the tropical and subtropical native forests of South and Central America, Africa south of the Sahara, South and South-east Asia and parts of Oceania; the arid semi-desert, steppe and savanna zones of Central and South-west Asia and South-east Europe, Northern, North-eastern and South-west Africa, Australia, Western North America, and Southern and Western South America; and a miscellany of smaller swamps or wetlands, waterless or rockbound islands and other intractable types of terrain scattered over the earth.

Parts of these areas are exploited, usually temporarily or periodically, by nomadic herdsmen of reindeer, camels, goats and so forth, by fur trappers and lumbermen, by mineral prospectors and miners or drillers, and by scientists and others, but so locally and insignificantly that on a global scale they still rank for practical purposes as uninhabited and unused lands. It may safely be presumed that in view of the intensive pressures to occupy additional land, the high degree of adventurousness and readiness to accept prolonged hardship on that account, and the increasing ingenuity in applying new technology with the backing of governments and the encouragement of international agencies, there is little land currently suitable for human use which has not yet been harnessed to it.

Further technological advances and a greater degree of desperation to accommodate the population explosion will no doubt result in further encroachments on this hard core of unexploited lands in the near future. At present there is little room for argument that the area currently under misguided attempts at human use which are doomed to failure, with disastrous long-term results for its fertility status, much exceeds the unexploited area which might on a realistic view be made to justify exploitation.

It is exceedingly difficult to quantify the virtually unused block of lands still consisting of large natural areas within the biologically productive residue. Its main components would be;

Tropical hardwood forests beyond commercial reach
Coniferous forests, mainly arctic and subarctic, beyond commercial reach
Temperate woodlands beyond commercial operation
Arctic tundra, and arctic-alpine tundra
Arid semi-desert and steppe, not supporting continuous grazing
Miscellaneous wetlands, islands and so forth

On the basis of estimates for the principal countries concerned (prepared by FAO) the total can hardly be put lower than 10 million square miles, about half of this being forest.

The second block within the biologically productive residue consists of land which is regularly humanly exploited on a substantial scale, but which retains a considerable element of natural ecosystems in its composition. Obvious examples are commercially exploited forests, and many grasslands and rough grazings, carrying domestic livestock.

From this must be distinguished a third block characterised by a degree of human intervention and management which has for the most part superseded natural ecological inheritances. This includes crop agriculture, factory farming, built up areas, and sites used for communications, mining and defence. These three blocks may roughly be distinguished as *unconverted natural ecosystems, converted natural ecosystems* now in regular human use, and *artificial ecosystems* virtually replacing their natural predecessors. If it is right to estimate the first block as roughly 10 million square miles, and as we know from land use statistics that the third covers some 4 million square miles, the second should cover around 26 million square miles, making it much the largest of the three. It includes about 10 million square miles of commercially exploited forests (an almost negligible part of which consists of actual plantations), about 8 million square miles of regular meadows and pastures, and large areas of grasslands ranging from moors and high upland grazings to savanna and steppe. As we shall see later it is this immense block which has suffered and continues to suffer most heavily and extensively from human misuse and failures in conservation. (For comparison, Africa covers $11\frac{2}{3}$ million square miles, Europe 4 million, Argentina 1 million and Greece, England or New York State 50,000.)

So far our breakdown of the surface of this planet has been simply global, without much reference to its geographical distribution, which must now be outlined. A commentator with understandable human bias has ungratefully summed it up that we find "Too much water, too many mountains and deserts, and too much ice on the globe". Be that as it may, we have to live with the fact that the Pacific ocean and its adjoining seas cover just over one-third of the earth while another third is sunk under the Atlantic and Indian oceans. After deducting also the Arctic ocean and the Antarctic continent, which are of almost identical extent, we are left with roughly 27 per cent, or 52 million square miles, of mainly ice-free land, of which about one-third is in Asia, a somewhat smaller fraction in its westerly and southerly extensions, Europe and Africa combined, and in the two Americas, and a residue in Oceania of about one-fifth the size of any of these three main continental groupings.

While Africa and South America are almost strictly continental, with mainlands forming 98 or 99 per cent of their extent, North America and Europe have 25 per cent or more of their areas split off in islands or peninsulas. Oceania (although Australia is conventionally excepted from island status on grounds of size) may be said to consist entirely of islands. In all, the earth's islands cover nearly 4 million square miles, or about 7 per cent of its land surface, but nearly one third of this lies in the Arctic or subarctic zones of the Western Hemisphere—that is chiefly Greenland and Canada. Excluding inshore islands, which are within sight of mainland or of another inshore island, and the few exceptionally large single isolated islands such as Madagascar, the rest consists mainly of a great chain of Asian offshore islands from Sakhalin through Japan, the Philippines and New Guinea to Java and Sumatra, and of a widely scattered series of mainly small oceanic islands, mostly in the Pacific, but some in the subantarctic and arctic seas, the Indian Ocean and the Atlantic, where the West Indies form the largest cluster. Over most of the earth therefore islands are a scarce resource.

Asia is the most "continental" of the continents, containing an inner area as large as the United States which lies more than 1,000 miles from any sea-coast. Of the continental coastlines, totalling some 162,000 miles, North America has nearly 47 thousand, Asia about 43, Europe 23·5 (of which Great Britain contributes 5), Africa less than 19, South America less than 18 and Oceania just over 12.

Australia, with only 1·5 per cent of its surface over 3,000 feet above sealevel, is the lowest-lying continent, followed by Europe with 6·5 per cent. More than a fifth of North America, a quarter of Africa and a third of Asia are above this contour, but nearly 90 per cent of mankind live below 1,500 feet, shunning the loftiest third of the land surface. Of the earth's total area nearly 40 per cent is within the tropics and over 8 per cent within the Arctic and Antarctic circles, the rest being temperate. But owing to the irregularity of the oceans the Eastern Hemisphere accounts for nearly two thirds of the land surface.

When Thornthwaite assigned the earth's land surface between eight climatic types the Subhumid came out in the lead with 11·7 million square miles (Africa accounting for nearly 30 per cent) followed by the Humid with 9·2, over 33 per cent of it in South America. This was closely followed by Semi-arid (8·5, 40 per cent in Asia) and Arid (8·6, nearly 50 per cent in Africa).

Next came perpetual frost (7·6 of which nearly 75 per cent was in Antarctica), and the closely allied Arctic Taiga (7·2, 55 per cent in Asia), and Tundra, which alone was mostly concentrated in North America (almost 50 per cent of a total 3·3 million square miles). Finally the least extensive type was Wet, with 1·3 million square miles, mostly in Asia (about 60 per cent). A number of alternative estimates have since been made, with broadly similar results. Dry climates prevail over larger areas than humid, especially in high latitudes and around the tropic fringes (and in Asia also to the north of these).

Although convenient, it is an error to think that change in nature is limited to vegetation and animal life and the weather, with the rocks, landforms and oceans providing an unchanging framework and foundation for them. Everything is changing, although at differing rates which themselves are subject to great changes from one period to another. The growing probability of the hitherto hardly credible proposition of continental drift suggests that even the earth's geography has changed to an astonishing extent, shifting formerly tropical areas almost to the South Pole and putting whole oceans between former parts of a single landmass. Very few parts of the earth share the good fortune of the Amazonian rainforest in having come through from early geological times in roughly the same climatic zone without ever having been either sunk beneath the ocean or overlain by an icecap. This is no mere academic matter, since it has permitted biological specialisation to evolve and survive on a scale beyond comparison with the more ephemeral northern temperate fauna and flora.

The upthrust of mountain ranges has left a legacy of earthquake and volcanic activity along zones of weakness in the earth's crust which remains a serious factor for the countries affected, beside modifying climates, changing river flows and creating vast areas of intense erosion, sometimes in such extreme forms as avalanches and landslides. Known changes in sealevel have greatly altered the sizes and shapes of land areas, and have contributed much to enriching the earth's soils through the provision of limestone and other sedimentary rocks, and of low-lying areas attracting deposits of alluvium from extended river courses. These processes are continuing, and some of them may in the foreseeable future become susceptible to some engineering manipulation, on lines which could make man a partner in them.

Climatic changes have become more precisely measurable with the aid of recently developed techniques, such as pollen analysis and carbon dating. Among the important influences traceable are ameliorations of climate resulting in melting and retreat of glaciers, extended navigability in the northern seas, and extensions of range of birds and other animals, accompanied by improved opportunities for growing crops in certain hitherto unfavourable areas. It is in the nature of climatic changes that they are composed of fluctuating and sometimes contradictory trends, affecting not only such everyday factors as temperature, precipitation, sunshine and humidity but also the frequency of events such as storms, prolonged and severe frosts, droughts and floods. It is therefore almost impossible to predict their trends, or even to detect the difference between minor checks or temporary reversals and major or long-term changes of substantial importance.

At the present time there is much uncertainty whether the appreciable climatic amelioration registered in northern latitudes up to 1950 is continuing with some check or is being reversed. Indications of past advances and retreats of species critically dependent on specific climatic conditions could, if more thoroughly and widely studied, throw much light on these questions, so significant for the future environment, but hitherto such studies have been left to the chance efforts of a small interested band of scientists.

The physical basis of life provided by the land and the oceans, with their climatic and other accompaniments is therefore insufficiently stable and constant to enable plant and animal life to maintain the steady ecological "climax" conditions postulated by earlier ecological theory. It is more practical to think in terms of evolutionary tendencies continually working towards such a "climax" but commonly frustrated in attaining it, or interrupted whenever it is attained, by many contrary factors such as those mentioned above, to which of course must be added a great and increasing number of human influences. On such a basis we are still better off than if we had to assume mere chance operating in chaos, but we must renounce the simple idea of a particular "balance of nature" or of some pre-existing natural state which functioned with quite imaginary smoothness and stability until it felt the evil influence of man. Our alternative is to devise complex models to be studied by systems analysis.

There are even situations in nature, admittedly uncommon and freakish, where instability is a built-in factor in closed systems. A most literal instance of this is in a valley in the Fiordland National Park on the South Island of New Zealand, where the abundant rainfall encourages the growth of lush woody vegetation up gulleys so precipitous that when the mass develops to a certain point it becomes too heavy to maintain itself at that angle through its insecurely attached root system, and the whole structure crashes down the mountain side in a kind of vegetable avalanche, leaving the cycle to begin all over again.

An opposite instance on a much smaller scale is seen on the great shingle promontory of Dungeness, reaching out from Kent into the English Channel. Here the bare pebbles are colonised by lower plants which gradually trap enough moisture and soil for grasses to colonise and at the next stage the woody shrubs of broom (*Sarothamnus scoparius*). As the broom grows it uses all the available moisture without eventually finding this enough, and finally dies of thirst, leaving once more bare shingle for the displaced lower plants to restart the cycle. A somewhat similar but much more extended cycle has been found in the eastern desert of Jordan near Azraq oasis. The saline silty soils are colonised by two tall shrubs, *Nitraria retusa* and *Tamarix macrocarpa*, which check and accumulate blowing dust, thus creating low mounds, some of which rise to the scale of imitation sand-dunes. Eventually some of these attain a height outstripping the growth capacity of the deep-rooted vegetation, which dies back, leaving the senile "dunes" a prey to wind erosion which etches them into strange gaunt shapes before finally demolishing them. Such ephemeral natural structures are often important habitats for specialised animals, in this way resembling the fallen and decaying trunks and branches of trees which, when not tidied up by over zealous and ecologically ignorant foresters, play a similar role in woodlands.

The concept of the cyclical pattern is very important in ecology. In addition to cycles of ecological succession, such as burnt forests reverting by way of grassland, heath, scrub and pioneer trees to a fresh stand of tall forest, there is the cycle of energy flow which is fundamental to life. Plants are the only organisms capable of directly using solar energy to synthesise carbohydrates from CO_2 drawn out of the air and from water, at the same time releasing oxygen into the atmosphere. Plants also use this primary raw material to make fats, starch and also proteins with the aid of nitrogen from the soil.

Animal life of all kinds can exist only on a basis of nutrients made available through activities of plants. It is true that in certain areas, such as much of Antarctica and parts of deserts and barren mountain ranges, it is possible to find animals, especially birds, far from the nearest growing plants, but these are no exception. They are merely using their superior mobility, and that of other vertebrate or invertebrate prey ultimately supported by plant food, to range some distance from their nutritional base, usually, like the Antarctic penguins, for only certain seasons of the year.

This example does however bring out that, versatile as plants are, there are certain extremes of heat and cold and aridity, although not of moisture, in which no plant so far evolved can function. In borderline cases, such as Arctic tundra, lichens and mosses alone may be capable of colonising the bare surfaces, and preparing a foothold for such higher plants as grasses and sedges in the less unfavorable places. In such severe conditions vegetation of any kind may be a fluctuating cover, establishing itself precariously in some periods and then being eradicated by climatic or other circumstances becoming harsher for a time.

Just as man seeks to breed strains of crop plants capable of growing in more difficult situations, so natural selection has through long ages been evolving plants which can defy many of the most adverse conditions of heat, cold, dryness, salinity, acidity, lack of soil and other factors presenting a severe challenge to the almost infinite adaptability of even plants. On this adaptability depends the existence of all higher forms and complex ecosystems, in which animals and plants continually adjust to climate, to soil, and to one another.

Recent increases of knowledge and improvements in techniques have led to the realisation that there is no single right way of classifying the earth's vegetation cover, but a number of alternative approaches are each appropriate for some differing purposes. On the other hand there are many "wrong" approaches which are based upon muddles or misconceptions, or are slanted towards proving some arguable theory.

In organising the conservation section of the International Biological Program it became clear quite early on that if we were to succeed in surveying at all accurately and in analysing and interpreting reliably the immense variety of natural and humanly modified environments on earth we would need to review, revise and systematically apply the best available models of classification and identification of stable, recognisable groupings. The manifest requirements of a world program for the first time created conditions favourable to such a comprehensive and internationally co-operative approach.

A fundamental problem was that of relating the mass of detailed data derived from different specialist studies in different places to the necessary broad picture faithfully expressing the altogetherness of everything. A solution was found in surveying on each selected site a large number of plainly identifiable and readily measurable factors. These could then be grouped and analysed in relation to a number of classifications constructed with the utmost practicable freedom of bias for different purposes, at different levels of generalisation or detail, and for use with different classes of data. By punching the material for handling by computer it became possible to make different print-outs in answer to different demands or test questions, and thus to secure a rigorous cross-check on the consistency and credibility both of the original data and of the assumptions and methods used in handling them.

This parametric method is still in its early days, but it promises to provide a highly illuminating and powerful new instrument for measuring and reflecting, on a universal scale but on a selective and manageable basis, almost anything that we need to know about our natural environment.

One part of this work which it may be helpful to outline briefly here is the recommended treatment of vegetation descriptions. This excludes any extraneous elements such as climate and geology and avoids such vague terms as "woodland" or "grassland" which imply a blend of different factors. It relies strictly upon the *structure* (such as the height, and spacing of plants) and the *function* (such as adaptations to or defences against such conditions as fire, drought or salinity). It thus escapes the picturesque and attractive but vague and often confusing large categories in popular use, and also avoids reference to species or genera (as in "oak-wood" or "heather-moor").

This more exact and objective system relies on three primary structural groupings. First comes Closed Vegetation, where in some or all layers the plants are predominantly touching or overlapping. In the second, Open Vegetation, they are separated by not more than twice their diameters. In the third, Sparse Vegetation, even the most complete layer involves wider separation. (See Annex 1)

The majority of recognised Formation Classes (31 in all) belong to the Closed Vegetation group. Forest, defined as closed woody vegetation 5 meters or more tall, comes first, its primary subdivision being into Evergreen and Deciduous. Evergreen embraces such varied types as the *Dipterocarp* tropical forest of Malaya and Borneo, evergreen swamp forest, mangrove swamps, palm swamps, most cloud forest types, Canary Island laurel forest, northern pine and spruce forest, and the *Prosopis* forest of Hawaii and *Leptospermum* forest of New Zealand. Winter deciduous forest includes the familiar oak-hickory of Eastern Northern America and beech and oak of Europe, Taxodium (swamp cypress) of the south-eastern United States, most monsoon forests, and the deciduous thorn forest of, for example, Brazil.

Second comes scrub (closed woody vegetation 5 meters or less tall), again subdivided into evergreen and deciduous. Evergreen includes bamboo or reed brake, *Hibiscus* swamp in the Pacific, reed or rhododendron swamp, French *maquis*, Californian chaparral and Florida palmetto scrub, the dwarf pine scrub of Japan, the Alps and the Rocky Mountains, and the famous sage brush of the old Wild West. Deciduous scrub includes the willow thickets of the Arctic, the hawthorn thickets of Europe and Eastern North America, and alder swamps. The third group, Dwarf Scrub, predominantly woody but less than 0·5 meters tall, includes the rhododendron mat of the eastern Himalaya, the bearberry mat of northern Europe and America, the crowberry heath of the Arctic and sub-Arctic, and the *Vaccinium myrtillus* (blueberry/bilberry) heath of subarctic regions.

The fourth group, Open Forest with closed lower layers, includes the open spruce muskeg of North America, and the denser stands of the "savanna" of the upper Orinoco, or the Colombian llanos. The fifth, its counterpart in Closed Scrub with scattered trees, is characterised by Mediterranean maquis or Californian chaparral with only scattered pines, and by comparable saw palmetto scrub in Florida. The sixth, Dwarf Scrub with scattered trees, is typified by English *Calluna* heath with scattered pines, and the heath birch forest of Lapland. The seventh is the treeless counterpart, Open Scrub with closed ground cover, exemplified by Rocky Mountain *Krummholz* near the treelimit, by English broom scrub, and by subarctic open willow and birch scrub. The next (eighth) group, Open dwarf scrub with closed ground cover is familiar in Western Europe through the open phases of *Calluna* and *Erica* heath, and in Eastern North America through the corresponding phases of *Vaccinium* scrub.

The ninth, Tall Savanna, is defined as Closed grass or other herbaceous vegetation 1 meter tall or more with scattered trees, and is familiar, at least from pictures through the Acacia tall grass savanna of Africa, often so rich in spectacular wildlife. Low savanna, the tenth group, differs only in its herbaceous vegetation being under 1 meter tall, and may therefore merge with the last; characteristic examples are the *Juniperus virginianus* savanna of the Eastern United States, and much sphagnum and lichen bog or muskeg. The eleventh group, the last representing savanna, is Shrub savanna with scattered shrubs, not trees, among closed grass or other herbaceous vegetation. This is often seen in old fields reverting to forest, especially in the Eastern United States, in grass with scattered sagebrush in the American West, and in north temperate juniper heaths.

The twelfth group, Tall Grass, excludes both trees and shrubs, but attains over 1 meter in height itself. It is typified by marshes of *Scirpus*, *Typha*, and *Papyrus* in the tropics, and by tussock-grass in New Zealand;

the great prairies of the Mississippi valley were of this type. These examples should sufficiently indicate the possibilities of recording and comparing the earth's varied vegetation types on a simple objective system, set forth in detail in Annex 1.

This ingenious and rational classification, prepared by Dr. F. R. Fosberg, enables similarities and contrasts to be traced on a coherent and comprehensive basis for vegetation in all parts of the world, placing every example studied in a significant ecological relationship to every other. Unlike a number of alternative systems it avoids confusing elements of climate, soil and so forth with the purely vegetational approach. It does not pretend, however, to be more than a useful means of readily indexing what we learn and what we know, as a basis for deeper or more far-reaching study. It has the merit of being readily understood and can be memorised and used without much effort as a basis for comparing observations in various parts of the world. It thus offers a much needed tool for relating world vegetation to other significant factors.

On that part of the earth's surface which is covered with water, either salt or fresh, there is vegetation cover over only a very small fraction, if we exclude floating marine plankton which is outside the scope of this classification. Areas covered by ice, or devoid of any soil over the bedrock are similarly poor. With such major exceptions it is generally true that evolution has yielded a series of plant species so fully adapted that almost everywhere else one or more of them can be found striving to form as complete a vegetation cover over the surface as is physically possible in the given conditions of solar radiation and nutrient supply, and of soil and climate. Where complete cover does not exist it is not for want of trying on the part of the tough and ubiquitous plant population.

For many reasons it is important to be able to explain which types of vegetation cover are to be expected in which areas, either in undisturbed conditions or following various disturbances of either natural or human origin. We need such knowledge, for example, in order to be able to forecast reliably where certain crops will grow or certain animals can flourish. The Fosberg classification outlined above makes it possible to determine for any point on the earth's surface the broad structure and functional adaptation of the vegetation found there, irrespective of the species to which the plants belong.

To determine these species, either in the form of a straightforward list of floristic composition or in terms of the recognisable combinations in which different ecologically allied species occur, is the next stage. Having found that a given area is covered by closed vegetation with the crowns of plants touching or overlapping, and that these plants form closed woody vegetation 5 meters or more tall, the next question is whether these plants are evergreen, or whether at least the canopy layer is bare of leaves for a period during the cold or dry season. If the latter applies the subformation is Deciduous Forest, and this may be further refined as beech, oak, oak-hickory, beech-maple or other pure or mixed types of composition. An infinity of other detail can be added as knowledge permits and as requirements demand, with the assurance that anyone else in any other part of the world using the same system will obtain results which will enable truly corresponding types of vegetation to be reliably compared with one another in whatever respects may be desired. By systematic recording at key sites, and by feeding the results through a computer, it will be possible to make comparisons and analyses inside a day which would have been beyond the reach of a lifetime of effort hitherto. Just as the right scatter of raingauges and other recording instruments makes it possible to generalise soundly about the climate and weather of large regions, so the selection of ecological survey sites will afford a dependable view of the nature and state of vegetation cover, and consequently of the biological potential of one site as against another.

The answers may be conveyed in several alternative ways. They may be presented by symbols or markings on aerial survey or satellite photographs, photogrammetrically studied, or by a wide variety of patterns of conventional cartography, using different scales appropriate for different purposes. For example, if we imagine ourselves looking down from an aircraft flying at a normal jet cruising level of around 34,000 feet (c. 10,000 meters), we are seeing the earth beneath on a scale roughly equivalent to 1:1,000,000 or about 16 miles to one inch; at about 7,000 feet the equivalent scale is increased to 1:2,000,000, just over 3 miles to one inch, while by flying at just below 200 feet in a helicopter the detail corresponds to a scale of 1:25,000 or $2\frac{1}{2}$ inches to the mile. The first of these is equivalent to the largest-scale maps of regions of the U.S.A., Germany or France in The Times Atlas: the second to a first-class motoring map such as a standard Michelin Sheet and the third to the most detailed map for walking and planning on widespread sale by the British Ordnance Survey. For certain purposes however neither photographs nor cartographic representation will serve, and statistical tables, diagrams, printouts from the computer or textual description and discussion such as this, with suitable illustrations may be preferred. Sets of color transparencies, reels of film, television programs, or three-dimensional models may better meet the need in other circumstances. Nor must it be overlooked that in the more critical or exacting situations there may often be no substitute for going out again into the field, armed with the necessary instruments to measure and record whatever may be relevant.

All such techniques, moreover, are no better than the training and skill of those who use and interpret them, and it is only because in recent years so many different scientific disciplines and new professions have converged on the broad field of geography and biology, of land use, landscape and land management that it is now possible with some confidence to tackle these problems in depth and on a global scale.

The greatest obstacles to progress are lack of imagination about the earth and its infinitely varied wealth of resources; lack of organised, coherent, accessible knowledge concerning many of the key factors; and widespread failure to seek out, learn and apply even such knowledge and experience, already fairly substantial, as now exists.

It is a particularly serious handicap that the main practical require-ment and opportunity for a concentrated point of synthesis of know-ledge about the environment happens to coincide, in terms or organised studies, with a no man's land between ecology, geography and land-scape. None of these studies is as strongly manned or supported as might be expected in view of their significance to our civilisation. This weakness is naturally most marked on the fringe between them. Until the fortunate if belated chance arising from the new task of the terres-trial conservation section of the International Biological Program there has never been any concerted effort in this borderland of sciences sufficiently concentrated and internationally effective to provide the necessary impetus and resources for a real step forward. At the same time several other sections of the IBP are making progress in tackling related ecological problems in depth. Without such complementary efforts no synthesising activities could at this stage yield more than some-what superficial results. The development of the International Biological Program itself continues to be crippled through absurdly inadequate resources.

For purposes of survey it is convenient to adopt an inventory basis, taking stock simply of the vegetation as we happen to find it. Obviously, this can be no more than a beginning of the real task. Ecology is a dynamic process functioning over a vast time-scale, and what at one moment may appear to the untrained eye a permanent pattern of forest, grassland or open water can have developed from some totally different phase and be destined soon to change into something once more unrecognisably altered. Until the end of last century Woodwalton Fen in Huntingdonshire was an open expanse of reedswamp and peatland intersected by a few artificial channels of water. In this state it became famous among naturalists, and from about 1912 onwards was gradually acquired as a nature reserve for the Society for the Promotion of Nature Reserves. At the same time powerful drainage pumps rapidly lowered the water-table of the entire surrounding area, but the effect that this increasing dryness would have on the fen was not at that period appreciated. A *laissez-faire* management policy was continued until it was realised with a shock some forty years ago that the so-called Fen was well on the way to growing into a dense swamp woodland, of poor quality and of little scientific interest. By that time the economic depression and World War II imposed a long delay on remedial measures, and it was not until 1954 that the Nature Conservancy was able to lease Woodwalton and begin a long-term program of rehabilitation.

Even so it took ten years' work to clear scrub and trees from one-eighth of the Fen's 514 acres, owing mainly to the patient research needed in order to avoid damaging the surviving fen flora and fauna in the process, and to the complex system of water-level management required to ensure the possibility of permanence for the new regime. One notable aspect was the relationship to neighboring agricultural interests, who were originally hostile to the "sterilisation" of such valuable land, but were entirely converted by experience of the inestimable value for them of such a vast sponge of peat ready to soak up huge quantities of floodwater, which would otherwise frequently have inundated much farmland. Although normal rainfall in this area is lower than almost anywhere in England it is liable to severe sudden downpours, which in 1968 caused deep flooding of nearby villages in early July and again in August. This is one of the most efficiently and scientifically farmed areas in Europe and it is a revealing commentary on the limited environmental understanding of agricultural authorities and of farmers that even in such circumstances it should have needed the chance presence of a nature reserve to prove such an elementary point.

An equally striking contemporary instance of ecological succession surprising and putting into reverse specialists who might have been expected to be aware of it occurred in the early years of Harvard Forest at Petersham, Massachusetts. Here an area of some 2,300 acres of woodland has been owned and managed in the interests of forest research for some sixty years. The condition of the different stands of trees has been recorded fully with photographic aid at intervals throughout the period, so that the results of natural evolution and of various silvicultural treatments can be traced.

Until the last decade of the 18th century the precolonial forest had remained virtually intact here, but during the next 40 years, up to 1830, clearances for agriculture had eliminated forest from some 60–70 per cent of the "town" area. During the third quarter of the 19th century this local agriculture ceased to be competitive, and as abandoned land reverted to forest it became dominated by naturally-seeded stands of white pine, the readiest pioneer species.

During the half-century or more needed for the pine to grow to commercial maturity American forestry was also growing up. As its own seeds came largely from Germany it early became dominated, like British forestry later, by an obsession with conifers. Harvard Forest was created at a time when the white pine crop on the abandoned Massachusetts farmlands was being harvested, with the intention among foresters of replacing it by similar crops *ad infinitum*. This plan took no account of the seral nature of white pines, which only colonise cleared land, and which serve as nurses to a variety of native deciduous species, maturing under the pine cover which they are destined to replace when it is felled or dies off. Fortunately the research adopted at Harvard Forest early disclosed the ecological unreality of the original forestry plans for it, and enabled much to be learnt in the course of the ensuing switch towards working with rather than in defiance of nature.

Hugh M. Raup, the former Director of Harvard Forest whose work on this and other sites has contributed so much to ecological understanding, made comparisons between such results of agricultural abandonment after the mid 19th century, and adjacent lands which had been maintained as woodlots throughout the agricultural period. He concluded that in general "the present stands, although they differ so greatly in history, are scarcely distinguishable from one another in structure and species composition".

Ingenious methods of reconstruction of earlier forest types led him also to conclude "that the old forest was not far different from what we have now. There is every reason to believe that its species composition has changed but little. Probably there were more large trees in certain habitats than we now have, though we believe that the number of very old trees was never great." It was probably composed largely of even-aged stands or of well-defined age-classes, although ages varied greatly from one stand to the next.

This feature is largely traceable to two great sources interrupting the continuity of the forest—fire among conifers and hurricanes or violent storms of wind among trees generally. In New England four major hurricanes can be documented in the last 500 years, the most recent

THE ENVIRONMENTAL REVOLUTION
INTRODUCTION TO THE VISUAL SECTIONS

In reading and writing about the environment it is our misfortune to have to attempt to deal with so many essentially visual objects and relations through the medium of words. These are not only inadequate, but owing to the power of literary and pedagogic traditions have become loaded against conveying a true picture of nature in its integrity and its subtle ways of balancing diversity.

The inclusion of four clusters of pictures in this book is intended not to illustrate it in a traditional sense but to present a linked series of pictorial presentations of essential elements in the argument, as a complement to the text. This, it is hoped, may challenge and stimulate the reader to see through and beyond the verbal level.

Of these four clusters two are basic, one reviewing man's evolution and its impacts upon nature, while the second reviews the successive stages of natural build-up of ecosystems from the naked rock, ice or clear water to the ever more complex and animal communities composing the biosphere. The other two are secondary. One shows the emergence of landscape as a conscious approach to the visual, spatial and physical aspects of land use and land management, and the other illustrates the various forms of human restraint in utilising, managing or rehabilitating land, which together make up the world of conservation.

Every picture tells not one but several stories. The primary selection, placing and scale adopted are intended to help in quickly grasping each spectrum of transitions between such crude extremes as primitive versus technological man, simple versus sophisticated landscapes, and preservation versus ecologically guided conservation measures.

FIRST VISUAL THEME—MAN'S IMPACT

By visually outlining the first half-million years of man's impact certain key points become plain.

For around nine-tenths of this time there were various rival contenders for the title role of Man. *Homo sapiens,* the winner, has so far held it for a mere fifty thousand years of trial and error. Four-fifths of this was absorbed in primitive preparations for becoming civilised. Only during the past 10,000 years—a mere fiftieth of man's traceable existence—has anything dimly resembling a civilisation emerged, since they built Jericho. Until this 20th century much of mankind, and most of man's occupied territory, stayed at prehistoric or early historic levels of culture. Urban technological civilisation remained a comparatively localised affair, even within living memory. Its more general spread over the habitable earth and its intense and elaborate development through massive applications of energy and of scientific technology are entirely new.

The pressures and menaces now suddenly confronting us are entirely beyond all previous human experience. They have outstripped the sluggish pace of earlier social evolution. They tax the adaptability and resilience of nature, and challenge the still far too modest resources of the newborn movements for care of man's environment.

A first essential is for as many people as possible to grasp as quickly as possible what is going on. By making this theme vividly visible it is hoped to assist the reader of the text to picture himself the accelerating pace, the snowballing scale and the mounting complexity which have gone to convert a poor handful of small tools into a vast "technosphere" almost as difficult for man to understand and to master as nature itself.

About half-a-million years ago *Australopithecus*, (A.1), emerged as the first known type of man—first to quit the shelter of forests and live by his wits in open country, and first to devise tools, from pebbles. Competition for the star role of Man lasted some 450,000 years longer, before *Homo sapiens* finally won it. His latest rival, Neanderthal Man (A.2) made improved stone tools, used fire and lived in caves.

A.2

A.3

A.1

A.4

Already between 200,000 and 100,000 years ago a more advanced type known as Swanscombe Man (A.4), with a brain about as big as our own, was hunting in Kent. He was succeeded by tall newcomers, probably from SW Asia, who hunted with spears, used tools of wood and bone as well as fine flint, wore sewn skins or furs, and could paint animals on cave walls. The example (A.3) from the most famous of these prehistoric galleries at LASCAUX illustrates the stage reached after some 15,000 years of practice.

Speedier social evolution produced some 10,000 years ago
the Neolithic breakthrough
illustrated at Jericho, where
by 7,000 BC (A.5) the first
known town of some 2,000
people had been walled, a
spring used to irrigate a
primitive crop of wheat, and
goats partly domesticated.
The oxen treading out the
corn in Baluchistan in AD
1952 (A.6) show how slow
progress in many areas has
been since, contrasting with
explosive urban growth.

A.5

A.6

A.7

By about 1,450 BC this
Theban named Nebamun
goes hunting with his wife
and daughter and his trained
hunting-cat (A.8). His prey
is recognisably depicted, with
written commentary. He
might almost be one of us,
with his assurance and sophistication. Yet nearly 3,400
years later the last remnants
of the mountain forest of
Baluchistan are still being
borne away to burn (A.7) by
less advanced tribes. Cultural
levels diverge ever more
sharply.

A.8

A.9

With advancing culture human impact on the land includes ambitious structures, initially of natural materials, such as the still baffling pre-historic artificial mound of Silbury Hill, Wiltshire (A.9), seen dwarfing the modern Bath Road beside it.

In medieval times large-scale extraction of materials, such as peat for fuel on this zone of the Norfolk Broads (A.10), created man-made lakes such as the two Ran-worth Broads (foreground), one used for sailing, the other protected against it by a boom to serve as a Nature Reserve. The marshland, no longer much exploited for its reed, sedge and animal pro-ducts, is reverting to swamp woodland, more than a thou-sand years after its clearance.

A.10

At a certain stage human mobility and command of fire, edged tools and other devices readily leads to an indiscriminate and irresponsibly destructive exploitation of the land, involving lasting damage out of all proportion to its often transient benefits. This picture (A.12) of a gutted Australian woodland and abandoned shacks is typical.

The oceans cannot be so readily injured as a habitat but the more conspicuous and commercially exploitable of their living creatures are targets for the same senseless and self-defeating human selfishness. In A.13 we see eight whales, killed by the highly-armed whalers and awaiting their turn to be towed to the flensing platform near Leith Harbor, South Georgia, in the Antarctic seas. Thanks to its own suicidal folly the great whaling industry, which never learnt how to curb its own greed, is now also a corpse, but the damage it has done will live long after it.

Great mountains have played a peculiar role in man's evolution, having been widely named, revered and given high symbolic status, long before anyone thought of ascending them. While in touristically active countries mountains are becoming freely commercialised and overrun, this modest hut beneath Popocatepetl in Mexico (A.11) still marks a point where those who wish to mount higher must do it on their two feet, soon leaving the treelimit to head for the snowline, here above 15,000 feet.

A.12

Industrial Revolution technology, crudely applied in steam locomotives, ships and stationary engines, opened up vast natural areas to production at heavy cost to man and nature, before much more powerful engines, using new energy sources such as oil, more lately brought access to extended areas and opportunities of exploitation in depth. Compare this iron and wooden relic of early days preserved in Death Valley, California (A.14) with the modern ditch digger (A.16) daily making 350 feet of 10 feet × 11 feet trench for San Francisco's water supply.

$1440
Total Price

HAWAIIAN OCEAN VIEW ESTATES

Only $15 per month including interest after low down payment.

More land for the money than any other Hawaiian Subdivision. Full acre Estates for only 2½¢ per square foot. Final unit now open.
5400 The Toledo, Long Beach, California.

OFFICE - MARLIN PLAZA - KAILUA TEL. 258-161 237-233

(A.15) California real estate knowhow leaps the ocean to Hawaii to subdivide for development some 10,000 acres of lavaflow land stretching back high up the misty slopes behind this cosmetically landscaped shop-window plot on the west coast of the big island of Hawaii, still relatively unspoilt compared with what has happened on smaller Oahu around the State capital city of Honolulu. Little is left beyond the long reach of jet airlines and of jet-age commercial ingenuity.

A.16

The hand-tool has become a machine, the machine has become technology, and technology has enabled mass-production assembly lines to pour mechanised personal and household equipment into communities where people live. People, like nature, are now at the receiving end of the impacts of technology, and must adapt themselves to it or suffer in similar ways.

The greatest impact is made by motor vehicles, those dear monsters which appear to us singly as pets, but collectively demand the transformation of our cities and countryside, and the dwarfing of all other human activities in their favour. Los Angeles, here seen through an airborne fisheye lens (A.17) is perhaps the clearest example. Vast freeways suck away the community's vital strength, like Crown-of-Thorns Starfish devouring the living thin layer of coral on a tropical reef. No one wanted or expected this to happen. Our culture and our institutions simply leave us as defenceless in face of the imperatives of masterless technology as nature itself, until we awaken and band together with nature in enforcing principles both more natural and more human.

Technology mass-produces not only products but chronic problems for the environment. The Tyne at Newcastle in northern England (A.18) was once a clear fresh salmon river. Now loaded with refuse, sewage and run-off water, polluted with chemicals and detergents, deoxygenated by large-scale demands for cooling electric power stations, and visually degraded by destruction of trees and riverside plants it faces a slow painful struggle back towards health and the expression of renewed harmony between man and nature. Meanwhile, it mirrors the minds and values of its human neighbors.

Early conservation legislation to protect English timber reserves was the spur for Abraham Darby, early in the 18th century, to develop methods for regaining freedom of industrial operation by switching from charcoal to coal for iron smelting. He can hardly have foreseen that his independent gesture would open the way to a world-transforming steel industry which would use its freedom from environmental controls to treat the atmosphere we breathe as in A.19, photographed at Scunthorpe, Lincolnshire. Being, as it happens, near England's east coast much of this fouled air is carried by prevailing winds across the North Sea to Scandinavia where its unwelcome effects are becoming increasingly conspicuous.

Dumping vast quantities of toxic chemical in the atmosphere is by no means the only adverse byproduct of technologically wasteful methods of making steel. Demands on coal and on water have been so great as to result in large areas of derelict land being created by mining subsidence and surface spoil, as well as additional reservoirs claiming valuable farming land or sites of high scientific interest in the absence of timely development on desalination of sea-water or of multi-use coastal barrages.

What the ironmasters had to accept for conservation of forests for three hundred years all industry must now accept for all natural resources. The free-for-all is ending. Thamesside, as A.20 shows, has gone some way to minimise soot and smoke, but exhibits a further modern industrial problem in the amount of land absorbed for stacked materials or finished products which might by improved organisation be kept moving to leave the land uncluttered and to speed the economic turnover. Bad conservation is almost always also bad management and bad business.

A.20

By the mid-twentieth century human capacity for senseless waste and damage to the natural environment had mushroomed up to the megaton scale. On 25th July 1946, a few days after the first talks on launching an International Union for the Conservation of Nature, this nuclear explosion at Bikini (A.21) sucked up two million tons of water followed by that ominous cloud, whose shadow in a sense darkened the world. It ranged masses of mankind against the unrestrained licence of the old order, which remained ready to countenance and develop even such monstrous recklessness towards the survival of humanity and of the natural environment. Fall-out of dangerous radio-active atmospheric pollutants over much of the earth gave rise to health hazards and possibilities of genetic damage which could no longer be laughed off. Governments were compelled to bow to world public opinion to the extent of desisting eventually from indiscriminate nuclear tests. The trauma was felt this time not only by nature but in the hearts and minds of men, and is well symbolised by this picture.

No such single dramatic impact symbolised the simultaneous explosion of human population, and the rapid approach of standing room only for the human race. On that this final picture (A.22) is enough comment.

being those of 1815 and 1938, which blew down whole forests.

This work appears to have disposed of two hitherto fashionable ecological theories—first that before modern human disturbance the forest maintained itself in a stable "climax condition", and secondly that this primitive "natural" forest was entirely different from the revived forest areas which can be seen spreading over abandoned farmlands in New England, New York State and elsewhere. On the other hand it confirms that the renewed natural forest only develops from farmland through various seral stages, the most important being stands of white pine.

No such study has yet been made in England, but there is reason to expect that when it is it will be led to very different conclusions. Systematic clearance of primitive forest in England dates back around three thousand years, which is a long time even in the history of woodlands. Moreover it has been very thorough and almost complete, in that no major natural woodlands have been in existence as such for several centuries.

Few extant woodlands, even of a drastically modified character, stand on land which has carried trees uninterruptedly since early prehistory. Moreover, we know that certain species of trees once prominent in native woodlands have become scarce and local, and that others have been extensively planted in new areas, such as the two oaks, the Scots pine and the beech, or have been introduced from other countries, or even other continents, on a massive scale. In cases where woodland is now permitted to grow up spontaneously on former grasslands or on clear-felled sites it does not therefore in England, as it may well in North America, bear any marked resemblance in composition or in other characteristics to the native woodlands before human destruction and exploitation.

These examples serve to bring out the point that while it is usually safer not to assume that any given ecosystem of plants and animals is now identical with or even at all like what it was, say, a thousand years ago, every case must be investigated on its merits. Conditions known to be of artificial origin may, as Raup shows, closely approximate to the natural, while apparently natural situations may have been drastically modified by even long-past human intervention.

The borderline between the "natural" and the artificial can be very arbitrary. The badly damaged surroundings of a large dam can closely resemble those at the tail of a medium sized glacier on a mountainside. A place where geothermal vents cluster on the earth's surface, or the site of a recent lava-flow, can be very like areas of industrial dereliction. The distribution, frequency and pattern of humanly induced changes in

C

the environment, such as erosion, are often novel and readily identifiable, but there are few such abuses for which some close parallel is nowhere to be found in nature. It is even possible that at certain periods of intense seismic and volcanic activity the extent of areas temporarily blighted and the adverse impact on wild life may well have exceeded the corresponding repercussions of modern human interference.

The more successful plants are in exploiting the terrain as they find it, the more options are opened for alternative types of community to exploit their primary biological productivity. These choices can be made through three main mechanisms. The first is natural selection entirely independent of human interference. The second is human management or intervention of any kind to alter or limit the trends which natural selection would dictate, as in the case where grazing livestock are introduced, or timber is extracted from forest. The third is the more or less complete suppression by man of the natural ecosystem in favour of some artefact such as a ricefield, a sugar-cane crop or a plantation of conifers.

In all three instances the goal of successive choices is the maximisation of biological productivity. Partly through ignorance and partly because of the more limited range of end-products acceptable to him, man has often tended to misjudge the capacity and the finer limitations of natural ecosystems, in trying to manage them or supersede them by something more to his liking. In extreme cases, unhappily by no means rare right down to the present day, he has not merely been frustrated in attaining the desired biological dividend, but has ended by injuring or even destroying the future biological productivity of the site, as happens where unwise land-use creates widespread soil erosion.

In other instances, as in many African areas where native wild herbivores have been replaced by biologically less productive and less healthy cattle, he has been misled by uncritical subservience to tradition into practices of management which yield less meat at higher cost while also deteriorating the capital asset. This has been done not by supposedly ignorant natives but by Europeans advised by agricultural specialists of high standing. In other cases, of which sugar-cane in Barbados and elsewhere is an excellent example, managers keeping close to natural processes have been able to substitute for a useless plant cover a crop of high economic value maintaining a productivity per acre at least as high as that realised by any natural alternative plant cover.

In every case, whether the choice is made by natural or human agency or by a blend of both, three criteria are decisive. Does the choice make sense ecologically, as being the, or one of the, patterns of end-

66

product consistent with maximising biological productivity over a long period? Do the means adopted in fulfilling the choice harmonise with the physical and biological conditions governing the site, taking into account any biologically sound modification of these conditions which may be practicable in the case of human exploitation? Last, do both the goal and the means make sense in terms of the potential and the vulnerability of the natural or humanly modified environment involved?

The blind workings of natural processes, with all their limitations and dependence on trial and error, do in the long run tend towards maximum biological productivity through maximum diversity and ecological specialisation. Human resource management, from primitive days right down to the latest technological projects, has no such built-in tendency towards sound solutions. On the contrary its efforts to work through the minimum number of species, with minimum diversification and ecological division of function, aiming to concentrate biological productivity on the production of a single crop to be removed from the ecosystem with or without artificial replacement of the lost nutrients, is inherently dangerous and unsound. Attempts to disguise and counter-act these weaknesses by the massive injection of toxic chemicals and other supposed remedies can aggravate the situation.

The first ten thousand or so years of man's activities in growing crops, rearing livestock and harvesting timber, were spent in empirical advances without the benefit of ecological science. We are now in the final years of this primitive era, at a peculiar phase when primary producers have at least warmly embraced science in every form except the one most essential to their task. Chemistry, mechanical engineering, genetics, parasitology, physiology and others have during the past thirty years been massively integrated in agricultural practice, but ecology has continued to be rejected as firmly as the other sciences were before 1930. The reasons for this deliberate blindness are complex, but they are also transitory. The ecological revolution is about to overtake the primary producers and their blinkered technical advisers. Its coming has been visible for a long time, at least since the work of Darwin, of whom it was rightly said that he saw what everyone had seen but thought what no one had thought about it.

It was a tragedy that his thoughts so instantly horrified and antagon-ised the religious that their significance in relation to the living natural world and man's treatment of it was largely neglected for generations. Only very recently have ecological advances and improved methods of handling and interpreting ecological data enabled the central task which Darwin began to be resumed in a manner and spirit worthy of his pioneer leadership. To master the processes by which the earth has become clothed with living forms, capable of creating and sustaining the complex higher activities which we have inherited and enjoy and benefit from, and to adjust all human attitudes and practices to harmonise with and to further those natural processes, is one of the greatest tasks now facing mankind.

4

SEVEN CIRCUITS ROUND THE EARTH

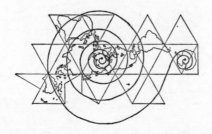

Even in the so-called jet age rather few of the world's leading decision-takers have ever set eyes upon more than an insignificant part of their native planet. Most of these few are familiar with a scattered series of cities and actively exploited areas, and have only the sketchiest idea of the natural environment in general. Lacking also any serious geographic and ecological education or training they are little better than absentee managers. The much wider population forming public opinion is in even worse shape. It is possible, indeed probable, that within the near future they will be in command of considerably more comprehensive, scientific and accurate information about the moon than they have about the earth. Such is the current state of environmental illiteracy that this discreditable and damaging ignorance is complacently accepted as natural and inevitable.

Those who have had the good fortune to see, both from the air and on the ground, a reasonable range of samples of the tropical, temperate and polar natural environments are still few, and unfortunately their sporadic efforts to communicate what they have seen cannot compare with the brief but massive and intensive message of the astronauts. Without any illusions about its adequacy this chapter has the task of trying to convey some idea of the kind of visual experience and of insight given by a traveller's view of the globe, as it looks to trained eyes. At least it can go beyond abstract and verbal generalisations, and can deal in more pictorial and substantial perspective with what is actually to be seen, by creating, as a substitute for first-hand experience, an imaginary aerial journey spiralling seven times round the globe, so as to make a strip transect crossing all the continents and oceans.

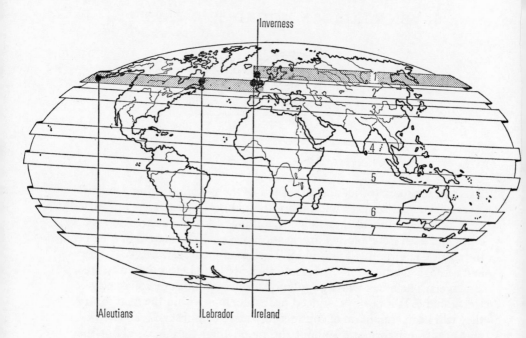

Starting in Highland Scotland from Inverness, within about 2300 miles of the North Pole, the first circuit, despite its high latitude, begins over temperate subhumid former forest lands and ice-free seas, thanks to the Gulf Stream. Trees can grow tall in such a climate, but this is not apparent since for centuries they have not normally been allowed to grow to maturity here before being burned or felled (see Plate C2). There is also a paucity of tree species in northern Europe, and especially in Britain, related to the very recent and drastic glaciation centered upon Scandinavia. For practical purposes Norway and Sweden are among the world's newest countries, having only as recently as six or seven thousand years ago emerged from under an ice-cap comparable with that of modern Greenland. As the ice melted and Scandinavia became unburdened of it the land rose by as much as 20 meters in southern Sweden and 250 meters in the north. Any thought that this all happened long ago should take account of the fact that the compensating lift is still continuing, that the immature drainage systems of

Scandinavia, including the recently-formed sump which we call the Baltic Sea, are still taking shape, and that soil formation and colonisation by plants and animals are still at a relatively early stage of evolution. Can it be entirely a coincidence that these newly-minted and fast-evolving lands on both sides of the North Sea have contributed to mankind some of its most adventurous and pragmatic races?

Paradoxically, however, it is the immensely old Fenno-Scandinavian shield which forms the original firm rock nucleus on which was based the later more southerly structural development of Europe, including such geologically recent if imposing erections as the Alps. It would therefore be more correct to regard the Scandinavian countries not as being new, but as old lands newly reopened to plant animal and human settlement after the last glacial interruption. The fact remains that, as lately as when man had already become a town-dweller in the Middle East, these lands were still utterly uninhabitable, in terms not only of neolithic but of modern technology. Man is pressing that closely in the wake of natural amelioration. Even so the world's most northerly band of major cities is still as far south as 60 degrees. This includes Bergen, Oslo, Stockholm, Helsinki, and Leningrad.

Passing eastward over Finland we leave behind the mild and moist oceanic influences and enter the drier, colder continental zone of northern coniferous forest, widely known by its Russian name as *taiga*. Except in parts of Siberia this immense forest, although natural and still largely intact, is a very recent colonist of its present area, between the largely destroyed temperate forests or the steppe to the south and the still perpetually cold, dry tundra, gripped by permafrost to the north, separating it from the ice-packed Arctic Ocean. Although much of this now tree-covered area was free of the last icecaps it was then so cold that the tundra held the treeline far south of its present limit.

Apart from the north-south line of the Urals this is a remarkably flat low-lying region, draining rather inconveniently into the Arctic Ocean, and presenting an opportunity and a challenge for major technological reconstruction of the river systems which nature has hitherto left in so immature and unsatisfactory a state. Up to now Soviet technology has dotted only relatively few factories and settlements throughout this zone, which remains, as it has been ever since pre-history, dedicated to no significant land use beyond the trapping of fur-bearing animals.

A quarter of the way round the globe, but still less than half-way across the Soviet Union near the Arctic Circle, the great Siberian plain ends abruptly after the crossing of the River Yenesei. In its place rises the great mountainous upland which reaches northward from Mongolia towards the Arctic Ocean, and which geologically forms the firm nucleus of Asia. Here is also the region of greatest seasonal temperature range on earth, from more than 70° below zero Fahrenheit in winter to more than 110 degrees in summer—values which at either extreme are matched in few other regions. Yet it was paradoxically only in this region, now of such climatic extremes, that trees were able to grow north of the Arctic Circle during the last Ice Age. There were, however, also local icecaps.

The second largest remaining tract of tundra in the eastern hemisphere is that which covers the whole north-east corner of Asia as far south as Kamchatka. Here was the former land bridge between Asia and North America, so important in the history of plant, animal and human distribution. Man crossed this way from the Old World to occupy the New, right down along the Andes, long before the more articulate and boastful Atlantic cultures of Europe made their quite recent "discovery" of the Americas. This crossing has been breached by the most northerly arm of the Pacific, beyond which, on the Alaskan as on the Siberian shore, the tundra bends far southward, covering the western flank of the coniferous forest (see Plate B5) down to the Alaska Peninsula.

Dipping southwards over the Bering Sea our course is set past Mount McKinley, the highest in North America, marking the hinge of that world range which runs with only minor interruptions from Patagonia up the Andes and Rockies to the Aleutians and thence through east Asia to the Himalayas, Caucasus, Taurus, Alps and Atlas. Alaska thus forms the link between the Old and New Worlds, between the Pacific and the Arctic Oceans, and between the vast empty northern wildernesses and the busy world of man. Here however, as at intervals in Siberia, occasional and sometimes large new projects (such as the newly found tundra oilfield near Prudhoe) interrupt the conspicuous predominance of surviving natural areas. We are traversing a zone to which man as a significant disturbing factor is a late comer, only now beginning to make a visible impact. Much more conspicuous is the impact of volcanic action, which earlier this century literally blew the top off Mount Katmai; of earthquakes, such as caused havoc in the city of Anchorage in 1964; of forest fires; and of floods, such as in 1967 devastated Fairbanks, seat of the University of Alaska. Not only the climate and the obdurate underlayer of perma-frost but the uncertainties of nature challenge the tough pioneer spirit so prominent among Alaskans.

Crossing the Alaska Highway, itself a monument to determination, and entering Canada near the confluence of the Yukon and its equally famous tributary the Klondike, we continue east through nearly a hundred degrees of longitude across the coniferous forests, the lakes and later the tundra of sub-arctic Canada—again an almost empty world. Leaving behind the transient sites of the gold rush and the western mountains our course leads over the Basin of the Mackenzie and the Great Slave Lake. Here place-names recall the more prolonged occupancy of the fur traders and the Hudson's Bay Company, whose returns of skins bought over the centuries unwittingly provided one of the more important stores of data for tracing cycles of animal abundance and scarcity. South-eastwards stretches one of the earth's greatest complexes of inland waters, terminating in the Great Lakes of the St. Lawrence system, while the crossing of Hudson Bay touches the southern fringe of the earth's greatest complex of islands, culminating in Baffin Island, Ellesmere Island and Greenland.

Approaching the coast of Labrador, where the clustered black spruces appear as miniature tree-symbols against a background of snow and ice, the mosaic of the tundra and the dark limitless northern coniferous forests end at last, never to reappear except on occasional alpine up-thrusts in lower latitudes. With increasing mileage and experience it ceases to be quite so surprising to reach, often quite abruptly, the end of dominant types of vegetation or land-use which have begun to seem endless. The patterns of the earth's diversity are themselves diverse. Some types, such as muskegs or peatbogs tend to be scattered in mainly small or very small units, while most of the world total of others may be assembled in rather few continuous tracts.

It should also be noted, as the North Atlantic lies below us wreathed in its characteristic fog-banks, between which icebergs can be seen floating, that the traverse of no less than 300 meridians of longitude without being more than momentarily out of sight of land is something that will not be repeated on the long journey ahead. Although at this point little over 2,000 miles broad, or just about the diameter of the moon, the Atlantic affords a first indication of the importance of the role of oceans on the surface of the earth. Rich marine fisheries and busy shipping routes, as well as its now congested airspace, lend a significance to this particular ocean crossing far greater than its relative size would suggest.

SECOND CIRCUIT—Shannon/Vladivostok/San Francisco/Portugal

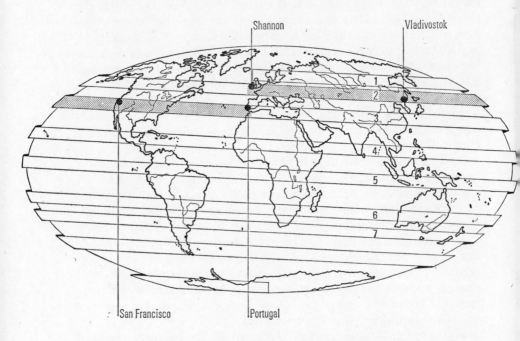

On this track the eastern landfall comes on the Irish coast near the mouth of the Shannon. Here the vivid emeralds and warm browns of the wet windswept landscape, with its worked patterns of blanket bog, and the countless pocket-sized walled farms, all of different shapes and layouts, introduce us to a range of ecosystems long ago empirically converted to human use. In its Celtic irrationality and charm this landscape is a reminder of the distinctive and persistent forms which partnerships between different human races and different lands can take. The tendency to overlook or underrate this valuable and highly significant diversity needs to be corrected.

Quickly crossing Ireland and St George's Channel we see a similar pattern momentarily repeated in south-west Wales, soon giving way to our first landscape of industrialism. Along Milford Haven modern landscaping has governed layouts of oil refineries and the new pattern of planned land use (see Plates D 8–9). Farther east the full impact and horror of earlier uninhibited industrialism, based on nineteenth-century

74

coal-mining and metal industries, is revealed in the valleys and coastal belt from Swansea to Newport. It is succeeded on Severnside by a newer larger landscape of technology, including a strip steel mill, the mile-long road bridge, the Filton aviation plant where the British proto-type Concorde was built, and two nuclear power stations. Nature matches this scale with the Severn's tidal rise and fall of more than 40 feet, one of the greatest on earth.

As our transect crosses southern England the contrast between the settled pastoral West country and the modernised and expanding cereal-based farming of the East opens a theme of interacting agricul-tural systems and landscape which from now on will be endlessly repeated. The ports of Bristol and London, London Airport, and the great built-up area of London itself, also bring our first conspicuous demonstration of the immense impact of modern megalopolitan civilisation on the face of the land. Across the North Sea the vast modern Europort of Rotterdam, the taming of the Rhine mouth through the ambitious Delta scheme, the great Ijsselmeer reclamation of land from water, and the uniquely domesticated, utterly flat water-meshed landscape of the old Netherlands between them impress on us even more strongly the scale and diversity of the potentialities developed by mankind for changing the earth. Without man nothing remotely like the country we now see beneath us could exist (see Plate C16). The spread of the adjoining Ruhr industrial complex across the German borders, and the scale of road, river, canal and rail traffic indicated by the transport network reinforce the same point. Megalopolis is much more than a normal big town magnified. It is a burst of technological vigor by which the towns themselves become dominated. The human scale, equally with the natural, is damaged by its cold imperatives.

We now cross the heartland of the oldest highly developed continent, from which has stemmed so much skilled production, so much learning, music and art, so many social advances and so much war and destruc-tion. In this ordered landscape the careful management of forests for long-term sustained yield, the drastic regimentation of watercourses and the well-tended patterns of farming point to a certain maturity of relationship between man and environment, marred however, in places by marks of pollution or unnecessarily brutal treatment during development. As pollen counts show, it is around 4,500 years since the primitive forests of this region went down before fire and axe. The contrast between the Teutonic, the English and the Irish landscapes gives cause for reflection. Each mirrors the people who made it.

Across southern Poland and western Russia we pass over the rich black-earth tracts of the Ukraine and the vast plains merging into the open steppes, so different from the endless coniferous forest belt of our earlier more northerly transect across the U.S.S.R. Southwards stretches the earth's greatest landlocked lake, the Caspian. Entering Asia again we are retracing towards their origins the routes of the successive conquering hordes, invincibly endowed with horsepower, which changed human history some three thousand years ago, and tamed the then greatest empires of south-west Asia and beyond. Until dramatically superseded by modern planned mechanisation this Cossack horsepower contributed to the military strength of Russia. Mechanisation however, although strongly based on a fabulous abundance of natural resources, could not save the Kruschev virgin lands reclamation program from taking a severe beating owing to a prolonged run of dry seasons, for which the engineers and politicians proved no match.

Gradually the soil grows more arid, the great rivers fewer and narrower, the contours steeper, and we are through the Dzungarian Gate and over the Gobi, the northernmost of the great deserts. Northwards of this track over Mongolia lie some of the coldest, most inhospitable and most thinly inhabited regions on earth, while southwards, and towards the Pacific coast, are concentrated not far short of one-quarter of mankind, in China and the neighboring lands.

Crossing the southern extremity of the Soviet Far East near Vladivostok, over the Sea of Japan and the northern Japanese island of Hokkaido, we are launched on nearly one hundred degrees longitude of ocean traverse, with the sobering thought that we are still at one of the narrower sections of the Pacific. Not a single island breaks the monotony at this latitude, before our next landfall on the Californian coast near San Francisco, already at the southern end of the great coastal forests of western North America.

Here is the home of the earth's tallest trees, reaching nearly up to 400 feet in the case of the Coast Redwoods, followed by other outstanding species such as the giant Sequoiadendron and the Douglas Fir. The well-known beauties of San Francisco are offset on the Bay by some of the most aggravated conservation problems in the world, and by the tendency of so many people attracted by the charms of California to destroy what has led them there.

Here, in sharp contrast to Europe, there has been no sophisticated tradition of living with and managing the land. No patient land-loving peasantry has been on hand to convert natural ecosystems into endless parkland, as Europe often appears to air travellers from other continents. On the contrary a natural paradise has been rapidly converted into what has been unkindly called God's Own Junkyard through the insensitive rectilinear subdivisions of real estate men, the get-rich-quick attitudes which have brought in millions of incomers, and the prevalent low level of awareness of landscape design and care. The intensive fruit-growing development of the San Joaquin Valley, the famous wonders of the Yosemite National Park (see Plate D4) and the surviving keenly appreciated wildernesses of the Sierra Nevada are conspicuous indicators that here is one of the world's decisive testing areas for conservation.

Far beyond is the crossing of the continental divide at the main ridge of the Rockies, and the long traverse over the former Western prairies which were converted after the coming of the railroad into highly cultivated lands supplying distant industrial populations. The meeting of the Mississippi and the Missouri near St Louis forms the earth's third longest river, possessing a force which sometimes enables it temporarily to defeat the efforts to tame it of the world's technologically strongest nation. Although little shorter than the Amazon its flow is less than one-sixth in volume, and its basin is less than half in extent, but economically vastly more important. The rapid and spectacular success of the exploitation of the Middle West has, perhaps more than any other single factor, led people during the past century to overrate the easy opportunities and to underrate the many obstacles when seeking to cash in on nature.

In the history of conservation an important place is held by a large tributary of the Mississippi, the Ohio River, which lies ahead on the same course. It was the deforestation and erosion of the upper basin of the Ohio which caused the calamitous floods of 1913. By unusual wisdom and good fortune the right conclusions were drawn, and effective long-term measures to prevent a repetition were set in hand. These measures have provided perhaps the best confirmation so far of the general correctness of the diagnosis and prescription offered by conservation. They have greatly influenced subsequent thought and action elsewhere, notably in the neighboring basin of the Tennessee, where the Tennessee Valley Authority has carried out successful large-scale projects over nearly forty years.

Leaving the historic Ohio valley we cross the long chain of the Appalachians, also well-known to conservationists for the Appalachian Trail, and for the Shenandoah National Park with its famous Blue Ridge Highway. Very soon we are over Washington D.C., which not only contains one of the greatest concentrations of conservation knowledge and effort in the world, but, through the National Capital Parks and other projects, is rich in demonstrations of conservation, landscaping and good design for land use, conspicuous even from the air.

Beyond Washington the coast is soon reached, and the course continues north of the warm but biologically poor Sargasso Sea—native area of both American and European eels—and over the Azores. Here, deep under the ocean, the junction of the main mid-Atlantic Ridge with its spur stretching eastwards towards Cape St Vincent has given birth to one of the few groups of seamounts rising high enough from the ocean floor to break its surface, as the Hawaiian and so many other volcanoes have done in the Pacific. The submarine topography as we now know it shows conclusively how the earth's crust has become torn and fissured here, just as in such terrestrial rift phenomena as the Dead Sea.

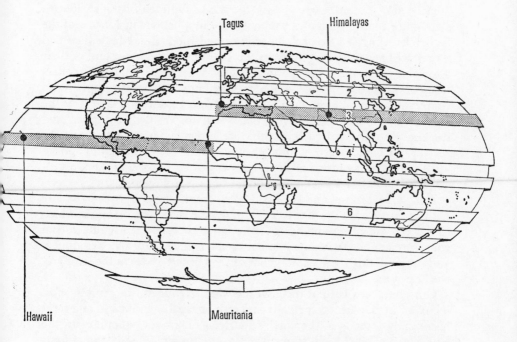

With our next landfall, in Portugal, we complete a second orbit of the northern hemisphere, over 1,500 miles southward of our starting point at Inverness. Here again, as in reaching Alaska, we are contemplating one of the great hinges of the world geography, and this time of history too. It is a hinge between Europe and Africa, between the Atlantic and the Mediterranean, between the regime of endlessly advancing depressions bringing year-round moisture and oceanic mildness to the north, and the North African Mediterranean region of hot dry summers and cool moist winters, buttressed by the Azorean high pressure system.

Crossing the extreme south-western coast of Europe south of the Tagus estuary in Portugal we see below, near Setubal, a small relic of the mixed deciduous woodland which was a key *refugium* during the maximum glaciation for many of the deciduous trees and plants which were to recolonise Europe as the ice withdrew, and to form the basis of modern European vegetation. Here, some 2,500 years ago, was the base from which small pioneer groups of men, having burst out from the closed world of the Mediterranean, began to acquire more wide-reaching and adventurous attitudes which prepared their occupation of western Europe, and especially the British Isles.

Here also, in south-west Spain, the Arabs founded in their Moorish state more than a thousand years ago the first centers in Europe of the higher learning, and especially science and medicine, which they had themselves acquired largely from the Persians at the other end of their astonishingly farflung dominions. It was by that path that the intellectual concepts and stimuli which we are here engaged in applying to conservation first filtered through to the West. Here much later, was the base from which Prince Henry the Navigator trained, equipped and despatched the Portuguese oceanic explorers, who were to open the seaways by which western man learnt to know and contrived to dominate and exploit so much of the earth previously beyond his ken, a process which has so far been going on for only around 500 years.

Here also, around the Gulf of Cadiz, were fought between the late 16th century and the battle of Trafalgar a series of seafights which closed the era of dominance of international trade by Mediterranean countries, and led to its supersession by the 19th century Pax Britannica, and subsequently by the emergence of the United States as the strongest world power.

Our course leads right through the Mediterranean, the largest, most self-contained, most ecologically and economically significant, and most historically famous of the earth's fourteen major seas ancillary to the four oceans. The Mediterranean is also the type region for one of best-known and best-liked climates, warm and dry in summer, moist but rarely cold in winter. The full range of varieties of Mediterranean climates is however only demonstrated in a country which would hardly come to mind as belonging here—Morocco with its peculiar band of altitudes, its span from ocean over mountains to desert, and its fortunate shape and situation.

The Mediterranean is rich in peninsulas, notably the Iberian, Italian and Greek, and in islands, headed by Sicily and Sardinia. It is also a center of major seismic and volcanic activity. Antiquities and remains of great past civilisation are thick on the ground. Egypt, Crete, Greece, Phoenicia, Carthage and Rome worked in relays towards the attainment of civilisation as we know it. They have also left evidences and legacies of long-continuing misuse of land and natural resources, indicated by wholesale erosion and deforestation.

Passing eastwards we encounter the faint traces of several of the earliest civilisations in Asia Minor and across the northern edge of the

Fertile Crescent in modern Syria and Iraq. It was probably somewhree in this region, perhaps as much as 10,000 years ago, that skilful exploitation of domesticated cattle, sheep, and goats enabled man to embark on animal husbandry, followed probably within another 2–3,000 years by the development of bread grains as a practical basis for the earliest systematic farm operations, and not long afterwards by the breaking in of draught animals to a primitive form of plough. Mixed farming, urbanism and empires arose in quick succession here, and soon began their spread throughout the world, which has continued into the most recent times. During this century large-scale exploration of oil has once more conferred on these Middle Eastern lands an international importance which they had long lost. By night the plumed flames light the desert, and by day it is scarred by the indignity of surface pipelines.

Geologically the Taurus and the linked Elburz range of mountains lead on to the vast and lofty Tertiary folding which centers on the Himalayas and the Tibetan Plateau. Here is the earth's most elevated and extensive highland region, from which issue two of its five longest rivers (the Yangtze and the Hwang Ho) as well as such other giants as the Mekong, Brahmaputra, Indus, Oxus, Ganges and Irrawaddy. While on its southern slopes this region carries major forest, to the west and north, from Iran to west China, its covering is the largest block of poor grassland on the planet. To the south again lies one of the densest great blocks of human population, especially along the Ganges Valley and between Bombay and Madras, but northwards the mountains interpose an almost empty high tableland separating from it to the east the greatest of all human concentrations in the Chinsese lowlands. For peculiar reasons this powerful mass of advanced and industrious people has for thousands of years led a self-contained existence within China. Should that inward-looking tradition ever be broken the fate of mankind could be changed.

Passing along a route above the crest line of the Himalayas we are able to appreciate this abrupt confrontation between some of the most impressive natural features of the earth and the teeming human millions, which here assume a numerical scale most menacing both to their natural environment and to their own future prospects as human individuals. How can such unwisely generated masses of mankind be educated, equipped, fed, clothed and served with their collective requirements in any way compatible with a civilised society? How soon and how abruptly will it prove possible to turn the flowing human tide? Can even a semblance of public order, civilisation and hygiene be maintained in such conditions?

Leaving India over Assam, which was until lately mistakenly regarded as the earth's area of highest rainfall, our course slants gradually southwards to meet the Tropic of Cancer over southern China, through the lower zones of the world's most populous lands. To the south, Vietnam is a reminder of the continuing horrors of mankind's obsessive tendency vainly to seek solutions of disputes by war; the means have here included wholesale attacks upon the natural environment by use of defoliants and other chemicals, as well as fire and immense quantities of high explosive.

Near Hong Kong the coast of Asia is crossed and the full breadth of the Pacific lies ahead, with the next mainland coast of Mexico as far distant ahead as Washington D.C. is distant astern of us. Once past the South China Sea, with Taiwan/Formosa to the north and Luzon, the largest island of the Philippines to the south we are crossing empty and in parts immensely deep seas, where sunken canyons reach down into the earth's crust 30,000 feet below the waves. Here is a zone of perpetual tension, seismic and volcanic, climatic and strategic. Earthquakes and typhoons, tidal waves and sea and air battles have within recent memory all in turn shattered its peace, and even nuclear test explosions (see Plate A21) have been thrown in for good measure.

Micronesia, where about three million square miles of ocean contain 2,141 significant islands totalling in land area only 687 square miles, is the first typically oceanic Pacific group, in strong contrast to the broad sweep of the continents. The "high" volcanic or limestone islands are counter-balanced by the flat coral atolls, often girdling large lagoons, and bearing as many as a hundred or more distinct emerging fragments of land, if the smallest islets are included.

Such belts of rapid and arbitrary change are a counterpoise to the more continuous continental expanses where gradual evolution proceeds with apparent order and cohesion. They are natural experiments, illuminating biological and geographic processes. For plants and animals, although no longer for man, they have provided isolated sanctuaries.

After the diminutive and now spoilt Wake Island the Hawaiian group lies to the north, starting with the small uninhabited leeward islands, last relics of a major cluster whose long-spent volcanic nuclei are eroded right down to sealevel. Passing eastwards, more recent and even current volcanic activity has thrust up islands presently much higher and larger, which are scientifically among the most remarkable spots on earth. One, Kauai, claims also to be the wettest, with an annual average rainfall of 486 inches and about 335 rainy days on Mount Waialeale. Another, the big island of Hawaii itself, is the tallest structure in nature, rising over 30,000 feet from its base on the ocean floor. No other island group so remote is so significant in so many different ways.

Biologically it evolved a higher proportion of endemic animals and plants than any other area, although a tragically large number of these have carelessly been made extinct. Humanly, despite some notable attainments, Hawaii emerged from prehistory only a couple of centuries ago, and promptly made up for lost time by using European arms, acquired by fair means or foul, to unify the eight inhabited islands into a pseudo-European kingdom. England was taken as the model, and hence the flag of Hawaii, somewhat anomalously for one of the fifty United States, still incorporates the Union Flag of Britain. Having rocketed up to international importance during the past three decades the State of Hawaii demonstrates how jet aircraft, modern mass mobility for tourism and modern strategic patterns can rapidly compensate for having missed the industrial revolution and the railway age. In the fast-expanding importance of the Pacific Hawaii as a center of communications, of learning, and of economic prosperity exercises influence disproportionate to its 630,000 inhabitants. An unfortunate by-product is the intense pressure for speculative development (see Plate A15).

After a further long stretch of featureless ocean, surpassing in breadth the entire North Atlantic, we reach the Mexican coast near the end of Baja California, an 800-mile long peninsula, paralleling the mainland shore a hundred miles beyond. The lack of rainfall and the heat make it mostly a seagirt desert, unique on earth, and thus still largely in its natural state. The scattered Indian tribes, who inhabited it up to a couple of centuries ago, were unintentionally exterminated by Catholic missionaries who brought them not only the white man's Christian religion but the white man's lethal diseases. The nearness of already crowded English-speaking California, with its restless and ingenious technologists, warns us to look on this peaceful condition as probably only ephemeral, and as a transient opportunity for launching real conservation ahead of or concurrently with development. The surrounding waters of the Gulf of the Pacific are rich in animal life. The Mohole project for drilling down right through the crust of the earth is being undertaken off these shores.

Having at last regained the American continental mass it is remarkable to find its breadth at this latitude slimmed down to a mere 600 miles, spanning a range of climates from hot and humid to cool and dry and back again to hot on the shore of the Gulf of Mexico, where the oilfield of Tampico is situated. At a similar distance across the Gulf of

Campeche we cross the north of Yucatan, famous for its remains of the great Mayan culture. The Mayans, despite their dense tropical forest environment, reached a high level of knowledge and achievement between 1,600 and a thousand years ago, long before the arrival of Columbus on the offshore islands of the neighboring West Indies (which he persisted in believing to be part of India).

Over these the course now runs, between the largest islands, Cuba and Hispaniola to the north and the much smaller Jamaica to the south, and thence on, southward of Puerto Rico, to the hinge between the Leeward and the Windward Islands. This lies between Antigua and Guadeloupe, at the outer edge of the Caribbean Sea, the American counterpart of the Mediterranean, but more southerly and almost wholly tropical, deeper and in much fuller communication with the ocean. Here is the birthplace of great hurricanes which usually travel out north-eastward over the Atlantic or hit the neighboring North American mainland, sometimes making their dying force felt even in Western Europe.

Here was played out the contest between European powers to determine how the helpless peoples of the Americas should be ruled, should worship and should work, and which alien tongue they should speak. The falling of North America under predominantly English-speaking rulers, while South and Central America continued within the Iberian cultures was a decisive step for land use as well as for so much else.

Our third Atlantic crossing is over a narrower part of that ocean, overflying the Cape Verde islands to the African coast in Mauritania, near the south-west fringe of the Sahara.

FOURTH CIRCUIT—West Africa/Arabia/Vietnam/Galapagos/ Amazon

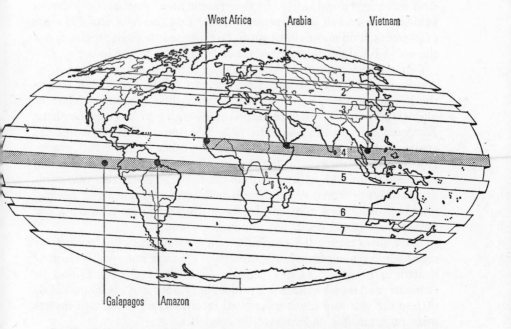

Southwards lie the rich moist forest lands from which originated the strangest and most tragic of all the great human migrations. During more than three centuries eleven million captured negroes were shipped across the Atlantic alive, while fully as many more died in transit. This slave trade from West Africa to work the European-owned plantations of the Caribbean and central and north America has left a vast and bitter inheritance of racial tensions, never greater than at this day. Men have to pay the price of treating men as callously as they have treated other natural resources.

Northward and eastward extends the earth's largest desert, the Sahara, forming today a more effective barrier to the spread of animals and plants, and of mankind, than the adjoining oceans. This barrier has at some periods been reduced by climatic amelioration, and there is growing evidence of the persistence until after Roman times of an important legacy of moisture and groundwater from the pluvial period accompanying the last Ice Age. Hannibal's elephants, still surviving in his day in North Africa were a biological windfall from this legacy. Even now much of the less accessible relict groundwater may still be tapped.

Since the 7th century the introduction from Asia of camels has enabled human travellers, initially the Arabs, to range over it a good deal more freely and safely. In very recent times mechanically driven vehicles and aircraft have opened it up farther, and have enabled some of its riches in oil and natural gas to be exploited through pipelines, but the uninhibited development of the Sahara is still in the future.

Our course runs south of the surprising mountain ranges of Hoggar or Ahaggar, and Tibesti, which form the core of the desert, but crosses the lower massifs of Air and Ennedi, with their peculiar mixture of alpine and desert life, before gradually emerging at last over northern Kordofan to cross the Blue Nile near Khartoum. This section of the course demonstrates how for man, as for other animals and plants, North Africa belongs to the Mediterranean, leaving the effective continental unit as Africa-South-of-the-Sahara. Even the vast communications potential of the Nile is nullified by distance and navigational obstacles, and above all by the surrounding desert, which allow passage to seasonal floods but to not much else.

Early this century the possibilities of gearing economic projects to social advancement from low standards of life were remarkably demonstrated here by the Gezira project. As a planned contribution to economic and social welfare this project has rarely again been matched, despite the vast and much advertised recent technical aid and investment programs for underdeveloped countries.

The Nile in Egypt demonstrates how unlimited human reproduction can quickly nullify the benefits of even so grandiose a scheme as the Assuan High Dam. For such an ephemeral gain the risk has been incurred of so sharply reducing the input of fresh water into the Eastern Mediterranean as to change its biological regime fundamentally, with unpredictable consequences. Lake Nasser, like other large man-made lakes, may prove, however, to be only a relatively minor foretaste of the modifications of geography which civil engineering will soon be used to impose.

Leaving Sudan, we pass the northern mountains of Ethiopia and the southern Red Sea before re-entering Asia at its south-western corner in the Yemen. Here, beyond a fairly narrow highland belt, begins another great stretch of desert, extending through the Rub al Khali, or Empty Quarter right up to the borders of Syria—the nursery of the Arab race, of the religion of Mohammed, and of the most tenacious nomad culture.

Although in principle the Sinai-Red Sea region might be expected to form a biological hinge between the Ethiopian, Palearctic and Oriental faunal zones this is in practice largely prevented by the impoverished and intractable desert terrain occupying so much of southern Arabia, Iran and Baluchistan. This has led Ethiopian and Palearctic desert forms to spread very thinly over a broad buffer band, with the result that we find the strength of desert influences dominating both the mutual impacts of fauna and flora and the persistent but continually erased interventions of man. Except for sheets of ice or marine transgressions, dry sand is the most effective environmental blanket for extensively cloaking or burying other influences.

Continuing eastwards we soon encounter the Arabian Sea, forming the northernmost section of the third great ocean—the Indian, only slightly smaller than the Atlantic, but contrasting with it and with the Pacific in extending north of the tropics only in its small northern outliers, the Red Sea and the Persian Gulf. Beyond the Arabian Sea the coast of southern India is crossed near the center of the Western Ghats, the long rather low mountain range dominating the narrow western coastal plain and receiving the first brunt of the monsoon rainfall which is the ocean's annual gift to India.

Asia, like America, is much slimmer in these low latitudes, and after only a few hundred miles over the South Indian uplands the coastal ricefields of Madras flank the next large tract of ocean, approaching the Bay of Bengal. The Andaman Islands, an outlying possession of India, interrupt the open sea area two-thirds of the way across to the next and last mainland Asian coast. This is crossed near the border between the southernmost tip of Burma and the even longer southerly tentacle of Thailand down the upper Malay peninsula.

Here, already past midway between the Tropic of Cancer and the Equator, we touch the slenderest and in some ways the richest and most remarkable of the equatorial lands. Vigorously exploited in modern times, especially from the Malayan border southwards, for rubber, tin, and other products, the peninsula has retained until the last few years much of its natural forest cover, and has hitherto escaped the worst of the Asian population explosion. It has, moreover, developed what is probably the world's most advanced system of land-use planning.

It was from the region stretching northwards from here that such early successes in domestication as the domestic fowl and rice-growing were achieved. Unfortunately the nature of the climate and the terrain makes the process of tracing these primitive exploits even more difficult than in drier countries. The plains of Thailand, Cambodia and South Vietnam, which we cross near its southern tip, must have played a significant role in man's transition from a hunter and food-gatherer to a tender of crops and a rearer of selected animals. Considering the probable duration of such human activities here the environment in general has not been too badly conserved.

Over the delta of the Mekong River, less widely known than it ought to be as one of the earth's great water-courses, matching in length the Mississippi and the Missouri, our eastward course now takes us for a second time out from Asia across the South China Sea (about a thousand miles southward of our previous track by Hong Kong). Here we enter what is, except for the frozen wastes of Arctic North America, the earth's most important complex of islands. On this occasion we intersect it only between Mindinao, second largest of the Philippines and Borneo, third largest of all islands, guarded at the north end, over which we pass, by the great mountain and new National Park of Kinabalu. Easing away southwards of the Micronesian ocean archipelagoes of Palau and the Carolines we pass along the north side of New Guinea, second largest of islands, where Asia gives way to Oceania, and where we leave the northern hemisphere on crossing the equator near Nauru.

Just before crossing the International Date Line (here 180° E & W) our course passes over the peculiar scattered group of coral atoll lagoons known as the Gilbert Islands, none of which rises more than 15 feet above sealevel, although Tabiteuea, immediately south of the Equator, is fifty miles long. It is such coral reefs, and the fewer but more impressive tops of great submarine mountains such as Nauru and the Hawaiian group, which make the Pacific so much the richest ocean in numbers of truly oceanic islands, through the central belt of which we are now passing.

Eastwards lie a few more scattered isles of the Phoenix and Line groups, which have the distinction of being among the latest to be annexed in the worldwide colonial expansion of the 15th-20th centuries, having offered nothing attractive to the colonial powers until the early days of trans-Pacific air travel.

Beyond these Line Islands extends a vast landless stretch of the eastern Pacific as far as the famous Galapagos group, straddling the Equator some 600 miles west of the South American coast. Galapagos is now increasingly influenced by conservation principles, mediated through the Charles Darwin Research Station, the world's first international biological station, and the source not only of much valuable scientific work but of films, writings and lectures which have done much to make real to world public opinion the urgency of conservation problems in remote lands.

88

Galapagos, although on the Equator, lies in the cold Humboldt current, which from here southwards produces such peculiar climatic effects along the west coast of South America, crossed near Guayaquil in Ecuador. Here is the most southerly part of the coastal lowland belt running down from Panama through Colombia. The northern part of that belt may yet, when properly gauged, prove to have the highest annual rainfall on earth. Yet to the south of our course, where the cold marine current touches the Pacific shore, begins one of the earth's most curious and ribbon-like coastal deserts.

Few parts of the earth show so steep a graduation of climate and ecology as the hundred-mile wide strip from the Pacific over the almost rainless Santa Elena Peninsula, the shifting agricultural areas of the coastal hills and the banana-growing and rice-growing lowlands, to the coffee-growing lower slopes from which rises steeply the Eastern Cordillera of the high Andes, dominated by the 20,000 feet dormant volcano of Chimborazo. Between the two cordilleras, from 7,000 to 9,000 feet lie the high intermont basins containing most of Ecuador's population, here largely pure-bred Indians.

This region formed the northern part of the famous Inca Empire which, in contrast to all the great early civilisations of the Old World, was not valley-based but mountain-based, hardly extending below the 7,000 feet contour. Like the Aztec, but unlike the even more impressive Mayan civilisation, it flourished until the impact of the Spanish invaders in the early 16th century, when its destruction was so complete that a traumatic cultural setback among the native peoples has persisted to this day. Nevertheless the rapid development of Spanish colonialism created a new strong urban base here a full two centuries before anything of the sort grew up in North America. This slower and longer maturity of human settlement has had far-reaching influences.

That human communities could exist at these high altitudes was due to the early discovery and exploitation of foods so valuable that their use has now spread throughout the world, particularly the potato, which was originally cultivated in these highlands. The llamas and alpacas, two cameline species now found only in a domesticated state, provided respectively transport and wool for clothing. The llamas however were not used in agriculture, nor was there a plough in pre-Columbian times, yet elaborate works of terracing, land reclamation, irrigation, and fertilisation with guano brought up from the coast were already developed. In terms of conservation the level of the pre-Spanish regime has yet to be regained here.

East of the Andes the land falls steeply, and becomes covered with the tropical evergreen forest called *selva*, broken on the upper slopes by a more open park-like blend of grassland and treecover loosely called *savanna*, or *llano*. Once known as "rain forest" this largest of the world's woodlands is characterised by pronounced climatic uniformity, with an even day-length, no distinct seasons or major fluctuations in temperature, and an enormous diversity of species—more than 4,000 species of trees alone have already been described from it. Although none grow so high as the redwoods of coastal California the canopy often reaches to between one and two hundred feet, and the trees are loaded with epiphytes, such as orchids and lianas or bushropes. Animal life is correspondingly rich and varied.

The basin of the Amazon, which begins at the Andean ridge, is much the largest of all river basins, draining 2,368,000 square miles, or more than the Nile and the Mississippi-Missouri together, while it brings down to the ocean as much water as the dozen next largest rivers combined. In length alone, however, it is slightly exceeded by the Nile. Although the Amazon is navigable by ocean ships for 1,000 miles to Manaus, Amazonia has so far almost entirely resisted development or exploitation, other than by the native Indians who inhabit it in now almost negligible numbers. The great forest, so impressive as it stands, occupies soil too infertile for cropping. The climate, the difficulties of access, the hostility of Indian tribes and health hazards render it unattractive for settlement in present conditions. It is therefore one of the few large parts of the earth where the making of a wise long-term land use plan with a clean slate is still possible.

So vast is the Amazon that it even has two tributaries, the Madeira and the Purus, which rank among the earth's twenty longest rivers in their own right. Although rubber was first cultivated along the Amazon from native wild trees the great bulk of it has long been grown in South-East Asia, to which it was introduced through the Royal Botanic Gardens, Kew.

Leaving South America just beyond the estuary of the Amazon our course diverges only gradually from the east-south-easterly alignment of the coast, one of the most suggestive indications of the original integration of South America and West Africa, postulated by the now increasingly accepted continental drift theory, and reinforced by the similar structures and ages of the precambrian rocks common to Eastern Brazil and West Africa.

Like the east Pacific, but unlike its central and western regions, the tropical Atlantic inhibits by its cold currents the growth of coral. Its only coral atoll, out of more than four hundred on the earth, is the Rocas Reef, just south of our course and westward of the island of Fernando Noronha. Here the Atlantic is at its narrowest. The nearest coasts of Africa lie well north of our course, which crosses the Gulf of Guinea south of Liberia, Ghana and Nigeria (in the angle once, so long ago, filled by the north-east corner of Brazil) touching land near Cap Lopez in Gabon.

FIFTH CIRCUIT—Lambarene/Aldabra/Java/Rio de Janeiro/ South-West Africa

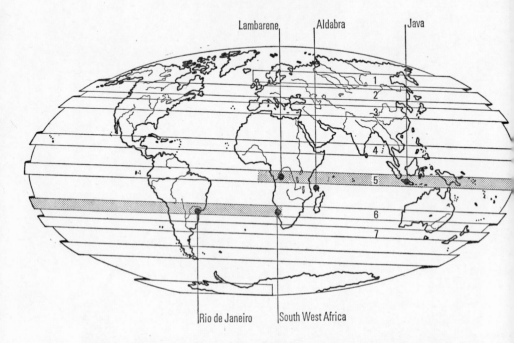

Lambarene   Aldabra   Java

Rio de Janeiro   South West Africa

Here, in beginning our fifth circuit we happen to pass Lambarene, made famous by the devotion of Albert Schweitzer—a reminder of the influence of many generations of European missionaries and idealists exerted in so many remote parts of the world.

The "rain-forest" of this area, widely used for shifting cultivation, differs from the Amazonian in being also substantially exploited for timber up to a considerable distance inland. Beyond that it falls outside the range of currently feasible commercial use, and is accordingly still a more or less intact natural area. Here we enter the basin of the Congo, the African equatorial counterpart of the Amazon, and second to it in size of drainage area and volume of flow. But while the Amazon flows east, and drains all but a small part of the broadest section of South America, the Congo is a west-flowing river, draining not more than about two-thirds of the width of Africa, well below its broadest part. Leaving it on the borders of Kivu, and crossing Lake

Kivu near Bukavu, we reach country rich in clues to the earliest progenitors of man, and pass between the heads of Lake Tanganyika, seventh largest on earth, and Victoria Nyanza, the third.

This great lake district of East Africa is also a region of wide high-lying grasslands, supporting the earth's largest and most spectacular herds of herbivores, such as elephants, rhinoceroses, wildebeest, giraffes, zebras and many species of antelope, together with their accompanying carnivores such as lions and leopards, and such other notable species as ostriches, crocodiles and vast clouds of flamingos on the lakes.

This is also a region of intense volcanic activity, and of towering mountain peaks such as Kilimanjaro and Meru. At the higher altitudes, between the treelimit and the surprising equatorial snowcaps, stretch alpine heaths remarkably like the *paramos* of the Andes, and the sub-arctic at sealevel. There could be no plainer demonstration of the relationship between high altitude and high latitude, in terms of climate and vegetation.

In terms of land use East Africa is memorable for the catastrophic repulse of one of man's biggest and brashest assaults on the natural environment, the post-World War II Ground-nuts Project, and for the equally conspicuous success of such world-famous National Parks as Serengeti and Tsavo, in combining conservation with a prominent role in the economic and touristic development of a somewhat poorly endowed region.

Here also began recently the most significant scientific studies of the relationship between natural vegetation, wild and tame large herbi-vores and human pastoralists, represented by the remarkable Masai tribe, tenaciously following their impressive traditional way of life.

Continuing north of Zanzibar the course passes north of Aldabra (see Plate B9), successfully defended by conservationists since Darwin from the conspiracies of short-sighted men to sacrifice its unique scientific value to projects of temporary expediency—most lately in the form of an aircraft staging post to support Anglo-American military interventions in the Far East. A scattering of other islands in the Seychelles and Chagos groups flank the course across the Indian Ocean to the Sunda Strait between Sumatra, the earth's sixth largest island, and Java, the thirteenth. The entry to this narrow strait is flanked by the small peninsula of Udjun Kulong, now a nature reserve and the key point in efforts to prevent the final extinction of the Javan rhinoceros. With its hundred million inhabitants (about two-thirds of them in Java, where the density averages nearly 500 per square kilo-meter) Indonesia is a leading example of the political, social and economic problems which can be created by excess of human population even on fertile and highly productive land, wisely managed and scientifically well equipped by the original Dutch colonists.

Continuing through the Java Sea, north of the islands of Madura and Bali, we cross the Wallace Line marking the faunistic boundary between Asia and Australia, and pass over a number of coral reefs as we enter the Flores Sea between Celebes and Flores. Here, more than anywhere else on earth, we are among a wealth of distinct seas flanked by an outstanding series of islands. Celebes ranks eleventh in their world order of size, and Timor, Halmahera, Flores, Ceram and others are all large enough even to outrank Jamaica. Reaching the last of these seas, the Arafura, we pass along the south coast of the second largest of all islands, New Guinea, and nearly touch the north coast of Australia at Cape York in passing through Torres Strait, past Papua and out into the Coral Sea.

Here begins the Great Barrier Reef, which runs southward for twelve hundred miles to the Tropic of Capricorn. Our route passes north of the New Hebrides, an Anglo-French condominium, and close to the Fiji Islands and Samoa, before which the International Date Line is recrossed. This part of the Pacific is one of the few parts of the world where colonialism still survives, the next archipelago being that of Tahiti, the famous center of French Polynesia. Just beyond, in the Tuamotu-Gambier Group, are five atolls where, despite strong protests, General de Gaulle's government chose to carry out nuclear bomb tests during the nineteen-sixties, an outrage against the natural environment of the Pacific.

From here eastward we re-enter the great empty quarter of the south-east Pacific, unbroken by land until we cross the South American coast near Iquique in northern Chile. Here we are confronted by the curious coastal desert of Atacama, resulting from the same cold currents which make this region of the Pacific one of the world's greatest fisheries. Although the coastal climate is moist and cloudy, rainfall is nil. Not only water but food and even building materials all have to be brought from the interior. Nevertheless, such are the natural resources of nitrate and copper and the capabilities of a flourishing money economy that this inhospitable littoral supports a number of sizeable towns, all seaports. Mineral extraction on a large scale adds locally to the already bare and forbidding character of the landscape, imposed by aridity, volcanic action and dust storms. In such exceptional cases even the more drastic earth-moving activities of man merely accentuate the work of natural forces inhibiting the growth of a developed vegetation cover.

The Andes are here at their broadest, spanning some 400 miles, with strongly marked Western and Eastern Cordilleras. The high plateau between the two contains great salt flats such as the immense Salar de Uyuni and lakes at more than 12,000 feet. Despite its clear rarified air and cold, windy climate this Altiplano carries nearly three-quarters of the population of Bolivia, in cities ranging above 13,000 feet (Potosi). Crossing the high *Puna* of the eastern slopes we again meet the great South American forest, here in a scrub woodland form known as the *Chaco* of Paraguay, with much open grassland.

We are now over the basin of the Parana, the fourth greatest on the earth. After passing the Brazilian border this river is crossed some way above the Gualra Falls normally the second greatest (and at its peak much the greatest) of the earth's waterfalls in terms of volume of water. The uplands east of the Parana are the greatest coffee-growing areas of Brazil, and are also large producers of cotton and sugar cane. Our course out to the Atlantic leads between Sao Paulo, the greatest industrial city of South America and Rio de Janeiro on the coast, both now with well over 3 million inhabitants, exemplifying a modern trend towards the build-up of massive urban concentrations in countries formerly dominated by crop and animal production. In Rio, as in the new inland capital, Brasilia, this trend is accompanied by bold and talented experiments in design, not only of large buildings but of landscape for recreation and leisure. Sadly also it shows some bad examples of shanty town suburbs created by improverished refugees from the country regions.

SIXTH CIRCUIT—Walvis Bay/Madagascar/South Australia/ Valparaiso/Tristan da Cunha

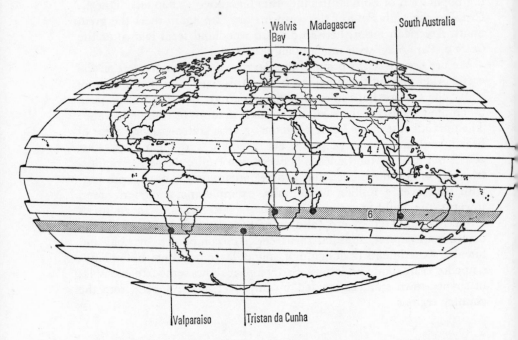

Continuing east, still just within the tropics, our course over the featureless South Atlantic reaches the coast of South-West Africa near Walvis Bay, in a zone dominated not by forest but by desert, the inland Kalahari being more extensive than any of the American deserts. Only around the Limpopo in Mocambique is there any substantial cultivation. Beyond the Mocambique Channel (actually quite a broad stretch of sea) the course leads over southern Madagascar, the fourth largest island on earth, which has a rich and unique fauna, including several rare lemurs.

It continues across the broad empty southern Indian Ocean to western Australia, crossing the coast at Shark Bay. After passing over a broad band of sheep country it heads across the central desert, second in size on earth only to the Sahara. Falling away gradually southwards here the course takes us over Lake Eyre in South Australia and into north-west of New South Wales. Annual rainfall at last begins to reach

20 inches on approaching the Darling River, a rival in length of the Danube and Indus, even though it is itself a tributary of the Murray. Here, towards the east coast, Australia's richest primary producing region is crossed well north of Sydney.

We now embark on the 1,300 mile crossing of the Tasman Sea, the first instalment of the South Pacific, passing on the way Lord Howe Island, of just over 3,000 acres, formerly remarkable for its rich fauna, much of which was exterminated through the careless accidental introduction of rats some fifty years ago. There are however still great seabird colonies on inaccessible outlying rocks. The coral reef on its west side is the most southerly in existence.

Our next landfall is the northern tip of the North Island of New Zealand, a narrow subtropical peninsula, with forests rich in treeferns, reaching out to bridge the gulf between the temperate grasslands more characteristic of that country and the moist islands of the South Seas. Well to the east, beyond 180 degrees (which on this section is no longer the international date line) lie the Kermadec Islands, resting on a submarine ridge which is closely paralleled to the eastward by the Kermadec Trench, one of the deepest in any ocean. The onward course passes well south of the islands of French Polynesia, and of Pitcairn and Easter Island, encountering no further land until the Chilean Juan Fernandez, only 400 miles off the South American coast. The smaller of this pair of islands, Mas Afuera, is a hundred miles farther out, and its peak rises above 5,000 feet. It has shared the fate of too many remote islands in being used as a convict colony. The other, Mas Atierra, was the home for four years of the Scots seaman Alexander Selkirk, whose experiences inspired Defoe to write Robinson Crusoe, and launched the peculiar modern obsession with islands as an escape from the world for laymen.

Crossing the South American coast near Valparaiso, its greatest commercial center, in an area liable to serious earthquakes, we quickly pass over the capital of Chile, Santiago, South America's largest city outside Argentina and Brazil. Chile is one of the world's most oddly shaped countries, 2,600 miles long but only averaging 110 broad, with the mountain range of the Andes taking up about half of that. It also shares with Colombia, alone in South America, the peculiarity of having both an Atlantic and a Pacific coast. It is in this region that the Andes reach their highest point in Cerro Aconcagua, just over the border of Argentina.

We cross Argentina on its broadest section, extending nearly 1,000 miles. The first part is a region of dry uplands, with occasional irrigated oases. Only 2 per cent of Mendoza Province is cultivated, mainly

D   97

for vines and alfalfa, with some olives and fruit-trees. Mendoza averages only 7·5 inches of rain a year; San Juan only 3. Continuing eastward the land drops below 200 meters onto the Middle Pampa, where we reach one of the great agricultural areas of the world, notable both for cattle and for growing fine crops of alfalfa for fodder, maize, and fruit and vegetables as we draw near to Buenos Aires, which is becoming one of the world's largest cities. Four hundred years ago the pampas were covered with tall coarse grasses, and the first land use to which they were put was for ranching cattle, horses and mules in large estancias, reseeded with more palatable European grasses. In the second half of the 19th century a complex network of railways was created and a switch took place to crop agriculture in many areas, involving a need for mass immigration from Europe, totalling over 6 millions between 1857 and 1930. The impact upon the fauna and flora has been one of the most widespread and intense ever recorded, illustrating vividly the nature and scale of modern conservation problems.

The course now leads out over the Rio de la Plata, joint estuary of the Parana and Uruguay rivers, and over Montevideo, capital of the small republic of Uruguay, before embarking on the crossing of the South Atlantic by way of the remote island group of Tristan da Cunha. Originally discovered by an early Portuguese explorer, whose name it bears, it remained uninhabited except for intermittent use by British and American sealers, until the early 19th century. A British garrison was then placed there for a short period, leaving behind it a nucleus of a civilian settlement which by 1961 had grown to 280 strong. At this point a surprise eruption of the supposedly extinct volcano caused mass evacuation to England, but after things quieted down most of the inhabitants preferred to return rather than to stay in England. This makes a peculiar exception to the main trend towards depopulation of remote islands, other than those exploited for external reasons.

SEVENTH CIRCUIT—Cape of Good Hope/Tasmania/Tierra del Fuego/Cape Crozier/South Pole

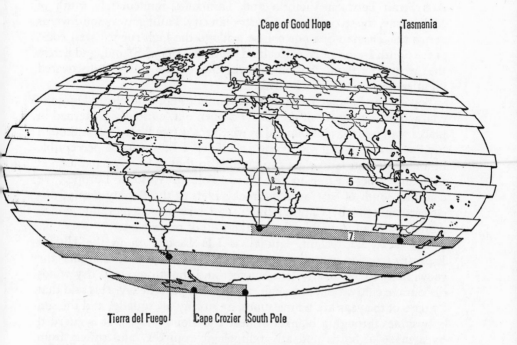

Cape of Good Hope Tasmania

Tierra del Fuego Cape Crozier South Pole

By correcting the course slightly to regain the latitude of the River Plate we are enabled to pass over the Cape of Good Hope. That we would otherwise miss South Africa entirely is a reminder of the relative poverty of land in the southern as against the northern hemisphere. There, in following a corresponding north latitude, we would cross North Africa from Morocco to Tunisia, Asia from the Lebanon right across to South Korea and Japan, and the United States from California to North Carolina, with unlimited land masses still farther north.

Owing partly to geographic and strategic importance, partly to having become the world's chief producer of gold and diamonds and partly to an unfortunately conflicting blend of population from Dutch, British and African stocks South Africa is a focus of international political and racial tension. From the standpoint of wildlife conservation South Africa now ranks high, with an outstanding series of National Parks.

99

The Cape region is remarkable also for possessing a peculiar flora of exceptional richness.

Now entering the Indian Ocean we are faced with a 6,000 mile journey over water, passing *en route* only the uninhabited French island of New Amsterdam, and coming well below Western Australia to the Bass Strait between Victoria and Tasmania, immediately south of Melbourne, the second largest Australian city. Falling away southwards across the Tasman Sea our course leads to the high rugged west coast of the South Island of New Zealand south of Milford Sound, and across the great Fiordland National Park, site of the lately rediscovered flightless primitive bird Notornis.

Beyond the Lake of Te Anau the mountains are soon cleared and the characteristic pastures of the lowland open out, curiously patterned in places with tree ribbons planted as windbreaks (see Plate C4). Although the South Pole is still so distant, its influence begins to be perceptible in a climate and landscape comparable to that to be expected a good thousand miles nearer to the North Pole in Western Europe. We continue south of east over the rocky islets of the Bounty group, discovered in 1788 by Captain Bligh, and near the memorably named Antipodes Islands, within the northern limit of drift ice.

Our next, far distant, landfall is Isla Desolacion in the Ultima Esperanza region, once more in Chile, where even in summer the snowline descends nearly to 2,000 feet and the strong, cold dry winds discourage cultivation, although rainfall is in parts heavy. It is said that "7 days of the year are tempestuous, 25 stormy, 93 squally, and the sun only shines through a blanket of mist and cloud on 51". It is guarded by a maze of fiords and an archipelagic complex, and suffers from earthquakes. Nevertheless, largely through British pioneers, a fair amount of development has taken place, and the remote town of Punta Arenas on the Strait of Magellan has nearly 65,000 inhabitants. To the north lies Patagonia, to the south the isle of Tierra del Fuego, with the world's biggest sheep farm, carrying a million animals.

Taking leave of the conventionally habitable world we now enter the Antarctic region, passing south of South Georgia into the northern limit of pack ice, and crossing the widely scattered group of South Sandwich Islands, closely flanked by one of the two deepest sea-trenches in the Atlantic. In an ever narrowing circle we cover the subantarctic waters, in which has been fought out the hitherto losing struggle of conservationists against the greed and short-sightedness of the great whaling interests. Crossing the Antarctic Circle at the Balleny Islands near the South Magnetic Pole we end our long spiral course by turning due south past Cape Adare and over the Emperor Penguin colony at Cape

Crozier, to follow the route of the early heroes of Polar exploration over the Ross Ice Shelf and up the immense corridor of the Beardmore Glacier to the South Pole, on a featureless tract of ice more than 9,000 feet above sealevel. In contrast to the North Pole, occupied merely by shifting pack-ice, the South Pole is near the fringe of the earth's thickest and most extensive icecap, the continued build-up of which is suggested by the rapidity with which the American base station structures erected so few years ago have already become underground rather than surface buildings.

Here our transect ends, on a continent never until lately inhabited, and now occupied only by a fluctuating population of between 1,000 and 2,000 men (with no women or children) almost entirely concerned in the fulfilment or support of international scientific studies. Thanks to Antarctic Treaty, and to the Agreed Measures accepted by its twelve signatory powers, this continent observes a series of measures for conservation of its fauna, flora and natural environment not only far in advance of any other international convention, but probably more comprehensive than yet exists for any single territory in the world.

CONCLUSION

In this long spiral transect by air we have performed in imagination a journey which no one yet has ever actually made, even with numerous stops. We have looked at our own more friendly and varied planet in much the same way as astronauts look at the cold dead moon. By this device we have, it is to be hoped, gained a somewhat clearer picture of the global distribution, nature and scale of some principal features of the natural environment and of human impacts on which we need more and more to focus our minds. Without neglecting the importance of relative area and general influences, we have also contrived to take brief notice of many of the most significant special points on the earth, which help to indicate its potential and to illustrate the story of its evolution, and its treatment at the hands of man. Such an exercise is no mere entertainment, but a basic necessity for civilised living in our world.

One impressive characteristic of the planet is its immense diversity, both in the mass and in detail. Superficially or inattentively an observer might start with the idea that one ocean, one desert or one forest must be very like another, but in practice they are nearly all distinctly different. There are two polar regions, both very cold, but one is a continent and the other an ocean. The cities of Singapore and Quito are both almost on the Equator, but in Singapore the average Fahrenheit temperature for every month is from 80 to 82, while in Quito it is always 55 except in August and September when it rises to 56.

Differing land-forms and physiography, differing climates, geology and soils, differing water regimes, differing past records of evolution, differing exposure to earthquakes and volcanic erruptions, to hurricanes, floods or sandstorms, and to invasions of plants and animals have created and are still bringing about an infinite variety of local conditions, sometimes also fluctuating greatly from one year to another, or converging or diverging at different seasons. While it pleases us to treat certain factors as permanent and unchanging this is entirely a question of the time-scale adopted; if it is long enough everything proves to be in a state of flux. We must always bear in mind that our natural environment is not only infinitely variable but continuously dynamic, undergoing ceaseless systematic changes which would be much more evident to us if we took more trouble to observe, record and measure them over more adequate periods and at a more adequate number of stations.

Nevertheless, by bringing to bear all the scientific and technical disciplines now available to us, together with the tools and techniques, ranging from aerial survey and cartography to biological assay, chemical analysis, taxonomy and statistics, it is becoming possible for us to identify and relate to one another all the varying combinations of elements and circumstances which are operative in each particular locality or situation. On this basis we can trace past, present and to some degree even probable future trends, given absence of human intervention, or the impact of defined types and degrees of intervention. With this sophisticated knowledge will come not only the possibility of applying much more professional skill in land use and land management but a much more comprehensive and flexible approach, which will have repercussions in many other human activities, and not least in government.

That the earth is not a flat pancake but a sphere has gradually come to be accepted over recent centuries by most of mankind, even though many offices still display highly distorted Mercator world maps. The model in most of our minds of the earth we live on is no less primitive.

THE MARKS OF MAN

IN considering the current environmental revolution it is not enough to be armed merely with a general outline of human evolution as it has led man to make various impacts upon the land, and with a general picture of the intricate living systems which have led to the present distribution pattern of vegetation and animal life. It is necessary also to review the many sorts and intensities of humanly imposed modifications of the natural environment to be found in different regions, ranging from the lightest ephemeral disturbances to the entire replacement of local fauna and flora by huge artefacts made of cement, steel and glass. Few people have eyes sufficiently trained to recognise many of the more subtle marks which man has left, or to distinguish between a genuinely natural environment and one which after more or less severe disturbance has regained a spurious likeness to wilderness merely because the marks of human interference have faded or have been covered over or removed. Even a list of the known sources and methods of human intervention may come as a surprise to many who have never reflected much upon the intricate interplay of man and nature with whose continuing repercussions we have to live. Only very recently has it come to be recognised as important to study and to be aware of such processes, as something significant for the health of mankind and for the wise use of resources. (See Annex 2.)

It is for many purposes convenient, and indeed inevitable, for us to distinguish between those changes which are natural, deriving from processes already at work before man first took a hand in the evolution of the environment, and those which are due directly or indirectly to man's intervention. But in doing this we must always bear in mind that what we find and experience is a given total situation, usually formed by a blend of both these groups of processes, which we cannot except within narrow limits arrest, expedite or reverse, so far as they have already entered into the system.

There are no doubt still certain spots on the earth where no man has yet set foot, and certain sea areas where he has at most passed quickly over the surface without leaving a trace or initiating any perceptible change. Even so, the spread of pollution through outer space and the stratosphere, through the atmosphere, and on and below the surface is so pervasive that it can nowhere be ruled out, and can almost everywhere be detected if the appropriate instruments are used.

A surprising indication of this was the recent discovery that, although we can be sure that toxic pesticides have never been used in or anywhere remotely approaching Antarctica, nevertheless these substances have decisively penetrated into Antarctic ecosystems. Radio-active fall-out from improper experimenting with nuclear weapons has resulted in universal deterioration of the environment. When we now speak of un-spoilt or undisturbed natural areas we can do so only with such serious qualifications in mind. Processes of this kind may be termed indirect and unintended human influences.

Also unintended, but no longer indirect, are the consequences of human visitation or passage. An aircraft disseminating a trail of more or less burnt-out oil residues in the air, or a ship or small craft doing the same in water, or a mountaineer kicking away into limbo rare crag-dwelling plants in order to gain a better foothold, or a party of horsemen breaking the vegetation cover on a steep hillside and leaving a trail of eventual erosion, may all be innocent of intent to damage the natural environment. Nevertheless, damage directly results from their intrusion, and in some cases it may prove cumulative and eventually far greater than even a specialist might have foreseen. On the other hand a skier on slopes shortly to be again covered with fresh snow, a swimmer running across the sands and into the sea, or a sailor steering his dinghy across a lake may leave no detectable effects.

It is, however, difficult, to be sure. Where footprints or wheeltracks persist, as in some deserts, they may form nesting places for certain species of bird, lairs for certain invertebrates or moist niches for certain plants which, for good or ill, would otherwise not be able to maintain themselves here. In some cases parasites, diseases or predators may be introduced with destructive effects upon some rare and specialised type not hitherto exposed to them. In a swamp on an island of Hawaii which is a last refuge for certain native species elsewhere exterminated it has been found that even a footpath used only once or twice a year by scientists has enabled exotic species to penetrate the habitat. Jugoslav conservationists have reported severe losses among chamois and other shy mountain beasts which have panicked over precipices at the sudden unaccustomed sound of clumsy attempts at yodelling and at the gaudy attire and strange movements of bands of tourists thoughtlessly thrust into this once quiet and peaceful world of the high peaks with the aid of an aerial cableway.

Precautions enforced during outbreaks of foot-and-mouth disease, quarantine for pets, and prohibitions on import by travellers of plant material are reminders of the biological hazards incidental to even apparently innocent forms of movement. Probably the worst ecological catastrophe of recent times, involving the virtual extermination within about a decade of one of North America's most biologically valuable trees, the American chestnut, was the result of an apparently innocuous import of a related chestnut from Burma infected with the spores which proved so quickly fatal to the American species.

These are instances of the damage which can result from even the lightest human contacts, where no harm is intended and probably none is recognised by the doers even after it has occurred. Where similar kinds of impact are on a larger scale, as with the passage of troops, a cross-country vehicle contest or the trampling of large numbers of visitors the damage is correspondingly greater, more evident to all, and more likely to prove irreversible.

In the dry air and intense cold of Antarctica rubbish is eternal, and it is almost impossible to bury or hide refuse except by bringing it to the coast and hurling it into unfrozen sea. Thus, despite the high principles of conservation accepted by the scientific population of the continent and its logistic supporters, the appearance of their settlements can hardly fail to remind the observer that where every landscape pleases only man is vile.

Similarly in North Africa tracks and debris of the tank warfare of the nineteen-forties will long adorn or mar the desert scene, while the endless proliferation of wheelmarks of later cross-country vehicles point strongly to the need for canalisation along defined routes, and for extensive sanctuaries free of the too enduring impression of wheels. Even on tropical Pacific islands the lush vegetation has so far failed to hide many scars of World War II.

With increasing mechanisation of transport many uses of wild areas which formerly left no noticeable trace have become seriously disturbing. Equipped with fourwheel drive on caterpillar tracks vehicles on reconnaissance penetrate over soft ground or up steep slopes or through waters which would previously have been inaccessible except to the most agile and adventurous. Foresters and lumbermen are especially notable for their inconsiderate and unwise use of vehicles leaving heavy scars behind them. Amphibious models, light fiberglass portable boats and rafts, hovercraft and other recent inventions bring unexpected and unwelcome visits to islands, swamps or coastlines which through their long proven inaccessibility have become the last refuges of rare animals and plants unable to survive under human pressures. Having lost their last natural defences such creatures are now left entirely at the mercy of human understanding, restraint and readiness unreservedly to enforce adequate safeguards. Far more serious research and experiment is needed to remedy the gross environmental damage inflicted by most types of vehicle and mechanical equipment used beyond where the pavement ends.

As has already been mentioned, a start in the right direction has now been made throughout Antarctica, and a network of protective measures, to be described later, is being gradually developed worldwide. For the rest, much depends on the spread of public appreciation of the harm which thoughtless human pressures can cause. Certain groups of people are alerted to these perils from the nature of the interest which takes them to the countryside, but even conservationists and naturalists not infrequently leave an area less pristine than they found it.

Litter of picnics, film containers and bits of packaging are found even after visits to wild places of those who most ought to set an example. Crude attempts at disposal, equivalent to sweeping the problem under the carpet, can even make matters worse. On islands off Pembrokeshire shearwaters from distant fishing grounds returning at night with food for their young waiting hungrily concealed in underground burrows have been frustrated by finding that some well-meaning visitor has meanwhile blocked the only entry with an empty tin of baked beans which cannot be shifted, and which condemns the chick to die of starvation.

Visitors to island breeding colonies, for instance terneries, have often kept the parents off eggs so long in chilly weather that the eggs have gone cold and failed to hatch. In other cases, by putting such large birds as herons and storks off eggs in areas infested by egg-eating species such as crows or gulls, visiting naturalists have given ideal opportunities for destructive raids while nests remain undefended. Where picnicking is regular, parties leaving uneaten food for scavenging species often unwittingly cause a build-up of their local numbers which, especially when bad weather interrupts supplies, leads to increased raiding of eggs and young of other species.

An interesting and possibly harmless instance is the concentration of sandwich-ivorous parties of the occasionally predatory Kea parrot of New Zealand at such points as the entry to a road tunnel where tourists have to wait for some time to pass through owing to rotational one-way traffic working. It is quite plain that this pattern of distribution is not natural but man-made.

Conversely, where specialised breeding habitats are favoured for some human open-air activity during the breeding season, reproduction can be so seriously interfered with as to lead to a drop in numbers, or to local extinction. The Little Tern and Ringed Plover, nesting on sand or shingle beaches, are frequent sufferers from this in England, while one of the last nests of the Kentish Plover, now extinct as a British breeding species for similar reasons, was only saved on a day of intense human trampling along the shore by a warden sitting down by the nest with his raised knees forming a bridge over the eggs.

When such occasional rare nesting species as bee-eaters make a breeding attempt in Britain it is usually necessary to put on relays of wardens to discourage incessant disturbance. Without such unpalatable and expensive protection the birds would not stand a chance. The menace is not primarily from those few consciously bent on destruction, but from bird-watchers too unimaginative and inconsiderate of the birds and of their fellows to refrain voluntarily from pushing in so close as clearly to amount to persecution leading to desertion.

Fortunately vigorous protective measures, backed by new stiffer laws against disturbance and a great deal of public information and propaganda have recently begun to create a healthier attitude and to inhibit such antisocial behaviour. Nevertheless the fact that it could become so pronounced among even those who would profess a keen interest in wild life is some indication of the vastness of the task to be faced in educating the mass of ignorant and uncaring mankind.

Unfortunately one of the first consequences of interest in nature is pressure to collect specimens. Often this appears mainly a response to primitive instincts and cravings, but as collecting can also be of great scientific and educational significance it is not easy to set up good distinctions. In the rather clear and limited case of collecting birds' eggs it is now generally accepted that as an adult activity this should be permitted only under licence in connection with scientifically justifiable investigations by research institutions, selected museums, and occasional individuals who are specially qualified for such studies. In some countries there is still some misguided feeling that an outlet should be provided for the hunting and collecting instincts of juveniles by making permissible the taking of eggs of common species. Unfortunately such statutory encouragement is impossible to reconcile with the teaching of conservation as a social responsibility, and it leads to destruction of the more accessible nests in the very areas where the fullest and most approachable bird population would be most appreciated by dwellers in and near towns.

Somewhat similar considerations apply with plants, especially with wild flowers. Discriminating and persistent plant collectors have made rarities so much rarer in their localised haunts that, as in the case of rare breeding birds, normal publication of distribution has had to be voluntarily censored, to the loss of naturalists generally. As a peculiar byproduct there have been cases of the secret planting and stage-managed discovery of extreme rarities in places where they never naturally occur, usually in order to enhance the prestige of the hidden manipulator. In other cases planting has been openly done either in an effort to restore lost species, or to "beautify the landscape", or, less controversially, to shift rare plants from an area where they are threatened by some impending development to a safer site.

Parties from schools and universities seeking to bring back impressive evidence of their prowess on field trips have caused serious damage to the flora, and sometimes also to the habitat. In certain extreme cases they have so irritated the local farmers or landowners as to tempt these themselves to try to extirpate a rarity in order to remove all excuse for what they regard as a tiresome form of trespassing across their land. It is often difficult to distinguish where naturalist interests cease and gathering or collecting for simple decorative or gardening reasons begins. Certain spectacular wildflowers, and ferns such as *Osmunda regalis* are freely sought, dug up and taken home by gardeners, whose destructive activities have sometimes been aided and multiplied by illadvised articles in periodicals giving details of suitable localities for such pillage.

Beyond this again commercialisation rears its head. In a certain nature reserve newly formed in the north of England a strong plea was made to permit continuance of an ostensibly innocent local custom of going in to pick bunches of Lilies of the Valley in May. Observation by the warden soon showed, however, that this custom was practised more intensively on a Wednesday than on all other days of the week combined. This led to the discovery that these flowers were actually being harvested to be profitably sold at the weekly Thursday market in a local town. The "custom" was then brought to an end.

Similar problems have arisen with the collecting of lizards for pet-shops, and of frogs for sale to laboratories, as well as of moss for the use of nurserymen and commercial florists. In many developing countries, for example in North Africa, highways are lined with boys and girls offering the passing motorist a wide variety of specimens of plant and animal life which are thought to have some cash value. Even geology is not exempt from such abuse, and leading geological conservationists have recommended prohibition of further fossil collection from certain unwisely exploited sites.

Scientists are apt to feel that as their studies in the field are so disinterested and for the common good, they should be treated as invisible men, entitled to do as they please, rather than as competing claimants for space. Seeing some suitable field or woodland they will in the most casual and informal way get permission to do investigations or experiments on it, without informing the owner, or even without themselves fully facing the fact that unless the *status quo* is maintained virtually without alteration on this land for perhaps five or ten years or longer the greater part of their work is going to be ruined and the reaching of tenable conclusions made impossible. When, as often happens, they find within a much shorter period that a drastic change is in prospect, or has actually begun to be carried out on the site, panic ensues, and help is urgently sought to secure a standstill.

Alternatively, investigations are initiated in some National Park or Nature Reserve without recognising, or without disclosing the fact that their successful completion will depend upon permission being given to carry through some operations perhaps incompatible with the objects or conditions governing the establishment of the safeguarded area, or with the plan of management, or with the interests of other parties. Examples are experiments demanding clear-felling of a forest plot, unlimited collection of fresh-water fauna from a stream, the introduction of extraneous species, or exclusion of the public from certain sites.

In earlier times, before biological and environmental studies shifted from a descriptive or observational to an experimental basis, such conflicts would rarely arise, especially since the fashionable attitude towards even drastic interferences with nature was then much more carefree. The time has now come, however, when just as science costs so much that its share of the Gross National Product must be budgeted in relation to other claims, so the future requirements of science for use of land must also be carefully considered and provided for if they are not either to be brushed aside or to create great difficulty and illfeeling by being belatedly asserted as an afterthought, at the expense of other plans developed earlier and with more regard for long-term land management. This refers especially to scientists from universities or other institutions seeking sites *ad hoc* as particular studies develop.

Cases are known where even university researches on university-owned land have been wrecked or injured by arbitrary actions of university land managers. In one case in America a bird population under study on the campus was largely killed off by sudden rash treatment with insecticides; in another in England a wood where damage to trees by rodents was in course of long-term detailed investigation was suddenly clear-felled without warning to the research workers belonging to the same university. Whatever may have been the merits in these particular cases they emphasise the need for fuller understanding and closer co-operation between scientists working in the field and the managements of the land concerned. On neither side has adequate thought or consultation been put in.

Current ideas of conservation practice, and recognition of the extent to which many supposedly natural areas have been modified in fact by man, are leading to a growing amount of controlled intervention in replacement of the previous *laissez-faire* attitude in the management of national parks and equivalent reserves. It becomes quite possible, therefore that differences of view and interest may develop between scientists working on applied ecology in furtherance of management plans and independent ecologists pursuing more fundamental studies in the same area. There is also room for conflict between zoologists studying the numbers or behavior of shy animals and botanists or freshwater biologists unaccustomed to the need for taking such factors into account as they move about or collect in the field. In short, many of the errors and omissions evident in the behavior of ignorant townsmen in the country are closely paralleled in some parts of the ranks of those engaged as specialists in the study of fauna and flora, who are no less in need of guidance in order to avoid causing damage or disturbance through thoughtlessness. If even scientific training helps little in this respect the implication is clear that the elements of considerate behavior in the natural environment should be a part of universal education.

Apart from scientists working in the field, and other naturalists, archaeologists, and investigators interested in adding to knowledge, wild places are also visited by painters, poets, seekers after aesthetic or spiritual experiences, ramblers and enthusiasts for tough or prolonged open-air exercise, pony-trekkers and tourists or holiday-makers. While many are solitary, or limit themselves to small quiet groups, some see nothing incongruous in invading the wilderness in small crowds, sometimes mounted or waterborne in canoes, boats or cross-country vehicles. Parties organised educationally are also sometimes large and are apt to convey young people who have had as yet no opportunity to derive a taste or sensibility for them into vulnerable wild places, which they would be better advised to visit when more mature and less heavily brigaded.

All the diverse types of visitor to wild country so far considered at least have it in common that they are drawn there neither mistakenly nor by chance, nor with a view to exploitation by bringing back anything more economically valuable than photographs or small souvenirs. In this they differ from soldiers, topographical surveyors, frontier guards, mineral prospectors or others who are sent on duty, or from hunters and fishermen who hope to bring back trophies even though their personal appreciation of the wilderness may be much more than merely incidental, and their readiness to learn and observe the rules of good conduct towards the natural environment is often excellent.

Certain other types of outdoorsmen are more exacting or more prejudicial to the environment or to others hoping to enjoy it. Skiers concentrate on particular slopes where they demand facilities often causing injury to landscape or undue disturbance to wildlife, and sometimes severe erosion, as on the Cairngorm in Scotland. Crosscountry drivers of vehicles cause even more disturbance and noise, as well as some erosion. Mountain climbers in any numbers raise on their favorite routes problems similar to skiers. Explorers of caves and underwater environments, although they have only lately appeared in any numbers, have already measurably deteriorated their favorite haunts, especially in the case of sub-aqua activities using spear-gun equipment. In some places seasonal wild crops, for example of bilberries (*Vaccinium*) bring parties of pickers into wild places: such inexperienced casual visitors are especially likely to be careless about common hazards, such as fire. Gipsies, although certainly experienced enough, are notoriously careless of the amenities and tender spots of the countryside on which they live. The same seems to be widely true of pickers of wild crops in most parts of the world.

All these are easy-going amateurs in the exploitation of wilderness compared with the more serious and dedicated specialists who carry on some of mankind's oldest vocations—the trappers, the lumbermen, woodcutters and charcoal-burners, the metal miners and the herdsmen. The impact of these on their chosen ground is in the long run very substantial, to say the least.

While trapping, legal or illegal, is widely practised for food and as a sport, it is probably most highly developed commercially in the northern forest zone, where the harvest consists of fur-bearing mammals. Early evidence from Russia points to widespread use as early as the 8th century of palisades with a few openings compelling the animals to pass pits, nets or bows with a trip-release. Fall-traps, spring-traps and nooses were also widely used. Marten, squirrel, beaver, ermine, sable, fox, lynx, otter, wolf and bear are known to have been trapped for fur over the past thousand years, but it is difficult to separate results of trapping from results of deforestation and other changes adverse to such animals. Trapping for fur in the northern wilderness still flourishes as one of the world's oldest non-agricultural types of gainful occupation. As a form of cropping it cannot be convincingly held responsible for impoverishing the fauna, which indeed shows far fewer extinctions of mammals persistently trapped than of those hunted.

Much forest destruction was done rather to replace trees by pasture or cropland than for the sake of timber, and fire was often used in preference to the axe, as it is to this day in South America. In contrast to such drastic changes in land use the activities of specialist lumbermen seeking trees suitable for boat-building or for major construction, or of suppliers of firewood, faggots or piles, or charcoal were highly selective, and must often have resulted in systematic and enduring changes in forest composition, almost always in the direction of eventually eliminating the favored material. Where traditional exploitation for charcoal can still be seen in progress its impact on the whole form, composition and ecology of woodland is impressive.

Apparently in England oak was one of the last species to suffer in this way. The demand for well-grown trees for constructing wooden ships and wooden buildings eventually caused a serious shortage which led to some of the earliest conservation legislation.

Initially such legislation was designed to reserve the more accessible timber of south-east England and the Midlands for naval and other priority uses, and to compel the ironmasters to relocate their massive consumption of wood for iron-smelting in more remote and less competively exploited forests to the west and north. In the event, however, the indignity and upheaval of this forced shift of their industry stimulated the iron-masters to tackle more assiduously the problem of substituting for the traditional charcoal a fuel not subject to the dictates of conservation legislation, namely coal. Abraham Darby, who had had to move in this way to Coalbrookdale in Shropshire around the beginning of the 18th century, found a practical method, which rapidly led to a greatly expanded and more varied production capacity, and was a principal factor making possible the Industrial Revolution and the modern steel industry. Thus early efforts at conservation yielded an immense unforeseen indirect dividend to the world economy, but they also triggered off countless new conservation problems, including those immediately arising from the rapid and unregulated growth of coal-mining to replace the withdrawn supplies of timber. Within England and Wales the modern wooded picturesqueness of the Sussex Weald and other former centers of iron production was bought at the price of the modern dereliction of so many once agreeable landscapes in the coalfields from Northumberland and Durham to South Wales.

Wherever in this way conservation requirements have laid restrictions upon industrial processes harmful to the environment the initial horror and resistance of industrialists to being forced to change their ways, and apparently to accept added cost burden, has been followed by a complex series of readjustments. In some cases effluents or wastes have proved to be economically capable of being utilised or reclaimed by improved techniques, or by finding new markets for them rather than pouring them into rivers or dumping them on "waste land". In other cases the cost of meeting more exacting requirements has been met by savings in other directions, while the direct benefit has been reaped elsewhere in such ways as cleaner air and reduced costs of cleansing and maintenance throughout the community, or improved fisheries, or a better environment providing site options which would otherwise have been closed by the presence of industrial spoil. Not infrequently, however, the immediate solution adopted involves other changes which may themselves give rise to further conservation problems.

Paradoxically it may be said therefore that restrictions imposed on industry by conservation, although often hailed as crippling handicaps, may result in making industry more efficient and stimulating new growth points, while on the other hand the net gains to conservation may prove more limited than was expected owing to indirect effects through substitution of materials or development of new processes which may themselves have objectionable results. It is often overlooked on both sides that ever since Abraham Darby's response to conservation pressures two and a half centuries back mankind has been embarked on a complex interplay between the successively enforced requirements of conservation and the successively revised techniques of industry, which merits more serious study than economists have so far given it, since the game is still far from ended.

Even when relieved of supplying the ironmasters British woodlands could no longer cope with demand, and no less than 17 Reports of Royal Commission status were called for between 1786 and 1793 to review the poor state of home-grown timber resources. Plantations were called for to replace the exhausted remains of primitive forest, but as the enthusiasms for landscape and agriculture of the great country landlords grew, their interest in forestry waned. England became one of the most heavily deforested countries in Europe, although still rich in hedgerow and park trees scattered throughout the land. By contrast selective or mass extraction, made good or not by natural regeneration, has continued to prevail through a large part of the earth's forests, and these may therefore rate as modified natural stands.

From its nature metal mining is highly localised, but being extractive, and often demanding fuel on a considerable scale, it has proved since early times one of the more serious means of scarring the earth's surface. Not infrequently the spoil-heaps remaining are toxic, and defy the colonising efforts of vegetation for a century or longer. Although detailed historical records are often wanting the nature of sites of former mine workings is such that the dating, extent and nature of the original interference can usually be determined with some accuracy, unlike the corresponding temporary activities of farming.

Of all opportunist exploiters of wild lands by far the most numerous, widespread and tenacious have been the herdsmen.

It is now probably some 10,000 years since the appearance, supposedly in the Middle East, of a new human occupation based on the care and exploitation of herbivorous animals, especially cattle, sheep and goats. The development and spread of this occupation, the elaboration of techniques of grazing management, breeding, and taking and processing the resulting products, and the far-reaching consequential social and economic adaptations must have absorbed millenia rather than centuries of effort before a reasonably settled and widely acceptable pattern emerged, enabling pastoralism to become one of the most important bases of economic, political and military power. Our concern at this point is to trace in outline the nature and scale of the successive impact of this dynamic and pervasive activity upon the land itself.

A first notable feature is the apparent close link in time and place between the origins of pastoralism and the origins of crop agriculture. Was this a mere coincidence, or did similar conditions and trends converge to create both more or less together? It is now authoritatively suggested that the origins were more widely spread in time and place than has previously been supposed and that the role of the Middle East was rather to combine and exploit discoveries largely made elsewhere. Considering the numbers of plant and animal species it would certainly appear remarkable that the prototypes of such staples of modern farming as sheep and cattle, wheat and barley, beans and clover should have all been found ready to hand in a single smallish region between the Nile, and the uplands of Asia Minor and Iran. Such a coincidence would be all the stranger since over a large part of the world, except for the favored mixed farming regions of the temperate zone, the trend has generally been towards complete separation of pastoralism from agriculture. The United States, Britain, France and Germany, Argentina and Australia are among the minority of countries where both can be carried on extensively with full success, and can be blended together on compact mixed holdings. Even in Swiss Alpine valleys a cool climate, deep mountain shadows, poor soil and other adverse factors compel farmers to concentrate on livestock rather than crops. It is this Swiss ecology which accounts for the fame and plenty of Swiss cheese.

In many parts of the Middle East, as in North Africa, the arid climate and irregularity of rains have throughout human experience led to great and unpredictable fluctuations in local moisture conditions, and in consequent capability for growing crops or carrying livestock. Thus, although the two pursuits are largely distinct, favorable rains in an area often lead the herdsmen to concentrate their flocks in the very places where cultivators are eagerly looking forward to the one or two good crops which they can expect in a five-year period. The amounts and incidence of rainfall on the higher ground, and the surprisingly severe winters up there, limit even for the most mobile herdsmen the value of the mountain grazings, except in such plateau areas as Highland Baluchistan, where a seasonal mass movement from the Indus Valley has long been regular.

While the climatic evidence is incomplete, and the means and rate of operation of the process are still in parts obscure, the broad conclusion is incontrovertible that extensive areas of the Middle East and East Mediterranean have been converted from substantial fertility to a status of negligible biological productivity since and as a result of the activities of man as a farmer and pastoralist during the past ten thousand years. Perhaps the nearest to an alibi that can be produced is the unlucky coincidence of man's early efforts with a prolonged climatic deterioration, in the absence of which the results would possibly have been less disastrous.

Chief share of the responsibility is undoubtedly attributable to man as pastoralist. In mountain and upland areas he has deliberately and massively destroyed forest cover, by fire and otherwise, in order to extend grasslands which, being then heavily overgrazed, mostly degenerated to a rough unpalatable vegetation cover, or even to bare rock. By thus removing essential plant cover from the higher lands extensive erosion, by gullying and otherwise, was set in train. Streams were forced to carry excessive loads of stones and detritus which led to their fanning out during flash floods and destroying much valuable alluvial lowland. As moisture retention was impaired, seasonal and perennial water yields were severely diminished, thus restricting the numbers and extent of adequately watered lands and creating increased competition for and pressure on them, leading in turn to degradation even of areas which under reasonable use could have maintained a high level of biological productivity.

The result, clearly traceable in the Bible lands, has been regression of former forest to steppe and of steppe to desert, while even areas within desert limits have shown a severe reduction in their already poor carrying capacity for plant and animal life. One unfortunate result has been the forcing of previously settled tribes from fringe areas once above and now below the margin of agricultural subsistence into nomadic living, in numbers beyond the carrying power of the areas now available for their exclusive use.

It is when pressure of nomadic influx with herds of hungry beasts is superimposed upon overoptimistic efforts of subsistence farmers to grow crops in the same areas of desert fringe that something has to give. Nature restores equilibrium at a lower level by replacing steppe or pre-desert with sheer desert. In this way the load of greedy and ignorant mankind is shed, but at a heavy biological sacrifice. It is humiliating and shameful to reflect that this process of desert-making by man, started by prehistoric illiterates, is continuing at this moment probably faster than ever before, for example around the Sahara, under the auspices of modern governments and international agencies which have so far done nothing effective to curb it.

That livestock should have been first domesticated in a zone of intense biological vulnerability to excessive grazing pressures must be reckoned one of the greatest tragedies of ecological history. Learning the hard way, at the expense of the natural environment, pastoralists acquired bad habits and stubborn prejudices which the millenia of bitter experience have barely yet begun to eradicate.

By an oddity of early history the neighboring zone northwards, which pastoralists discovered only many centuries later, was ideally suited for them. The miserably poor tribes of the advancing desert fringe were forced by poverty and crop failures to launch out as nomads in the desert. The early settlers in south Russia who found their well-fed herds breeding up to numbers which outran even the plentiful local resources, were more happily tempted to follow the rich grazing opportunities out into the heart of the open grass steppe. Abandoning cultivation they flourished greatly as equestrian herdsmen. Having occupied the belt from central Asia to the Danube Delta they successfully encroached upon and subjugated the biologically less well-endowed, although politically more sophisticated, imperial peoples to the south. While they cannot be credited with great skill or foresight in conservation the fact remains that, in contrast to the Middle East and the Mediterranean, their traditional homelands retain high fertility status to this day. Mainly no doubt this was because they were less vulnerable, and have not been so long or so badly misused, as for example those overrun some two thousand years later in North Africa by the camel-borne followers of Mahomet.

Farther north in Europe and Asia the lowland areas were better fitted to retain their forest cover until later historical periods, and it was rather on the uplands and mountain pastures that the main pressure of pastoralism fell.

Here it was above all the sheep, let loose in absurdly inflated herds on lands vulnerable through low fertility status, brief growing seasons and often steep slopes, which, in regions such as the Highlands of Scotland, worthily imitated the havoc caused by their counterparts on the desert fringe. In such areas, not content with preventing regeneration of the dying forests, the sheep men set fire annually to "the hill" in an effort to flog out of the enfeebled environment a few more years' supply of nutrients before finally converting it into what Frank Fraser Darling has aptly described as a wet desert.

The customs and attitudes of pastoralists and their ceaseless conflict with settled farmers, with civilised society and with nature are well and copiously illustrated in the ever-popular stories and films of the American Wild West. The emphasis in the films however, is upon the trivial foreground of human drama, rather than on the enduring ruin which is inflicted upon nature as well as on man.

In East Africa modern pastoralism appears to have come in late in the evolution of a culture with an exceedingly long established tradition of hunting, trapping and co-existence with a wide range of wild animals, including some of the largest on earth. A more tolerant and, let us say it, more civilised attitude to their animal neighbors and competitors was adopted by tribes such as the Masai than by pastoralists of European origin, and it is on this admirable feature of African culture that the world-famous National Parks of East Africa largely rely. The poor quality and condition of the African's cattle has often been adversely remarked upon, but recent research has indicated that keeping cattle in East Africa to acceptable standards of health and nutrition is often an uneconomic affair, whereas wild native herbivores ecologically adapted to local conditions produce more meat at much lower expense.

It is however only very recently that the wrong-headed attitudes maintained through the overtly religious approach of the Africans and the quasi-religious fanaticism of the European cattlemen have been effectively challenged under the inspiration and through the experimental demonstrations of conservationists. It was not ever thus, as is shown by these quotations selected over thirty years ago by Sir Daniel Hall from then recent official reports:

> "With the exception of certain parts of Zululand and Pondoland, every Native area is overstocked, and this overstocking will continue as long as Native cattleholding rests primarily on a religious rather than an economic basis."

The Report here quoted of the Native Economic Commission for South Africa (1932) shows that cattle increased from 707,315 in 1918 to 1,716,836 in 1930, while sheep, donkeys and horses also vastly increased.

The Kenya Land Commission reported in 1933 that up to 1920, when the British administration introduced veterinary measures to control animal diseases, signs of overstocking and consequent deterioration of land "were hardly noticeable".

Anticipating the role of human disease control in triggering the population explosion these measures roughly doubled the cattle stock in twelve years, with catastrophic results.

"Now, in many parts where there used to be grass, there is nothing but bare earth, and . . . owing to the denudation of the soil, such rain as falls quickly runs off the hard pan which has formed, or evaporates, and is of far less benefit to the land than when the soil was covered with grass." "Another serious factor . . . is that areas which used to be open grass plains are now being overgrown by dense thorn bush, which absorbs the moisture and plant food at the expense of any grass which may be endeavouring to re-establish itself." "In the Kamba reserve there are over a million acres, of which 32,000 are under cultivation. Mr. Scott estimates that the Reserve contains 190,000 cattle, with 57,000 calves, though he estimates its grazing capacity at no more than 60,000 head. There are also 260,000 goats and 50,000 sheep . . . over large stretches of the hill-sides vegetation has been almost wholly removed. The soil has been eroded down to the subsoil and its erosion will continue at an ever-increasing rate. On less steep slopes and on better land vegetation still persists, and though the Wakamba are primarily a pastoral tribe patches of cultivation are in evidence. But even there grazing has been so persistent that the ground is all beaten down into little stock-paths and has become in its turn open to erosion. "It is not too much to say that a desert has already been created where grazing formerly was good, and where even cultivation existed, and that the same desert conditions are steadily approaching the land carrying stock and cultivation. The droughts of the past two seasons have intensified the rate of destruction. . . ."

Sir Daniel, after mentioning the evils of replacements of palatable vegetation by worthless or injurious weeds, such as the "bitter Karoo" (*Chrysocoma*) which had taken over hundreds of thousands of acres of grassland in Basutoland added this graphic comment:

"The greatest danger, however, lies in the fact that over-grazing may so destroy the vegetation and bare the surface that soil erosion sets in. In all tropical and semi-tropical countries, even where the total rainfall is low, torrential rains occur. Normally vegetation breaks up

the violence of the storm and retains some of the water; the roots hold
the soil together, but wherever the surface is bare the flow gets concentrated and will begin to attack the soil at any break in the surface,
with astonishing rapidity. Of all live stock the goats are the worst
offenders; they graze more closely, on bushes as well as on the grass,
thereby never allowing forest growth to regenerate from seedlings, and
their sharp feet break the surface. Within historic times they have been
the chief agents of deforestation of the lands bordering on the eastern
Mediterranean, whereby the hill-sides "have been bared down to the
rock, and the lower reaches of the rivers choked with silt and converted into swamps. Greece affords notable examples of this destruction, but similar conditions are being set up in all parts of the world,
nowhere more, perhaps, than in the southern United States."

These somewhat lengthy quotations have seemed advisable for several
reasons. They are the testimony not of critically-minded conservationists, but of official agricultural advisers to the responsible governments. Sir Daniel Hall, who was himself Chairman of the Kenya
Agricultural Commission of forty years ago, could speak as a leading
international authority, and was able to describe most vividly and
instructively the essence of destructive processes of almost worldwide
occurrence. At that time the first extension and acceleration of these
processes was still within the memory of many of those concerned, who
unlike many of their successors today could never have any illusion
that the land had always looked so bad. Yet here we are, forty years
on, still feebly watching the same destruction biting deeper and spreading ever more widely. East Africa, which was the primary target of
these prescient reports is one of the few parts of the world where any
fundamental change of approach and attitudes is yet visible, and that
only in far too restricted areas, largely through the influence of conservationists.

A much more extreme example of the obdurate ritualisation to
which pastoral peoples are prone is presented by the sacred cows of
India. There was no doubt a time when the conferment on these
animals of that degree of reverence and immunity was socially beneficial, but the practice has long outlived its usefulness and become a
byword for senseless conservatism. Nevertheless the Indian political
forces in support of it remain astonishingly strong, and have proved an
obstacle for a time even to doing scientific research to measure its
effects upon the environment.

In such a country as New Zealand pastoralism assumes a much more
modern guise, but even here strong elements of irrationality are manifest

in the attitude to control of deer and in the passion for aerial top-dressing of inaccessible pastures, despite the fact that there is more abundance of good lowlands than is needed to rear all that New Zealand can hope to export. Despite the high level of education, pasture erosion, that hall-mark of land-use illiteracy, is widespread on the uplands of the South Island and in parts also of the North Island.

Disillusioned with the poor returns obtainable from degraded wild pastures, modern-minded pastoralists, often lured on by government subsidies in such a country as Great Britain have experimented with ploughing and reseeding of hill pastures and marginal grazings. It is probably too early to generalise about the results, but the number of cases in which such innovations have been abandoned after a few years and left to revert to a more natural state suggests a need for caution.

There are in all such marginal situations—and areas of wild grazing rarely survive to this day unless they are marginal—ascertainable limits to the potential biological productivity in the particular circumstances. There are alternative patterns of management under which differing shares of this potential biological productivity can be put to economic use, either on a basis of eventual exhaustion or subject to sustained yield. Unfortunately the vast majority of pastoralists, large and small, rich or poor, neolithic or modern, have been reluctant to learn all they could about the productivity aspect, and have been too impatient, greedy or blindly optimistic to restrain their use of the range within limits necessary to produce the optimum yield.

All over the world it is common to see pastures where merely the crude device of halving or further reducing the number of stock on the area would give more meat, more milk or more of other desired products such as wool, and thus yield a more valuable income. Substitution of superior for inferior breeds and often also changes in the periods of grazing and resting the land, changes in the kinds of herbivore pressure (e.g. cattle as well as sheep, or wild herbivores instead of cattle or sheep in inhospitable or inaccessible areas) would in many cases bring further improvements.

It is sad to think that in a world so desperately in need of more protein for hungry people and better conservation for deteriorating environments so many millions of acres are being used to yield much less food than they might, with needless and enduring damage or even destruction to the natural environment, simply because so many agricultural authorities and institutions are failing to make the necessary effort to learn to demonstrate and disseminate sound methods of pastoral management.

Much of that large fraction of the earth's productive surface which is under the sway of pastoralists represents a twilight zone. It is not an environment consciously reshaped by human intervention, nor does it necessarily retain any close resemblance to a natural state. It is land blindly and injuriously modified, over centuries or even millenia, by a type of human being, remarkably similar in outlook in all countries, who combines living nearer to nature and yet more ruthlessly and chronically abusing the natural heritage, than almost any other. Beduin or gaucho, cowboy or Highland shepherd, rancher or cossack, the herdsmen's international is, with not many exceptions, at one in telling the time by the same clock—a clock which has long since stopped. Our earth is the victim.

In the course of history, and with ever increasing frequency in modern times, another class of wild land has developed which is wild in the sense of being now unused and uninhabited, but to the discerning eye is not in a natural state, on account of former, perhaps long-past settlement or exploitation. Ancient earthworks or walls, prehistoric trackways, terraces and early field boundaries, planted lines of trees, salt pans or collapsed heaps of mining spoil, middens or structural foundations, sunken vessels or sacred places once occupied by shrines or monasteries are among the better-known indicators of early examples. More recent disturbance may be marked by fragments of mineshafts, abandoned and over-grown railways, concrete "dragons' teeth" or pillboxes, trenches, aircraft runways, jetties or landing-places, rusting fences or foundations of vanished buildings, or more subtly, in Eastern America by former farm fields colonised by *Andropogon* grass and *Juniperus virginianus*, by clumps of nettles in a European woodland, by other tell-tale weeds elsewhere.

In some cases such sites lie bare, perhaps for centuries, where severe erosion has been triggered off, or toxic deposits have been left over. The steep, naked "badlands" adjoining Jericho, one of the world's earliest cities, are a dramatic example. Others are quickly revegetated but with some degraded pattern of second growth which may only very slowly, if ever, revert to the type of plant cover before human disturbance occurred. Others again, such as large ruins, may acquire a new fauna and flora perhaps more specialised and scientifically interesting than they had before. This can also happen with old excavations, such as many of the Norfolk Broads, or such sites as the Hills and Holes of Barnack, from which stone was quarried for some great English medieval churches, such as Peterborough. These must be distinguished from similar works abandoned much more recently, which usually remain for some decades in a raw state and have not yet had much opportunity to attract a fresh fauna and flora. (In certain conditions however the process can work fast; it took only a few seasons in parts of central London for sites of large building complexes destroyed by bombing during 1940–44 to be transformed spontaneously into quite rich habitats for plants and animals.)

Where persistent ill-advised attempts have been made to farm vulnerable land by unsuitable methods huge areas have had to be abandoned in a severely deteriorated state. H. H. Bennett, then Chief of the Soil Conservation Service of the United States, and a leading authority on the subject, thus summarised the position which he found in South America:

"In the old agricultural areas of the Andes and on portions of the Mexican Plateau soil erosion and continuous cropping together have ruined or ɪimpoverished a very large area of land . . . twelve Latin American countries have suffered from severe erosion to the extent of about 70 million acres now available for cultivation. In some of the twelve countries" (which included Colombia, Venezuela, Ecuador and Chile) "the estimated amount of land ruined or severely damaged ranges from around 50 to something over 60 per cent of the arable area. . . ."

"On much steep land, where the original growth was heavy forest and the soil was mellow, absorptive of rainfall, and productive, erosion across the centuries has disastrously affected a large total area, forcing abandonment of thousands of acres and migration of thousands of farm people . . . In some parts of the Andes land that once produced from 15 to 25 bushels of wheat to the acre without fertilizer, is now either abandoned or is producing only 1, 2 or 3 bushels an acre. . . ."

The clearing off of the forests followed by extensive steep-slope cultivation has had a profound effect on water supply "in many regions".

(Bennett, pp. 165–166, Plants and Plant Science in Latin America, Soil Conservation in Latin America 1945.)

One class of disturbed natural environment is so wide-spread and old-established in the tropics and sub-tropics that it calls for special notice here—former sites of shifting cultivation. This was defined by Sir Daniel Hall as

"the practice by which the cultivator clears a patch in the bush and crops it for a period of three years. He then abandons it for another clearing, and does not recur to the same land until a varying number of years have elapsed, during which the land accumulates fertility again and the weeds of cultivation die out."

He quotes testimony to the ill effects of this practice both from Asia and Africa.

"Vast areas of good forest land have been ruined in southern Asia by this destructive practice."
(Willis, J. C. Agriculture in The Tropics 1914.)

And from the Report of the West African Agricultural Conference, 1927

". . . the ever-increasing search for new land results in the denudation of the virgin forest, which is replaced by a secondary growth of inferior quality, and is here and there completely ousted by the pernicious weed *Imperata*."

Although from its nature usually practised in conditions of low population density, shifting cultivation can easily result in at least temporarily spoiling from a dozen to twenty acres for every acre currently in production. This leaves out of account all land which, owing to more serious soil impoverishment or colonisation by weeds, is still not worth further cultivation even after a rest of thirty or fifty years.

Recent discussion has tended to show more sympathy towards the practice, and this is perhaps best summed up by Professor John Phillips in *The Development of Agriculture and Forestry in the Tropics* (1961), where he writes:

"Existing in seemingly endless variations according to locality and people, this practice possesses some marked virtues and some definite weaknesses. Its main weakness is that it cannot impart a sense of stability and thus of the value of trying to improve the areas only periodically occupied. But it is unwise to attempt to persuade cultivators against it until some other procedure has been demonstrated as more efficient, less potentially dangerous to vulnerable soils when its rotation period is short, and at the same time suitable for introduction into relatively simple communities."

Commenting on the frequency of poverty and malnutrition in tropical areas where luxuriance of vegetation would raise higher expectations, Professor Phillips, from his exceptionally wide experience, lists a dozen factors in the low efficiency of subsistence crop production. These include ignorance of crop husbandry, poor seed, inefficient tools, a widespread although luckily by no means universal ignorance of simple techniques for conservation of soil and water, poor drainage and lack of understanding of flood control, excessive irrigation, losses in fertility due to leaching, compaction and erosion, poor land use, such as removal of protective vegetation needed for water yield, and other factors principally affecting sedentary cultivation.

Whatever arguments may justly be maintained in defence of shifting cultivation, it is common ground that the practice is inseparably linked with a low population density and low standards of life. By bringing about a human population explosion before beginning effectively to provide an acceptable substitute for shifting cultivation western civilisation has acted with foolhardy irresponsibility towards both the peoples concerned and the natural environment. The inevitable result is growing pressure to convert land already rightly classed by its cultivators as fit to sustain only very infrequent cultivation into land subjected to more frequent or even sedentary cultivation, without any justification in terms of enhanced potential productivity. No doubt some land under shifting cultivation will, at a price, be eventually transformed into regular cropland. Much more will be abandoned in a permanently and irreversibly impoverished state, to be added to the realm of sub-Man's gifts to sub-Nature.

A more encouraging but in some ways more peculiar category of wild lands is formed by the growing tracts subject to some kind of protection or conservation as National Parks, Nature Reserves, Game Reserves, Forest Reserves, National Monuments, Wildlife refuges, and Wilderness areas, not forgetting underwater parks. Regarded in terms of condition and land-use these vary from areas in an intact natural state and still exempt from any kind of significant human disturbance, to similar areas now so heavily visited as to be on the verge of losing such status, and others which are deliberately and sometimes drastically managed or provided with facilities in order to form what may be termed a substitute natural area.

Such areas, however styled and however managed, all have the common function of expressing mankind's need to afford protection, most of all against man himself, to samples of natural or semi-natural environment which might otherwise be lost, to the detriment of future generations. The goodwill to which they testify may, however, be feeble, or ephemeral, or may be overridden by other forces, or may be swamped by excessive numbers of incompatible ways of taking advantage of the opportunities provided. Not all so-called National Parks have been selected or are effectively maintained as wild lands. The true condition and use of such areas must be critically examined before deciding whether they qualify as wild lands or not.

It is only within the past decade that the somewhat narrow implication of the term "National Park" has been effectively translated into the concept of a contribution towards a comprehensive world network, and a fulfilment by each nation of the trusteeship obligations towards mankind as a whole inherent in its possession of outstanding natural areas. Three main instruments of this advance have been the United Nations Lists of National Parks and Equivalent Areas, already twice revised and amplified since its original production in 1961; the International Commission on National Parks, which serves as a continuous working party to review and encourage progress; and the frequent regional or technical meetings between managers and advisers with responsibilities in this field in different countries. Among such meetings special mention must be made of the training courses and centers which have recently been initiated, and will ensure that parksmen all over the world will soon form a single brotherhood and use common skills.

At present, however, it is still not easy to assess the number and extent of such protected areas, and the contribution which they offer towards a world series of first-rate examples of every natural habitat. The latest United Nations List accepts 1205 National Parks or equivalent natural areas in some 80 countries, with a total area of about 97 million hectares (385,000 square miles). Of these 37 million hectares are in North America (north of the Rio Grande), nearly 5 million in Central and South America, about 40 million hectares in Africa, about 3 million in Europe, about 4·85 million in Asia (both excluding the U.S.S.R. which has 3 million) and 4 million in Oceania, of which 2 million are in New Zealand. It is very difficult to digest the full significance even of this still very inadequate world series, partly because they are so varied in almost every respect and partly because to become at all well acquainted with the majority of them is almost beyond the grasp of any one person. (Although I have been unusually privileged in this respect I have only been able to visit 149 of these National Parks or Reserves in 27 countries, distributed among all continents except Antarctica, which almost deserves now to be classed as one immense National Park of continental dimensions).

No one who sees a number of them can fail to admire the immense and often heroic efforts which have gone to their creation and development up to their present scale and their present standard. Even on the map of the entire earth they form an appreciable element—about 0·75 per cent of the land surface, with Antarctica excluded. It is clear, nevertheless, that a very few pioneering countries still contribute by far the greater share of them; U.S.A. c. 25%, Canada c. 10%, S. and S.W. Africa over 8% and E. Africa nearly 7%, making up about half the world total area. Many countries and many habitats are still badly under-represented, despite the vigorous recent expansion.

There is also much confusion, not only among the public but among many of these responsibly concerned, over the objects of acquiring and managing such areas, and the extent to which differing concepts of these are compatible. It is still unclear how far quite different types of areas under different management are needed to satisfy the varied needs for conservation of natural environment and wild life, scientific studies in natural conditions, preservation of fine scenery and landscape, tourism, education, enjoyment of wilderness, maintenance of forest reserves and provision for outdoor sports and recreation. For present purposes it is sufficient to note that while National Parks and other protected areas include many valuable examples of natural areas they also include many—such as the so-called National Parks of England and Wales—which are largely in private hands and are exposed to much exploitation. They must therefore clearly rank as humanly modified habitats under economic uses, and as such do not qualify either by international standards or by common sense as genuine National Parks. It is to be hoped that this somewhat muddled situation, and the confusion of purposes and misuse of words accompanying it, will soon be sorted out. Meanwhile the renaming of the responsible agency as the Countryside Commission instead of the National Parks Commission is a step forward.

One of the most rapidly growing and most diverse and elusive types of land use is for what may be termed loose-boundary outdoor recreation. Traditional organised games such as football, baseball, cricket and tennis, together with competitive swimming and many others, are governed by such exacting requirements for both players and spectators that they must generally be played where the necessary purpose-built facilities exist. Golf and horse-racing are somewhat different, in that the availability of naturally suitable sites where they can be dovetailed in still tends to outweigh in importance as a location factor the existence of easy access or the convenience of special facilities. Hunting, shooting and fishing, gliding, sailing and skiing lean still more heavily on availability of wild lands and waters, although, especially for the last two, the modern trend is towards creation of increasingly elaborate base and access facilities. Walking or rambling, climbing, bird-watching, canoeing or the pursuit of other natural history and outdoor studies or hobbies are generally most flexible and independent of a need for fixed structures or transportation, and are consequently with some exceptions the activities most compatible with preservation of areas in a natural state.

Such preservation is, however, increasingly threatened by a series of converging adverse trends. The number of persons engaging in many of these activities is rapidly expanding, nearly all over the world.

INTRODUCTION

Natural processes which have created the natural environment that we now enjoy begin with water or land devoid of living beings, but have been able sooner or later to bring about permanent colonisation by living plants and animals. Once established upon an area such organisms develop complex relations with one another and with their environment, each of which can be considered as an ecosystem, distinguished from others by local conditions, biological composition or other factors. Ecologists who study the relations between living organisms and their environment are accustomed to think in terms of cycles of growth and decay, of inputs and outputs, of a standing crop or biomass representing the capital asset, and of biological productivity which can be measured in terms of gross or net primary production by plants and of secondary production by animals.

What is important for the present purpose is to grasp that what we call Nature, even if we see it as if it were a fixed state, is actually an ever changing product of a highly dynamic system functioning according to subtle and firm principles and rules which cannot be changed by man although he may disrupt or modify their operation at particular points.

Our analysis of these processes is still very incomplete and has to be developed from many different angles. For this visual presentation it seems best to start with the emergence of land devoid of living things and to follow through the emergence first of conditions suitable for life and then of vegetation and animals, rising from the poorer and more elementary and more thinly dispersed to the richer, more complex and more densely concentrated groupings. Throughout, the various ecosystems work mindlessly and incessantly towards further evolution, repairing damage or recovering from catastrophes and reverses where these occur and profiting by the most favorable periods and conditions. Yet many of them are vulnerable, brittle or susceptible to all kinds of adverse factors. One of the most alarming aspects of man's relations with nature is his capacity hamhandedly to inject or strengthen dangerously adverse factors without realising it.

Man himself, as the computer is beginning to show, is much less of a godlike unique rational individual and much more part of a series of social patterns than he usually cares to admit. Part of the problem of harmonising mankind and nature is to understand the basic patterns essential to the well being of each, and to reconcile their unconformities.

More and more people have lately become keenly aware that the earth is only one among the planets. The picture opposite (B.1) taken from Apollo 8 homeward bound from the Moon centers upon the North Atlantic, with the North Pole near the 11 o'clock position, South America below the center and the United States and West Africa at upper left and upper right.

B.2

Creation of new land by volcanic thrusts from the seabed can still show us the catastrophic processes which have enabled the patterns of vegetation to gain foothold, as here at Surtsey off Iceland in November 1963 (B.2).

Less abruptly, as here in Antarctica (B.3), new land can offer itself for plant colonisation by slow emergence from under an icecap. That has been the way that much of the land of northern Europe and America has been shaped.

B.3

Even close to the Equator, as here in the Andes of northern Colombia (B.4), mountain chains have upthrust to yield scenes of snow, ice, cold lakes and bare rock faces far above the altitudinal limits of tropical vegetation.

By contrast, at Katmai in Alaska the *taiga* forest of spiky conifers (B.5) holds its own against the fringing arctic tundra near sealevel in a country whose soil is largely within a grip of permafrost.

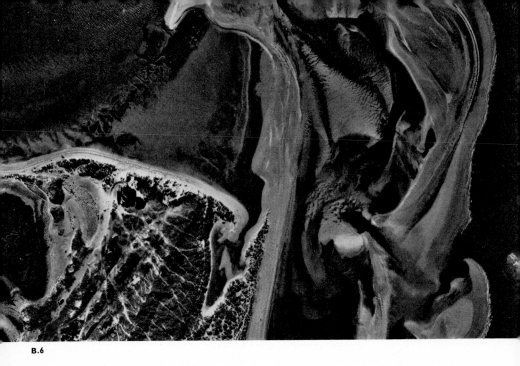

B.6

Other natural environments offer themselves more gently to plant cover through sea-waves depositing sand guided by offshore currents, as here at (B.6) Blakeney in Norfolk, where the wind's subsequent work of dune-building is equally clear on the more mature area of the lower lefthand quarter.

Beneath this is a fringe of saltmarsh, dependent on shelter from direct wave-action, whose complex structure is better shown in B.7, taken farther south on the Essex coast.

B.7

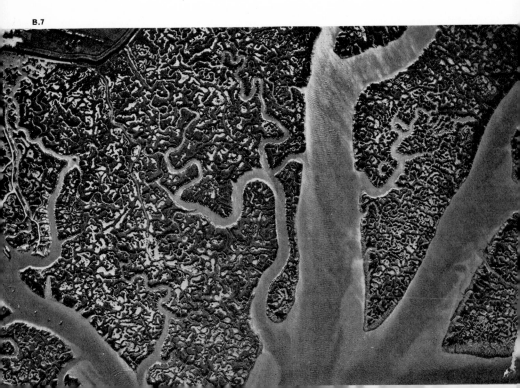

B.8

In such arid lands as Arabia, where the famous Wadi Rum in the south of Jordan is shown in B.8, the handicaps of lack of moisture are aggravated by over-grazing of camels, goats and sheep, while such woody shrubs as the Haloxylon here pictured are widely destroyed for fuel (compare A.7).

Only in still remote and inaccessible areas such as Aldabra coral island atoll in the Indian Ocean can such an almost perfect defensive stronghold be found as these Noddy Terns enjoy on this mushroom-shaped overhanging islet (B.9).

B.9

B.10

In fertile humanly populous lands natural or semi-natural vegetation has survived only on sufferance, through its usefulness or from sentiment, like the Cotswold escarpment beechwood in B.10, which withstands cutting without losing its character. Similarly such a wetland (B.11), as the Neusiedlersee near Vienna, survives by being conserved for sport and because no one has got round to draining it.

B.11

B.12

Tropical forest, shown in B.12, looks luxuriant yet contains surprisingly little worth exploiting at the high costs involved within its low-turnover system where most of the available nutrients are locked up within the standing crop. Even sub-tropical swamp forests such as this cypress swamp in the Florida Everglades (B.13) yield only slowly to the real-estate man and to creeping drainage.

B.13

B.14

Great assemblages of wildlife are not usually found in tall forest but, as in this African acacia savanna under Mount Tanganyika (B.14), in more open places, partly kept open by the constant mowing of herbivore jaws. Others, such as the great gannetry of Grass-holm off (B.15) Pembrokeshire, get all their food at sea, and are content to nest so tightly crowded that each bird is within pecking distance of the next. Natural ecosystems provide diverse answers to diverse problems.

B.15

Their incomes, mobility and equipment are also tempting and enabling them to push further into hitherto undisturbed places, and to create more serious and lasting disturbance or environmental injury than their predecessors. Fresh means of locomotion, such as four-wheel drive vehicles, tracked vehicles, helicopters, light fiberglass or portable boats, such as inflatable dinghies, and amphibious vehicles, hovercraft, snocats, marsh-buggies and so forth are steadily adding to the range and intensity of visiting pressures. Being often impelled primarily by a craving to escape from urban conditions obscurely felt to be intolerable, many of these new recruits to wilderness exploration are lacking in any background training and conditioning which would enable them to appreciate and minimise disturbance incidental to their incursions, and they are thus liable unwittingly to prove more damaging than they realise or intend.

The tendency of commercial interests to exploit, both in general advertising and in marketing of many products, the perennial charm and attraction of the outdoors, and the intense exploitation of every opportunity for expanding tourism with the aid of Press articles, pictures, television, films and other media ensure that opportunities of which they would never have dreamed and places of which they would never have heard are brought alluringly to the attention of many people with more money and leisure than sense or sensibility.

A steadily increasing jet of unpurified human effluent from affluent humanity is thus played upon vulnerable coastlines, lakes, mountain valleys, and above all, islands. The resulting development is so rapid, so widely sprinkled, and so varied that it becomes every year more difficult even to ascertain or to chart the current extent of such encroachment upon the earth's remaining natural areas. Nothing short of a daily lowlevel patrol and photographic record made by helicopter could give a reliable situation report.

Only relatively remote or inhospitable areas, which offer as yet no temptation for human settlement, exploitation or location of facilities, can now remain immune from all but light impacts at infrequent intervals. Where any significant attraction exists these are quickly followed by more substantial encroachments. On the Swiss Alps, for instance, it is now difficult to find a mountain landscape unbroken by the silhouette of one or more grand hotels crowning summits which would look better without them. Chair-lift terminals, mountain roads and railways, huts, tall tele-communications masts, concrete markers, pipelines and penstocks, dams and spillways, pylons and power-lines are increasingly frequent and prominent features of much of the world's grandest scenery. It is saddening to reflect that a less greedy and less insensitive civilisation could have achieved almost all the same benefits without creating any such trail of damage and destruction.

It is at this point on the spectrum that we pass over from natural areas still entitled to be regarded as in a wild state to a degree of human encroachment resulting in a hybrid or transition zone between the wild and the man-made. The line of increasing human influence on land use leads from here through such intensive categories as forests of native species under regular management and exploitation, managed pastures and meadows, amenity woodlands, coverts, windbreaks, hedgerows, and country parks forming conscious imitations or adaptations of nature, to such living artefacts as plantations, orchards, nurseries, gardens, market gardens and land under field crops, where the plant grown may often be unknown in a wild state and the biological processes are regulated and supplemented. Game preservation, managed river and lake fisheries, zoological and botanic gardens, golf links and other essentially biological forms of land use fall within the same group. The common element here is the step from exploitation or use of areas, either remaining in a natural state or directly derived from it, to deliberate substitution of a new man-made ecosystem, departing increasingly both in its species composition and in its functioning from the earlier natural patterns.

The next major step is that from managed biological uses of land to non-biological uses for such inert artefacts as buildings (whether dwellings, offices, factories, shops, streets or power stations), and other structures, such as bridges, ports, and airports, roads and railways, mines and depots.

Logically a distinction should be made between types of land use which merely superimpose some load of inert materials on the surface and those which either destroy the surface (e.g. some forms of extractive industry) or leave it permanently impaired (e.g. by deposits of toxic wastes). Uses of the first group are reversible simply by demolishing and clearing away the structures, while those in the second can be remedied, if at all, only by specific and usually expensive and slow processes of reclamation and rehabilitation. It is here that we reach the other end of the spectrum of landuse from the virgin natural area.

It must, however, not be overlooked that comparable intervention is beginning to affect the sea as well as the land. So far much larger parts of it are touched only by occasional passage across the surface or by submarine, although even this can leave a trail of oil pollution or conceivably nuclear radiation. More frequent or mass shipping movements can involve also collisions, wrecks and the addition of domestic or fishery waste products leading to ecological changes. Dumps of atomic waste material, submarine cables, and fixed structures such as rigs drilling for oil or natural gas become increasingly numerous and significant in shallower waters. Even wholly artificial islands have already made their appearance inshore, as off California. The use of the sea as a container for almost unlimited dumping of effluents from shore-based communities and industries is assuming serious proportions.

Summing up, the spectrum of land use which is most significant for conservation begins with undisturbed, unmodified natural areas which still form true wilderness. Next come wild lands visited only infrequently and subject to light and innocuous use, followed by wild lands which have been subject to exploitation in the past, or are currently being slightly modified without losing their essential character, except perhaps on a very restricted local scale. Managed lands, which follow, fall into four main groups; those which are being drastically managed away from a still traceable natural base, those where the natural base has been fully replaced by substitute man-made ecosystems such as field crops, those where biological elements have become subordinate, minor or non-existent, and finally, spoilt or damaged lands in need of rehabilitation. While many conservationists naturally and properly prefer to concentrate their attention on the earlier parts of this spectrum the existence of the whole, and the need for bringing science to bear upon the care of every type of environment, call for the continuous study and forethought of governments and of all concerned with public policy at any level.

THE ROAD TO CONSERVATION

MAN finds the road to conservation only through first taking endless wrong turnings. Inevitably the bitter results of unwise use and exploitation of the natural environment must be deeply experienced and lamented before the errors, omissions and neglects which led to them can be appreciated and identified. In theory advantage may be taken of mistakes made at other times or in other places to find the right approach without endless repetition, here there and everywhere, of abuses of the natural environment. In practice this is only just beginning to be done. Unfortunately mankind has a stubborn preference for learning the hard way. Even after this there may well be a relapse. The same lessons, having been forgotten, may need to be re-learned even in the same territories. Successive cultures, successive planes of culture, and even large organisations seem particularly prone to forget and to have to start all over again.

Certain quite primitive cultures somehow acquired and acted upon a better understanding of some of the essentials of conservation than is yet widely shared by modern western man. Certain early civilisations, such as those of ancient China and the Incas of Peru, developed highly sophisticated approaches and techniques which they used on a large scale; for example in constructing successive terraces on steep slopes to hold the topsoil in place. Just as there are basically well-adjusted and competent performers at such activities as driving vehicles on the roads, so there are better-adjusted and on the other hand more accident-prone cultures in relation to the natural environment. That to which western readers belong is, on the record among the most disastrously accident-prone in this respect ever to have existed on earth. Accident-proneness can be related to ignorance, lack of skill, carelessness, defects of personality or preoccupation with other incompatible aims. Probably all five are contributory causes here.

That we are poorly adjusted to our environment and how this has come about, are two of the main points which have to be grasped in order to bring a more civilised approach into existence. Each generation of men inherits and accepts as normal a certain pattern of environment which is more or less rapidly changing, largely unobserved, into some quite different pattern. Often that change is for the worse, in terms of such objective criteria as biological productivity, soil status and moisture regime. Each generation, therefore, mistakes for a natural permanent environment what is actually the outcome of a peculiar blend of natural and human forces, and mistakes a temporary transition phase for a settled end-product of evolution. Such false assumptions discourage thought and investigation concerning the natural and human forces responsible for the current situation, the means by which they operate, and the extent and rate to which they themselves are undergoing change and thus exerting changing types of influence upon a natural environment itself in the midst of change already dictated by previous impacts or interventions. The process is highly complex and dynamic, and is unlikely to be handled with skill or success by people who do not realise that it exists, or who brashly suppose that the particular views and attitudes which they themselves hold are the only ones possible for their community.

Certain cultures in human prehistory and history, although without explicit understanding, happened to take shape on lines harmoniously adaptable to the requirements of conservation. For these people cared for the land, its vegetation and its wild life, aware that its continued well-being was of value to themselves. But as well as applying sound principles of irrigation, terracing and fertilisation to the land they farmed, some were also interested in cultivating, preserving and propagating unusual and beautiful trees and plants. Some made gardens, woods and forests, and parks. Others were interested in wild animals for a wide variety of reasons and they learnt how to conserve stocks of these animals in face of adverse pressures.

Although some of the examples I have chosen from different periods in history to illustrate these points may not at first look like early attempts at conservation, this is what they are. For in all these cases there is an effort to secure harmony with natural processes, or an attempt to understand, preserve and encourage wild life, even if the reasons for what was done seem unusual to us.

In the earliest civilisations, for whose rulers the wise use and improvement of readily available natural resources were of intense and continuous concern, such activities as agriculture, irrigation, gardening, forestry, hunting, fishing, outdoor leisure pursuits and even astronomy and other forms of science and technology were still bound together with a unity and intimacy of contact which we are belatedly struggling to renew today. All, too, were closely linked with religion. The earliest records, dating back a mere 5,500 years, begin more than 20,000 years after the earliest known cave paintings, of the Aurignacian period in

France. During that final 20,000 years of prehistory fire had come into use, dogs, sheep, goats, pigs and cattle had been domesticated, agricultural crops had begun to be grown and building, shipbuilding and the first cities had developed.

Much had already been done which affects the natural environment to this day, although only on a localised basis. In the absence of more adequate information, however, it would not yet be profitable to carry back any discussion of the emergence of conservation so far. Work in progress on sites of the earliest known large settlements in Turkey has revealed evidence of bull baiting and of games with other wild animals, going back some 10,000 years, and implying complex and sophisticated relationships between man and wild life which may well have had much earlier origins.

For the five and a half historical millenia we have some help, although until recently only fragmentary, in four distinguishable forms. Certain structures or artifically modified areas can be traced as serving ends directly related to what we would now recognise as conservation, such as terracing, managed forests, parks or game preserves, gardens, and places protected by tabus or religious edicts. Closely related to these are relics of practices and devices primarily for exploitation, but serving incidentally some conservation need, such as dams, tanks and cisterns, irrigation channels and eventually agricultural, forest and fishery research and experimental areas, flood control works and so forth.

At the level of written records similarly two forms of evidence can be distinguished — official statements, reports, enactments and decisions on the one hand and unofficial descriptions, projects, studies, experiments, ideas and discussion on the other. Our knowledge of man's progress along the road to conservation is derived from questioning these four types of sources. Contemporary unofficial written sources, although now the most copious and readily available means of learning about conservation activities, contribute during more than 90 per cent of the period little of significance. It has also to be borne continually in mind that until very recently conscious appreciation of conservation was very rare. Available direct and straightforward evidence is correspondingly scarce, and we have to make do with imprecise and incidental indications.

As the earliest civilisations in Egypt, the Middle East and the Indus valley were based on irrigation to open up new fertile lands, they depended not only on advanced mathematics, astronomy and measurement of time and space, but also upon experiments with the rearing of aminals and the cultivation of plants suited to local needs and conditions. At Jericho irrigation has been traced back at least to 7,000 BC. It came naturally, therefore, to the early rulers here to create places which blended the roles of forest and horticultural nurseries, botanic gardens, zoological gardens, game reserves, parks and pleasure grounds. Here they could relax, reflect, observe, demonstrate, impress visitors, make love, and amuse or be amused by favorites.

Thotmes or Thutmosis III of Egypt, soon after 1,500 BC, recorded at Karnak the animals and the trees and other plants which he had brought back from his Syrian conquest. He already had a menagerie including lions, apes and giraffes. From this same period date the earliest known garden plans, one of which, from the reign of Amenophis III, shows a large rectangular walled enclosure, with shady avenues inside and outside the walls, two orchards, and four vine pergola walks leading to the house. There are four water-gardens with waterfowl and lotuses clearly shown, surrounded by grass plots and flower beds. Evidently such an elaborate plan must have had many forerunners. When climatic changes, natural catastrophes or military stresses led to the displacement of human communities people also naturally sought to take their plants and animal stocks with them to new homes, where their survival might depend upon selective breeding. Conquerors tried to propagate valuable plants or animals used by their defeated adversaries.

As the earliest gardens were so largely in arid lands they made much of water, often artificially led in. In constructing gardens dependent upon irrigation it was most convenient to base the design on a pattern of straight lines and on a jealously enclosed inward-looking layout unrelated to its surroundings. As the garden-inventing civilisations of the Middle East were so bound, and it was from them that the western world became much later stimulated and taught about gardening, many gardeners to this day use rectilinear and geometrical patterns in climates and conditions where they are unnecessary and may not be appropriate. This historical accident has contributed to a marked degree of estrangement and lack of communication between the fraternity of gardeners in general and the conservationists, ecologists and even landscape designers, with whom they might be expected to find more in common. "Nature abhors a straight line", said Kent, one of the leaders of the breakaway from classical practice in the early eighteenth century, but many gardeners still cling to the paths of rectitude and the conflict has not yet been resolved in the West. The separation is indeed so widely taken for granted that it may even seem odd to insist that gardening and conservation belong together, as pursuits aiming at harmony between man and nature.

In Chinese practice, it is true, both formal and informal gardens were prized, and studied with loving care from quite early times, even before the Christian era, but owing to the remoteness of China and to Chinese secretiveness, the knowledge and experience thus gained did not become available elsewhere until very late, except in Japan.

During the 5th century AD Japan was already inheriting from Chinese sources such still surviving cults as the planting of cherries and the keeping of tortoises in ornamental gardens. Pines, oranges, peaches, wistaria, orchids and, naturally, chrysanthemums were already used and admired there by the time the Englishman Alcuin was creating modern Europe's first center of higher studies for Charlemagne at Aachen in the late 8th century. Unfortunately, although Japanese gardens have continued to symbolise landscape and to demonstrate a long tradition of appreciating its principles, Japan, like other Far Eastern states never in practice "leaped the fence, and saw that all nature was a garden . . ." as Horace Walpole so vividly expressed it in describing William Kent's 18th century innovations in England. On the contrary the Japanese tradition became more and more intensive and miniature, running to tray gardens, box gardens and fascinating but somewhat unreal dwarf trees, all tending to produce a substitute in and around the home for the values otherwise to be sought in wilderness. Tiny delicate pools with graceful bridges and gateways, and countless kinds of symbolic rocks formed the nucleus of miniature Japanese landscapes; lawns and flower beds were absent or secondary.

It was in Mesopotamia that the concept of a park and the practice of planting stands of trees were first put on record, in Assyria and in Babylon. Tiglath Pileser I, around 1100 BC, claimed credit for having brought cedars and box "from the lands which I conquered, trees which none of the kings my forefathers had planted: these trees I took and planted them in the parks of my country, these trees I planted in the parks of Assyria". Solomon, about a century later, followed a similar course.

Steppe art of the same period, from c. 1250 BC, reflects an intense preoccupation with animals such as the stag and other game, but ignores the domesticated beasts on which the prosperity and dominance of the steppe tribes rested. Recent careful investigation by American archaeologists of prehistoric remains in south-western Iran shows that while bones of gazelles and other wild animals are prominent, side by side with those of domesticated forms, for some time after 7500 BC the villagers had apparently ceased to do effective hunting by around 5000 BC. It was presumably at about this stage of population growth and settlement that wild game stocks began to be sustainable only in more remote areas, or under strict protection and reservation in favor of a privileged few for whom the necessity of conservation would be inescapable.

Some centuries later Sennacherib formed at Nineveh c. 700 BC "a royal park which was in part a botanical garden and a pleasure resort, and included an artificial swamp" —perhaps the earliest known instance of wetland conservation. It was planted with "a great variety of trees collected in the course of Sennacherib's campaigns" (David Oates, Studies in the Ancient History of Northern Iraq, British Academy 1968). He claimed to have "levelled mountain and field" in making his parks and gardens.

Nineveh itself was not to endure much longer, but after the Persian conquests its eventual successor capital Persepolis, under Darius, saw a partial repetition of the pattern of introduction of tree species from elsewhere, before it in turn was captured and destroyed by Alexander the Great. The fact that one of the Seven Wonders of the Ancient World was termed the Hanging Gardens of Babylon, together with evidence of tree-planting on the terraces of temples and other structures in this region, indicates the importance already attached to the artificial perpetuation of living plants.

Already in these early days some of the main and chronic problems of securing the effective practice of conservation are manifest. It is not something which is felt spontaneously and directly as a human want or need. The requirement for it, and the appropriate remedial measures emerge only indirectly, and often gradually and obscurely, as a by-product of other situations or activities. The meeting of this requirement and the adoption of new practices rarely offer any substantial or early reward, and often cut across established customs and vested interests. Where great power and resources accumulate in the hands of an innovating ruler or group, or an enlightened corporation, lay or religious, some bold initiative may be taken more or less arbitrarily, but its continuation under different successors is precarious, unless its advantages are unusually big and evident, and unless the necessary power base itself survives. Changes in outlook, changes in technique, changes in organisation and other factors besides fluctuations in power can easily lead to the abandonment of such conservation measures.

The most frequently recurring or sustained class of localised conservation in early times is undoubtedly that related to the preservation of game and of hunting grounds. An odd blend of factors seems to have brought this about. Up to the neolithic period gathering of wild foods and hunting were the normal basis of human economy, and on that basis the effective limit of population density was about 0·4 persons per square kilometer, or roughly 1 per 1000 acres. In the transition, while primitive farming was still subsidiary, the ceiling rose towards 1 per square kilometer. The slash-and-burn system raised it to between 2 and 3, the early fallow system to between 4 and 10, the medieval 2-field system to between 10 and 15, and the 3-field system to between 15 and 35. (For comparison rough estimates of past populations of England and Wales range up to about 1½ millions—10 per square kilometer during Roman times, about 1·2 millions 900 years ago at the Norman Conquest, or about 8 per square kilometer, about 5 millions at the end of the 17th century, or c. 35 per square kilometer and about 47·3 millions in 1965 or c. 330 per square kilometer.)

The critical shifts in human pressure on the environment have been linked first with the adoption of cultivation, and secondly with the growth of cities and of technology. The first enabled human population density to rise from under 1 to up to 35 per square kilometer, and the second has made possible the modern population explosion, involving hundreds per square kilometer.

The first of these critical shifts must have created in most instances a steady and conspicuous drop in wild game, partly through increased hunting pressure, partly through forest clearance and pressures of domesticated herds on the habitat, and partly through disturbance. At the same time the burdens and fetters of farming began to tie the mass of cultivators firmly to small pieces of land, and to create a social and psychological as well as an economic gulf between them and the wider-ranging pastoralists and hunters. The latter eventually proved militarily stronger, and the overthrow of the earlier south-west Asian empires by the equestrian peoples from the steppes created an association between royalty and aristocracy and arduous field sports which has not yet entirely vanished.

The conditions compelling a choice between local extinction of game through such pressures and the creation of effective game reserves and protective laws seem first to have emerged in Iran, as has been shown above, before 5,000 BC. The dilemma however no doubt remained very localised during three or four millenia, during which customs, tabus and assertion of privileges no doubt helped to take care of it.

The details of great hunting scenes in ancient reliefs presuppose large stocks of game which it can be inferred probably meant some method of maintaining such stocks in game reserves. Around fifteen centuries ago the royal appetite for slaughter of wild game animals in Iran seems, from carvings, to have been immense and could only have been satisfied by previous rounding up and corralling of sufficient numbers under artificial conditions.

Fuller light is thrown on the situation by the detailed and well-preserved hunting scenes carved in a cliff near Kermanshah in west-central Iran during the Sassanian Dynasty (226–641 AD). (See Charles A. Reed, Peabody Museum, Yale, Postilla No. 92 Nov. 5 1965.) By implication the Red Deer (*Cervus elaphus*) had already been exterminated by then in this part of Persia, since the deer shown as quarry are definitely fallow deer. These were driven in advance into holding pens in a large compound, from which they were driven out at the right moment by men on Indian elephants, and then guided by galloping horsemen into the center of the arena, where the king, on horseback, shot them with arrows. The dead deer were then loaded on dromedaries and carried away, no doubt for a feast.

A pig hunt in a swamp is also shown in detail, with the king hunting from a boat; again the pigs were driven in hordes by elephants, which owing to the terrain were also used for carrying away the dead ones. Although, like many later artists, the sculptors here were sometimes at fault in their representation of animals running, they display very accurate observation of other details, except the plants which are shown too vaguely to be identifiable. While wild pigs still survive in the area successfully the Mesopotamian fallow deer have long been reduced to a small remnant. They were indeed believed to be extinct until their rediscovery in very small numbers during the past twelve years.

The use of pens, corrals, decoys and other devices for artificially concentrating numbers of birds or mammals at points of no return where they could be satisfyingly massacred is one of the oldest human inventions. It has been practised on creatures as varied as deer and wild boar, young seabirds and geese, ducks on the water and even bands of whales. The trouble involved and the hopes of regular repetition were no doubt among the earlier incentives for conserving a nucleus of breeding stock.

Sometimes it may happen that through religious or social circumstances measures contributing to conservation may become embodied in custom or law, and may thus acquire the status of a permanent and general practice without being dependent upon particular organisations or individuals to maintain them. Common lands in England and Wales, and equivalent areas in other countries protected against exploitation by continuing collective or personal rights over them, illustrate this type. Even when such rights to graze cattle, take firewood or dig peat fall into disuse their legal survival prevents the land from being built up or otherwise exploited.

An interesting case of conservation buttressed by religious tradition arose through the selection as a place of meditation and retreat by St

Cuthbert about AD 680 of the Farne Islands off the coast of Northumberland. To safeguard his solitude and to fulfil his ideals he insisted that the wild life, and particularly the breeding eider ducks, should be left unmolested. So powerful and enduring has his influence been that the tradition, although not always fully respected, has never died out, and is still a live influence after nearly 1,300 years.

In England the demarcation of infertile land for reservation of stocks of deer and other game goes back to Saxon times, although the Normans, who so much enjoyed and developed this system of "Forests" are popularly credited with their invention. Whether from energy and sportsmanship, or lack of ingenuity, or some other reason hunting in these forests seems always to have stopped short of the mass killing of corralled animals deprived of any chance of escape, depicted in many ancient and medieval scenes, such as Paolo Uccello's vivid 15th century painting of a night hunt in a forest, in the Ashmolean Museum at Oxford.

Dudley Stamp (In *Man and the Land*, p. 94) guessed that the medieval acreage of "royal Forests, chases and other land for sport" absorbed some 5 million acres out of 37 million in England and Wales. Since such areas incidentally afforded protection to all other animals and plants, including trees which were strongly defended against injury or destruction, the system must have done much to retard or prevent the extinction of native species and the destruction of all samples of the natural environment. Nevertheless Germany, for example, has now a far greater wealth of surviving natural areas, especially of woodland, than can be found in England.

Similarly the art of falconry, so keenly studied and fostered by the Emperor Frederic II in Germany and Italy in the thirteenth century, was inherently a well-matched contest between predator and prey, which generated its own skills and its own courtly rituals and restraints. The qualities of the quarry were hardly less studied and valued than those of the hunting creatures. Frederic's Asiatic contemporary Kublai Khan was at the same time independently pursuing similar interests, including the setting of closed seasons for hunting birds. Another contemporary, St Francis of Assisi, gave an outstanding lead for bird protection in Italy, which it has taken his fellow-countrymen seven and a half centuries to begin to follow.

The setting aside of Crown lands, the influence of court practice and example, and the preaching and influence of a few recognised saints or holy men were prominent among the few channels for promoting conservation up to the end of the medieval period. After that period new means gradually became available, of which enforceable general legislation was the first.

THE BRITISH STORY

IT is convenient, in reaching the more modern period, to treat separately the development, partly overlapping in time, of the British and the American conservation movement. With due respect to the valuable contributions made by other countries it is from these two sources that most of the main principles and structures now widespread in the world of conservation have stemmed. In point of earliness only the British claim first place.

As we have seen in the previous chapter, early conservation was haphazard. The first enforceable legislation in England was under King Henry VIII when an Act was passed by Parliament in 1534 "to avoide destruction of wilde-fowle". The conservation aim of this was shown by its protection for the eggs of herons, spoonbills, cranes, bitterns and bustards, while the birds themselves were left unprotected, even in the breeding season. The interests of falconers was evidently paramount here.

The next subject of official concern in England was the standing crop of timber, especially of mature oaks, threatened by deforestation and by the rapidly growing demands for charcoal in the process of iron smelting. Religious tensions and national rivalries following the Reformation stimulated the increased production of iron cannon and of gunpowder and ammunition, which led the movement towards more wholesale exploitation of woodlands and thus created a shortage of accessible timber. That in turn alarmed the Navy and led to what we now recognise as the earliest series of conservation laws in England.

A key figure in this development was John Evelyn, a man of keen powers of observation and tender conscience. His sense of guilt from the destruction of trees, on which his family's fortune had been based—his grandfather and father were suppliers of gunpowder—led him to devote great efforts to studying and promoting the planting of trees and the re-establishment of woodlands. Tree-planting had been done before in a number of isolated instances both in Scotland and in England during the 16th century, but it was mainly through Evelyn's efforts in the second half of the 17th century that it first acquired the status of national policy and of a national upper-class habit, directed towards the rehabilitation and improvement of depleted natural resources and devastated landscapes.

As so often happens, however, many of Evelyn's keenest converts and disciples switched their efforts in directions which he had not foreseen or intended. Much of the ensuing treeplanting was designed not to produce more timber but to enhance the sporting interest of estates by aptly designed coverts for foxes and pheasants, or their landscape beauties and amenity through ornamental plantings, often with exotic rather than with native species. All this, magnificent as its results appeared, made little impression on the economically minded, and must if anything have strengthened the national tendency to regard such activities as conservation as luxuries for the rich rather than as essentials of national good housekeeping.

Evelyn also launched pioneer ideas in care of the environment in his *Fumifugia*, in which he envisaged using a kind of planning control to banish from cities such as London industries liable to give off noxious fumes and smoke, and to use trees and shrubs of suitable species planted in the right patterns and locations to create more favorable and salubrious conditions.

These ideas, although not implemented, received the blessing of Charles II, who himself showed how to enhance urban amenity by developing the collection of waterfowl (started by his grandfather James) and by the making of artificial "lakes", which have ever since given to St. James's Park in London its special quality and appeal among parks of national capital cities. The unmatched extent and picturesqueness of London's inner Royal Parks today stems from such regal patronage and use.

It is on record that the exile in the Low Countries of Charles II and several of his intimates had interested them in the ideas on landscape and its appreciation which painters and others there were at that time elaborating. The word landscape is itself derived from the Dutch *landskip*. Dutch painting in the 16th and 17th centuries is rich in scenes expressing the complex interrelations between man and his natural and man-made environment. Already as early as 1576 the Bois de La Haye had been set aside to be preserved intact as a natural area. In this great period of Dutch civilisation landscapes shared with paintings, tulips, architecture and costume a connoisseur level of appreciation among discerning patrons.

Immediately after the Restoration the ancient styles were revived in England. Then the leaders of English taste suddenly began some two and a half centuries ago to turn their backs on the rectilinear or geometric basic design almost universally accepted for gardens throughout the previous three thousand years, and surrendered themselves to what they took to be nature's alternative pattern. It can hardly have been mere coincidence that this abrupt and drastic change immediately followed after, and was guided by members of the same compact social group as the political new deal beginning in 1688, under which the strict limitations of constitutional monarchy and Parliamentary control were firmly saddled on the British crown. The gardens of Versailles breathed absolutism and academic tradition; those of England did homage to nature and commented on the unwisdom of man presuming too much.

Writing in 1709 the 3rd Earl of Shaftesbury, member of a leading political family of the period, aptly expressed the connection:

"I shall no longer resist the passion growing in me for things of a *natural* kind; where neither *Art* nor the *Conceit* or *Caprice* of man has spoiled their *genuine Order* by breaking in upon the *Primitive State*. Even the rude *Rocks*, the mossy *Caverns*, the irregular unwrought *Grotto's* and broken *Falls* of water, with all the horrid graces of the *Wilderness* itself, as representing NATURE more, will be the more engaging, and appear with magnificence beyond the formal mockery of princely gardens."

Here is at the same time a challenge to pompous, artificial hierarchical values, personified by his contemporary Louis XIV of France, the Sun King, and a championing of the deeper significance of the natural environment with the clear implication that it ought to be conserved.

Thomas Burnet a few years earlier in 1684 had put in its extreme form the contrary view of an imaginary unnatural Nature in *The Sacred Theory of the Earth*.

"If the Sea had been drawn around the Earth in regular figures and borders, it might have been a great Beauty to our Globe, . . . but finding . . . all the marks of disorder and disproportion in it, we may as reasonably conclude, that it did not belong to the first order of things, but was something succedaneous, when the degeneracy of mankind, and the judgments of God had destroyed the first World . . ."

David Daiches has commented on this in verse full of a twentieth century wit which would surely have been appreciated in Queen Anne's day, when noble members of the Kit Kat Club were reacting in much the same way, and were preparing to spend their wealth and to dedicate their great estates to realising on the land the vision of the philosophers, poets and painters.

143

Burnet! You wring my heart full sore.
I had not realised before
How crooked, twisted, bent and curled
Is this our poor distorted world.
I look below and at my feet
I see misshapen grasses meet.
Above me, in the endless sky,
The malformed clouds float sadly by . . .

While sky and meadow, field and tree
Are just as ugly as the sea.
Enough! I shut my burdened eyes
And do my best to visualise
A world where all is neatly framed
And Burnet need not feel ashamed. . . .

Such ordered creatures play their part
In boosting their Creator's art.
How trim the patterned ocean's strand
In perfect square of yellow sand!
I note the rocks that bound the seas —
Triangular (isosceles)
Neat fishes as they swim adduce
The square on the hypotonuse.

A nymph approaches—creature fair
How straight and even is her hair!
Her eyes two perfect circles are;
Her bosom is rectangular.
Am I delighted? I am not!
—Burnet, you talk the damnedest rot.

At certain places it is possible to see clearly marked on the face of the land turning-points in human attitudes towards it. One of these is in Kensington Gardens, London, a monastic possession and source of water in the Middle Ages, which was taken over as a deer park by Henry VIII in 1536, thrown open to Londoners a century later by Charles I, and newly landscaped in broadly its existing form nearly a century later again, under the direction of Queen Caroline, by Henry Wise and Charles Bridgeman. Looking down from a tall building at Lancaster Gate the foreground is dominated by the stone-paved layout of basins and fountains in the classical style, from which there is a dramatic transition to the naturalistic and romantic Long Water and Serpentine, converted from a previous series of ponds along the valley of the Westbourne Brook. (The very word serpentine and the sinuous curves which it evokes are close to the heart of the new landscape school.)

Simultaneously, but on a smaller scale, a similar abrupt change in landscape style was made by Lord Burlington and Kent in the later part of the gardens of the new villa at Chiswick; unfortunately the planned restoration of this long neglected garden is still in a most imperfect condition.

The rapid and complete victory of the new approach not only gave its exponents a monopoly of designing the great landscapes which the rich landowners of the 18th century commissioned on a scale never matched before or since. It also, less happily, led to the uprooting and complete replacement of many important examples of earlier styles. From the tentative early irregular but still basically rectilinear and statue-studded essays of Bridgeman and Kent between 1700 and 1740 to the more boldly naturalistic enterprises of the mid-century under Capability Brown and his successors this far-reaching revolution was conceived and guided by a small handful of gifted and wealthy patrons and their talented professional aides.

Various attempts have lately been made to trace the origins and early growth of the English landscape movement, but the more we probe and analyse these the more subtle and complex they prove to be. The Baconian systematic and philosophic approach to the secrets of Nature; the Navy's dire need for great oaks to build its wooden walls against the French and the Dutch, the tedious but fruitful days spent by Charles II and his courtiers in exile among Dutch landscapes before the Restoration; the Whig reaction against the despotic politics and the regimented gardening of Louis Quatorze; the heightened prestige of land ownership and the emulation in land improvement which so valuably absorbed so many manhours and so much commercially earned capital around the days of Queen Anne; the eagerly collected and keenly admired paintings of Claude, Poussin and Salvator Rosa; the travellers' tales of Chinese gardens emancipated from the cold rules of geometry; the explorers' booty of strange exotic trees and new plants which challenged the skills of the new nurserymen, and the taxonomic resources of the new school of botany, led by Ray and later by Linnaeus; the requirements of architects for fresh and grander settings to display their great new country houses to best advantage; and the sporting passion for pursuing the partridge and the mallard with the newly improved firearms and the fox on the newly improved horses all contributed to the explosive creative mixture from which the appreciation of landscape so suddenly emerged fully-fledged.

Literature, both in prose and poetry, contributed much towards distilling the imaginative outcome of reflections stimulated during foreign travel, or by looking with fresh eyes at the legacy of classical times. Through it the head and the heart were brought to enjoy a rare reconciliation, as the new landscape both echoed and stimulated the awakening desire to become better attuned to nature as a means of escaping from the cares and deformations of a too rigidly crystallised society, and of releasing personal tensions through a leisurely and undirected immediate contact with the living environment.

Without forgetting that advances towards conservation were largely made possible and demanded by other and earlier developments in economic, social, cultural and technological fields it is important in tracing their evolution to bear in mind that changes in attitudes and ideas have throughout been accompanied by identifiable innovations, not only in physical shape on the land, but in terms of emerging new skills and occupations and of institutional or legal patterns generalising, enabling and regulating the form and method of changing practice and requirements.

On the physical plane, for example, demarcation and restriction of movement between one unit of land management and another have been provided since prehistoric times by earth banks, stone walls and in flat wet areas by channels of water. In England this process began in the Neolithic period some 4000 years ago, and there are still farms in Cornwall and elsewhere which are parcelled up today by dry-stone walls into the same fields which were laid out in the Iron Age more than 2000 years back. As the banks became grown up with bushes and trees, such as can still be seen widely in Devon and Cornwall, the possibilities of establishing biological barriers were demonstrated.

The 17th and 18th centuries in England saw a vast increase in hedgerows, and to a much less extent in lines of trees as windbreaks (and also in the newly invented ha-ha or sunken walled obstacle invisible in the wider landscape). Besides separating fields these devices were used to convert roads into sheltered avenues, to separate farms from highway verges, and to insulate the new fast turnpikes along which ran the horse-drawn coaches carrying passengers and mail. The flow of water was controlled by levees and flood banks, weirs and locks, and by diversions along leats, canals or other artificial channels, and underground through culverts, land-drains and sewers. Water was also conserved for power by such devices as small dams forming hammer-ponds or mill-ponds, and for navigation or water supply or amenity in reservoirs and other artificial pools, often linked with distribution through surface channels, drains and canals or piped systems.

Trees were also planted on a grand scale in plantations for timber, for game coverts or for amenity and climatic amelioration. The newfound mastery of growing trees and guiding water, together with earth-moving, were the main physical tools which made possible the landscape and land use revolution of 18th century England.

But these in themselves would not have been availed without the stimulus and guide of the new concepts and feelings concerning man's relation to nature, and the new skills developed by the early landscape gardeners and designers, foresters, horticulturists, agronomes, land agents, factors, and others, who nursed and developed the necessary techniques and practices, and sorted out how and where to apply them. Considering the novelty and the large scale of so much that had to be done it is remarkable how many gifted men came forward to do it.

In the background, often with a long time lag, legal and institutional innovations followed, providing an infrastructure of regulatory and enabling powers and resources.

The newly emerging attitudes and understanding of nature were nursed to maturity among minority groups in society. They formed a small band of lively, contemplative, economically and politically independent men who looked at nature no longer as a threat or a sinister mystery but as man's natural home, to be studied, admired and managed with affection and appreciation, but also with a relaxed and confident mastery. Although they were small in number they formed a central nucleus which gradually grew in size and influence over the years. They kept their ideas alive and visibly present for the expanding leisured class to see and appreciate. They acted as points of focus for the growth and development of ideas about conservation, and so enabled those who did appreciate the many intangible values of nature to have examples around them to copy. Parks, pleasure gardens, sporting estates, and designed landscapes were freely planned by those who could afford to do so.

But just as this movement was gaining many adherents in all walks of life, science, technology and industry made enormous advances and Britain entered upon the period of the Industrial Revolution.

The landscape of England, the first to be deliberately and skilfully improved by professional effort, became immediately afterwards the first to be crudely devastated by the industrial revolution. It is an odd coincidence that of all the centuries and all the territories where man has made his impact felt on the land it should have been a single small country in a single century where both these almost opposite types of impact should have strongly and abruptly occurred. In the middle decades of the century men of taste were arguing keenly over the compatibility of cornfields and grazing cattle with classical architecture and with fine landscape. Within the same lifetime the dilemma had changed to one of accommodating pithead gear, spoilheaps, cotton mills and tall factory chimneys alongside scenes of the most discriminating and cultivated design. In a number of cases the same landowning families were involved on both sides of this conflict, and were themselves profiting from the spoilation of their own estates.

In a sense there were three sides, since the contemporary agricultural revolution, itself a product of the same social group in the same country, was already making demands which were becoming difficult to reconcile with accepted landscape design when they were equally suddenly over-taken by much more intractable demands of industrialism. The problem was especially acute in such coalfields as Durham and south-east Northumberland, South Yorkshire, Nottinghamshire and Derbyshire, parts of the West Midlands, south-west Scotland and South Wales. It also affected the non-ferrous metal areas of Cornwall, and the localities rich in iron ore and other resources now quickly being extrac-ted on a large scale.

On a naïve view it might have been counted a blessing that the great new challenges of industrialism in terms of landscape and land use should have first developed in a land and under a ruling class so experienced and so appreciative of such problems, but practice worked out differently and often disastrously. Instead of studying and experi-menting with means of reconciling the new industrial operations to the landscape the leaders of taste and politics and the makers of money and holders of managerial authority in the new industries were almost unanimous in behaving as if the problem did not exist, and as if the land required for industrialism was almost infinitely expendable.

It was not so much a defeat as an abject surrender to the invasion of half-baked greedy materialism and to the ascendancy of barbarian values in aesthetics, in ecology, in economics and in social respon-sibility. It initiated a new Dark Age for the natural environment, and placed the bulk of available human ingenuity and resources at the disposal of developments disastrous to the trustee interests of those generations towards their descendants. Unfortunately, too, owing to its dynamic technology and mobility, it spread throughout the world much too rapidly for its dangers to be measured and guarded against anywhere else.

The very prestige of England at this time tended to mould opinion in favor of tolerating evils in which the English themselves saw no harm. Late Georgian and Victorian England bought prosperity for a minority at the cost of running up an overdraft on the environment which will yet take longer to repay than any line of credit from the Bank of International Settlements.

Creditable exceptions must be made of the constructors of the canal system, notably Brindley, of the improved roads, notably Telford, and also some of the railway builders, notably Brunel, whose often hastily designed alignments, bridges and earthworks have on the whole fitted admirably well into the landscape.

Factory industry with its dark satanic mills, mining with its pollution of earth, air and water and its massive destruction of land forms, and housing for workers formed with few exceptions the worst examples of how not to treat a human environment. But for the good fortune that these outrages in some cases could be seen to foster lethal diseases, which could be plainly seen to be killing some of those responsible for them, the necessary political support for beginning remedial measures would have been even further delayed than it was. Such measures were however narrowly restricted to the field of sanitation and public hygiene. Wealthy England a century ago was not willing or able to support a single landscape designer of the caliber of the great 18th-century virtuosos, or to maintain a single school of study of the massive complex of environmental problems which stared it in the face.

Land ownership, land use and land management in Britain during the past two and a half centuries have been characterised by a remarkably consistent blend of great merits and severe defects. Even while many country-dwellers were subject to repressive and arbitrary treatment, exploiting their economic weaknesses, the land itself was handled with a sense of the interdependent relationship between man and nature, and of the need for taking care of both the human community and the ecosystem. This broad and organic approach was the antithesis of the distorted and artificial approach of classical economics. By setting themselves against the divorce of land from nature and society and its subjection to a real-estate market economy British landowners have rendered another notable service to civilisation. Their conservatism has proved of great value in maintaining almost intact far into the twentieth century the landscape inheritance derived from the seventeenth and eighteenth, complete with trees, hedgerows, field patterns, wild or feral rivers, pools and marshy places.

The failures, however, were serious. While many were tree-lovers, they were literally unable to see the wood for the trees. Consequently this country-loving, sporting, gardening and farming nation has been left without any substantial appreciation or understanding of forests, as distinct from game coverts, amenity plantings or lowgrade timber factories. Even Crown plantations from the early 19th century exhibit that peculiar blend of ecological hamhandedness and aesthetic insensitivity which, with honorable exceptions, have been the hallmark of the British forester during the past century and a half.

Again, while many were nature-lovers they eagerly embraced the opportunities afforded by landownership for working off upon beasts and birds, especially predators, such feelings of aggression as could not be satisfactorily released by exercising their hereditary penal jurisdiction as justices of the peace or their hereditary military traditions, now actively deployed mainly in Asia and in Africa. Their enthusiasm and resources subjected much of the land to a peculiar and strict regime of game preservation operated by a biological police force of gamekeepers, stalkers and water-bailiffs, which was on the whole effective throughout its jurisdiction in preventing other forms of human interference with animal life. Unfortunately its own obsessive and misguided century-long campaign against avian and mammalian predators gravely unbalanced the equilibrium in favor of pests of agriculture and forestry.

While the feudal landowners of Europe had been tied to royal or princely courts the prime outdoor pursuit had been a highly organised and formal type of stag-hunt through forest avenues designed for the purpose. As the free English country gentlemen sought outlets for their manly vigor and their keen sporting instincts they turned rather to fox-hunting and to shooting ducks, pheasants and partridges, for all of which the new pattern of landscape proved ideally suited, and thus endeared itself to many whose aesthetic sensibilities could not react to it. The landscape of pre-Victorian England, like that of Virginia, thus came to express a special concept of liberty which goes with firm constitutional guarantees, philosophic enlightenment, a more than reasonable dose of liquor and the hunting of the fox.

Decisive and far-reaching as was the impact on the land of the new approach, its practical legacy was curiously limited. For the vast majority who were not great landowners, who had not been consulted or received much explanation of what was going on over their heads, and to whom such rich men's pastimes were almost as esoteric as managing a stud of racehorses, the enjoyable aesthetic results of naturalistic landscape carried no more than the most tenuous message in relation to their own tastes and activities. They duly admired these works, as their betters told them they should, but the deeper significance of the new relation implied between man and nature was probably largely lost upon them, except in so far as it was conveyed to them by the brilliant succession of poets, from Pope and Thomson to Coleridge and Wordsworth, who so enthusiastically embraced the new feeling.

The rejection by English 18th-century gentlemen of the earlier stiff and geometrical conventions of gardening and of landscape, and the triumphant spread of more naturalistic and informal styles, gave however, a great sense of release and of free inspiration and enjoyment, which readily also attached itself to scenes of wild nature.

Even mountain and marine scenery, hitherto regarded as uncouth and horrible, attracted increasing appreciation and at times unbridled enthusiasm. Men began to climb mountains for fun for the first time. A social foundation was created both for modern conservation and for modern tourism, which have only recently begun to understand how much they have in common.

The best of the great landowners struggled with marked success to apply to their urban estates the high aesthetic standards, the civilised spatial and land use planning and the economic responsibility and self-restraint of the best-managed country holdings. In London ducal Bloomsbury and Belgravia, and elsewhere Eastbourne, Bournemouth and Sidmouth, for example followed the fine lead given in 18th century Bath and in Edinburgh's New Town. The concept of what later, in America, became labelled the city beautiful was always kept alive in this way, but too many landowners fell to the lure of quick profits and the pressure for quick development to satisfy expanding industry and multiplying population. The standards in the majority of 19th and early 20th century towns and town quarters fell very low. Easier travel encouraged raw commercialism to take over too many tourist attractions and "beauty spots".

The lineal heirs to the new rural landscapes cherished them, luckily, with far more care and consideration than their inventors had accorded to their predecessors in design. They have thus largely survived to delight and inspire us today, when many of the great country houses and parks are much more freely open to the public than ever before. But this entire heritage has hitherto been largely meaningless for most new owners and managers of land, especially public authorities and private firms, which have assumed often without recognising it, so much of the responsibility for the well-being of English landscape today. It is in the circumstances fortunate that more of the benefit of this great heritage has not been thrown away, during the long interval when power over it nearly passed to men who did not know and did not care.

In one unique region the impacts of early tourism and of the post-feudal landowner coincided without successfully merging. Settled peace within Britain after the Union of the English and Scottish Parliaments was incompatible with the perpetuation of the traditional clan economy in the Scottish Highlands. After an unsuccessful attempt to put the clock back through the 1745 Jacobite rebellion the Highlands were pacified and opened up through road-making, which encouraged an intolerable increase in population. Early in the 19th century the Malthusian stage was reached and events demanded massive population redistribution, the handling of which was exacerbated by the inhumanity and meanness of a few of the landowners and the intensely close ties between man and clan and between man and land.

In the accompanying revolution in land use two new interests stepped eagerly into the breach—the pastoralists with their sheep and the field sports enthusiasts with their plans to turn over the land to the pursuit of stag and grouse, salmon and seatrout. Whether these developments were inevitable, or were in the true interests either of the Highlands or of Highlanders is open to question, but in the prevailing conditions of rabid economic *laissez-faire* and of ignorance and unconcern south of the Highland line they happened in quite a short time. The incomers from the south shot and fished, often with more enthusiasm than skill, and their standard of wildlife and game management was very much lower than they fondly supposed it to be. They brought in a good deal of money, but not enough to create a new viable Highland economy, which in any case was the last thing they wanted to see.

By intermarrying with the laird's families, and by their overwhelming superiority in political, social and economic power, they were able to preserve this highly artificial state of interrupted social evolution and ecological succession for a full century from around 1840. This period saw a steady impoverishment of soils and vegetation, of biological productivity and of wildlife. Yet to a great many British people, influenced by the summer court at Balmoral and by such popular artists as Landseer and Millais, what they saw in the Highlands was the essence of untouched wilderness, and of wild nature as it should be. It had masses of purple heather, blue mountains, waterfalls, stags and shaggy Highland cattle. It looked romantic and picturesque; it was free from the crudest kinds of intrusion by industrial man; therefore it must be genuinely natural.

Yet the Highland grouse-moors with their constant over-burning of heather and persecution of predators were as crudely and heavily managed as many agricultural areas. The regime for the Highlands was largely escapist in its objects, and sportsmen, artists, poets and tourists agreed in not seeing what they did not want to see, either in the human or the natural scene. Even the hard-bitten sheep men, whose hard-biting sheep were rapidly degrading the vegetation and scenery, shared in this euphoria of *la vie en rose*, or rather, *en pourpre*.

Meanwhile in a separate compartment of the English mind, interest in natural history in its widest sense went on making progress. In the early seventeenth century the first botanical garden had been established at Oxford. In about 1700 the Chelsea Physic Garden had been created in London by the Society of Apothecaries and from this same period date the beginnings, under Sir William Capel, of what nearly a century later blossomed into the Royal Botanic Gardens, Kew and became one of the most important centers for the systematic study and propagation of plants. With the British Museum, founded in 1753, this period marked the beginning of what has since become a substantial official participation in the study and application of biological knowledge. The work of basic classification of plants and animals, begun in the late 17th century by Ray with Willughby and others, had been carried to a decisive point within the next century largely under the leadership of the great Swedish biologist Linnaeus. Explorers such as Captain Cook, Sir Joseph Banks and many others reached out so widely around the globe and enabled so much material to be amassed that it became possible to probe more deeply into the working processes of nature. In the middle decades of the 19th century Charles Darwin and Alfred Russel Wallace carried such probing deep enough to undermine much of the accepted theological and intellectual foundation of earlier western Christian culture. Indirectly the impact of this contribution towards a new approach to natural environment was immense, even though Darwin himself, except for isolated interventions as in the case of Aldabra, showed much less active interest in conservation than his American contemporary George P. Marsh.

Unfortunately Darwin delayed publishing his theory so late that the new rulers and manipulators of Victorian Britain were firmly in the saddle in time to contain and stifle some of its most significant implications, especially when these were acutely distasteful to the Anglican Church. The obvious need for large-scale follow-up in the sphere of biology and environmental studies was coldly ignored. Such sciences as ecology and ethology, whose importance is only now coming to be widely understood, were starved of the resources which were meanwhile by comparison lavished on chemistry and physics, as being more "useful" and also much less productive of thoughts dangerous to the System. Indeed so much energy had to be diverted by biologists to compelling dominant conservatively-minded authorities to accept the new Darwinian outlook that there seems to have been little left over in Britain to follow it up positively in terms of first-rate intellectual effort. The opportunity which Darwin had opened of responding to the environmental threat and challenge of the industrial revolution was therefore largely lost, and this great potential plus was converted into yet another minus.

After the successful foundation of the Linnean Society in the 18th century, and of the Zoological Society of London and a few others around 1830, the build up of voluntary effort faltered until after the Great Exhibition of 1851, when a number of societies concerned with various branches of knowledge were initiated, both nationally and locally. With few exceptions, however, these early bodies devoted themselves to discussion, field excursions and a limited amount of publication and collecting. Action in any external field, such as for conservation, was alien to their outlook, as well as being beyond their capabilities.

Unlike the United States Britain was densely furnished with antiquities of known significance, including many earthworks, burial mounds, standing stones and other prehistoric monuments, trackways and fortifications which were proving less and less able to withstand man's destructive interference. Even in the 19th century it was recognised that something must be done, and a first Ancient Monuments Act was passed in 1882 involving the creation of an inspectorate with certain limited powers of custodianship.

Some of the sites concerned, and others in the hands of the Crown such as the Royal Parks and the New Forest, were also of significance for the life sciences and for nature conservation, but no additional provision was made to take care of these special preserves until the 20th century was well advanced.

Even sites already supposedly enjoying legal protection, such as the common lands, came under increasingly greedy private pressures, which fortunately at last stimulated the organisation of an effective counter-movement, headed somewhat oddly by the Corporation of the City of London which took decisive action over Epping Forest (1882) and Burnham Beeches (1879), and by the Commons, Open Spaces and Footpaths Preservation Society, founded in 1865. That Society, however, concentrated on the preservation of existing rights. The seizure of opportunities to acquire new open spaces and sites of historic or natural history interest remained unprovided for until the foundation in 1895 of the National Trust for Places of Historic Interest or Natural Beauty. While the need for such a body had become painfully clear the particular means of constituting it was suggested by a slightly earlier initiative in Massachusetts—the first of many examples of the indebtedness of modern British conservation to American pioneering.

Simultaneously a few leading ornithologists became anxious over the widespread destruction, in the absence of any legal close season to protect them, of seabirds, birds of prey and others. Wanton shooting from boats at Flamborough Head was particularly criticised, and, after this had been taken up in Yorkshire through an Association formed for the purpose, An Act for the Preservation of Seabirds was passed in 1869, and was soon followed by others widening the scope of bird protection. In the 1880's similar concern about destruction of birds to meet the demands of fashion for plumage led to the forming first of a Plumage League and then in 1889 of a Society for the Protection of Birds, the nucleus of the modern Royal Society of that name. The scope of the movement was broadened and deepended by a remarkable immigrant from Argentina, W. H. Hudson, one of the most outstanding writers on nature and a fine all-round naturalist. His experience of the destruction of wild places and wild life in South America intensified his appreciation and gave weight and conviction to his warnings of the losses to come. He laid the moral and intellectual foundations of a more substantial movement in Britain for the protection of wild life, starting with birds, and bringing together sentiment and science. Hudson also helped to correct the parochial inward-looking tendencies which were common to British as well as American preservationists.

Although the Zoological Society of London at that time concerned itself little with such matters the cause of safeguarding the world's wildlife from extinction was keenly supported by a number of prominent men such as the Duke of Bedford, who single-handed saved Père David's deer from the extinction which was overtaking it in China by importing and nursing up a fine stock in his park at Woburn. Such efforts were underpinned in 1903 by the foundation of the Society for the Preservation of the Fauna of the Empire, long fondly known on account of its nucleus of elderly big game hunters as the Repentant Butchers Club, and now officially entitled the Fauna Preservation Society.

The next year, 1904, became equally significant through the formation of the British Vegetation Committee. From it sprang the British Ecological Society (1913) and the close-knit band of distinguished phyto-sociologists which, under the inspiration and guidance of A. G. Tansley, was mainly responsible for placing on a fully scientific basis the eventual national system of nature reserves and of measures for nature conservation, nearly half a century later.

In these early years of the century, when conservation in the United States was already recognised as a major concern of the President and of Congress, the movement was represented in Britain by well under a dozen growing points, all still so new and small that it would have needed the eye of faith to perceive their potential significance for the remote future. Even where public figures such as Sir Edward Grey became interested their support was given only in their private capacities. The historic walk through the New Forest, taken in June 1910 by Grey and the ex-President Theodore Roosevelt together, made much more stir in the United States than in Britain. It is an index of the relative backwardness of British public opinion on the broader issues that only fifty years later, when American and British naturalists repeated this walk to celebrate the anniversary, did it prove possible for the first time to get the word "conservation" freely printed in British serious newspapers and used by the British Broadcasting Corporation on radio and television.

Although the eccentric naturalist Charles Waterton had created a short-lived private bird sanctuary at Walton Hall in Yorkshire in 1843, and watchers had been employed during the 19th century to protect rare breeding birds on certain small areas in Shetland, in Norfolk and elsewhere, some sixty years more slipped past before a serious start was made towards publicly acquiring as nature reserves sites of unusual scientific interest. With characteristic confusion of aim several of these, such as Blakeney Point Norfolk, were vested in the National Trust before it became realised that the Trust's obligations for public access, its delicate relations with local interests and its lack of specialised scientific management would lead to conflicts of management policy.

Shortly afterwards, in 1912, the energy and leadership of Charles Rothschild led to the beginnings of the Society for the Promotion of Nature Reserves, and the making of a first national list of sites whose scientific interest qualified them for special reservation. By that time, however, World War I was imminent, and although the list was duly submitted to the Government it was swept away in the post-war economy drive, not to be revived for yet another thirty years. Unfortunately also, after the early death of Charles Rothschild, the momentum of his drive for voluntary action gradually ran down, and the executive, overweighted by entomologists, conspicuously failed to establish effective ecological management of its primary nature reserve Woodwalton Fen, and of others, which showed ominous deterioration.

As the leadership of the pioneer organisations grew more elderly and timid the period between the two world wars was largely one of frustration, redeemed only by the brilliant campaigning of a new group of leaders of the amenity movement, including such men as Patrick Abercombie and Clough Williams-Ellis, and by an upsurge of more modern ideas and organisation among field ornithologists.

Unfortunately these exceptions aggravated rather than corrected the splintering tendencies of the potential conservation movement. The Council for the Preservation of Rural England, the first attempt at a co-ordinating body (1926), put the accent so strongly on country as against town and on preservation as against management that despite vigorous and practical leadership it tended to leave inadequately covered the natural history and recreational interests on one side and those of planning for future environments of people on the other. The pioneer work and thought of Patrick Geddes, Ebenezer Howard, the founder of garden cities, and others were poorly followed up in their own land.

A gulf widened between the nostalgic lookers-back who deplored the decay of destruction of the over-mature and obsolescent but delightful 18th century landscape and those who, lacking their taste and imagination, looked forward, often in crude and vulgar terms, to something more contemporary. The loud gasp which went up from the faithful when Prime Minister Stanley Baldwin unveiled in Hyde Park, as a memorial to W. H. Hudson, Epstein's uncompromising sculpture of Rima truly expressed the timid and negative spirit of that time. For all their high aspirations and successful proselytising work the apostles of amenity committed themselves to a line destined soon to be out-dated and to lose much valuable potential support. This was to bring about a rapid rundown of the movement after World War II, and to leave a legacy of serious problems in reuniting the outdoor naturalist and recreational interests with those of the aesthetically and historically minded, and with the growth of tourism.

In ornithology the creation of many local societies and clubs, and of the new British Trust for Ornithology (1931) with its research twin the Edward Grey Institute at Oxford, also complicated affairs initially. However by mobilising a rapidly growing force of amateur bird observers, trained to a high standard through co-operative work in the field, and effectively served by a lively central office, the Trust was able to bring ornithologists at last out of the 19th century and to provide a young vigorous seasoned nucleus from which such new conservation bodies as the county naturalists trusts could be built up. In Norfolk (1926), West Wales (1938) and Lincolnshire (1946) it was the ornithologists who led and organised the new model, because they had accustomed themselves to doing rather than merely looking on and arguing, and because they recognized the pleasures and gains of teamwork. Once this new approach had been demonstrated in practice it was soon followed up by the new Mammal Society of the British Isles (1954), the British Trust for Entomology, and by naturalists trusts in almost every remaining county of England and Wales, with the Scottish Wildlife Trust (1965) north of the Border, acting as a natural history counterpart to the successful National Trust for Scotland (1931).

Aided by the new forces of radio and television, and by luckily finding from its ranks some of the most skilful performers on these media, the movement was able to capitalise on the great asset already created by a band of first-class nature photographers and filmmakers, and thus to go over the heads of a largely ignorant newspaper Press and educational Establishment to make direct contact with people of all ages everywhere. Initially this appeal was mainly escapist, but after something of a struggle in the late 'fifties it was broadened out to voice the aims and show the problems and achievements of conservation.

In this connection steps were taken to create a co-ordinating Council for Nature (1958) able to speak for, serve and provide a united image for all the varied bodies concerned with nature from any standpoint. The efforts of the Council's Information Unit in providing the Press with a constant stream of reliable news, which was eagerly disseminated, and the organisation of National Nature Weeks and of the Conservation Corps for young people opened countless eyes to the constructive opportunities and values of nature conservation. They made a reality of the force of public opinion, which had long potentially existed but had never been made articulate and effective except in isolated controversies.

This would not have been possible without the coming to fruition from 1949 of Tansley's project of an official service with the twin tasks of expanding and expediting ecological research for the benefit of conservation and of acquiring and maintaining a national series of nature reserves. In *Our Heritage of Wild Nature; A Plea for Organised Nature Conservation*, in 1945 Tansley had spelt out simply the more technical report presented to the government in 1943 by a committee (under his chairmanship) of the British Ecological Society, on Nature Conservation and Nature Reserves. He also took account of the report entitled *Nature Conservation in Great Britain* by the Nature Reserves Investigation Committee, sponsored by the Society for the Promotion of Nature Reserves at the request of the Minister for Reconstruction, and no doubt also of some simultaneous proposals from the Royal Society. It is an ironic commentary on the workings of the British system of government that it should have been possible under heavy German bombing, and subject to petrol rationing, blackout and absence on military service of so many ablebodied observers, at last to carry through, within a mere couple of years, a survey and review, which had clearly been urgently needed since the previous century. This was thanks to the wartime suspension of working of the normal British mechanisms for ensuring inaction.

Tansley endorsed the N.R.I.C. contention that "the Government should take formal responsibility for the conservation of native wild life, both plant and animal", but stressed the impossibility of discharging such an obligation without countrywide research on fundamental ecological problems to make possible scientific management of Nature Reserves and other areas. He thought that there was "a good deal to be said for amalgamating the Service with the control of Nature Reserves, since these would be indispensable places for a considerable part, although by no means the whole, of the work of research . . .". Its results in ecological knowledge would be exactly what is required for the enlightened administration of a Reserve. He concluded in favor of constituting a new "Ecological Research Council, parallel with the Agricultural and Medical Research Councils, and employing the Research officers and maintaining a central office to act as a clearing house for ecological information. This Council might at the same time take control of National Nature Reserves . . .".

It was still necessary for these problems to be considered by two official committees, one for England and Wales, under the chairmanship initially of Julian Huxley with Tansley as his deputy, and one for Scotland. Their Reports (Cmd 7022 1947 and Cmd 6784, 1948) greatly amplified the discussion and recommendations, but followed a similar line.

This time they were promptly considered and readily accepted by the Government, on the advice of the Lord President of the Council Herbert Morrison, whose main personal interventions were to insist that the new agency should have a fresh and distinctive title, and to present its Royal Charter personally to the Charter Members (of whom I was one). In fulfilment of his wishes the name chosen, about the New Year 1949, was the Nature Conservancy. (As soon as news of this had crossed the Atlantic the identical title was adopted, regardless of the confusion bound to be involved, by an unofficial conservation organisation of an entirely different type.)

There was obvious practical merit in combining the functions of research, of advice and information and of managing nature reserves as well as experimental stations in a single professional body as Tansley had proposed, and the system has worked most satisfactorily. It is odd in the circumstances that this pattern should have been a new invention, that it has not yet been fully and successfully matched anywhere else in the world, and has several times been the target of ignorant and highly placed critics eager literally to tear it apart.

Within fifteen years of its creation the Nature Conservancy had acquired more than a hundred National Nature Reserves, had designated some 2,000 statutory Sites of Special Scientific Interest, and had built up a multi-disciplinary staff of well over a hundred scientists, backed by grant-aided workers in universities and elsewhere, with some 40 post-graduates at a time under training. (So effective was this training policy that one of them, Dr M. E. D. Poore, was able to take over as my successor in directing the Conservancy in 1966).

Some had originally supposed that the creation of the Conservancy would mark a *nunc dimittis* for the voluntary movement, but this was far from being my view. As has been indicated above, the years of the Conservancy's growth were also years of unparalleled growth throughout the voluntary movement, without which many of the opportunities would have been lost. I was impressed on a visit in 1955 by the frank and confidential relationship between official and voluntary bodies working in this field in the United States. Although the official posture in Britain has usually been more aloof I was encouraged to find that it was by no means difficult to break the ice and to establish more friendly teamwork, given the right initiative.

Unfortunately, although top-level exchanges were maintained between the governing bodies of the Nature Conservancy and the National Parks Commission, their respective staffs and supporters found little common ground. Originally it had been taken for granted that the dominant partner would be the National Parks Commission, but its over-enthusiastic promoters misjudged the reaction to their project of the County Councils, already by 1949 much aggrieved by the encroachments of Whitehall and the curtailment of their jurisdiction. These County Councils felt no sympathy towards surrendering in some cases the planning control of the greater part of their areas to new nationally-controlled authorities, and although Ministers were among the promoters of the new Commission they gave in to the County Councils.

Few public men at that time understood or cared about the plans for a Nature Conservancy, which went through Parliament virtually unopposed, and with all the powers of acquiring land, if necessary by compulsory purchase, of employing wardens and estate staff and of running their own affairs without Departmental interference which had been denied to the National Parks Commission. The Commission was left therefore as essentially an advisory body, although with an accepted right to voice publicly its often dissident views.

As years passed and hopes of some rectification were falsified the Nature Conservancy, in concert with the nature movement, took the initiative to bring about an understanding and alliance with the amenity and outdoor movements and with the National Parks Commission in respect of the general care of the countryside. The first step was the creation, on the Conservancy's initiative, of the Council for

Nature in 1958, and the welcome for non-naturalist bodies in such demonstrations as National Nature Week.

Then, through the personal concern of the Duke of Edinburgh, all the bodies and interests directly and substantially involved in the care and use of the countryside were convened in 1963, and again in 1965 to two Countryside in 1970 Conferences under his chairmanship. In a cordial atmosphere the many differences of interest, style and practice were reviewed and found to form no sufficient reason for maintaining barriers and conflicts based largely on tradition or on misunderstandings. Among the many constructive results was agreement that a wider and stronger Countryside Commission should be developed out of the National Parks Commission in England and Wales (with a newly created counterpart in Scotland where no National Parks Commission had existed) to oversee and contribute to the maintenance of the amenities of the countryside as a whole. The somewhat artificial preoccupation with certain areas mistakenly labelled National Parks (in disregard of international definitions) was therefore at least qualified and balanced by a more constructive and wide-ranging responsibility, making the Commission a true counterpart to the Conservancy, with its equally catholic responsibilities for conservation. The two together could now underpin the local authorities in such tasks as safeguarding the integrity of the coastline, and keeping a check upon the indiscriminate conversion of open country to plantations or reclamation for agriculture.

Unfortunately the modernisation of the natural history movement which was carried through in the later fifties and early sixties has not yet been matched by an effective modernisation of the British outdoor recreation and amenity movements, which remain cast in a somewhat nostalgic and anachronistic mould, with certain notable exceptions. Whatever may be thought of the merits of the particular case the determined effort in 1966–7 to revolutionise the policy and to unseat the leaders of the National Trust was a warning (promptly heeded by the Trust) that a phase of general modernisation is now called for.

Already in 1908 it could be said that conservation in America had arrived; the same could not be said for Britain before 1963 at earliest—a timelag of over half a century.

But as so often happens, once sluggishness was overcome there were plenty of advantages to be gained from starting with almost a clean slate.

THE AMERICAN STORY

F o r historical reasons the modern advances in care of the environment were not until very recently visible on a worldwide scale, but were largely concentrated in Great Britain and a few immediately neighboring European countries, and on the eastern and western seaboards of North America, with only a few small and rather feeble focal points elsewhere. During the 17th and 18th centuries the most dynamic center of growth was in Great Britain; during most of the 19th and the first half of the 20th it had shifted to North America.

William Penn's far-sighted and significantly named settlement of Pennsylvania (1681) made provision from the outset "to leave an acre of trees for every five acres cleared," and pioneered in employing a forester to prevent mismanagement of trees. No doubt this inspiration owed something to John Evelyn. Near Philadelphia too John Bartram the "king's botanist" set up the first botanical garden in North America, in 1730, just over a century after the establishment at Oxford of the first in England. The value of such gardens was demonstrated two years later when the Chelsea Physic Garden in London, created by the Society of Apothecaries some fifty years previously, shipped to America the first cotton seed, from which a great American industry developed. (The seed of much else in American history and culture invisibly accompanied it.)

In America, too, there were enterprising landowners eager to improve and embellish their estates by the conservation of soil and water, of vegetation cover, of game and wild life. They included such founding fathers of the United States as George Washington at Mount Vernon, William Hamilton at Philadelphia and Thomas Jefferson at Monticello. These were largely dependent for literature and technical experience on their English counterparts, but they did not hesitate to strike out on fresh lines. For example, while in England the indiscriminate planting of exotic species soon became almost an obsession, Jefferson in 1806 anticipated modern conservationists in resolving, as his *Garden Book* records, to treat his mountainside in a "disposition analogous to its character". Accordingly, he would use only indigenous trees and plants.

From this time on American and British attitudes and lines of development have conspicuously diverged, at least up to 1960, since when some renewed tendencies to convergence may be traceable. In England and Scotland the great landowners might be attacked for abusing their great political influence, and for failing in some of their responsibilities towards their tenants, their workers and the rural community generally, but they were hardly vulnerable to severe reproach over their steward-ship of the soil, their care for wild life and their progressive attitude towards agricultural improvement. Far from making fortunes out of the land they were much more apt to pour into it wealth derived from commerce and other external sources.

While the British economy before 1850 was largely based on develop-ing industry and commerce on a fairly modest but prosperous agricul-tural substructure, the future of the United States was clearly seen to depend on opening up the shifting frontier and on bringing into use the vast continental natural resources. These resources, being from the outset largely in federal hands, created an entirely different type of drama and tug-of-war between federal government and nation. Washington D.C. had the dual and sometimes irreconcilable respon-sibility of enabling resources to be so exploited as to yield the most rapid practicable expansion of the national economy and, as trustee and arbiter, restraining all kinds of abuses against the land itself, the citizens generally and innumerable interests directly concerned. This was a process from which no important prospective beneficiary could afford to be dissociated. In its course dollar pressures would evidently tend to prevail in the absence of articulate, sophisticated and well-organised bodies to act as champions and spokesmen for the public in-terest, and to insist upon politicians taking their decisions accordingly.

While this situation began casting its shadow early it was only very gradually, partially and belatedly recognised by American public opinion. The national bias and traditions did not favor the development of public, least of all of federal, intervention in the use and management of land. But as early as 1789 a colleague of Benjamin Franklin, Dr Nicholas Collin, rector of the Swedish church in Philadelphia had warned (perhaps on the strength of the views of the city's founder William Penn):

> "Our stately forests are a national treasure, deserving the solicitous care of the patriotic philosopher and politician. Hitherto they have been too much abandoned to axes of rude and thoughtless wood-choppers."

He seems to have been moved mainly by considerations of ornament, of amenity as we would now call it, but a few years later, in 1806, James Fenimore Cooper's father William, in his *Guide to the Wilderness* warned against a future scarcity of timber because "the soil being all fit for culture, will be all cultivated, and the wood of course wasted". This theme was echoed by his son in a best-seller novel in 1823.

It was in the 1830's that the seeds of the great American conservation movement began to sprout up. This part of the story has been excellently reviewed by Hans Huth in his *Nature and the American* to which I have to acknowledge heavy indebtedness over the next few pages. George Catlin, a lawyer and painter who set out to illustrate the Indian tribes in the west, published in a New York newspaper in 1833 the suggestion that forests up the Missouri

> "might in future be seen (by some great protecting policy of government) preserved in their pristine beauty and wildness, in a magnificent park, where the world could see for ages to come, the native Indian in his classic attire, galloping his wild horse . . . amid the fleeting herds of elks and buffaloes . . . *A nation's Park* containing man and beast, in all the wild freshness of their nature's beauty!"

The popularity of Catlin's lectures, with his pictures, no doubt helped to impress this novel idea on informed opinion.

Ralph Waldo Emerson in 1835 in his *Nature* sought to put an end to the shallow moralising and romantic sentimentalism in which the subject was then drenched, and to substitute for it a new approach, uniting natural history with human history as a means of releasing new spiritual force. In 1844, very likely stimulated, as Huth suggests, by Catlin's proposal, Emerson voiced the more practical idea that "the interminable forests should become graceful parks for use and for delight."

Emerson's conviction that "the reason why the world lacks unity, and lies broken and in heaps, is because man is disunited with himself", through failing "to look at the world with new eyes" proved an inspiration to the more single-minded Thoreau, whose work provided America with a solid and distinctive philosophy in this field.

Writing at this early stage in the history of conservation the verdict must be that they were defeated in their attempt to vindicate the unity of man with nature as against a short-sighted materialism given a veneer of respectability by a classical culture. Perhaps those who have the opportunity to return to the matter next century may be able to qualify this verdict in the sense that they were merely far ahead of their times.

America was well served also after the mid-century by the widely read popular writings of John Burroughs from 1865 onwards. Huth aptly says "Man in harmony with nature was Burroughs' concern", and his influence strongly affected the growth of public interest and concern on the subject. The great museums, which had been initiated by the Englishman James Smithson's gift to the American nation in 1826, strongly reinforced this practical and straightforward approach.

John Burroughs however was not attracted by wilderness, and he once accused John Muir, the prophet of the Sierras, of being "crazy about trees and wild scenes" and even called him "mountain-drunk". Under the pressure of all this conflicting indoctrination many Americans must have felt somewhat confused, but at least they embraced with enthusiastic energy the passion for exposing themselves to nature and to wilderness which continues among them to this day. Some indeed embraced it too uncritically. Already in 1860 Thomas Starr King gave tongue to the reproach that most summer travellers

"bolt the scenery, as a man driven by work, bolts his dinner.... Sometimes they will *gobble* some of the superb views between two trains, with as little consciousness of any flavour or artistic relish, as a turkey has in swallowing corn." This distressed him greatly since

"To learn to see is one of the chief objects of education and life."

Gobbled or not, the intake was now beginning to be digested, and the effects would soon appear. The first movement towards parks in the United States had been directed towards making some of the cities more habitable. After serving as a cow pasture since 1639 Boston Common began to be landscaped in 1830. New York however by 1853 had lost all but 117 acres of public open space. The repercussions on hygiene and on public order and decency set off a reaction. It first assumed the uniquely American form of a popular movement for scenic cemeteries.

Dr Jacob Bigelow of Boston, an adversary of traditional burial customs, was the pioneer. After six years campaigning he succeeded in bringing to fulfilment Mount Auburn Cemetery, opened in 1831 four miles outside Boston—"the first example in modern times of so large a tract of ground being selected for its natural beauties and submitted to the processes of landscape gardening to prepare for the reception of the dead". It seems odd now to read of parties of pleasure coming out to it from the city, sometimes at the rate of six hundred visitors a day, and of the idea being quickly imitated by New York, Philadelphia and other cities.

Politicians and others responsible were left in no doubt that there was a demand for parks for the living as well as for the dead. The point was hammered home by the pioneer American landscape architect, Andrew Jackson Downing, who urged that it was the duty, and should be the policy of republics to further the taste for parks and gardens which *all* may enjoy. The public park would promote general goodwill, and mix all classes.

The scenic cemeteries proved to have brought about a glorious resurrection of nature in the American way of life. The first witness given of this was in New York, where the demand voiced in July 1844 by William Cullen Bryant for a new park eventually led to action. Beginning with an authorisation for land acquisition in 1851 it culminated seven years later in the appointment of Downing's famous pupil, Frederic Law Olmsted, to direct the design and execution. Olmsted's plan, partly based upon Paxton's Birkenhead Park in England, formed the foundation for development of park design in North America. As Huth puts it he "almost single-handed introduced large-scale landscape architecture to America". But, owing to a temporary difference Olmsted left New York from 1863 to 1865 on a highly fruitful interlude in California, at that time separated by an arduous and perilous transcontinental journey from the east coast, and only fifteen years old as a part of the United States.

The new State had begun with a world-famous gold rush, and in 1852 the discovery of the first of the great mountain sequoias had touched off a controversy in the Press over the desecration of cutting down such splendid trees. This attracted the public support of James Russell Lowell, editor of the *Atlantic Monthly*, who proposed a society for the prevention of cruelty to trees, commenting that "we are as wanton in the destruction of trees as we are barbarous in our treatment of them". With the backing of Oliver Wandell Holmes and others, the first battle in the history of the American conservation movement had begun.

Almost at the same time a small punitive expeditionary force against the so-called Yosemite Indians had first penetrated into their now world-famous valley fastness, quickly acclaimed as "the most striking nature wonder of the Pacific". Articles, sketches and the recently developed medium of photography brought it vividly to the awareness of Americans everywhere. Horace Greeley, visiting it in 1859, no doubt expressed a widespread view in hoping that the new State of California would immediately provide for the safety of the Mariposa Grove of Big Trees, its twin wonder.

It was, by great good fortune, to Mariposa County that the forty-year-old Olmsted came, at the height of his powers, during his temporary exile from the heart of affairs in New York. How great these powers were is shown by the fact that within little more than six months after his arrival a project for transferring to the State of California an area including both the Yosemite Valley and the Mariposa Big Trees "upon the express conditions that the premises shall be held for public use, resort and recreation and shall be held inalienable at all times" had been worked out and sent across the continent to Washington, passed there through Congress and received President Lincoln's signature as law. Olmsted, whose first impressions of Yosemite had not been wholly favorable, was now appointed first chairman of the Governor's commission for the Yosemite Park. Although technically the first National Park was Yellowstone, created by Act of Congress nearly eight years later, in 1872, for practical purposes the pioneer role was fulfilled at Yosemite, where the first such park management plan ever made was worked out by Olmsted and sent to the State Legislature in 1865.

That the significance of this advance was at once understood is shown by Samuel Bowles' record of a visit to California, also in 1865, by an influential group led by Colfax, Speaker of the House of Representatives. Commenting on this "admirable example" Colfax singled out Niagara Falls, parts of the Adirondacks, and of the Maine lake scenery as meriting similar treatment. The concept of a series of National Parks was foreshadowed.

The Civil War was over, Lincoln was dead, the transpacific railroad was one-third of the way to completion and slavery was about to be abolished. For the first, but by no means the last time a war-torn nation turned its thoughts, among other things, to caring for its natural environment and scenery. Even Olmsted's early return to New York did not check progress in California, and the spread of the national park idea. In 1868 John Muir, who was to carry the torch with so much dedication and success, arrived in California; among his converts were Emerson, and later Theodore Roosevelt.

General C. C. Washburn who led an expedition to Yellowstone in 1870 was briefed before setting out on "the project of creating a park". Here again action followed speedily, with two official expeditions in 1872 and an Act of Congress by March 1872, necessitated by the accident that as it was in a mere federal territory at the time Yellowstone could not be given legal park status through any other channel.

Other advances towards conservation were already in train. In 1864 George Perkins Marsh had published in New York his path-finding *Man and Nature; or, Physical Geography as modified by human action*, revised ten years later as *The Earth as modified by Human Action*. As United States ambassador in Italy Marsh had concluded that the fall of the Roman Empire had been partly due to its neglect to conserve forests and soils. His insistence on the public importance of what we now call conservation was influential in forming opinion, and his words written in 1874 still read well:

"It is desirable that some large and easily accessible region of American soil should remain as far as possible in its primitive condition, at once a museum for the instruction of students, a garden for the recreation of lovers of nature, and an asylum where indigenous trees . . . plants . . . beasts may dwell and perpetuate their kind."

Similar views had been expressed to Congress in support of the project for a Yellowstone National Park, special emphasis being laid on the opportunities for scientific research. Yet these were the voices of a very small minority. During the first half of the 'seventies, while Yellowstone was being created, the slaughter of buffalo on the prairies amounted to something like 6 millions, and this was not untypical of the squandering of natural resources which was soon to exterminate the enormously abundant Passenger Pigeon and to create genuine alarm for an impending shortage of forest timber.

In 1873 Congress passed a Timber Culture Act requiring settlers who were granted plots to plant one-quarter of them with trees, but it proved unenforceable. The basic problem was clearly the conservation of existing forests, and it was at this time that John A. Warder of the New American Forestry Association first used the word "conservation" in its modern sense. "Arbor Day" to encourage tree-planting was launched in 1872.

Clashes between champions of conservation and those interested in uninhibited exploitation of the public domain were now inevitable. An early victory for the conservationists was gained at Niagara Falls, where the spoliation of the environment and squalid commercialism became an international scandal, leading to official protection for the U.S. and Canadian Falls and their surroundings from 1885.

The bitterness, intensity and scale of the ensuing struggles, and the vast areas and interests at stake, now forced the development in America of a pattern totally unknown in Europe. Strongly backed by influential journals, and led by outstanding publicists and professional men, the conservation movement still desperately needed big money and massive organised support.

The forces against which it had to contend stood to gain large fortunes from railroad promotion, land development, oil and lumber extraction and other activities largely dependent upon federal concessions and grants. Naturally they picked spokesmen and supporters, or cultivated less direct forms of influence in Washington. Unless conservation could reinforce its strength within public opinion by effective matching deployment in the rooms and corridors of power its most important battles would be lost.

In the closing decades of the 19th century it so happened that the conventional agenda for the Congress and the Federal Government was remarkably light. The issues of Slavery and North versus South had been settled by arms, and it was important to play down their aftermath while time went about its very necessary healing role. Foreign Affairs and Defence were secondary while isolationist America could still shelter securely behind a Monroe Doctrine itself securely underwritten by the British Navy. External trade was relatively unimportant. The great domestic issues dominating European politics were largely held in check by the steady mass flow of new immigrants dominating the labor market, and by the vast politically unadventurous farm population. It was therefore less difficult than European comparisons might suggest to secure Congressional time for problems of conservation in a wide sense.

There were also more positive favorable factors. In defiance of predictions by such European economists as Bagehot, the Gross National Product of the United States had immediately after the Civil War begun expanding at a pace never before achieved anywhere over any substantial period. This expansion was buoyed up by mass immigration of willing workers, by fresh technology eagerly embraced, by crude but effective innovations in the structure of finance, commerce and industry, and by the large-scale tapping of hitherto unused resources.

This dynamic condition, which increased the frequency and aggravated the seriousness of manifest blunders and crimes against the principles of conservation, also led to questioning of the abstract academic doctrines of classical economics, and to intense controversy on a quantitative basis concerning real resources and the reality of dangers of exhausting them. The seeds of resource economics and of econometrics were thus sown in America, and bridges were built between economists and natural scientists, a long lifetime earlier than in Europe, where the sterilities of the fluent theorists held unchallenged sway until the great depression of 1929 onwards and the leadership of Keynes at last inoculated public opinion against them.

At the same time public spirit and feelings, by no means unjustified, of guilt to be expiated, released a stream of surplus wealth for the endowment of foundations, colleges, and other institutions, on the model which James Smithson had set. In this way there soon arose a large and able band of scientific, professional and technical leaders interested in resource problems from different angles. A start was also made in developing the unrivalled series of Federal services in this field, beginning in 1885 with the Department of Agriculture's division of economic ornithology (later to become the U.S. Biological Survey, and eventually the Fish and Wildlife Service), and immediately continuing in 1886 with the Division of Forestry. This however had to wait a dozen more years before being given by Congress the necessary powers to employ foresters, to protect the forests and to manage the Forest Reserves which had now begun to exist on paper, under a clause approved by Congress in 1891.

All these developments in the United States during the three closing decades of the 19th century may be said, for the first time in any country, to have put conservation on the map as a serious public issue. Success, however, was bought at a high price. Devoted and industrious as the pioneers of the movement had shown themselves, their origins, experiences and casts of mind and temperament were so diverse or even discordant, and their numbers and resources so slight, that they had been able to create no more than a sketchy precarious and lopsided foundation for the heavy political superstructure which was soon to be improvised. The impulse so surprisingly ignited at Mount Auburn cemetery had run quickly through New York's Central Park to Yosemite and then back by Yellowstone to Niagara, gathering on the way a force more worthy of its goal. But as politicians, administrators and technical men were attracted, the starry-eyed types of men who had pioneered it tended to be elbowed to the flanks. The resulting tensions, conflicts and divisions have overshadowed the American conservation movement ever since.

In terms of its underlying significance between 1890 and 1920 that movement has been acutely analysed by Harold J. Barnett and Chandler Morse, who wrote (in *Scarcity and Growth*, Baltimore 1963):

"Conservation", a coined term, was a part of the "Progressive" political reform program at the turn of the century. It was also a major social movement underlying that program. Conservation doctrine, it is true, began with a focus on natural resources. But in the quest for political support, the doctrine was broadened to include other Progressive social welfare ideas. In terms of ideas, Conservation ranged all the way from abstract metaphysics to practical everyday activity of the individual—it concerned all the various natural sciences, economics, political science, public administration, sociology, engineering, art, and public health. . . . To look at the Conservation Movement as a set of social values, and a successful and practical political force derivative from these, clarifies some of its features which are difficult to understand. The internal contradictions of the Movement resulted from efforts to enhance its political appeal, and to ally divergent groups and interests. . . .

Its political and social character explains its heterogeneous support and membership, its dynamism of subject matter approach and goals; and its later metamorphosis, senescence and relative decline."

To Europeans and others approaching current conservation problems afresh, the attitude and assumptions accepted in the United States are apt to be totally incomprehensible without some such clue. And as the memory of these homeric struggles fades even in the United States, confusion and frustration can arise even there on account of the still present legacy of those high ideals and low politics.

Karl Polanyi is quoted by the authors as having, apparently oblivious of that movement, accurately summed up its essence;

"What we call Land is an element of nature inextricably inter-woven with man's institutions. To isolate it and form a market out of it was perhaps the weirdest of all undertakings of our ancestors.

Traditionally, land and labor are not separated; labor forms part of life, land remains part of nature, life and nature form an articulate whole. . . .

. . . The economic function is but one of the many vital functions of land. It invests man's life with stability; it is the site of his habitation; it is a condition of his physical safety; it is the landscape and the seasons. We might as well envisage his being born without hands or feet as carrying on his life without land. And yet to separate land from man and organise society in such a way as to satisfy the require-ments of a real-estate market was a vital part of the utopian concept of a market economy."

This was published nearly twenty years before the thalidomide babies, but the implied comparison with them of our distorted and deformed civilisation is apt. Dogmatic and blinkered economists, like hasty and irresponsible chemists, can inflict damage beyond their powers of imagination upon delicate organisms such as ecosystems and unborn babies. Unhappily, while the peddlers of thalidomide have at least been stopped, better late than never, the peddlers of mischievous prescriptions for a market economy in land are still busy on the job in every continent except Antarctica. Indeed private preliminary enquiries have already been initiated for real estate on the moon.

Despite its hybrid origins and its sometimes confused objectives the first conservation movement in America was based on a series of philosophic and economic ideas which were of more than ephemeral significance. One of the consequences of the great emphasis placed since Judge William Cooper's days on the catastrophic prospects of exhaustion of natural resources was to encourage attempts at quantitative estimates and forecasts, working towards a complete inventory of natural resources, and of the rates, objects and techniques of their utilisation. As is well known many of the forecasts of impending exhaustion of timber, coal, oil and other materials proved to be grossly exaggerated. If it had not been so we would already be living in an economy seriously crippled by chronic shortage of vital primary products.

Yet the exercise, even in its earlier unsophisticated phases, was salutary and valuable. It helped to correct the logical fantasies derived by classical economists largely from their own inner consciousness. It posed great issues which could not be answered in terms of *laissez-faire* or of a market economy. It stimulated research and the growth of professionalism where British economic liberalism in contrast bolstered up the amateur. It educated opinion to the importance of numeracy in economic policy. It helped to restrain the grosser abuses of the handout to private interests of federal lands and resources, known as the Great Giveway. It drew attention to the need for withholding temporarily or permanently certain lands and waters from certain or from all uses in the interests of trusteeship for the environment and for the future. And it triggered off much investigation and research which has helped to provide the tools for more modern management of the economy. Compared with such lasting benefits the fact that particular forecasts and warnings at various times were often wrong is relatively unimportant, except in so far as it tended to delay advances by playing into the hands of critics and opponents.

Conservationists were also fairly united in attacking instances of apparent waste or unwise use. Barnett and Morse distinguish four categories here.

> "The first type of waste is the destructive use of a particular natural resource where it would be possible to obtain approximately the same type of product or service in a less destructive way.
>
> "For example, if arid grazing land is turned to crop production, with subsequent erosion, this is waste. It is wasteful to pollute streams. . . . The second type of waste is failure to procure the maximum of sustained physical yield of useful extractive products from nature's renewable resources. . . . Crops, fish, livestock, timber and hydropower should be produced to the limits".

Not to do so is equivalent to leaving fruit to rot, and in view of man's voracious appetite is likely to increase consumption of non-renewable substitutes, which is also wasteful.

A third type of waste is the use of technology or practices which do not obtain the maximum yield of extractive product from the physical resources destroyed. For example, in mining much usable material may be left in spoil heaps instead of being recovered and processed.

The fourth is the corresponding failure on the plane of utilisation; for example burning coal in inefficient appliances.

Such arguments are deployed in aid of minimising needless destruction and disturbance of environment and resources. The wide publicity given to them, and the need for satisfying resource authorities upon them, have had important effects in stimulating increased industrial efficiency, often in circumstances where this was unlikely to be brought about by market influences. In leading to the creation of referee public agencies with first-class specialist expertise in particular areas of resource management the movement has also compelled the often technically ignorant heads of both private and public concerns to employ more and better trained professionals, and has thus assisted in the recently accelerated technological revolution. It is unlikely to be a mere coincidence that the great impact of the first American conservation movement was followed, after the time-lag to be expected, by a technological transformation of American industry. The conservationists may have been felt by many at the time to be a great nuisance, but they seemingly brought in their wake great gifts of future wealth.

The concept of the "balance of nature", and the interdependence of biological and other physical processes in maintaining environmental quality and biological productivity was also a basic tenet of the conservation movement. The worldwide discussion and speculation touched off by Charles Darwin's *Origin of Species*, although not the original source of such a concept, no doubt greatly reinforced and refined it. In contrast however to the strong and early stimulus given to studies of major natural resources, the first American conservation movement was relatively ineffective in bringing about the necessary intensive ecological researches, many of which indeed have only recently begun.

As early as 1871 Doane's report on Yellowstone to the 41st Congress had emphasised "as a field for scientific research, it promises great results; in the branches of geology, mineralogy, botany, zoology and ornithology, it is probably the greatest laboratory that nature furnishes on the surface of the globe". Perhaps these "great results" may yet appear during Yellowstone's impending second century of existence: they have not been apparent during its first. The reasons for the disappointing progress of ecology and its prospects for the future are treated in chapter ten.

Not only ecology but other earlier elements contributing to the first American conservation movement also failed to hold a leading place.

Landscape design, after its early achievements in scenic cemeteries, in city parks and in the uniquely American invention of the Parkway (before 1887) proved unable to maintain its momentum, becoming content with a somewhat localised, although significant and often qualitatively impressive contribution.

National Parks made a slow start, the first additions after Yellowstone being Sequoia and General Grant, with a twenty-year timelag. The first National Park indeed preceded the establishment of a National Park Service by 44 years.

The impact of the new American way of life brought its most devastating examples around the turn of the century. During each of the thirty years up to 1896 it is estimated that an average of 1,200,000 passenger pigeons were killed. At the beginning of the century there are believed to have been 3 to 5 billion; by 1915 the species was extinct, simultaneously with another well-known American bird, the Carolina parrakeet. The most spectacular American mammal, the bison, was so recklessly slaughtered during the same period that its extinction was averted more by good luck than good management.

American ornithologists responded to the challenge by forming in 1885 a group which gave rise to the powerful National Audubon Society. This was followed up two years later by the Boone and Crockett Club, formed by a far-sighted group of hunters at the instigation of the future President Theodore Roosevelt, then aged only twenty-eight and at the outset of his lifelong leadership for conservation. Soon afterwards the crusading Sierra Club was formed in California by John Muir to act as a vigilante group for conservation. These were only a few of the more significant voluntary bodies whose creation both confirmed and strongly reinforced public concern over many aspects of conservation. Missionary work was needed on a vast scale, but above all it was urgent to identify the targets for action and to ensure that action was taken.

Against the longest odds in the story of conservation the moment when national political action became all-important happened to bring to the fore in Theodore Roosevelt a dedicated outdoorsman and naturalist who possessed great gifts for leadership and for politics, and who, through the timely assassination of his predecessor, was to become the youngest of all Presidents of the United States, in 1901 at the age of forty-two. It was a relatively dull and uneventful period of history, with no great external events to dictate his agenda, and being free therefore to dictate his own he chose to dramatise and to force a showdown on some of the main issues of conservation.

His persuasive powers, still recalled for us by innumerable Teddy

Bears, his blunt outspokenness and his immense political toughness forced his detested adversaries the "land thieves" to fight for their lives. He mobilised on his side not only conservationists but many who disliked powerful empire builders enriching themselves, who liked to see the authority of democracy vindicated against them, and who were sympathetic to a more dynamic and assertive role for the Presidency, and a more positive and responsible attitude on the part of the Federal government towards the American inheritance and its wise use. It was not only that he forcefully upheld his vision of conservation; in doing so he educated the American nation to a larger view of its destiny, and of values transcending the quick buck.

His advent however was far from solving all conservation problems. His energetic, skilled use of his great personal and constitutional powers revealed how immense and intractable these problems remained, and how much had still to be done to define and understand them, as a precondition of successful action. Initially he had, in Stewart Udall's words "replaced the century-old policy of land disposal with a new presidential policy of withdrawal-for-conservation". But that only made sense either for wilderness areas or as a step towards a better thought-out program of development and wise use than had yet been dreamed of.

Like many crusading movements borne triumphantly to power on an emotional and negative platform of aims the conservation movement began to find itself out of its depth, confused, and even more gravely divided into warring factions. To one, led by the Chief Forester Gifford Pinchot, conservation meant simply a comprehensive and well-planned management of natural resources of every character, based on sound ethical and economic grounds. To him it was wasteful not to put resources to productive use provided this was done on a sustained yield basis. Aesthetic, spiritual and scientific objects were hardly within his range of sympathies, and he parted company bitterly with the protagonist of the other view, his former friend the eloquent John Muir.

Pinchot, as the organisation man with immediate access to the President, disposed of greater effective power, which he used even to exclude Muir from the culminating conservation event of Roosevelt's presidential term. This was the Conference of Governors at the White House in 1908, which discussed the interrelationship of soil exhaustion, erosion, timber famine, scarcity of water and diminution of wildlife. This memorable meeting, with its far-reaching and enduring consequences in establishing conservation as a major theme in the policy-making of the States as well as the Federal government, was designed to be followed up by a corresponding international conference, but there was no time for this before the President vacated his office, and his successor declined to undertake it.

When Theodore Roosevelt's presidency ended in 1909, before he had been able to carry out his intention of convening an international conference on conservation, he found himself able to travel about the world. In doing so he used his regained freedom of movement and his high news value to look into conservation matters and to issue widely publicised statements about them. In this way something of the sense of high importance and the strong feelings about conservation which had hitherto been contained within the United States first impinged upon world opinion. Conversely, the news of these excursions reported back home conveyed a vague first impression that perhaps some day the rest of the world might become involved in such issues, and that conservation might become a significant American export.

At that time however other countries were entirely unprepared to take up the subject as one of general public concern, and they were largely preoccupied with the stormy international and internal crises immediately preceding the First World War. Equally Americans other than Roosevelt tended to regard conservation as a purely domestic affair, and showed little enthusiasm for missionary work elsewhere. Although the seeds had been shown they were to lie dormant for a long time.

Reaction meanwhile set in within the United States under the new President Taft. His Secretary of the Interior, Richard Achilles Ballinger, was out of sympathy with the conservationist line of conserving in Federal hands the title and ultimate control over publicly owned land and natural resources. Ballinger sought to revert to the 19th century doctrine of encouraging rapid development by getting these resources into the hands of private enterprise as fast as possible. As the Roosevelt administration's policy had involved building up powerful federal offices, notably the Forest Services under Gifford Pinchot, to vindicate and enforce the public interest the immediate effect of this reversal was to create something of a civil war in Washington. Owing to clumsy mishandling of a test case Ballinger and Taft became discredited and the conservationists won on points, but the resulting suspicion and ill-feeling, involving the Department of the Interior on one side and the Department of Agriculture on the other, were to continue for many years.

In the center of these conflicts was usually Gifford Pinchot, who combined the basic standpoint of a dedicated production forester with a keen sense of political tactics and expediency, balanced when necessary, as in 1909, by a readiness to denounce the immorality of the special interests. These he contended, were the sole opponents of conservation because they sought private monopoly control in order to gouge the public. Yet within the administration Pinchot was far from opposing a monopoly provided that it was held by the Forest Service. Warring philosophies, warring economic and commercial interests, warring official agencies and warring voluntary bodies grew in strength as the American conservation movement came of age. The chronic struggles, the staggeringly copious documentation, the entanglement of broad or basic issues with ephemeral situations and clashes of personality, and the continual blending with intricate manoeuvres in national and local politics make the evolution and significance of conservation in modern America a forbiddingly intractable subject of study. These complexities go far to explain its surprisingly limited influence and impact on the rest of the world.

This influence has, nevertheless, made itself strongly felt through a number of dramatic events and innovations. Among these were three great natural catastrophes—the disastrous Ohio River floods of 1913, the vast wind erosion of the Dust Bowl States in 1934–5 and the New England hurricane of 1938. None of these was unique, but each made a deep impression on American and world opinion, as news stories carrying the message of nature's capacity to humble man's pride by hitting him unexpectedly hard. The impact of the Great Depression on land use and the economics of farming was even greater, and equally lasting in its influence on attitudes and policy. Less sudden, but no less significant has been the recent explosive growth of leisure activities out of doors, which was partly anticipated and stimulated by the creation of the National Park Service in 1916, and itself led to the establishment of the Bureau of Recreation in 1965. The Soil Conservation Service, The Tennessee Valley Authority and the Fish and Wildlife Service are the other main administrative innovations which have had most marked influence internationally.

Although destruction of life and property by catastrophic river floods has occurred from time immemorial modern technological civilisation finds the continuance of such disasters difficult to accept. The most direct reaction is to tame the offending river by high banks, dams and other flood control works. Experience shows that while this can be successful in certain situations it is technically impossible or prohibitively costly and inconvenient in others. An alternative approach, less favored in the United States than in Britain, has been to zone flood-plains of rivers against residential or other types of development, and to keep at least the key parts of them under forms of land use not seriously vulnerable to flood damage.

A third approach is to go back to the stage before heavy rain is able to enter the main river as run-off, and to check its onrush by a series of buffers, beginning with protection forests at the top of the catchment or basin and with stream regulation works and small impoundments on the higher slopes, and continuing with larger emergency holding dams and other devices, including restriction on quick-acting drainage, in order to spread the flood crest over a longer period and to prevent it rising so high as it otherwise would. Linked with such devices is an elaborate network of automatic raingauges and reporting stations to enable precautionary steps to be taken and any necessary flood warnings to be issued in good time.

The successful development of this last approach has been largely due to the constructive response evoked by the loss of life and damage to property inflicted upon the Ohio Valley in 1913. The Ohio Conservancy Act of the same year created the Muskingum Conservancy District to protect a drainage area extending over parts of 18 counties. Supervised by a body of local judges, and armed with powers to finance itself by levy, the District acquired land and constructed 16,000 acres of reservoirs designed to contain a rainfall runoff 36 per cent higher than that which caused the 1913 disaster. Far from needing to rely on any levy the District has incidentally created recreational and timber assets which more than cover its running costs, and has proved that, given fore-thought, flood control can be made to pay in financial as well as in social terms. Unfortunately, although Muskingum has been there for all to see over the past half-century, its lessons remain unlearnt by the majority of watershed managements, especially in other countries.

A great dividend has accrued to America from the extensive and profound studies of terrestrial water, and the many practical experiments in water regulation, management and use, which are the outcome of conservation concepts and pressures. This intelligent approach is in marked contrast, for example, to the scientifically illiterate attitude until very recently maintained by most authorities concerned at all levels with the water supplies of Great Britain.

It is illustrated by the imaginative and sustained researches of the Forest Service of Coweeta Laboratory and Experimental Area in North Carolina, and at Fraser in the Rocky Mountains, Colorado, and of the Soil and Water Conservation Research Station at Coshocton, Ohio. The work at Coweeta has included controlled experiments to measure changes in runoff associated with different patterns of timber-cutting on upper catchments, different types of streamside vegetation, and different types of farming, including a precise reconstruction of the contribution made by "hill-billy" farming to soil erosion. At Fraser the main concern has been to ascertain the contribution to water yield from snow on the higher stream basins, and how it can be regulated by spreading the summer snowmelt over a longer period. At Coshocton it was found that more than 80 per cent of erosion of local farm lands was due to intense summer rainfall, which affected woodlands not at all and grasslands only negligibly but took away as much as 20 tons of topsoil per acre where corn (maize) was planted in straight rows on hillsides. Such experiments have made it possible to understand where land use practices have been at fault, and how to check and so far as possible remedy the damage.

In terms of water control the largest, most spectacular and world-famous of conservation projects has been the Tennessee Valley Authority. Although actually created in 1933 under President Franklin Roosevelt it had its origins in steps taken by his cousin Theodore in establishing the Inland Waterways Commission in 1907. In his letter appointing the Commission the first Roosevelt wrote:

> "It is not possible to frame so large a plan as this for control of our rivers without taking account of the orderly development of other natural resources. Therefore, I ask that the Inland Waterways Commission shall consider the relation of the streams to the use of the great permanent natural resources and their conservation for the making and maintenance of prosperous homes."

One of the first public acts of the new Commission was an inspection trip with the President down the Mississipi Valley as guests of the Mississipi Valley Improvement Association. By establishing the principle of unified river basin management, irrespective of State boundaries, and combining flood control, power development, irrigation, drainage and purification the Commission let loose in the world a potent and constructive new idea which was widely welcomed as enabling conservation principles to be effectively applied in practice to vulnerable regions which had suffered greatly from their neglect, both by blinkered government departments and by short-sighted and greedy private interests. The usual timelag and obstruction prevented a practical demonstration until the breakdown of the conventional management of the American economy in the Great Depression after the Wall Street crash of 1929 left the way clear for the second Roosevelt's administration to go ahead.

Even so the opportunity might have been lost but for the lucky chance that during World War I the Federal Government, anxious over the supply of munitions, had started building at Muscle Shoals on the Tennessee a dam and power plant for the production of nitrates, which was completed only after the war ended. Bills passed by Congress, on the initiative of Senator George Norris, to operate this plant under Federal ownership and management and to supplement it by a series of others were vetoed successively by Presidents Coolidge and Hoover. Given the urgent need and demand for productive works, and the discredit into which the opposition to it had fallen, it was not difficult to resurrect this project as the Tennessee Valley Authority, established in May 1933 to plan and build dams and to operate them primarily for the purposes of promoting navigation and controlling floods, and incidentally to make and sell electricity. Reforestation, soil conservation and agricultural and industrial development were also among the functions of this most notable and successful experiment in conservation and in government. It was an irony of fate that the Muscle Shoals nitrate plant, the original cause of contention and provider of the opportunity for action, was entirely obsolete by the time that the TVA was set up. By 1955 the TVA had reforested 240,000 acres; had provided a navigable waterway carrying $1\frac{1}{2}$ billion ton-miles of freight, and by reducing flood crests had saved damage downstream estimated at 61 million dollars by 1956 and a far larger sum in the conditions of acute flood threat in the following year.

It is hardly necessary to describe in more detail this world-renowned conservation project, the greatest and most comprehensive yet achieved anywhere. That it has still no real counterpart in other American river basins is an index of the veto power still exercised by opponents of conservation. Elsewhere the TVA has been imitated in, for example, the Damodar Valley Project in India, but several attempts to follow it have been castrated, like the original plan for the North of Scotland Hydro-Electricity Board, or nipped in the bud by hostile influences, official as well as private. Although by Theodore Roosevelt's standards it came nearly thirty years late, by those of conventional politicians and administrators it was at least forty years ahead of its time.

Catastrophe and conspicuous economic waste could follow mishandling of the soil just as readily as from mishandling of inland waters and watersheds. This lesson was brought home most massively, by another coincidence just after the worst impact of the Great Depression had led to the Franklin Roosevelt New Deal and the launching of the TVA. Ever since early settlers had pushed into the semi-arid lands of the Middle West occasional drought years had caused the abandonment of cultivation and the loss of soil by wind erosion. In 1934–5 however the scale of the trouble increased so spectacularly that it was possible to show Congressmen the soil of the dustbowl states passing in brown wind-borne clouds over the Capital in Washington, and blotting out the sun. This happening was put to good use by Dr Hugh Bennett, head of the

Soil Conservation Service, who was then up before a Senate Committee asking for extra money to combat this menace. Pointing to the window he testified "There, gentlemen, goes part of Oklahoma now". To such a dusty argument it was impossible to give a dusty answer, and the money was voted.

Bennett deserved his success, having worked for thirty years to stir up practical interest in the misuse of land through soil erosion, culminating in 1928 in an official bulletin entitled *Soil Erosion a National Menace*, which proved prophetic soon afterwards. This was effective at least in securing funds for research, undertaken in ten stations, which fortunately was well enough advanced by the time the government and public opinion were ready to take action.

It is typical of the blindness which besets efforts for conservation that with few exceptions the State Colleges of Agriculture and the Department of Agriculture itself were uninterested in the problem. The new Soil Erosion Service had to be set up in 1933 within the Department of the Interior, to be transferred to Agriculture and renamed the Soil Conservation Service only after two years, when the national urgency of this essentially agricultural abuse had become plain for all to see.

Like the TVA the program of soil conservation was not simply technical and administrative, but involved getting down to the grassroots in political and social as well as in biological terms. Recipes could be sent out from Washington, but countrywide action required detailed and sustained teamwork by groups of neighbors. The answer was the soil conservation district, a voluntary model grouping which was adopted eventually on a vast scale throughout the States. This linking of social and technical devices echoed the findings of Theodore Roosevelt's Countryside Commission, which he set up in 1908 under the inspiration of Sir Horace Plunkett, the Irish pioneer of rural co-operatives, who happened to be ranching in Montana when Roosevelt himself had been a distant neighbor as a young man. Plunkett's ideas were simultaneously and equally belatedly brought to fruition in Britain though the Agricultural Marketing Boards and the ensuing development of agricultural research, experiment and advisory services. The time-lag, as usual, was more than a quarter of a century on both sides of the Atlantic.

In spreading the principles and practice of contour ploughing to guard against erosion the Soil Conservation Service has in a literal sense been conspicuously successful, as any air traveller over the United States can verify. Another landscape-changing innovation has been the multiplication of small pools created by earth dams or impoundments to provide water for farm use and amenity. One of the results of these pools has been a large increase in waterfowl. Encouragement for game-birds has been given by planting suitable shrubs for food and shelter, often in the form of hedgerows, which, ironically enough are being increased in this way with Federal help in America at the same time that the legacy of hedgerows in England is being rapidly destroyed in many areas, with Treasury subsidies, in the name of farm improvement.

While large and widespread results have thus been achieved by applying conservation science to the use of land and water in the United States the problem of safeguards against hurricanes, tornadoes, line squalls and other catastrophic climatic events has proved more intractable. Similar methods of scientific study have however been developed, and it has at least become possible to give generally reliable warnings of the build-up of such hazards as it occurs.

Wildlife and fisheries, like forests, soils and water came high on the list of misused and heavily damaged natural resources in America. Although President Grant in 1875 had vetoed the first animal protection bill ever to be passed by Congress (for the protection of bison which were then being slaughtered at the rate of a million a year) federal intervention on behalf of wildlife had come earlier even than action on behalf of forests. A bureau for this purpose has existed under various names since 1885, and various State bird protection laws since 1886, while the Federal Lacey Act, which suppressed commercial dealing in wild birds, was passed in 1900. The first federal wildfowl refuge was created in 1903 at Pelican Island, Florida, and already by 1916 an effective international basis was secured for North American bird protection through the Convention for the Protection of Migratory Birds—a legacy of Theodore Roosevelt's friendship with the British Foreign Secretary Sir Edward Grey, then in the final year of his long term of office.

In no field has public opinion been more continuously and vigilantly manifested through an impressive series of national State and local voluntary bodies, such as the National Audubon Society, the North American Wildlife Institute, the National Wildlife Federation, the Izaak Walton League of America and many others. Yet there is something uncomfortably marginal and precarious about the status of genuine wildlife conservation, unprejudiced by external considerations, in the modern American scene. One factor in this has been the preponderant sectional bargaining power and lobbying capacity of commercial interests based on the sale of guns and ammunition, fishing tackle and other articles used in field sports. The resolute and effective blocking of moves to control the indiscriminate sale of firearms, even after the two Kennedy assassinations and those of Martin Luther King and others, is testimony to this hidden power over Congress. The *New Yorker* showed on 20th April 1968 that Americans killed by privately owned guns within the United States since 1900 totalled about 750,000, "or a third again as many as have been killed in all our wars". In 1966, for example, such domestic casualties were $3\frac{1}{2}$ times greater than American military casualties in Vietnam.

For whatever reason there has been a conspicuous contrast between the continuity of policy and of administration under excellent leaders of the Forest and National Parks Services and the frequent tampering with Fish and Wildlife, accompanied by far too frequent changes in a procession of by no means always distinguished Directors. Brash and heavyhanded special interests are forever inciting Congressmen to breathe heavily down the Wildlife Service's neck. The luckless Service has recently run into more and bigger trouble in relation to the indiscriminate and destructive use of toxic chemicals. Except during Dr Ira Gabrielson's all too brief regime it has rarely had the benefit of a firm hand at the helm and of a personality able to impress Congress and to put up resolute defence against outside pressure.

In earlier times National Parks were in a comparably weak position. At one time while "exclusive control" of Yellowstone rested with the Secretary of the Interior the Superintendent was an army officer appointed by the Secretary for War, and all improvements were managed by another officer of the Army Corps of Engineers, not answerable either to the Superintendent or the Interior Department.

After establishing Yellowstone in 1872 Congress waited fifteen years to add in 1890 the three Californian areas Sequoia, Yosemite and General Grant as forest reservations. There was still much confusion about the definition, status and management requirements of a National Park. As there was still no Service nor even any responsible official in Washington to sort matters out, all kinds of errors and abuses inevitably crept in, including the granting under political pressure of National Park status to unsuitable areas such as Platt in Oklahoma, a few hundred acres surrounding some sulphur springs which had given rise to a town of the same name whose inadequately treated sewage contaminated the medicinal springs.

On the other hand the necessity for separate legislation in respect of each proposed National Park was impossibly unwieldy as the only means of preserving anything anywhere. Sometimes a bill would go through in a single day, but more often years of political warfare were needed. For tree-covered areas the Forest Reserve Act of 1891 could be and was used, since it enabled the President to "set apart and reserve ... in any part of the public lands wholly or in part covered with timber or undergrowth, whether of commercial value or not, as public reservations". The first three Presidents enjoying these powers used them to reserve some 27 million acres and the fourth—Theodore Roosevelt—added about 148 million before the power was taken from him by Congress. But as the Acting Superintendent of Sequoia expressed it in 1896

> "these lands present the curious anomaly of parks with guards, but with no law to punish, and a forest reserve land under practically the same conditions as the parks, with ample law to punish, but no guards to enforce."

Poachers of game, graziers with large flocks of sheep, unauthorised timber cutters and tourists starting destructive fires could all get by with impunity, and did so on a vast scale. Even squatters pursuing private claims to land within the parks, were a major threat, and at Yosemite the State of California so abused its trust from Congress that after commercialisation had become a public scandal the valley was taken back under federal control.

Meanwhile from the 1880's onward the pillaging of antiquities had belatedly led to the passage in 1906 of an Antiquities Act which authorised the President to set aside by proclamation historic spots, landmarks structures and "other objects of scientific interest". It led to the reservation as so-called monuments of battlefields, forts, birthplaces of the famous, rocks bearing inscriptions, pueblo cliff dwellings, Missions, big trees, caves, natural bridges, the Grand Canyon, cactus desert, cliffs, glaciers and dunes and islands. It was all in a good cause, but it brought many anomalies, such as the emergence of a National Monument, Katmai in Alaska, as the largest area in the United States system of National Parks, of which it should logically be one.

Although it was obvious that the sound development and administration of National Parks called for some specific provision of resources and allocation of responsibility, no progress was made for years, even by such able champions as Representative John Lacey of Iowa who had introduced a bill "to establish and administer national parks" in April 1900. Nearly twelve years later President Taft sent a special message asking Congress to act. The 62nd, 63rd and 64th Congresses all dickered with bills for that purpose, before the National Parks Act finally passed in 1916.

Thanks to the wise counsel of Frederick Law Olmsted Jr. plain words were inserted into the law to safeguard the parks against being encroached upon by special interests. The new Service was directed to promote and regulate the use of national parks, monuments and reservations.

"by such means and measures as conform to the fundamental purpose of said parks, monuments and reservations, which purpose is to conserve the scenery and the natural and historic objects and the wild life therein and to provide for the enjoyment of the same in such manner and by such means as will leave them unimpaired for the enjoyment of future generations".

In view of the endless obstructions and machinations of the special interest groups its inclusion was most satisfactory and creditable, and it has been a charter for safeguarding the parks ever since.

An even more surprising stroke of luck followed. The Secretary of the Interior, Franklin K. Lane, received at this time a complaint about the administration of Sequoia National Park from Stephen T. Mather, a member of the Sierra Club who had made a fortune out of borax and was able to devote his energy to outdoor interests, Secretary Lane replied tersely that if Mather did not like the way the parks were run he should come and manage them himself. In this irregular manner was recruited one of the most outstandingly successful conservation administrators on record. With his many influential contacts, high aims, great powers of persuasion and his personal financial independence he set to work to build up a strong, well-organised and well-informed support movement for the parks at all levels, from which it continues to benefit. It is questionable whether any other public service in the world has been able to acquire so large and devoted an army of individual supporters. If need be, when Congress would not find essential funds Mather would find them from his own pocket. His weakness was intermittent ill-health, but before he died in 1930 he had given the Service a status, a direction and a capability of growth of which it has made good use. While it can be criticised on various points it is, all in all, one of the most original and effective social inventions so far developed in the world of conservation.

The creation of the Park Service had been strongly opposed by the Forest Service. It has been one of the handicaps of conservation in the United States that these two great Federal services, organised by two outstanding conservationists, should have developed under different Departments with conflicting philosophies and programs, and should so often have found themselves disunited or actually in conflict in face of their powerful and unsleeping common adversaries. Among the recurrent threats which both had to withstand were proposals for mergers and rationalisation of federal lands administration. These, however attractive on the plane or organisation charts, could have undermined the political and technical basis on which their efficiency and indeed their survival rested. As things were a Director of a great ability and integrity, Newton B. Drury, lost his post in 1951 rather than acquiesce in a political decision, later recognised as wrong, to permit the Bureau of Reclamation to build two dams in the Dinosaur National Monument.

By the middle 1950's it became clear that the success of the Park idea and the vast expansion in leisure and the recreational movement was far exceeding the capacity of the parks to cope with visitors. To face this situation Director Conrad Wirth devised and successfully negotiated Mission 66, to re-equip and reinforce the parks at a cost over ten years of 786 million dollars.

Although the National Park Service has been much strengthened the fact remains that the Forest Service is twice as large in staff as it and the two Fish and Wildlife Services combined. And even these are far from being the only important federal agencies concerned with holding land available for public recreational use. During 1959–62 the field was exhaustively surveyed by the Outdoor Recreation Resources Review Commission under Laurance Rockefeller, which took a bold forward view. One result was the creation of the new Bureau of Recreation, backed by the Land and Water Conservation Fund set up under an Act of 1965, which began with an appropriation in its first year of 251 million dollars. Through this mechanism is co-ordinated all Federal acquisition of lands and waters for outdoor recreation. Additional co-ordination will be secured through the preparation by the new Bureau of a Nationwide Outdoor Recreation Plan. Among specific plans in train are those for a national system of wild or scenic rivers, a nationwide system of trails and an expanded series of national seashores. Under the happily-named Wilderness Act of 1964 systematic additions are being made from suitable forest park and wildlife lands to the National Wilderness Preservation System.

So immense and complex has the American conservation movement grown, and so deeply are its values and ideas embedded in American public affairs, institutions and ways of life that its precise evolution and influence are increasingly difficult to trace. It continues to be a mass of inconsistencies and contradictions—passionately upheld yet constantly let down or repudiated, rich in public spirit and yet often aggressively sectional, massively manned by trained professionals and yet often amateurish and unsure of itself, deeply concerned over the future and yet too often hag-ridden by the legacy of the past.

During the past few years introspection and inquest have become fashionable, with more and more conferences, seminars, and other discussions of all kinds seeking to evaluate the performance and problems, to identify future trends and needs, and to correct the course and structure. Many of these discussions have been enlightening, but identifiable results have often been disappointingly slow to emerge. Yet evidence of expansion, of the quicker digestion of much new knowledge, and of mounting effort to work out a more harmonious common approach is plentiful, and despite the massively destructive forces arrayed on the other side there seems reason for a fair degree of confidence.

Conservation in America is again changing its meaning and shifting its center of gravity. A dominant theme is the sensitivity to harmful and arbitrary interferences with the natural environment, and especially with such aspects as purity of water and air, freedom from noise, and protection from unilateral acts prejudicial to people as consumers or users of common natural resources. Whereas most previous conservation demands have manifestly been mobilised and brought to fruition mainly by effective pressure group tactics this public reaction gives an impression of having made itself politically effective more through the unmistakeably clear and firm views of a great many citizens not specifically organised in this context. If, as thus seems possible, ordinary people are able directly to influence Congress and the White House on such matters through sheer resolution and awareness of the issues the entire character of the American conservation movement as mainly a tournament between the chosen champions of battling interests could be altered.

Another comparable trend is the mounting strength and social awareness of the mixed host of participants in the allied activities of outdoor recreation, sport and leisure, including vacation travel and tourism. As leisure increases the opportunities for this host to become more articulate and to develop attitudes and requirements to be reckoned with are obvious.

A further visible trend is away from sentimental approaches towards a more practical demand for scientific and technical answers to many questions hitherto handled empirically by officials and private managers. The application of ecological and other scientific studies to conservation of the natural environment and to land use and land management is becoming recognised by public opinion, somewhat ahead of the still disappointingly limited efforts at organising it on the part of Federal and other public agencies, and of the universities and scientific institutions.

In view of the almost overriding national preoccupations with the situation in Vietnam and in America's own great cities it is encouraging to observe how much serious attention the care of the environment continues to claim, and how ready it is to contribute to America's future civilisation.

TOWARDS WORLDWIDE ACTION

DURING the first two-thirds of the 19th century there was an important input from Europe, and especially from Britain, into the build-up of thought and attitudes of the embryonic American conservation movement. That movement, however, as has been shown, grew up in its own way and in its own time, with a minimum of interest in problems beyond the wide American frontier. In Europe effective internationalism was almost equally feeble and slow-growing. When it came it was for long to be virtually confined to working with immediate neighbors. Since 1870 an American Fisheries Society had formed a nucleus which broadened out in 1902 into what was to become the International Association of Game, Fish and Conservation Commissioners. Effectively, however, the international status of this venerable organisation goes back only for a half a century, and it is essentially a U.S.-Canadian affair.

Mention has already been made of Theodore Roosevelt's attempt at the end of his Presidency to convene an International Conservation Conference in Washington. As a first step delegates from Canada, Mexico and Newfoundland met at the White House in February 1909. Recognising the need for conservation practices to cross political boundaries they recommended the President to call a world conference on "the subject of world resources and their inventory, conservation and wise utilisation". Although the sands were running out for Roosevelt diplomatic soundings were taken with favorable results. The Netherlands agreed to act as host. Invitations actually went out to fifty-eight nations to meet at the Hague in September 1909, but the project was killed by Roosevelt's successor Taft.

Although a world initiative remained barred the matching interest of Canada offered certain opportunities. The building of the Canadian Pacific Railroad gave rise to claims by workmen to rights in certain hot springs. (The Hot Springs National Reservation created in 1832 in a small town in Arkansas had similarly been the precursor of the United States system of National Parks.) Having bought out these claims the Dominion Government established around them the first of Canada's National Parks—Rocky Mountain, later renamed Banff—in 1885. Two others followed before 1900, including Waterton Lakes (1895) which was 37 years later to be twinned with Glacier across the border as the Glacier-Waterton International Peace Park. In 1911, five years before the United States, Canada passed an Act setting up a Park Service, and by building up a network of 28 National Parks totalling more than 18 million acres Canada has kept up comfortably with the growth of National Parks in the United States.

Owing to this kindred interest and neighborhood, conditions have been favorable for the development of international co-operation on a U.S.-Canadian basis. The most highly developed example arose from the North American Migratory Birds Treaty of 1916, which called for legislation in both countries and led to an impressive build-up of organisations and staffs, tending, like the birds themselves, to operate with little regard for the political frontier. As duck-shooting or hunting is a large-scale sport, supporting and supported by great commercial interests in the United States, and as so many ducks and geese are bred in Canada but spend the shooting season in the United States, a ready-made basis has existed for the deployment of U.S. dollars in support of Canadian conservation effort. This deployment is co-ordinated through the annual North American Wildlife Conferences and their associated special meetings, especially that of the National Waterfowl Council and the four Flyway Waterfowl Councils. Only those who have personally attended these gatherings can appreciate fully the scale, complexity, technical expertise and political backing involved in them.

The system thus supervised is the reverse of a talking-shop for pious hopes and abstract ideas. It is a highly successful operational and management network, with its eyes and ears all over North America, and with the necessary manpower, boats, aircraft, vehicles, funds and, not least, legal authority to ensure that what is decided at the top level is usually fulfilled in practice.

Broadly its objects are to

"Maintain a total population of nesting, migrating and wintering waterfowl in the United States not less than that which existed in the period 1950–6 . . . Maintain regular seasonal migrations of waterfowl in the United States so that each State may have the opportunity to share in the benefits of the resource.

Manage migratory waterfowl for the benefit and enjoyment of people—meeting all recreational, aesthetic and scientific needs for this resource as equitably as location of habitat and requirements of preservation of this renewable resource permit."

Not only the substance but the precise wording of this statement by the Bureau of Sport Fisheries and Wildlife are eloquent of the American approach, with its blend of technical political and user considerations. The massive increase in waterfowl populations since this system was created is testimony to its effectiveness in regulating shooting pressures and in maintaining the necessary habitat despite human and climatic factors. (The number of pools available for waterfowl in the great breeding area of southern Alberta, Saskatchewan and Manitoba has fluctuated owing to seasonal variations of moisture between 6 million in 1955–56 and half a million in 1961.) In terms of completeness of integration, area and scale of operations, and influence at the grass-roots, this is one of the most significant international operations yet devised, not only in conservation but in any human activity. The lesson has been learnt and unreservedly accepted that Ducks Unlimited means Sovereignty Superseded. There are many subjects besides ducks where the same lesson applies, but few where it has been mastered.

On United States initiative a series of attempts has been made to organise co-operation on conservation policies between the countries of North and South America, but hitherto with only limited and somewhat disappointing results. Mexico followed Canada in signing a Migratory Birds Treaty in 1937. In 1942 the Convention on Nature Protection and Wildlife Preservation in the Western Hemisphere was signed in Washington, following in its general lines a previous London Convention of 1933.

Perhaps the most successful American initiative was the First World Conference on National Parks, held in Seattle in 1962, and the related development in Brussels and New York of a U.N. List of National Parks and Equivalent Reserves. Attended by representatives of 63 countries this well-organised conference, with the full backing of the National Park Service, managed at one stroke to bring into existence a close-knit worldwide group of national park managers and promoters, and to give powerful impetus to the broadening and deepening of the parks movement, both internationally and in many individual countries.

That National Parks had by that time a respectable history as something more than a North American peculiarity was largely due to a few other countries which had been quick to adopt the idea in its earlier years. Pre-eminent among these was New Zealand, where the scruples of the Maori chief Te Heuheu Tukino regarding the future trusteeship of his tribe's holy places in the mountains gave rise to the device of handing them over in 1887 to Queen Victoria, as "a sacred place of the crown and a gift for ever from me and my people", for permanent safeguarding, through the creation in 1894 of the Tongariro National Park. Thus stimulated, only a few years after Yellowstone, New Zealanders followed the same example to preserve much of the outstanding scenery in their scenically rich country, of which more than 6 per cent is now held in National Parks. Although Australia got off the mark even earlier with the Royal National Park near Sydney (1885), constitutional obstacles inhibited large scale development there.

In Africa also the idea emerged early, with President Paul Kruger's 1898 designation of the Sabie Game reserve, which finally in 1926, through the efforts of Lieut-Colonel Stevenson Hamilton, became the Kruger National Park, now ranking with its 1,817,146 hectares as the third largest, and one of the richest in wildlife in the whole world. Other southern African areas go back to the same period, including Umfolozi, Hluhluwe and St Lucia Game Reserves, Natal (1897).

During the past thirty years the build-up in both southern and eastern Africa has been so massive as to create a National Park coverage second only to that of western North America. The need for international co-operation over standards and legislation emerged earliest here, and led to the signature in London in 1933 of the Convention Relevant to the Preservation of Fauna and Flora in Their Natural State. Of outstanding significance also was the creation by the Belgian Government in 1925 of the Parc National Albert in the then Belgian Congo. This was to be the first Park devoted to systematic scientific research, under l'Institut des Parcs Nationaux du Congo Belge (1933), which, through the inspiration of Professor Victor van Straelen, was to publish about 300 volumes describing the results of the *"exploration scientifique"*.

In so small and sophisticated a country as the Netherlands there was little room for National Parks of a spacious character, but devotion to the care of landscape and wild life was no less intense. When in 1904 the city of Amsterdam proposed to use as a refuse dump the nearby Naardermeer, one of the few breeding strongholds of the rare Spoonbill and the uncommon Purple Heron, the public reaction was strong. The following year saw the creation of the now powerful Vereniging tot Behoud van Naturmonumenten in Nederland—the Society for the preservation of Nature Monuments in the Netherlands, which promptly bought the Naardermeer as the first Dutch nature reserve. From the stink of Amsterdam's refuse arose one of the pathfinding nature conservation bodies of the world. The Spoonbills and Purple Herons remain in undisturbed possession to this day.

Among other significant contributions made by the Netherlands to the scientific care of the environment special mention must be made of the enterprise of the Forest Service in creating entirely new landscapes with native trees and shrubs, notably on the reclaimed lands which were once under the Zuyder Zee or Ijsselmeer. Nowhere, too, was the

INTRODUCTION

An environment becomes a landscape only when it is so regarded by mature people, and especially when they take action to shape it in accord with their taste and needs. Nature can produce the raw material of scenery unaided, but even natural scenery exists only when man appreciates it. To transform it into landscape demands the magic powers of the seeing human eye and the loving human hand.

For example, the wild scenery offered by the uplift ridge of the Scottish Highland Boundary Fault as it runs west past the Trossachs (C.1) and crosses the shore of Loch Lomond to continue as a row of wooded island stepping-stones now forming a National Nature Reserve, has only in modern times emerged as one of the world's most famed landscapes. This has been due to its romantic appreciation by visitors and the sensitive care of local people, in tending its trees, pastures and farmland, and in the design of buildings and works.

In the even wilder setting of the Cairngorms (C.2) the slowly decaying forest of Scots Pines, now overstocked with Red Deer, appear romantically attractive, while the clumsy plantation does not. Ecologically both are unsound, but ruined woodlands have charm just like ruined abbeys.

The Japanese, apt pupils of China, long since seized upon their handsome pine (*Pinus densiflora*) as a keynote in their landscaping and in art. By selection, symbolism and miniaturisation they created in their gardens (C.8) imaginary counterparts of wider landscape, which have almost made them content to forego the real thing.

Gardens, being intensive and inward-looking, have traditionally excluded wider landscape values until the authoritarian 17th century so grandiosely inflated them that, (as at Vaux-le-Vicomte—C.10—the prototype of Versailles) they became dominant. Up to that time the rural scene had been composed largely of artless layouts of arable, pasture, meadow and waste as at Laxton (C.9) or of dense forest.

The English landscape revolution around the outset of the 18th century reversed tradition by assimilating gardens and pleasure grounds with broad vistas over a country-side remoulded into a kind of endless park able to permit productive as well as recreational and aesthetic uses. Special attention has been paid here to illustrating how this was done. Trees and water took pride of place over flowering plants, uneconomic mainten-ance was minimised by doing what came naturally instead of fussily insisting upon tidiness and formalism, and attempting always to keep growth at a certain favoured phase. Exotics were freely introduced.

Much later the plantsmen responded with the free-growing Paradise Garden full of choice plants from many countries, but the brilliant initiatives of the 18th century were not followed through, and their bold innovations became museum pieces. Later land-scapes have tended to seek pleasure for the eye, or concealment of the ugly, or to reflect a fragmentary functional approach through windbreaks, crop-patterns or coverts, rather than to provide a comprehensive living pattern.

A comprehensive contemporary style of landscape, genuinely expressive of its uses and of the attitudes of those who dwell in it remains to be devised, except to some extent for parkways and motorways. In the Netherlands however, where the Dutch Old Masters made landscapes which still delight as in picture galleries the Dutch New Masters are bravely presenting us with great new landscapes on the ground—see C.16. A civilisation deserving the name has the same kind of needs for landscape as a man or woman has for suitable dress. In its absence there can be no harmony between man and nature.

Certain natural features are outstandingly appealing to the sensitive human eye. Fast-running streams, lakes mirroring mountains, trees and green glades or meadows are among the most universally admired. The relatively flat-topped granite mountains of the Cairngorm group (C.2), with their glacial cirques and scree-clad escarpments are unspectacular, but seen as they are by many in late summer they gain splendor from the tracts of purple heather on their flanks, and romance from the diverse forms and colors of the Scots Pines, self-sown and unfortunately deprived of natural regeneration for many years before the Nature Conservancy began to restore it by rotational fencing. The only visible building, Derry Lodge (lower left center) is flanked by artificially planted conifers which if much farther extended could have ruined the scene.

Another country beside Scotland, Japan, also enjoys a distinctive species of Pine (*Pinus densiflora*) which has been given world fame by many talented painters, and is here seen (C.3) growing on the lovely island of Kinkazan, off north-eastern Honshu. Unaccustomed to being crowded within tight forests these pines suggest freedom, ease and grace by their open spreading crowns, while their tufted foliage and warm-tinted trunks lend diversity and liveliness to any scene of which they form part. They remind us how nature has prompted and stimulated man's enjoyment of landscape.

Such fertile but windy grass-lands as those of southern New Zealand give frequent reminders of the virtues of trees as wind-breaks, but the attempts to grow them as such (C.4) demonstrate rather abruptly that land-scape has principles and conditions of its own, and is not brought into existence merely by a succession of well-meant but unrelated and at times meaningless plant-ings. Here is a countryside in search of a landscape and in time no doubt it will find a worthy one.

By contrast the modern or-ganisation of farms on the borders of Shropshire and Herefordshire (C.5), marked out by many hedgerows with scattered compact village communities and with trees concentrated on the escarp-ments has spontaneously produced a landscape so pleasant that even the dense coniferous monocultures in the right background are unable to spoil it.

A very different functional pattern (C.6) is produced near Wisbech St Mary, Cam-bridgeshire, where the flat drained fenland is farmed in large open hedgeless patches of arable, in which trees are almost confined to the high-way verges and the farm surroundings. Only the crazy variations of the crop pat-terns and the endlessly dif-ferent shapes and sizes of fields save it from an Ameri-can mid-western monotony. Reminders that nature ever had a share in the now wholly-man-made scene are few and muted.

C·5

C.6

A ricefield in northern Honshu, Japan (C.7) is in itself no less functional and agriculturally efficient, but by respecting the contours and landforms it achieves a rightness both as landscape and ecologically. The Japanese have by recent research traced both the secondary phases and the primitive ecological state of their main agricultural types. This scene can be regarded as neatly fitting an appropriate artefact of applied biology within a seminatural environmental setting in which even the rooflines of the buildings pay respect to the scale and lines of the landscape.

A Japanese landscape garden is so rich in miniature symbolism to be pondered intensively on one spot (C.8) that one may suspect such surrogates for extensive landscape of having to some extent drawn attention away from the countryside itself. For whatever reason, modern Japan is a strange mixture of refined susceptibility and apparent gross insensitivity to the requirements of landscape. We may hope that this will prove to be merely a transition stage, leading to renewed dominance of the great Japanese tradition.

In England, by contrast, no native tradition is traceable beyond some three centuries ago. Here in C.9 is a plan of Laxton, drawn with such care and skill that it apparently shows us just how a typical open-field English village looked three-and-a-half centuries ago, on the eve of the landscape revolution. It is a kind of implicit rather than explicit folk-landscape, poles apart from the grandiose, formal, symmetrical, highly self-conscious and mannered designs which were about to burst upon Europe from the school of Le Notre who created the gardens of Vaux-le-Vicomte (C.10), as it proved to serve as a prototype for the even more magnificent and dazzling influential Versailles.

C.8

C.9

Partly for political and security reasons the French kings preferred to live outside Paris, while Charles II, as much a countrylover as his contemporary Louis XIV made London his main home and tried to bring the country into it, with results which dominate the capital's planning to this day (C.11). The old Court had been at Whitehall, between the Thames and St James's Park, which remained the focus as the royal residence has gradually shifted west by St James's Palace to Buckingham Palace. The stately avenues of the Mall—itself named after one of Charles II's favourite outdoor pastimes—and Birdcage Walk—named after a second —converge on the newest Palace which lies between the bird-haunted lakes of St James's Park, with Duck Island at its far end, and its own newer gardens at the bottom of the picture. Try to imagine London without this great nucleus of inner parks, stretching far out of the picture, or even with an alternative landscape design in the French grand manner. The imagination boggles. It has been said that the center of British sovereignty lies at the bottom of St James's Park lake midway between Buckingham Palace, Parliament and Whitehall. It could equally well be said that the center of British civilisation lies very close to this astonishing juncture of urbanism and the countryside.

Charles II, although never for a minute able to forget his enforced role as a constitutional monarch, had leanings towards absolutism which were exhibited much more openly by James II. His dramatic flight, followed by the new political settlement, reinforced the feeling of the English leaders against everything connected with despotism. As a symbol of independence they developed their landed estates and their commercial wealth in ways ostentatiously divorced from the Court. They were inspired in this by Pope, Addison and other gifted writers. Charles Howard, Earl of Carlisle, who had twice headed the government on critical occasions, was quite content to withdraw to Yorkshire and devote most of his life to creating one of the decisive contributions to the new naturalistic landscape by his work at Castle Howard (C.12). Although he retained the lavish use of temples and other features of solid masonry he broke away from the geometrical regimentation of trees and shrubs, and from a symmetrical basis of design, even permitting the river, after accepting his "Roman Bridge" to follow the serpentine line which was most agreeable both to it and the new English taste in landscape.

At Stourhead (C.13) far away in Wiltshire a newly wealthy city family named Hoare threw up an even greater genius, the younger Henry, who created, well out of sight of his house a landscape garden which is recognised to-day as one of the great works of European civilisation. Again he relied considerably on classical temples, grottos and statuary but his landscape is dominated by the lake which he made by a skilfully sited dam. Unfortunately, as we see it to-day, it is also dominated by great masses of rhododendrons and other exotic flowering trees and shrubs.

In the next generation the great designer Lancelot (Capability) Brown broke right away from masonry and flowerbeds to create such landscape as Ashburnham (C.14) which are perhaps the most essentially English of all. In doing so, however, he ruthlessly swept away some good examples of earlier styles.

By looking at the evolution of Stowe, Buckinghamshire (C.15 a, b and c) we can see the "Softening and Broadening" trend at work from 1739 (a), through 1769 (b) to 1797 (c).

C.15a

C.15b

C.15c

As a modern contrast, but still much influenced by these English examples, we see the masterly new landscape designed on Walcheren, by the Netherlands Forest Service beside the Veersche Meer, a small part of the immense new Delta Plan.

C.16

C.17

Finally we see from another part of the European Continent, South Germany, the dominant role in landscape renewal of the modern motorway.

importance of systematic scientific research in support of conservation earlier appreciated.

Another country early in the field was Switzerland. Here the dangers of indiscriminate interference with the forest cover of mountainsides had been learnt from bitter experience in the Middle Ages, resulting in official protective ordinances as early as the 14th century, and the development of methods of forest and torrent management by the 18th. As a land of peasant pastoralists, however, Switzerland developed early an intense persecution of predatory birds and of such mammals as the Brown Bear and the Wolf. The Red Deer and other game species were also exterminated before the need for conservation was appreciated. Switzerland has since developed an elaborate system of regulation, including examinations which must be passed by anyone seeking a licence to hunt game. A thorough knowledge of wildlife, of safety precautions and of the law is insisted upon.

The scientific challenge presented by the larger lakes of Switzerland was recognised by the great naturalist A. Forel whose comprehensive and systematic studies of the hydrobiology of Lake Geneva were largely responsible for establishing the modern science of limnology or fresh-water biology. Unfortunately the obvious conclusions in terms of required conservation measures were not drawn by the cantonal authorities, with the result that these still picturesque sheets of water are among the most heavily and critically polluted in the world.

Swiss interest in the National Park idea arose towards the end of the first wave of park creation. Unlike other countries Switzerland has always deliberately concentrated upon a single Swiss National Park, which, after being launched by voluntary effort, was officially adopted by the federal government in 1914. The area chosen was on the Italian frontier, and was originally planned to be extended into Italy, but here great obstacles were encountered. No doubt this and other problems turned the thoughts of its founder, Dr Paul Sarasin of Basel, towards international co-operation. At the 8th International Zoological Congress at Graz in 1910 it was he who secured the formation of

"A committee charged to establish an international or world commission for the protection of nature. . . . It would have as its mission to extend protection of nature to the whole world from the north pole to the south pole, covering both continents and seas."

The 14 naturalists chosen for this committee from participants in the Congress belonging to Europe, America and Asia agreed on 18th August 1910 to use the good offices of the Swiss Federal Government for circulating to Ministers of Foreign Affairs resolutions inviting them to

(1) encourage protection of nature where appropriate through existing national organisations for fauna, flora and sites, and

(2) Nominate delegates for an international commission for the protection of nature to be convened by the Swiss Federal Council.

After some delay in awaiting the official published proceedings the Swiss government was able in June 1911 to approach those of Germany, U.S.A., Argentina, Austria, Hungary, Belgium, Denmark, Spain, France, Great Britain, Italy, Japan, Norway, the Netherlands, Portugal, Rumania, Russia and Sweden, all of whom except Japan and Rumania eventually agreed in principle. An International Conference for the Protection of Nature was accordingly held in Basel in November 1913. It unanimously resolved upon an Act of Foundation of a Consultative Commission for the International Protection of Nature, to be situated in Basel and to form a clearing-house and propaganda channel for international nature protection.

Unfortunately the days of European peace were fast running out, and after the outbreak of war in 1914 the project fell into suspense. Neither the United States, which had proposed a wider international conservation conference in 1909 nor Great Britain were among the adhering countries. After the war ended efforts at revival were also abortive, despite a further international conference in Paris in 1923, and the surviving Swiss promoters lost interest.

The initiative now passed to the Low Countries, where in 1925 P. G. van Tienhoven took the first steps towards setting up an office. An attempt in 1927 to secure British support at a meeting in London once more proved abortive, but in July 1928, at a meeting in Poland of the International Union of Biological Sciences, a proposal for a commission for International Protection of Nature led to a resolution to establish, mainly for documentation purposes, an International Office for the Protection of Nature. In 1934 this office at Brussels was accorded legal recognition, but once again war was looming, and after being hurriedly transferred to Amsterdam in 1940 it was compelled to cease functioning.

In 1946 Julian Huxley, then chairman of the official committee to draw up plans for conservation of wild life in England and Wales, proposed to bring a party to inspect the Swiss National Park. In the event he was unable to be with it. Its members, of whom I was one, found to their surprise on arriving at Basel that the Swiss hosts had taken the opportunity to assemble a number of conservationists from other European countries and to arrange a miniature impromptu international conference, meeting both before and after the field excursion. For this we were entirely unbriefed, and had no choice but to reserve our position. This was the more difficult because at that time the British economy was war-shattered, London itself was badly bomb-damaged, and even the initial plans for a British organisation to under-take the conservation of nature remained to be fully formulated. More-over, experience with the newly-fledged United Nations and with such international agencies as UNESCO strongly suggested that the high ideals and ambitious programs of such world bodies tended to make little progress towards practical performance and achievement unless they were given an injection of British administrative manpower and expertise of a quality which at that time could not easily be spared. Dr van Tienhoven also was very reserved concerning the future of his own office, and the agreed conclusions were accordingly indefinite.

The Swiss promoters, however, persevered, and exactly a year later, on June 30–July 1 1947, they assembled, after better preparation, a conference at Brunnen drawn from 24 countries, at which it was agreed to establish a Provisional International Union for the Protection of Nature. Julian Huxley, who had meanwhile become the first Director-General of UNESCO, energetically embraced the project, and con-vened in 1948 at Fontainebleau a meeting, at last definitive, at which a draft constitution, obligingly prepared at my request by the British Foreign Office, was adopted. In contrast to those of other international unions of a strictly scientific character this constitution provided not only for membership by non-governmental national bodies but also for inclusion of international organisations whether intergovernmental or unofficial, and of public services and governments themselves. The initial signatures thus included 18 governments, but not until 1963 did actual governmental membership surpass this figure. Jean-Paul Harroy was appointed Secretary of the new Union, with an office in the Natural History Museum at Brussels, provided by the generosity of the govern-ment of Belgium. The first President was the President of the Swiss League for the Protection of Nature, Dr Charles Bernard, Swiss-born but then of Dutch nationality.

Thus the choice of founder officers aptly recalled the Swiss and Dutch-Belgian origins of the movement, which soon developed a distinctly recognisable and integrated international character.

Fresh developments now followed in quick succession. Mindful of the frustrations of 1909 a number of interested Americans pressed to take advantage of the new United Nations agencies in order to mount, forty years later, a first world conference on natural resources. With enthusi-astic support from Julian Huxley at UNESCO and from some other quarters this was convened in 1949 at Lake Success near New York. It was not a very successful conference but it marked a breakthrough for conservation onto the agenda of intergovernmental business.

The following year, at the International Council for Bird Preservation meeting at Uppsala in Sweden, another significant step forward was taken, which led, four years later, to the international Convention for preventing pollution of the sea by oil. This International Council sprang from early and quite independent origins, going back well into the 19th century. In 1868 German agriculuralists and foresters, meeting in Vienna, were persuaded that indiscriminate slaughter of birds, particularly on migration in or through southern Europe, could lead to increased damage by insect pests. They sent a resolution to the government requesting concerted international action for the protection of animals useful to agriculture and forestry. The idea won some support, although the concept of "useful" and "harmful" species, long so firmly believed in certain influential circles, has failed to withstand later scientific criticism.

In 1876 a draft convention was circulated to various European countries. A State center for research in economic ornithology now began to take shape in Hungary, almost simultaneously with the similar initiative in the United States Department of Agriculture. As in America, there were strong political cross-currents involved. Hungarians were becoming very restive as junior partners in the Hapsburg Austro-Hungarian Empire, and had only been partly pacified in 1867 by the strange device of the dual monarchy, having Vienna and Budapest as twin capitals. Politically such a creature was hardly more viable than its ornithological symbol, the two-headed eagle. Influential Hungarians seized on the movement for international bird protection as an opportunity for Budapest to snatch from Vienna a diplomatic initiative. In the event however it was at Vienna that the first International Ornithological Congress was held, in 1884, as one of the pioneers among the now countless regular international gatherings concerned with particular branches of science and learning.

The Vienna conference and its follow-up were, however, so mismanaged that the international ornithological commission appointed to draw up a proposal never met, and the atmosphere of scandal allowed the Hungarians to make a fresh start. The arbiter in these disputes was that enthusiastic royal ornithologist the Crown Prince Rudolf, whose sudden and mysterious death by shooting at Mayerling in 1889 complicated matters further.

In May 1891, however the long desired meeting in Budapest—the Second Congress—took place under the presidency of Professor V.

Fatio. It demanded an international convention for the protection of birds useful to agriculture, to be promoted by the Ministers of Agriculture of both Austria and Hungary. A conference met in Paris, in 1895, to discuss a French draft, and was followed by the Third International Ornithological Congress, also in Paris, in 1900. This at last led to an International Convention for the Protection of Birds Useful to Agriculture (1902), signed by twelve European countries, not including Great Britain. In 1905 the Fourth Congress met in London and devoted one of its five sections to economic ornithology and bird protection, which helped to bring British naturalists in touch with international ideas and activities. Here Walter Rothschild gave an important paper on Extinct and Vanishing Birds. One of the results of this gathering was the extension of protection of penguins, which had been first legally provided in the Falkland Islands as early as 1864, to put an end to their slaughter throughout the British Antarctic territories.

At the Fifth Congress in Berlin in 1910, almost simultaneously with Paul Sarasin's more comprehensive initiative at Graz, it was resolved to set up a standing 14-nation international committee for bird preservation to report to the next Congress, drawn (except for the U.S.A.) entirely from European countries, including Great Britain. Like the Sarasin initiative this was overtaken by the first World War, but unlike it, was successfully revived soon after the Peace treaties.

Through the initiative of the American Dr Gilbert Pearson, with strong support from London, the International Committee for Bird Preservation was established there in 1922. This well-run organisation, with its National Sections now in over 50 countries, has during nearly half a century of activity set an example of scientifically well-based and administratively and politically sound recommendations for practical bird protection. Many of these have been successfully adopted over a wide range of countries. Particular attention has been given to problems of wildfowl conservation, in recent years delegated to the International Wildfowl Research Bureau, and to the prevention of deliberate oil pollution at sea. This has also recently devolved on the British Co-ordinating Advisory Committee on Oil Pollution and its opposite numbers overseas, who have secured the ratification of two reasonably effective international conventions. It is notable that this worldwide evil, so damaging to tourism and holiday interests, to fisheries, yachtsmen and others was brought under control only through the initiative and organised effort of bird protectionists, who may claim to have been the earliest and, at least until very recently, the most energetic and successful arm of the world conservation movement.

Botanists and horticulturists have not developed commensurate interest and effort for safeguarding plants internationally, although leading botanists such as A. G. Tansley through his phyto-sociological excursions, W. H. Pearsall and F. R. Fosberg have been tireless in calling international attention to conservation problems. Foresters have inevitably been more widely and deeply involved in conservation, but their strongly traditional attitudes and activities have by no means always been received with approval or admiration by other conservationists, with whom they have until recently had too little effective communication.

Entomologists have been involved chiefly through such specialised activities as the Anti-Locust campaign and measures of biological control, although in certain limited fields such as lepidoptera the collection, protection and even the introduction and farming of rare species, especially of butterflies, has long been a focus of effort in a few countries individually.

Although the fate of conspicuous mammals has long been a major concern for conservation, mammalogists as such have taken less part than sportsmen such as big game hunters. Only recently also has non-hunting amateur interest developed to a stage of effective organised study and intervention, and even then only in a small minority of countries.

Limnology has been successful in attracting substantial resources, deployed through many important and well-staffed scientific institutions but here again, organised effort in support of conservation has lagged until the very recent start of such efforts as the joint Project Aqua of the International Biological Program, the Societas Internationalis Limnologiae and the International Union for the Conservation of Nature.

In contrast to terrestrial ecology, freshwater and marine studies have attracted endowments for strong scientific institutions since Philip Henry Gosse first popularized aquaria at the London Zoo and elsewhere in the mid-19th century, Anton Dohrn by using his personal fortune managed to launch the Stazione Zoologica at Naples in 1873— the forerunner of more than 500 existing marine stations. At the same time H.M.S. Challenger pioneered the study of oceanography on a 3½ year cruise of 69,000 sea-miles round the world. The interest of navies, of the fishing industry and more recently of others including oil interests have given to marine studies, including ecology and conservation, a coherent if narrow purpose and a steady large-scale support which has been conspicuously lacking on land. While agriculture has almost wholly divorced itself from its primitive food-gathering and hunting origins fisheries are still geared to catching what nature spontaneously yields. Conservation problems for fisheries are thus much closer to the care and management of natural areas, and hydrobiology has contributed much to our understanding of population dynamics in nature, although the resulting knowledge is still imperfectly integrated with that emerging in the almost literally watertight compartment of terrestrial ecology.

In these and other ways the painfully slow development of a generalised world conservation movement has been accompanied, and in some fields far outpaced, by growth in more specialised areas and directions. Since about 1950, however, the broader and more comprehensive approach has made much faster progress. The reasons for this are not easily traced. No doubt one of the greatest previous handicaps was the absence of any authoritative and financially strong specialised intergovernmental agencies of worldwide scope.

The creation of the United Nations, and particularly of its Food and Agriculture Organisation (FAO) and its Educational, Scientific and Cultural Organisation (UNESCO) in the late 1940's laid a solid foundation of which conservationists were quick to avail themselves. The simultaneous growth of international aviation, and the multiplication of international contacts and conferences which it permitted, removed another major obstacle.

In principle it would have seemed reasonable to expect that the organisation and application of conservation measures would go ahead country by country up to an advanced stage before the need for international co-ordination and mutual help called for a secondary development of supra-national effort. In practice the cart had to be put before the horse. Up to 1950, with the partial exceptions of the United States, Canada and the Netherlands, there was no country yet equipped with a network of official and unofficial bodies able to speak and act with any degree of knowledge and coherence over the broad range of conservation problems. Great Britain, in particular, having only just launched the Nature Conservancy, was still most inadequately qualified or equipped for the task. Although other countries differed in their respective strong and weak points all were alike in their unreadiness to come to a conference table with properly based scientific appraisals of their problems, and with competent organisations to handle them.

It was in these circumstances that invitations to a series of international conferences with broad and varied agendas in places as far apart as Caracas and the Hague began to pour in quick succession on the small and motley band of naturalists, professional biologists, publicists, educationists, administrators and others interested in conservation. In the beginning, attendance being open to all, responsible or irresponsible, operators or passengers, specialists or laymen, the proceedings were at times confused and confusing, and the outcome could be as disillusioning as in Romain Gary's *The Roots of Heaven*. Readiness to pass sweeping and strongly worded resolutions was in inverse ratio to knowledge of the relevant facts as a whole and to capacity for securing action upon them. Fortunately the lack of any alternative channel and the obvious urgency of the task prevented a drop-out of the best men, which might otherwise easily have occurred. At the General Assembly at Copenhagen in 1954 a partial transformation was achieved from an indiscriminate gathering of enthusiasts of every type and calibre to a more technically oriented and informed type of organisation, under the Presidency of Dr Roger Heim, Director of the Natural History Museum in Paris and a leading conservationist.

The following Technical Meeting in Edinburgh in 1956 demonstrated the value of this transition. As its President I expressed the point in these words at the First Plenary Meeting on 21st June:

> We are now getting through the period of propaganda, of senti-ment and of generalisation, and we are getting down to hard prob-lems. . . . We must first of all know the facts. We must never be wrong about our facts. Secondly, knowing the facts, we must know what the facts mean; we must interpret them. Thirdly, we must frame and carry out courses of action which will produce the best results in a given situation on those facts.

In addition to delegates from FAO and UNESCO, the meeting was attended by representatives of the Academy of Sciences and the Ministry of Agriculture of the U.S.S.R., the U.S. Forest Service and Soil Conservation Service, the British Ministries of Agriculture, Fisheries and Food, and of Housing and Local Government, the Nature Conservancy, National Parks Commission, Forestry Commission, British Broadcasting Corporation, National Coal Board and Central Electricity Board, the Scottish Home, Education, Agriculture and Health Departments, the Royal Scottish Museum, the North of Scotland Hydro-Electric Board and the Hill Farm Research Organisation (Agri-cultural Research Council), the Directors of National Parks of the Union of South Africa and of Natal, the Game and Fisheries Department of Uganda and of Sudan, the Forests Department of Soudan, the Netherlands Ministries of Education, Arts and Science, and of Agricul-ture, Fisheries and Supplies, the Ministry of Public Instruction of Italy, the Indian Board for Wildlife, the West German Federal Ministry of Food, Agriculture and Forests, the French National Museum of Natural History, the Service des Eaux et Forêts, the Ministry of Agriculture and the Inspector-General of Historic Monuments and Sites; The Department of Agriculture, Fiji, the Naturfredningsraadet,

Denmark; the Ministry of Culture, Czecho-Slovakia; the Vice Gover-nor-General and the President of the Institute of National Parks of the Belgian Congo, and the Commonwealth Scientific and Industrial Research Organisation, Canberra, besides many non-official bodies, institutions and universities. The attendance of such a wide range of governmental participants best indicates the impressive, if still patchy, advance of conservation as a subject of international public importance. The unusually full representation of United Kingdom official organisa-tions was due to special persuasion exercised by the Nature Conservancy as organiser of the meeting. Two of its four Themes, the Rehabilitation of Areas Biologically Devastated by Human Disturbance, and the Relationship of Ecology to Landscape Planning, were of special interest to these. From this time onward British participation, especially in support and follow-up efforts for worldwide conservation, was substan-tially reinforced.

The necessity to devote more time and resources to follow-up action on international conservation was recognised and assisted by a wider spacing of General Assemblies of the International Union, from every year to every second year, and, after 1958, every third year. The Union had, on American insistence, changed its name in 1956 to the International Union for Conservation of Nature and Natural Resources (in place of the previous narrower "Protection of Nature") and having got together a provisional worldwide nucleus of collaborators it could now profit by both geographical and functional devolution, both of which were pressed ahead.

Already in 1955 a young freelance ecologist from the United States, Dr Lee M. Talbot, had been sent by IUCN to make a reconnaissance of the threatened species of wild animals in the Middle East and South Asia. In 1958 the Athens General Assembly focussed attention on problems of the Mediterranean, including erosion and other human pressures. This Assembly constituted the highly successful International Commission on National Parks, which initiated action for the United Nations World List of National Parks, and Equivalent Reserves. It then undertook the detailed follow-up resulting in a much amplified and improved second edition in 1967, which has given an effective stimulus to governments to improve both the coverage and the quality of management of their National Parks. Through the efforts of the com-mission, first under H. J. Coolidge and later J. P. Harroy, the world resources of expertise for establishing and managing national parks have been made available wherever they are most needed, with highly encouraging results.

The next Assembly, in Warsaw in 1960, brought a strong accession of professional zoologists and wildlife managers concerned especially with the ecology of large herbivores, among whom the United States and Russian contingents were prominent. Closely related with this aspect was intensified concern over the conservation of wildlife in Africa, which was given practical expression in the African Special Project, steered by E. B. Worthington. After this conference met in June 1960 independence was secured within a few weeks by Madagascar, Congo (Kinshasa), Somalia, Dahomey, Niger, Upper Volta, Ivory Coast, Chad, the Central African Republic, Congo (Brazzaville), Gabon, Senegal, Mali and Nigeria. Many regarded it as certain that under the new African governments all prospect of conservation of nature would be ended.

Although warned on high authority that they would be wasting their time the conservationists of the International Union resolved to make a supreme effort to win the new African regimes over to conservation from their earliest days. The focus of this effort was a meeting, called the Symposium on the Conservation of Nature and Natural Resource in Modern African States, held at Arusha in Tanganyika in September 1961. To that meeting came not only the familiar band of international and expatriate conservationists working in or for East Africa, but some fifty new faces of leading African scientists, game wardens and politicians, on whom the responsibility for future decisions would largely rest. Greeted warmly as partners, at a time when the ending of colonial regimes was being taken with an ill grace and with bitter forebodings in many quarters, the African participants responded keenly and contributed much to the success of the Arusha meeting, not least through their sense of humour. It was understandable, one of them remarked, that Europeans should be smitten with anxiety over the future of Africa's large animals; after all they knew what they themselves had done to the large mammals of Europe. Have no fear, however. For Africans their wild neighbors were a welcome and essential part of their peculiar heritage, and they would no more be destroyed than Europe would knock down its cathedrals. Indeed many Africans bore animal totems and regarded these animals as their brothers. Tourists coming to see them would be welcomed, but it was to be hoped that the tourists would refrain from treating the Africans as if they themselves were simply a form of wild life.

A highly satisfactory declaration was made on this occasion by Julius Nyerere, head of the government of what was shortly to become independent Tanganyika:

ARUSHA DECLARATION

The survival of our wildlife is a matter of grave concern to all of us in Africa. These wild creatures amid the wild places they inhabit are not only important as a source of wonder and inspiration but are an integral part of our natural resources and of our future livelihood and well-being.

In accepting the trusteeship of our wildlife we solemnly declare that we will do everything in our power to make sure that our children's grandchildren will be able to enjoy this rich and precious inheritance.

The conservation of wildlife and wild places calls for specialist knowledge, trained manpower and money, and we look to other nations to co-operate in this important task—the success or failure of which not only affects the continent of Africa but the rest of the world as well.

Uganda's independence followed in 1962, Kenya's in 1963 and Zambia's in 1964. These four states, with Congo (Kinshasa) held the most important National Park responsibilities.

So well did the new African states respond that, against all expectations, both the number and the effectiveness of management of National Parks in Africa notably improved after the end of the colonial regimes. This satisfactory situation was confirmed in 1963 when the 8th General Assembly of the IUCN was held in Nairobi—the first world conference of its size ever to be held in East Africa. A particularly encouraging feature was the rapid acceptance by governments that wildlife constituted their best attraction for tourism, which was rapidly establishing itself among the most important favorable items in their balance of payments. Nature conservation had emerged as a demonstrable national asset.

At the same time other objectives had been achieved in other continents. In 1934 the Government of Ecuador had sought support internationally for implementing a decree to safeguard the unique fauna and flora of Galapagos, and in 1941 a project for a scientific station there was only defeated owing to World War II. In 1955 the IUCN had organised a fact-finding mission to the islands, and this was followed by other investigations to select a site and prepare for action. Galapagos had provided Charles Darwin with an important part of the stimulus and evidence for his theory of evolution. At the International Zoological Congress held in July 1958 in London on the centenary of his statement only a single resolution was passed, urging the creation for this purpose of a Charles Darwin Foundation. It was created in Brussels a year later through the tireless efforts of Professor Victor Van Straelen. The Charles Darwin Research Station was duly built and put into operation in 1962. In 1964 the *Golden Bear* arrived from San Francisco with a strong international party of scientists to inspect and reinforce the varied and important studies already initiated by the Galapagos Scientific Project in the fields of general ecology, pedological, geological, botanical and zoological sciences, marine biology and conservation problems.

Hard on the heels of the African Special Project, which was taken over as a going concern by the FAO, IUCN turned to South-East Asia. After considerable study and preparation a conference was mounted in 1965 at Bangkok on Conservation in Tropical South-East Asia, which promptly triggered off much increased activity, not only in mainland states, but in Indonesia and the Philippines.

Europe meanwhile had not been neglected. In November 1962 IUCN's MAR conference, at Les Saintes-Maries-de-la-Mer in the French Camargue, reviewed the sorry state of conservation of European and North African Wetlands, including deltas, estuaries, marshes and swamps, lakes, waterways and other aquatic habitats. One result was a first definitive list of European and North African Wetlands of International Importance, which has been vigorously followed up to secure action in many of the countries concerned. The MAR conference showed that the bulk of the knowledge and interest then available was concentrated among ornithologists. This resulted in the virtual omission of such important areas as peatmoors, which are less interesting ornithologically than botanically. An attempt to correct this deficiency at the ensuing International Botanical Congress proved abortive through lack of support, but eventually, nearly five years later, the Nature Conservancy managed to bring together the necessary specialists at Attingham in England to launch Project TELMA with the object of filling this gap, at least for northern Europe and prospectively later for the world.

Meanwhile the Nature Conservancy, with the International Wildfowl Research Bureau, had in October 1963 launched a vigorous follow-up on the ornithological front through the First European Meeting on Wildfowl Conservation, held at St Andrews, Scotland, a pivotal point for international wildfowl migrations at that season. The meeting was selectively restricted to a small number of wildfowl biologists, government officials, conservationists and leading wildfowlers or shooters from seventeen countries. It assembled an up-to-date picture of the wildfowl situation throughout Europe, and of existing conservation laws, refuges and reserves. It reviewed adverse and beneficial developments affecting wildfowl, the implications of future plans and the possibilities of co-operation between hunters and conservationists. In this way it not merely mapped in some detail a course of future action, but created a compact responsible and close-knit group able and willing to get on with it in nearly all parts of Europe, west of the U.S.S.R. At a Second Meeting at Noordwyk in the Netherlands in 1966 the scope of the effort was further reinforced by the keen participation of the U.S.S.R. which itself agreed to become the host country for the third meeting in Leningrad in 1968. Unfortunately this eagerly awaited meeting became a partial casualty of the immediately preceding Soviet occupation of Czecho-Slovakia.

In the meantime there had been gradually developing at Strasbourg since 1949 a belated inter-governmental effort towards European co-operation in the shape of the Council of Europe, whose 18 member states work through a 147-member Consultative Assembly drawn from national parliaments and a Committee of Ministers with executive functions. Disillusioned by long experience of the dilatoriness and ineffectiveness of European governmental participation in conservation, naturalists and conservationists generally felt little enthusiasm for placing reliance on such a body until official readiness to make its interventions practically effective had been demonstrated first in other fields. In 1963, however, the Council's Committee of Ministers decided to set up a European Committee for Conservation of Nature and Natural Resources as a specialist body composed of experts to assist them in their work, and to advise and propose action on all matters concerned with nature conservation.

Although admirable in principle this step gave rise to some anxiety, since no explicit recognition was at first given to the valuable role which the European-based International Union for Conservation was already playing in promoting, within Europe as elsewhere, the identical aims of improved conservation of nature, of natural resources and of land-scape. Nor was allowance made for the technical advantages of con-ducting such functions as bird protection and conservation of wetland habitats through the efficient mechanism which had been developed by specialists during many years of governmental neglect of such problems.

Even now, while Governments such as that of the United Kingdom were very ready to gain credit by voting at Strasbourg for such good causes, they proved miserly in responding to requests to provide any extra resources for carrying out the resulting additional work, otherwise than at the expense of existing conservation commitments already suffer-ing from grossly inadequate financial support. Even finding manpower of the right caliber to attend meetings of the new Committee on top of so many competing engagements proved a chronic difficulty, not least for advanced countries to whom both the Council's staff and other countries naturally looked for the greater part of the technical and administrative experience, working time and information required.

As usual, the willing horses rallied round and somehow made things work, but with the best intentions the Council added yet further to the disproportion between the extensive international overheads of European conservation and the wretchedly insufficient manpower and money which the member states were ready to find for such purposes within their own frontiers. In this field the Council's initiative was not so much a means of enabling all the various national efforts to be co-ordinated as a missionary course to bring home to member governments the extent and consequences of their own joint and several continuing defaults on their obligations of trusteeship.

This situation was recognised by the Council of Europe's decision in 1967, on United Kingdom initiative, to organise for 1970 a European Conservation Year to promote wider understanding of conservation aims, to create awareness of the problems and potential, and to stimulate appropriate policies and action.

In a very different part of the world another well-organised effort had also been making great progress under the more strictly scientific auspices of SCAR—the Scientific Committee for Antarctic Research of the International Council of Scientific Unions. After a period during which it was feared that a grab for Antarctica among the powers would be followed by the dreary pattern of military fortification, ill-conceived commercial exploitation and indiscriminate destruction of wild life, wiser counsels prevailed. Through the Antarctic Treaty of 1959 the twelve nations engaged in research there during the International Geophysical Year agreed that "Antarctica shall continue forever to be used for peaceful purposes, and shall not become the scene or object of international discord." In effect all territorial claims within the continent were indefinitely frozen, without being either withdrawn or internationally recognised, and rights of access, including overflight, and of inspection of aircraft, ships and stations, were mutually accorded. Strategic and commercial interests being thus restrained, science and conservation emerged in the role, much more satisfactory here than elsewhere, of residuary legatee. At last there was a continent for science.

No time was lost by SCAR, as scientific adviser to the Antarctic Treaty Powers, in drawing up a series of Agreed Measures for giving effect to a program of conservation based on the most enlightened approaches and practice of advanced countries. The enforcement of these Agreed Measures was rendered legally complex and tricky by the exclusion from Antarctica of the conventional mechanisms of national sovereignty, although in practice it was made easier by the fact that access to the continent has hitherto been too difficult and costly except for personnel sponsored and supported through official scientific programs linked with SCAR. In 1968, however, the long arm of tourism began to reach Antarctica, and the definition and enforcement of ground rules became more urgent. For once, conservation was not overtaken by the speed of these developments, but several important issues of demarcation of special conservation areas and species and the regulation of sealing and other activities in the surrounding seas remained to be cleared up on the basis of agreements reached in principle, and of powers which the contracting governments were obtaining from their legislatures.

Full documentation on the Antarctic Treaty, the Agreed Measures for the Conservation of Antarctic Fauna and Flora and the consequential British legislation "to enable effect to be given to measures for the conservation of Antarctic fauna and flora..." are given in the Antarctic Treaty Act 1967 (London; HMSO, 2s.).

The Treaty itself had looked to the continuation and development of international co-operation in scientific investigation through exchange of plans, personnel and data. It had forbidden nuclear explosions in Antarctica and the disposal there of radioactive waste material, but had left to follow-up meetings the definition of means for the "preservation and conservation of living resources in Antarctica".

The resulting Agreed Measures for the Conservation of Antarctic Fauna and Flora constitute a landmark for several reasons. First, their provisions are drafted in the accurate language of scientists dealing with scientific matters, and succeed in breaking away from such pet fallacies of the lawyers as a distinction between "animals" and "birds". Secondly they constitute the first comprehensive and detailed attempt to implement scientific principles of conservation on a continental scale, in a single clearly presented instrument. For example, Article VII requires participating governments "to minimise harmful interference ... with the normal living conditions of any native mammal or bird" and specifies that

"2. The following acts and activities shall be considered as harmful interference;

(a) allowing dogs to run free

(b) flying helicopters or other aircraft in a manner which would

207

unnecessarily disturb bird and seal concentrations, or landing
close to such concentrations (e.g. within 200 meters)

(e) discharge of firearms close to bird and seal concentrations (e.g.
within 300 meters)

(f) any disturbance of bird and seal colonies during the breeding
period by persistent attention from persons on foot."

The British Antarctic Treaty Act of 1967 forbids any person of
British nationality "while he is in any part of Antarctica" to

"wilfully kill, injure, molest or take any native mammal or native
bird," or
"gather any native plant within a specially protected area, or drive
any vehicle within such an area."

The basic penalty provided for offences is a fine of up to £50, but for
destruction of seals imprisonment is authorised.

While it is sad that even the picked personnel in Antarctica have not
proved able to regulate their own conduct in these matters sufficiently
strictly to obviate the need for formal control on such lines the law in
this remote and only transitorily peopled continent is undoubtedly far
closer to fulfilling modern conservation needs than that for most if not
all advanced countries.

In contrast, the selfish and short-sighted attitudes of states and
commercial interests had been exhibited at their basest, as late even as
the nineteen-sixties, in the case of whaling in southern waters. Here was
no success story but a dismal tale of man at his almost incredibly
stupid worst in relation to the cropping of an obviously exhaustible
natural resource. The situation was well summed up at the 1967 annual
meeting in London of the International Whaling Commission in a
statement by the celebrated aviator General Charles A. Lindbergh,
whose dismay at the destruction he had witnessed in flying over the
earth had converted him into a keen conservationist:

"Mr. Chairman; Gentlemen: I am here representing the International Union for Conservation of Nature.
The IUCN notes that the harpooning of blue and humpback
whales has, for the first time, been discontinued in all oceans. The
IUCN compliments the International Whaling Commission for its
part in bringing this about. Our satisfaction is mixed with distress
in the knowledge that harpooning was discontinued because of the
near-extermination of both species, rather than because of responsible planning for the use of important ocean resources.

The IUCN again calls attention to the fact that over-exploitation to obtain short-term profits has reduced a great ocean resource to a small fraction of its optimum yield potential at a time when growing human populations desperately need additional meat, oils, and meals.

The IUCN continues to urge adoption of kill quotas that will rebuild whale stocks to the point of maximum yield within the shortest practicable period of time. Obviously, the quota of 3,200 blue-whale units for the 1967–8 season is too high to accomplish this objective. The IUCN recommends the adoption of quotas for each whale species as a major step in reaching maximum-yield populations. Experience shows that the present B.W.U. system has led to the destruction of one whale stock after another.

The present whale crisis is an outstanding example of the danger of uncontrolled and irresponsible exploitation of natural resources. The IUCN believes that the ability of the International Whaling Commission, and the governments it represents, to program a return to optimum-yield stocks has significance reaching far beyond the whaling industry. It is an indication of man's ability, in general, to turn this planet's natural resources to his own essential needs, with all the implications this involves."

Behind the temperate wording of General Lindbergh's unanswerable statement lies the plain fact of the total default of the International Whaling Commission, and of the governments controlling it, in their duty to defend the asset entrusted to them from a rake's progress of greedy and wholly unjustified destruction, the consequences of which must be felt long after those guilty of it are dead. In such unworthy hands too often lies the power to determine whether or not the world of tomorrow will be worth living in. Their criminal negligence, their ignorance and their rapacity stand in dark and evil contrast to the disinterested struggles of so many conservationists to save our descendants from being robbed of their inheritance.

The action, still incomplete and only partially effective, towards controlling deliberate pollution of the sea by oil has already been referred to. Shipping interests, especially in the United States, often proved obdurate in blocking action until they were compelled to change their attitude through the slow and massive marshalling of world-wide public opinion by the conservationists. The more modern-minded and intelligently managed oil industry was less backward in appreciating, and more active and resourceful in seeking to meet the demonstrated need for reconciling seaborne tanker operation with the observance of tolerable care for the marine environment. Once it was made clear in

1950 that conservationists had the wit and the means to gather samples of oil pollution on the seas and shores and to secure its precise analysis in order to determine its age and origin the silly "explanation" that it was all due to the breaking up of vessels sunk during the war was soon dropped, and the oil companies collaborated realistically by experimenting on the nature and speed of drift in oceanic conditions. A swing of technical effort into studying the problem soon produced acceptable and effective innovations for minimising the release of oil at sea, such as the gloriously simple *"load on top"* method. Progressive ports such as Copenhagen led the way in developing facilities which deprived stick-in-the-mud shipowners of the excuse for treating tidal waters as a common sewer, and in devising more advanced codes of practice which they were gradually induced or compelled to observe.

Unfortunately their rearguard action against elementary decent standards of conduct in their use of the high seas monopolised so much of the small available conservation effort that other aspects of the growing maritime traffic in oil could not be tackled soon enough. The traditions of the sea are of long standing, but the attempt to retain them in unmodified form in face of vast increases in the tonnage, speed and capacity for injury even to distant environments of a modern large tanker was unwise and indefensible.

In Britain the establishment of the new oil port of Milford Haven in a fine natural harbor which had been included, through a serious error of judgment, in the Pembrokeshire Coast National Park gave an opportunity to test the possibilities of handling large quantities of oil by modern methods with an acceptable minimum of damage to the natural environment and the landscape. Given from the outset the right terms of reference, directives and limiting conditions, the new port authority created under the Milford Haven Conservancy Act of 1958 and the incoming oil companies proved agreeably co-operative. The layout and design were satisfactorily settled to reconcile economics of scale and modern technique with high environmental standards.

The snag which soon emerged was that the good intentions and enlightened understanding at the top level extended only most imperfectly and feebly down the line to those who continued to perform their duties with the laxity and squalid disregard for amenity to which they had long been accustomed. Avoidable spillages of oil into tidal water, and also avoidable accidents leading to spillages proved unacceptably common. At the cost of a considerable diversion of manpower and of risking unpopularity, the Nature Conservancy monitored the whole performance in detail, and by bringing lapses immediately to the attention of top managements concerned was able, through their willing co-operation, to secure a gratifying reduction in such incidents, which some of those involved had wrongly argued to be unavoidable. Once it was shown that offences against the environment were no longer to be dismissed as venial or trivial the necessary standards were readily achieved. Experience, however, showed that most detailed vigilance was required on the part of the Conservancy, the port and the oil companies in close co-operation.

An interesting by-product of this Milford Haven exercise was a research study of the effects on living organisms of emulsifier detergents used in a well-meant attempt to clean beaches heavily contaminated by oil. This research showed that so far as marine life is concerned the remedy is much more destructive than the disease.

Armed with such practical knowledge the Nature Conservancy, as the British Government's official adviser on conservation, urged that new codes of practice for the movement of oil in both inshore and international waters should be worked out, with the co-operation of those concerned, in order to minimise the obvious hazards due to movements of such perilous cargoes in fog or bad visibility and in congested conditions. In reporting to Parliament in December 1961 the Nature Conservancy stated:

"In November 1960 the Conservancy prepared a draft sub-mission to Ministers, pointing out that the immense expansion of oil traffic in British waters has created what amounts to a major new hazard.

On 25th January 1960 a collision off Portsmouth between the tanker "Gorm" and the "Santa Alicia" resulted in some 1,200 tons of oil being discharged into the sea, forming a nearly solid floating mass. As a result of this incident arose the Coastal Resorts Oil Pollution Committee, initiated by the Portsmouth City Council, which sent a deputation to the Minister demanding immediate remedial and preventive action.

In July this was followed by the "Esso Portsmouth" disaster at Milford Haven, and shortly afterwards the 26,000 ton tanker "Bideford", while pumping fuel oil aboard at Fawley, left a valve open and heavily polluted Southampton Water with oil. The Master was fined £500. Almost at the same time two oil tanker barges, which were rashly attempting to move cargoes of fuel oil and petrol up the Severn in dense fog, collided and blew up with the loss of several lives and the destruction of a railway bridge over the Severn at Sharpness.

The Conservancy raised the question whether safety margins for the movement of oil ought not to be as strictly defined and as thoroughly policed as those relating to aircraft and mining hazards, and whether the good intentions of the authorities and oil companies concerned were being adequately fulfilled by those actually carrying out the operations."

After summarising further serious incidents the Report added:

"During the year the Conservancy have discussed possible remedial measures with the Ministry of Transport and have consulted the National Parks Commission and the Council for the Preservation of Rural England. The early warning system was initiated earlier this year, whereby coastal local authorities and others—including the Conservancy—are notified of the approach of offshore oil pollution ...

Efforts to solve this widespread and extremely serious problem must now be focussed on the conference in London on 26th March to 13th April 1962 of the Inter-Governmental Maritime Consultative Committee (I.M.C.C.). The object of the Conference is to review the present situation regarding oil pollution of the sea; the working of the International Convention for the Prevention of Pollution of the Sea by Oil, 1954; any amendments to the provisions of the 1954 Convention proposed by Governments; and the practicability of securing complete avoidance of the discharge of persistent oils into the sea.

Meanwhile the Conservancy will continue to watch the position closely and to bring home to all concerned the importance of making really effective efforts to ensure that accidents do not happen through carelessness or negligence."

No warning could have been more specific, better-timed or more prophetically vindicated by subsequent events than this message, ordered by the House of Commons to be printed five years and 108 days before the *Torrey Canyon* struck. Meanwhile in 1966, 89 named vessels had been reported as leaking or disposing of oil in British coastal waters alone.

Unfortunately negligence at sea was sheltered by negligence in Whitehall, which with customary blind stubbornness refused to recognise the problem until forced to do so by a catastrophic shock to public opinion.

On 18th March 1967 one of the largest ships in the world, the 118,000 ton tanker *Torrey Canyon*, sailing under a Liberian "flag of convenience" with an Italian master and crew, was approaching the Isles of Scilly at full speed. Carrying over 119,000 tons of crude oil from the Persian Gulf to Milford Haven, Captain Rugiati had for several days been on a course intended to pass some five miles west of the Bishop Rock, and therefore of all the Isles of Scilly. Despite all modern navigation equipment available it proved, when radar contact was made at 6.30 a.m. on the 18th, that the Scillies were on the port bow, not to starboard as they should have been. A Great Shearwater homing to its small island breeding territory on Tristan da Cunha could not have afforded so wide an error as six miles; for a 20th century great ship it was lamentable. The master was called, and he came up on the bridge soon after 7 a.m. He was anxious to save half an hour on the last lap of the voyage to Milford Haven and decided on that ground to take the risk of passing through the rock-strewn and heavily fished channel between the Scillies and Cornwall. At 8.18 a.m., four miles east of St Mary's he made the even rasher snap decision to pass through the seven mile wide shallow sea passage, heavily used by fishing vessels, between the Scillies and the Seven Stones. In doing so he gambled on being able, while still at full speed, to make a sharp turn to westward, but this was baulked by a fishing boat in the way. His correct reaction would have been to abandon this foolish manoeuver at once and to head out eastward, leaving the Seven Stones to port, but he let the opportunity pass. The rocks were now right ahead, and although a turn was attempted it was now too late, despite desperate warning signals from the Seven Stones lightship. The *Torrey Canyon* struck. To save half an hour Rugiati had incurred a financial waste of around £10 millions and inflicted perhaps the greatest single injury ever caused to the tourist and holiday industry in peacetime, apart from incalculable damage to the natural environment and to wildlife.

In Whitehall and Downing Street the previous complacency was soon to give place to panic action. Almost incredibly, however, complacency still ruled on the *Torrey Canyon* itself. Although the experienced coxswain of the St Mary's lifeboat, already alongside, warned that the ship might break in two, Captain Rugiati as late as 11 a.m. decided to cancel distress signals, and salvage plans went ahead. In a vain attempt to save the ship from the consequences of his folly the master began pumping crude oil into the helpless sea. By the evening some 5,000 tons of pumped or leaked oil extended over eight miles of water between Scilly and the Wolf Rock off Cornwall. By early evening the Navy was at work spraying the oil with a detergent more lethal than the oil itself to marine life. The nauseating stench of the oil smeared across the sea could be smelt in an aircraft three miles downwind.

Next morning saw the world's largest single patch of man-made pollution, twelve miles long and up to six miles wide, formed by some 20,000 tons of crude oil drifting towards Cornwall. A conflict of interests soon developed between those concerned with minimising the oil pollution disaster to the coasts and to marine life and those who still hoped to refloat the giant tanker, holed in 19 tanks, and tow her precariously along the whole length of the English Channel to Amsterdam. For example, a floating boom around the wreck would check the further fouling of the sea, but would increase the fire and explosive risk to the shattered hull.

Whitehall, which had been deaf to repeated pleas over the years to establish an efficiently co-ordinated operational organisation for just such emergencies, now had to improvise one in a matter of hours under the critical eye of the Prime Minister, who by coincidence was about to take an Easter vacation at his island retreat within a few miles of the wreck. The Treasury, which had grudged a few thousand pounds to insure against this clearly foreseeable risk, was now forced to squander some £2 million on a largely futile defensive and cleaning-up operation.

Only after ten days of vacillation was the fact faced that the *Torrey Canyon* could not be salvaged, and must at all costs be prevented from disgorging the remaining third or half of her immensely injurious cargo. Salvage efforts, brave and skilful as they were, had led only to expensive delay, to an explosion costing the life of the Dutch salvage chief, and to the further spread of oil pollution. At last, on 28th March, ten days after she had struck, the *Torrey Canyon* was heavily bombed by Royal Naval aircraft with R.A.F. support, and through repeated attacks the remaining oil was apparently successfully burnt up in the hull.

Nearly 5,000 men and women, including a sizeable part of the Army's strategic reserve, had been deployed in palliating the damage caused by probably less than 25,000 tons of oil which came ashore before the wind shifted. By April 5 the impact had been diverted to the North-west coasts of France, where a state of emergency soon had to be declared and again large military forces had to be sent to aid the civil authorities in an equally hastily improvised and extravagant defensive operation.

That the damage to beaches and fisheries was not much greater was due much more to the good fortune of winds which unexpectedly carried the oil in another direction than to good management in what was inevitably a botched-up improvisation. By an irony of fate the Chancellor who had to pay the bill for this extravagant negligence was the man who, when out of office, had done most to encourage and guide the campaign to persuade governments to awaken to the danger—the Rt. Hon. James Callaghan, M.P., with whom I had had the pleasure of visiting Washington some years earlier in a successful effort to enable the international convention of 1954 to win ratification by the United States Senate.

On May 4 1967 the Inter-Governmental Marine Consultative Organisation met in London to tackle the action which it ought to have taken, and which had been clearly indicated to it, half a dozen years earlier. Thus are the affairs of our world conducted by those whom we entrust with that responsibility. Had it been spent in time a small fraction of the money and manpower frittered away on cleaning up after the *Torrey Canyon* would not only have obviated that and other disasters, but would have provided a first-class world-wide preventive and remedial organisation for the positive care of the oceans and their shores. Industry and transport must run, oil must move where it is wanted, but in moving it a discipline no less rigorous than that applied to the much greater hazards of air traffic must be accepted by those engaged in the trade, in circumstances where the record shows a culpable laxity of due care and attention.

Since this section was written the House of Commons Select Committee on Science and Technology has issued its report on the problem, entitled Coastal Pollution (no. 421 HMSO 7s.). This report gave rise to much publicity on account of its forthright criticisms, not only in relation to specific matters under review but concerning the conduct and efficiency of the British system of government revealed by the episode.

Under "Central Government's Role" they state:
"Crying over spilt milk is never profitable but the tears may sometimes engender a determination to spill no more. . . . without wishing to hark back unduly to the unalterable past, we nevertheless believe that given the knowledge that was available at that time (1966) to I.M.C.O., shipowners, the Oil Industry, and various Government Departments it is surprising, to say the least, that more comprehensive plans had not been laid to meet the obvious possibility of a major spillage occurring near our shores."

Their inquiries showed that even after the disaster four days elapsed before the calling in of the Government's Chief Scientific Adviser, himself an eminent biologist with much knowledge of the background issues involved. Among many disturbing conclusions the report found serious reasons to doubt the justification for employing detergents on which the Government had squandered £1·3 millions, or more than the entire annual grant to the Nature Conservancy.

In quoting the views of the Marine Biological Association the report strongly agreed with their conclusion that

"We are progressively making a slum of nature and may eventually find that we are enjoying the benefit of science and industry under conditions which no civilised country should tolerate."

As a footnote Lloyds Register disclosed that in the relevant year 1967 world merchant shipping losses at 833,000 tons were higher than ever before in time of peace, and that over half that total was wrecked by striking rocks or other hidden obstructions, the increase over the previous year, being no less than 188,000 tons. These figures further emphasise the collective negligence already pointed out, which should be a cause of shame to all concerned in it.

Pollution of the seas by oil is a good example of the recently acquired capability of man for injury to the natural environment on a global scale, both through lack of conscience and through lack of due precaution. It is not, unfortunately, unique.

Perhaps the greatest demonstration of human folly and irresponsibility is provided by the recent development of unimaginably destructive nuclear weapons deliberately designed to inflict widespread indiscriminate damage on human populations and their environment in some hitherto fortunately postponed holocaust, while meanwhile requiring tests which greatly increase radio-active fall-out, with consequently aggravated risks of genetic and other injuries. Since the design and refinement of these devices has become the task of an important section of the world's scientific community, and since they are commissioned and controlled by the most powerful states at the highest governmental levels, the task of bringing them under control with a view to their progressive abolition clearly far exceeds the capabilities of the conservation movement. Owing to its obvious urgency and to the hair-raising implications of "overkill" and "megadeath" it has stimulated worldwide psychological reactions akin to those which sustain the more emotional sections of the conservation movement, and has led to the emergence of organised opposition on somewhat analogous lines, initially largely dominated by shared feeling of horror but becoming progressively more amenable to the self-discipline of technically and politically practicable patterns of organised expression.

It may be merely coincidence that the only specific success so far achieved has not been in the direction of "banning the bomb", but in the much more limited area of restricting tests of nuclear devices, where the immediate object is almost indistinguishable from that of the conservation movement. Some of the leading scientists concerned, especially in the internationally influential Pugwash Conferences, have ideas and aims which interlock with those of conservationists. It seems certain that this much younger but much more widespread and politically articulate movement will continue to evolve and gather strength until the objectives of nuclear disarmament are achieved, unless a globally lethal nuclear war breaks out first. For the present it probably remains more correct to regard the two as unconnected except for some underlying common interests, but it is to be expected that as time goes on the already implicit mutual support between them will become more explicit and articulate, and that these twin surges of thought and feeling against the destructive and degrading misuse of the earth's precious resources and of mankind's potentialities will tend to coalesce. The more fundamentally they are viewed, and the longer they run, the less division can be found between them.

A third distinct area of international interest in restraining the misuse of science for injurious applications, even in an ostensibly good cause, is provided by the great expansion of toxic chemicals for use in crop production and animal husbandry. Here, as in the case of oil pollution at sea, the dangers and inconveniences involved touch many interests, but once more it has been left to the nature conservation movement to put the problem in perspective on a basis of incontestable facts, and to force changes of practice and regulatory action.

The first International Technical Conference on the Protection of Nature, organised by the International Union and by UNESCO at Lake Success, New York in August 1949, included a well-balanced review of consequences detrimental to man from the generalised use of insecticides or of modern herbicides. Emphasis was laid on avoiding "the blind use of DDT—in time" and on using such products only where absolutely necessary, and discouraging indiscriminate commercial or private spraying. Research, selectivity and control were essential. Three specialised agencies of the United Nations, represented at the meeting, were requested to establish a joint permanent Commission on Pesticides. Despite the admirable sentiments expressed the record of the meeting indicates an undercurrent of unjustified complacency on the part of the interested parties. For example, the representative of the U.S. Department of Agriculture "assured the meeting that there are enough experts at the disposal of the U.S. Government to fulfil the task of the controlled use of insecticides". In the light of twenty years' further experience it can only be concluded either that this statement was not true, or that the experts referred to were not well used.

In the United Kingdom these dangers were investigated in detail by an official Working Party on "Precautionary Measures against Toxic Chemicals used in Agriculture" whose report appeared in 1955. In the case of chemical herbicides for control of roadside vegetation studies were sponsored jointly by the Nature Conservancy and the Agricultural Research Council, resulting in the issue by the Ministry of Transport in 1955 of an official circular to all highway authorities cautioning against the spraying of herbicides for such purposes except in strictly limited situations. This circular, although resented in some quarters at the time, was widely effective in saving the English countryside from the abuses and excesses which would otherwise undoubtedly have occurred. Both initiatives served notice on commercially interested groups, and on public administrative and technical officers susceptible to their propaganda, that the application of these dangerous substances would in future be carefully watched and strictly supervised in the overall public interest. In contrast to developments elsewhere it established in Britain early a position of strength from which later generally acceptable codes of practice and conduct could be successfully negotiated.

While some of the most powerful pesticides and herbicides originated in European laboratories it was in the United States that their production and use first rocketed. When the world situation was next technically appraised at the 5th Technical Meeting of the International Union in Copenhagen in 1954 another spokesman for the U.S. Department of Agriculture proudly announced that "Since 1945, Americans have used 300 million pounds of insecticides annually to fight their insect enemies". Among these which he endorsed with enthusiasm were aldrin and dieldrin, which in the light of later research had to be virtually banned in the United Kingdom, on account of their damage to wildlife. He added that

"Use of many of these new chemicals has been widespread in the United States. Millions of acres of crops are now being treated annually. Close observance shows that when wildlife losses occur, they represent weakness ... in not establishing safe application procedures, and in not disseminating necessary information to the public."

This rosy view was not borne out even by other U.S. official representatives, from the Fish and Wildlife Service, such as Dr Clarence Cottam who stated:

"Past and current losses incidental to the chief objective of control have been largely unnecessary. They were and are the result of carelessness or, more commonly the lack of sufficient knowledge and judgment to make the wisest use of these controls. . . .

The profit motive seems to insure that the amount of funds available for the development of new control agents is almost unlimited, but unfortunately there is little incentive and almost no

prospect for immediate financial returns to stimulate study and testing
of these control agents to ascertain their relationship to and effects
upon wildlife and its habitat. The U.S. Fish and Wildlife Service
currently had funds for employing but one full-time scientist to study
the effects of these control agents."

This contrasted with an officially estimated usage of some 444,000
tons of 21 different insecticides, herbicides and algaecides in 1951, plus
3½ million gallons of carbon tetrachloride and 225 million tons of lime,
talc and similar dilutants.

Among other contributors to this important discussion Mr C. Potter,
head of the Department of Insecticides and Fungicides at Rothamsted
Experimental Station, stated:

"It cannot be too strongly emphasised that the insect-plant community is an integrated ecological complex and that the problem of
the destruction of harmful and beneficial insects cannot be viewed
as the isolated effects of chemicals on a few species of obvious importance."

After much further discussion at a high level the Technical Meeting
made a number of practical recommendations which would now be
almost universally acceptable. These included:

use of the most specific product by means least hazardous to wildlife
use strictly in accordance with scientific advice as to quantity and
quality
if widespread applications appear necessary a qualified biologist
should assess local conditions and possible effects, and advise on
precautions or limits
if biological control or other alternative measures exist they should be
preferred
manufacturers and distributors as well as governments and scientific
institutions should collaborate in research on dangers to organisms
other than pests and weeds
each government should set up a committee to collect and correlate
information on the effects of chemical control products on wild life
and to exchange information internationally
governments and industry should be requested to call the attention of
users to the dangers of inconsiderate use of chemical control products.

Unfortunately, in the absence at that time of any incontestably
catastrophic results on a sufficient scale to arouse public opinion to
irresistible demands for action, governments and industry as usual

chose to ignore this wise advice, so well justified by later events. As a partial exception the United Kingdom, thanks to the efforts of Sir Solly Zuckerman as scientific adviser to the government, and to those of the Nature Conservancy and several unofficial bodies, developed, rather gradually, the kind of organisation and policy which had here been recommended. In particular an Inter-Departmental Advisory Committee on Poisonous Substances used in Agriculture and Food Storage arranged in 1957 with the representatives of industry for a voluntary notification scheme under which the industry agreed not to market a product without first fully informing the Committee of its nature, and of grounds for regarding it as effective and safe, and obtaining the Committee's approval to its use. Where this approval was made subject to certain precautions these precautions would be stated on the label. Also in 1957 the voluntary conservation bodies concerned agreed with the Nature Conservancy to arrange with the industry both for research tests to be carried out, during the course of product development, on birds, insects and fishes (mammals being already covered) and to undertake systematic field observations. The societies agreed to provide observers in areas where contract spraying was taking place, or where field trials were arranged by manufacturers.

A peculiar hitch now arose. Although it was widely and deeply felt that the expanding indiscriminate use of toxic chemicals in agriculture must involve risk to wild life, extensive inquiries failed to provide "any substantial evidence to prove that these chemicals are causing any important or widespread reduction in bird or mammal populations". It was not therefore possible to obtain the necessary funds and scientific manpower to undertake field trials or fundamental research at that stage. A good deal of quiet progress continued, however, and in 1959 a high-powered official committee with wide terms of reference was created to make fresh recommendations. In January 1960 the Nature Conservancy set up a unit under Dr N. W. Moore to investigate the effects of toxic chemicals on wild life. The manufacturers, who had collectively imposed a voluntary ban on future sales of alkali arsenites, now symbolised their enlightened and co-operative approach by inviting Lord Hurcomb, a senior member of the Nature Conservancy and President of the Council for Nature, to speak at their annual dinner, where their Chairman referred to the risk to wild life as

"a very complex problem depending as it does on ecological studies" and in expressing gratitude for the co-operation of conservationists and of the Nature Conservancy said "We want to establish this as a real working partnership . . ."

The first widespread incidence of deaths of birds and mammals in agricultural districts, which were later shown to be caused by poisoned seed dressings, occurred in England in the Spring of 1960.

While it would be too much to claim that the emergency found the authorities fully prepared, the necessary groundwork had been largely completed and both investigation and action followed at a relatively rapid rate. In 1961 the Nature Conservancy reported to Parliament that "Events during the past year have shown that the serious concern felt by conservationists and the urgency which they attribute to this problem were fully justified".

Spring sowing in 1961 had resulted in "heavy and widespread casualties of birds and mammals". Within a six-month period there had been over 300 reported incidents from forty-four counties, affecting 48 species of wild birds and 11 of mammals. As the Conservancy summed up:

> "There were two main difficulties in the way of producing firm evidence as to the cause of wild life casualties: firstly, there were not enough investigators to find significant numbers of corpses in the areas most affected, but this problem was soon overcome, mainly through the efforts of the voluntary societies; secondly, there was the difficulty of determining by post-mortem analysis, whether a particular chemical had caused death." Much intensive work by the Government Chemist and others was needed to develop the necessary refined techniques. This was expensive—"it costs as much to analyse the organs of a dead bird as to analyse the organs of a human being."

Among the dead were some 1300 foxes and large numbers of game-birds such as pheasants and partridges. The immediate effect was to drive the influential but hitherto somewhat aloof landowners and followers of such field sports as shooting and fox-hunting into a working alliance with nature conservationists, which was to survive the emergency and to open other doors for the future.

On 25th April Lord Shackleton initiated a debate in the House of Lords on the catastrophic casualties caused to game and wild life by the use of toxic chemicals in agriculture. He pointed out that, were it not for the actions of private individuals and societies, the public and the Government would not have the information necessary to assess the seriousness of the situation. The Government spokesman assured the House in reply that the Government were not complacent, although by this time all were aware that this was just what they had been.

The Nature Conservancy and the conservation societies now pressed for a complete ban on the use of seed-dressing containing aldrin, dieldrin and heptachlor, which, it was now beginning to be conceded, were mainly responsible for the mass killing of wildlife. In the event a compromise was agreed, involving a ban at the time of spring sowings. Meanwhile, before the somewhat feeble report of the official committee was received, the House of Commons Select Committee on Estimates came out in June with a condemnation of the piecemeal approach of the Agricultural Departments and recommended to Ministers "a comprehensive enquiry into the effect upon agriculture, upon public health and upon the ecology of the country of all chemicals used in agriculture". The Ministers were also urged immediately to ban the use as seed-dressings of aldrin, dieldrin and heptachlor and "to make the fullest use of their resources to assist the Nature Conservancy in fulfilling its responsibility for the conservation of wild life".

A decisive victory had been won for scientific conservation over an extremely powerful but stupid opposition. The significance of this event was greatly enhanced by the most creditable readiness of so many enlightened individuals and interested firms to come out for constructive co-operation with the conservationists. Unfortunately such public-spirited industrial leaders were much less in evidence in other important countries, notably the United States.

This was tested when in 1962 Rachel Carson published in the *New Yorker* and then in book form as *Silent Spring* her devastating and well-informed indictment of such follies as the U.S. Department of Agriculture's ill-conceived campaign to eradicate the fire ant with heptachlor in Alabama and neighboring states, and the gypsy moth with DDT on the north-east seaboard, and in Michigan. Compared with the record in the United States that in Great Britain was comparatively blameless. Although *Silent Spring* immediately became one of the most dramatically successful of best sellers in North America the continued opposition of vested interests has hitherto blocked the adoption in the United States of such measures for comprehensive scientific supervision and control as have been accepted and applied by all concerned in Great Britain since about the period when the book first appeared.

Attention must next be turned to the role played by the great media of information in the worldwide task of educating people about their environment. In this task *Silent Spring* was a landmark for several reasons. Not only was it an instant and enormous best-seller on both sides of the Atlantic; it was also the work of a former biologist of the Fish and Wildlife Service and a peculiarly gifted populariser who in the course of it provided one of the best and most widely read simple accounts of what ecology means to ordinary men and women. Its theme was thus basically scientific, and only secondly aesthetic or sentimental. It challenged the misusers and mismanagers of land on their own ground. Even if its success in bringing about fundamental changes of attitude and policy in the United States has hitherto been oddly and disappointingly partial its message continues to penetrate. By it Rachel Carson has amply earned the same epitaph as John Brown.

There had, of course, been other well-read and effective books on conservation before *Silent Spring*, such as *The Rape of the Earth; A World Survey of Soil Erosion* by G. V. Jacks and R. O. Whyte in 1939 and a notable cluster in 1948–9 including Fairfield Osborn's *Our Plundered Planet*, William Vogt's *Road to Survival* and Aldo Leopold's *Sand County Almanac*. These and many other works had done much to stimulate and guide the development of the worldwide conservation movement in the absence at that time of an adequate group of close-knit and effective institutions, official and unofficial.

From the 'fifties on' books became powerfully reinforced by the increasingly vivid and practical aid of the camera, through black-and-white and color still pictures and cinematograph films, both documentary and fictional. Bernard Grzimek's *Serengeti Must Not Die* and R. Gary's *The Roots of Heaven* may be mentioned as examples.

It would be difficult to exaggerate the impact and influence upon world opinion of the pictorial accompaniment of the conservation movement. Ever since what has since come to be called the coffee-table book was pioneered by *Picturesque America* in 1872, and the early photographers had brought back their astonishingly good photographs of Yosemite and other scenic gems of the West, the growing conservation movement had been stimulated by and recruited with such aids. Already for over thirty years enormous panoramas had literally unfolded to the American people the appearance of their great natural heritage, with far-reaching results in imprinting even upon habitual town-dwellers a nostalgia for the wild frontier. Such literary leaders as Longfellow and Dickens were deeply impressed by "the largest picture of the world", a canvas three miles long of the course of the Mississippi River. This, as Dickens reported, as "an indisputably true and faithful representation of a wonderful region—wood and water, river and prairie, lonely log hut and clustered city rising in the forest".

As new media have been perfected each in turn has been used by most devoted and skilful operators to bring home to immense audiences the wonders of nature. Anyone who has visited any of the world's great national parks and scenic or wildlife spectacles must marvel and rejoice that through modern photography and cinephotography their most impressive aspects should be so vividly and fully shown to so many

223

millions who can never be there. It is true that there can be no substitute to a naturalist for the tang of the place itself, for being able to seek his own goals in his own way, for the emotional preparation of journeying to it and acclimatising himself gradually to its atmosphere. The experience brought home to us by the masters of the camera and the sound-track is different, especially to those whose first-hand experience of the wild is nil or negligible, but it is no less worth having. Without it even the most tireless traveller can hardly hope to acquire even a sketchy overall awareness of the variety and complexity of the earth and its contrasting ecosystems.

The breadth and depth of this impact on mass consciousness, which has hardly yet begun to be appreciated, may be attributed mainly to four factors. First comes the perennial attraction and charm of nature itself as a subject, infinitely varied, and reinforced by man's age-long conditioning to it, recalled all the more poignantly in the subconscious of those who in modern city living have grown up cut off from their heritage. Second is the outstanding technical capability conferred by techniques adding realistic color, sound, and movement to visual representation, as a medium for transporting the viewer from the closed room to the open wilderness. Third has been the fortunate unbroken succession of exceptionally gifted practitioners who have applied their mastery of these media to this field. And finally account must be taken of the vastly expanding channels for bringing the results quickly, economically, conveniently and effectively before millions of people whose interest, however genuine, is often passive or subject to many competing claims. With all its blind spots and built-in bias our modern civilisation has, in spite of itself, allowed to the popular presentation of nature and of natural environment an effective share much larger than might have been expected from its ruling values and traditions. It is to this successful competition for viewing time, listening time and reading time that the conservation movement owes much of its impressive actual and enormous potential strength. In the low terms of commercial television the public may not yet have bought the product, but they have at least been familiarised with it.

It is true that this rather happy situation is far from universal; it applies principally in Europe and North America, Australia and East and South Africa, but is visibly developing elsewhere. The message and coverage of the subject are also far from adequately presented, with an emphasis on escapist of sensational aspects and a widespread avoidance of many of the chronic problems and abuses which most need to be brought home to public opinion. The role played by different media also varies. In Great Britain, for example, since 1960 television and the commercial cinema have played an outstanding part, aided by the lucky coincidence that certain leading naturalists such as Peter Scott and James Fisher have proved outstandingly talented and popular performers on these media. Radio and books have also helped, but there has been a conspicuous dearth both of writers deeply interested and fully informed about conservation and of journalists who as editors or commentators have had any understanding of the essential issues. Newspapers have given wide publicity to news which has been supplied to them, and to outside articles and correspondence on the subject, yet compared with the arts, sports, fashion, business and many other subjects the Press has failed badly in its handling of conservation and of the public's incontestable interest in nature.

The same has been true of the greatest exhibitions, notably Expo '67 in Montreal, which purported to deal with the theme of Man and Nature but signally failed to understand what it was all about. This is the more remarkable since smaller and more specialised exhibitions, such as those organised in London for National Nature Weeks, have shown that the subject lends itself well to this medium. The first National Nature Week gave rise, through the inspiration of the Duke of Edinburgh, to the successful employment of a far more specialised medium, the Study Conference, bringing together picked spokesmen of many different national interests concerned with The Countryside in 1970. While these Conferences attracted little mass publicity they had a great influence in focussing, through their study group reports, the integrated views of a wide range of traditionally conflicting or isolated interests, and persuading many leaders of opinion and policy-formers to reshape their efforts on converging lines. Museums, Zoos and specialised wildlife collections in the countryside or in holiday areas have also been persuaded to take an increasing role in the conservation movement, for which they form a valuable extra shop-window and workshop, not only educationally but in terms of techniques of animal rearing and care.

In the United States interpretive services provided in National Parks and elsewhere, and camps run by bodies such as the Audubon Societies have long been important. Some of these methods, such as nature trails, are now being developed successfully in other parts of the world. Conducted tours to interesting places under specialist guidance also form a growing point. Lectures continue to play a part, but in the more advanced countries this is being squeezed within ever narrower limits by newer media. Among these the production of more comprehensive atlasses with a wider range of diagrams and information, and the growth of cartographic, computer and model-making techniques are significantly extending the range of tools used for the study and dissemination of knowledge of the natural environment, at all levels from the most fundamental to superficial and mass dissemination.

Not only the general public but conservationists themselves often take for granted or ignore this unusually close and happy relationship with so many significant media. As a key aspect in the evolution of the subject it deserves to be more often borne in mind. The medium has multiplied and given extra dimensions to the message; perhaps, in turn, the message has stretched and stimulated the media which have fully embraced it, and helped them to outgrow literary attitudes.

Nevertheless this continuous and widespread stimulation of interest among so many who are without any previous orientation or training in connection with the natural environment, and who do not join or make contact with any of the relevant societies or institutions is at least one of the main causes of the characteristic flabbiness and ineffectiveness at the rank-and-file level of the world conservation movement. Its generals can rightly point to an immense volunteer reserve army, but they have no organised channels or means for actually mobilising it, except on very rare occasions when it may elect to mobilise itself. Nor in the meantime do they dispose of more than the bare minimum of reliably serving personnel and resources to conduct anything beyond a series of effective rearguard actions.

The first major effort to correct this weakness was made in 1961 through the formation of the World Wildlife Fund. After the failure of successive efforts to create a firm financial and membership base for the International Union for Conservation of Nature and Natural Resources at its original home in Brussels a drastic reorganisation was decided upon, involving in 1961 the removal of its headquarters to Switzerland, where the idea of such a Union had been launched half a century earlier. At the same time it was recognised to be unrealistic to expect a body so constituted and composed to serve at the same time as an effective organ for mass publicity, for fund-raising and for acting as an international partner agency to secure the acquisition and scientific management of threatened natural areas. Such functions called for expertise and organisation of a financial, legal, operational and public relations character which was scarcely compatible with the scientific, policy-forming, inter-governmental administrative and educational pre-occupations of the IUCN.

Action was once more triggered by Sir Julian Huxley through some articles late in 1961 in *The Observer* on the dangers threatening African Wildlife. These drew a criticism from Mr. Victor Stolan that whatever else might be done catastrophe was inevitable, "without a vigorous and immediate action to raise the great funds needed". When this was referred to me for advice I found that Peter Scott, then a Vice-President of the International Union, and Guy Mountfort, a leading international ornithologist and business man, shared my view that there was indeed a case for an immediate large-scale international effort to raise really substantial funds. Although my early soundings in the United States in March 1961 proved unrewarding I prepared an outline scheme which was approved in April by the International Union's Executive Board at Morges, Switzerland where the Union's new twin body was to share a house with it. The name World Wildlife Fund, and the Giant Panda symbol were quickly chosen. Prince Philip, Duke of Edinburgh, not only readily consented to become President of the British National Appeal but enlisted the support of Prince Bernhard of the Netherlands as first Patron and later President of the International Trustees.

The Fund was fortunate in attracting keen support at the highest levels from the outset, and in establishing effective world-wide contacts among key figures in international and national conservation. Through the Survival Service of the International Union it was soon provided, by means of the Red Data Books, with much more comprehensive, scientifically thorough and up-to-date information concerning threatened species than had previously been thought possible.

Based on such improved intelligence the Fund was able to start a flow of reliable news about conservation to the world Press and other media which greatly enhanced the quality and expanded the coverage of generally available information. It also helped to give a more balanced and less sterile or negative emphasis by placing in perspective particular threats and alarms. Frequent visiting missions and individual journeys to critical points gave encouragement to previously isolated local champions and informants, and conveyed to governments a new awareness of world vigilance over their treatment of the natural environment and wildlife.

Although conservationists continued to hold many different views, and to act differently in pursuance of different priorities in certain cases, no one publicly disputed the value or challenged the international leadership of the new co-ordinating body. Its strong legal and practical components enabled it to go in and sort out successfully many tangles and, aided by the power of the purse, to offer matching grants for the realisation of many projects which would probably otherwise have foundered or been delayed until too late.

Nevertheless it was a disappointment to the promoters that, possibly owing to the adverse economic climate of the "Sixties", and to the lack of a feeling of participation and responsibility among so many of the interested public, the total funds raised and applied did not prove much greater. It was only in July 1968, after nearly seven years of effort that the total of grants made (to 225 projects) exceeded £1 million (US $2,788,648: Swiss Frs. 12 million).

These projects have however included many first-class achievements such as the rescue, in co-operation with the Spanish Government, of much of the famous Coto Donana wildlife paradise. The Fund's early decisive intervention to save the White Rhinoceros in Uganda, was summarised by the territory's Chief Game Warden in these words:

"... I must stress the tremendous value that the World Wildlife Fund has been to white rhino conservation in Uganda. Firstly the grant has been directly responsible for stopping poaching in the Ajai's Sanctuary" (home of the main stock of 50-60 rhino). "Secondly, it has given the Uganda Government time to find the money required to take over the responsibility of looking after these white rhino permanently."

Individually, and where they happen, such achievements can transform the situation. Globally, they still show up as a disturbingly limited contribution to a vast and urgent problem. Nevertheless, both at world and at national level, as well as locally, they are helping to build up new growing points and centers of effective influence for conservation, at a gradually accelerating pace. In 1968 grants totalled nearly half of the whole amount channeled by the Fund during 1962–7. It is normal experience that the public takes time to adjust to supporting such new charitable causes, and there is no cause to despair of a healthy future growth, whatever impatience may be justly felt at all that is meanwhile being sacrificed, while available resources remain so small.

As the Uganda Chief Game Warden's testimony mentions, one of the main factors demanding a strong and well-endowed world organisation for conservation is the tardiness of governments in recognition and fulfilling their responsibilities in this field. Few, in fact, have so good a record as those of East Africa. In far too many countries it still rests with private initiative either to prod the sluggish authorities into action or even to assume heavy financial and other responsibilities for action which governments ought to have taken.

This widespread failure of politicians and administrators to do their duty is largely traceable to major defects and faults of leadership in three great fields of human endeavour—science, education, and the professions.

Modern science in its origins was closely linked with natural history, and even with activities which we would now include in conservation.

This remained true right up to the days of Darwin, a mere century ago. More recently however the lavish patronage of armed forces, of certain industries and of the State have swung its emphasis away from general biology and from studies basically concerned with the environment, and have led to disproportionate artificially induced expansion in physics, chemistry and certain other branches, including recently the competitive exploration of outer space. This distortion has had not only quantitative but qualitative effects, through offering greater opportunities and prizes, and conferring better status and experience of public affairs, on scientists remote from the mainstream of studies related to the earth and its living creatures. Such studies have thus not only been relatively starved of resources, but have been very thinly served by outstanding scientists capable of providing statesmanlike leadership for their integration and further development.

The imagination to perceive that biology, for example, would need a wide range of undisturbed natural areas available for permanent study, and the energy and leadership to set about securing such areas while there was yet time have been among the casualties of this situation. Only such invaluable mavericks as Sir Arthur Tansley, F.R.S. and Sir Julian Huxley, F.R.S., with their few counterparts in other countries, have worked effectively and continuously within the world of science to prevent this responsibility for the future from being totally neglected. In face of growing evidence to the contrary many biologists have idly assumed that the necessary areas for field studies would always be held available for them by someone else without their needing to give the problem a thought. Meanwhile science and technology have themselves developed into substantial users of land, in some cases threatening the fulfilment of conservation needs. This ostentatious and general unconcern of science with conservation has naturally communicated itself to governments. In view of the almost magic mystique which scientists have acquired among ill-informed politicians and administrators it has tended to pass beyond a merely negative influence and to become a positive incitement to disregard conservation arguments.

Redress arose not from any rational recognition of this blind spot, but in a curiously roundabout manner. Following earlier international polar investigations it was decided after World War II to mount a much more ambitious world program, which became the International Geophysical Year 1957–8, embracing Antarctic exploration, oceanic, meteorological and glaciological research, and the launching of satellites into space. Promoted by the International Council of Scientific Unions, this program attracted massive participation from the U.S.A., U.S.S.R., U.K. and other nations undergoing rapid expansion in these scientific fields. The relative poverty and insignificance of biology was thrown into sharp relief. Led by Sir Rudolph Peters, then President of the I.C.S.U., and by G. Montalenti, then President of the International Union of Biological Sciences, the suggestion circulated in 1959 that a biological year on the same model might do much to catalyse and unify biological research.

Prolonged discussions shifting from Neuchatel to Lisbon and then by Amsterdam to London yielded only a tepid response. It became apparent that such fashionable studies as molecular biology and genetics had little to gain from such a program. The potential was promising only for those branches of biology relating to factors which differed widely in their manifestations in different parts of the world, and therefore especially for ecology, fundamental and applied. Unfortunately it was in this area, with certain exceptions, that scientific development and organisation was least advanced, and that capacity and enthusiasm for world-scale co-operation were feeblest.

Despite repeated disappointments and discouragement the scientific leaders sponsoring the idea did not lose heart, and at a meeting in May 1962, convened, as it happened, at the headquarters of the International Union for Conservation at Morges in Switzerland, the Preparatory Committee created the previous year held its first meeting, and agreed on the broad lines of a possible program. This was revised and elaborated at further meetings in the following year in Rome and Edinburgh, and was accepted by the 10th General Assembly of ICSU in Vienna in November 1963. The idea of a "Year" had had to be stretched, owing to the nature of ecological problems, to a period of some 8 years of which three were devoted to preparation under the Special Committee (SCIBP) and the remaining five were to see the Program run under the guidance of National Committees, of which more than 50 have been formed. In effect there are seven distinct but closely related programs in terrestrial, marine, freshwater and human ecology, in the use and management of biological productivity for human welfare, and in conservation, of which last I am the Convener.

Unluckily the period when money could be fairly freely secured for good scientific projects was already at an end by the time that the IBP was finally worked out and agreed upon. The ensuing chronic financial stringency of the later 'sixties not only prevented the initiation or severely restricted the execution of many parts of the program, but also detracted from its capacity to assist and encourage biology to catch up with more favored branches of science. Despite all such obstacles and inhibitions the Program is making considerable progress, not least in the realm of conservation.

At any rate the inclusion of conservation as a main element in this worldwide, strictly scientific enterprise means that a start has been made in neutralising the effect of previous scientific apathy, and educating governments in the essential role of conservation in future scientific plans.

In September 1968 the representatives of over sixty nations at the International Biosphere Conference in Paris lent strong support in this direction, and in December 1968 further backing was provided by a unanimous resolution of the United Nations Assembly to mount a special review of environmental problems.

In education it is also necessary to neutralise the adverse repercussions from traditional apathy or hostility towards science and to stimulate educational use of the full potential of biology which has always been handicapped by fear, neglect and lack of appreciation among too many teachers. These difficulties have been aggravated by the recent intense preoccupation in scientific circles with mathematically measureable indoor controlled experiments on specialised particles rather than whole organisms. Ecology and other field studies have thus been brought under suspicion of barely ranking as scientific. The study of living creatures has ceased, for many of its practitioners, to require being able to recognise any one of these when it is met, or to begin to understand how they manage to live in nature.

Under such influences it has been a hard struggle to achieve the build-up recently begun of university departments working in ecology and in studies of the natural environment and its conservation. The United States, surprisingly, made an indifferent start in this field, partly no doubt owing to the unwise pressure exerted earlier by missionaries of conservation, who sought through political channels to impose a propagandist type of conservation teaching on state educational systems.

In Britain, while ecological studies at university level have existed for around forty years at Oxford, they have unfortunately remained fragmented and have never become as effective as they should have been. The launching, on the initiative of the Nature Conservancy, of a post-graduate course in conservation and ecology at University College London in 1960, jointly run by the departments of Botany, Zoology and Geography, represented the belated start of a modernising trend which has spread to Aberdeen, Edinburgh, Bangor, Wye and other centers. This has been ably backed up by the field centers of the Field Studies Council, which had been created, perhaps a little before its time, by Sir Arthur Tansley in 1943. Problems and developments in this field are described and reviewed in *Science Out of Doors*, the report of a study group under my chairmanship in 1963.

In the United States since 1958 a fine effort has been made to modernise teaching of biology in schools through the Biological Sciences Curriculum Study of the American Institute of Biological Sciences. Guided by Dr Bentley Glass and a steering committee including research biologists, teachers of biology in high schools and educational specialists and administrators, the course in biology for secondary schools was entirely rewritten under the direction of Dr Arnold B. Grobman in three variant forms. A "Green Version" placed emphasis on living creatures and their evolution and ecology, a "Blue Version" on the molecular level and a "Yellow Version" on the cellular, but 70 per cent of the material was common to all three. The whole project was subjected to testing and verification in all its aspects with immense thoroughness and imagination, and the experience and results have been placed at the disposal of educational authorities throughout the world.

Such action was long overdue. In Britain an official publication issued in 1960 by the Ministry of Education had roundly stated:

"The place which is occupied by advanced biological studies in schools, especially boys' schools, at present, is unfortunately that of vocational training rather than of an instrument of education." A large fraction of the teaching was aimed to help budding doctors through their first examination ". . . and the contribution which the study makes to the pupil's education is so small that it is doubtful whether such a subject ought to find a place in a school at all."

To have reached the nineteen-sixties with a type of biological education thus officially stigmatised as perhaps worse than useless is an indication that it would be difficult to overstate the scale of the default in this field of British educationists.

To this default is traceable a substantial part of the failures and weaknesses at political, administrative and management levels, which so greatly increase the difficulties of securing scientifically sound and socially satisfying action on the care of the natural environment. Perhaps even more serious in the computer age is the denial to the nation's students of such an ideal educational background for assimilating information theory, and learning to feel at home in a world where communications problems assume ever greater significance.

An effort in the direction of modernisation was eventually made through the medium of the Nuffield Foundation Biology Project. The Nature Conservancy made repeated initiatives both at a specialised level and through such wider channels as the Countryside in 1970 follow-up conference on educational aspects at the University of Keele in March 1965. This led to the creation of a Council for Environmental Education, which was finally launched into operation in 1968. Although the teaching of biology in a modern spirit and by modern methods must on any objective analysis rank among the essential responsibilities of a worth-while educational system the record unfortunately shows that serious attention has only belatedly begun to be given to the question after prolonged external pressure, notably from conservationists, who are so badly handicapped by the prolonged defects in this field of education.

As Annex 3 shows, there is a flow pattern to be traced from the fundamentals of minerals, soils, water, land surface, vegetation, and animal life and atmosphere, through the relevant research studies and the educational and information processes to the professions and technologies, and thence to such fields of application as agriculture, forestry, fisheries, water conservation, engineering projects, landscaping, recreation and so forth. The natural environment in its various aspects provides, in effect, the tangible raw material for many intangible human processing activities which, at different levels and in differing combinations, make use of this material to serve all kinds of human needs.

In this flow pattern a key place is held by the professions which actually shape man's impact on the land—the foresters, agronomes, agricultural advisers, land managers, developers, regional and local planners, civil and mining engineers, economists, bankers, lawyers, administrators and others. If the scientific knowledge and outlook acquired through the sum of research efforts is not effectively communicated to these professions through education, training and information, then the management of the supreme asset formed by the natural environment will fall short of the standards which can reasonably be expected. And that, of course, is precisely what it does. Inadequate in coverage and indifferent in quality as is much of the information and understanding so far available concerning the natural environment it is already sufficient to sustain a vastly superior standard of professional performance, in selecting the best land uses and in attaining the most beneficial combination of sustained yields, than is so far visible in practice. The blind spot in human awareness, education and training in regard to the natural environment and natural resources extends to the professions as well as to education and science where its outline has already been traced.

That it also extends to the workings and the personnel of governments and of international organisations is not so much a further weakness as an inevitable consequence of the three areas of weakness just mentioned. These authorities are staffed and ruled either by more or less educated laymen, whose outlook and knowledge derives from the normal educational system with all its failings and gaps, or by generalist professionals with higher training in law, economics, accountancy, or sometimes general science. Of these the economists, whose influence on investment projects is immense are, except partially in the United States, equipped for their task with an ignorance of the land and its special problems which is usually almost absolute. The same is true, more or less worldwide, of accountants and general scientists, while lawyers differ only in that a fair proportion of them have special knowledge of certain highly restricted and irrelevant aspects of land problems, such as tenure and trespass.

At a more detailed and critical level of project design and co-ordination, advice and recommendations usually come from agricultural or forestry technicians, hydrologists and geologists or, above all, from engineers, with whom none of the groups mentioned previously are in a position to argue constructively. This is unfortunate since the education and professional formation of these technical specialists is far from providing them with a sound basis for judging the environmental, social and economic implications of the courses and projects which on narrow technical grounds they are led to recommend.

Inevitably, therefore, the recent history of governmental and international authorities in taking decisions and adopting policies concerned with land and natural resources is one of the blind leading the blind.

The relatively disappointing and often harmful results of the vastly expensive and well-intended international efforts over the past two decades to promote through economic and technical aid an advance in standards of life in developing countries reflect the collective failure of these authorities to achieve a thorough and balanced scientific assessment of the complex of problems confronting them. They also indicate a grossly excessive reliance on the counsels of blinkered economists and narrow technicians seeking to resolve problems beyond their understanding by the repetitive application of the limited techniques and ideas forming their entire stock in trade. Among instances coming to mind is the trumpeted world conference going under the name of UNCTAD—the United Nations Conference on Trade and Development, first convened at Geneva in 1964. Far from initiating a new era, as was promised, it served mainly to demonstrate the bankruptcy of constructive ideas and of scientific principles among the imposing galaxy of experts assembled.

Two test cases of first-class international significance which threw a vivid light on governmental attitudes to conservation were those of the Serengeti National Park in 1956 and of the island of Aldabra in 1967.

In the first of these the British administration of the then UN trusteeship territory of Tanganyika (the scene of the disastrous Ground Nut Scheme which squandered more than £30 million in the 1940's through neglect to take ecological advice) found itself embarrassed by some problems in administering the Serengeti National Park as it had been constituted in 1951. The fundamental problem was the reduced carrying capacity of the area owing to uncontrolled deforestation and reduced water yields, aggravated by the bringing into agricultural use of neighboring areas which had previously in unfavorable years been available as a safety buffer zone for the vast herds of wildebeest, zebras, antelopes and other herbivores moving seasonally from one grazing area to another on a shifting migratory pattern. The practical and political problem was what to do with the Masai tribesmen and their increasing stock of cattle who for these and other reasons were being forced into competition with the park's wildlife.

The harassed administrators first turned their thoughts to amputating a large area from the Park and handing it over to pacify the Masai, of whom they stood in awe. As these thoughts gained currency, however, in a White Paper issued in 1956 they came to realise with surprise and distaste that the international conservationists found these proposals highly objectionable, and were in a position to intervene to some effect with the Colonial Office in London on the matter. Under intense pressure the Governor eventually agreed to seek ecological advice, and the Fauna Preservation Society sent out Professor W. H. Pearsall, F.R.S., an outstanding plant ecologist, to make an ecological survey and to advise on the scheme. A Serengeti Committee of Enquiry followed, leading to a revised White Paper containing a compromise which was held at the time to be satisfactory, providing for a large extension in the form of broad corridors for migrating herds towards Lake Victoria and the Masai Mara Game Reserve across the Kenya border, but taking out the highly important Ngorongoro Crater of some 1,500,000 acres as a "Conservation Area" to be shared between the Masai and the wild herbivores.

Although the administration, once convinced of the high importance of the conservation aspects, made a creditable effort to satisfy these, the handling of the affair allowed grossly insufficient time for an ecological survey and assessment of such magnitude and complexity. In particular it did not permit a proper comparison and integration of the hastily sponsored survey with work of the utmost significance simultaneously being carried out over a more adequate period by Dr Bernard Grzimek and his son, and by a group of American range ecologists, whose findings were about to revolutionise scientific knowledge of the management of such vast herds of herbivores, numbering some 600,000 head in 1960. In his best-seller book and highly successful film *Serengeti Must Not Die*, Dr Grzimek quite justifiably used some of these data to attack the compromise adopted by the Legislative Council of Tanganyika. The embarrassment resulting from a certain conflict of views among the ranks of conservationists was however probably far outweighed by the resulting sustained international publicity for the Park and the Conservation Area, which obliged the government and enabled the reconstituted National Parks Trustees to face their responsibilities for the area with a new perspective and attitude. Right or wrong, the 1959 settlement has therefore yielded results in practice which are as satisfactory as could reasonably have been expected from the standpoint of conservation, for which it undoubtedly represented a decisive victory of the utmost value elsewhere.

The Aldabra story was very different. This Indian Ocean coral atoll, some 600 miles east of southern Tanganyika, had long been famous among scientists for its unique forms, including the spectacular giant tortoises, rivalling those of Galapagos. Only lack of water and other amenities had saved its fauna and flora from the fate which had long since overtaken the Dodo at not great distance away. From time to time sanguine exploiters had cast eyes on it, and on one such occasion Charles Darwin himself had come out as a champion in its defence. During the 1950's a further threat arose, but after discussions with the Colonial Office the more objectionable proposals were dropped, although a commercial lease was given which brought certain injurious results on one island.

After 1960, however, a much more serious peril arose. Deprived one by one of the continental military air and naval bases on which so much money had been squandered in Africa and Asia, those who ran the collapsing British Empire east of Suez were forced to conclude that a less ephemeral line of communication could be created only by using small oceanic islands with populations too small and unsophisticated to follow the normal practice of making them untenable. As this even threatened to occur on so obscure an island as Gan in the Maldives, where serious trouble was encountered, it was finally perceived that true political safety could be found only on islands where the population was approximately nil. By a transparent device, therefore, while territories were annually being subtracted from the Empire, a new one was suddenly added to the list—the British Indian Ocean Territory, as it was grandiosely proclaimed in November 1965. This consisted of a handful of outlying specks of land, no more than about 1,000 guaranteed politically impotent inhabitants, and less than 100 square miles of land surface. Here was to be the last stand in the Indian Ocean of the British Raj, or at least of its air marshals. They had first, however, to secure the annihilation of the British admirals' rival force of aircraft carriers, the survival of which would probably have defeated the financing of their plan for a land staging airfield to move airborne reinforcements to the Far East.

With the usual unwarranted secrecy plans were made to locate an airfield neatly upon the scientifically most important area of Aldabra, with a harbor at the other end of the atoll, linked by a road involving disturbance of the entire intervening area. No plan could have been devised to cause more extensive and irreversible damage for a limited and ephemeral objective, since the useful life of such a facility could not have begun until the middle 1970's and on all precedents would have been unlikely to outlast the '80's. In the opinion of such independent authorities as the Director of the Institute of Strategic Studies the project could not be justified in terms of any known or intelligible strategic requirement. In the opinion of the Royal Society and of the Smithsonian Institution, which collaborated effectively in London and Washington, it would have caused irreparable harm to scientific interests of world significance. Successive groups of visiting scientists undertaking a high-pressure survey of the atoll brought to light a wealth of detailed information which vindicated this assessment. The British Ministry of Defence, when pressed, attempted to suggest that the need for this facility was largely to satisfy the Pentagon in Washington. Unfortunately for the Ministry excellent scientific contacts through United States channels revealed this argument as another distortion of the truth; Whitehall was as usual trying to find an alibi for a project of its own which was coming under unexpectedly heavy fire.

Although by November 1967 the arguments publicly given for the project had been so shattered by criticism that it would clearly have been an improper use of public funds to proceed with it, the Ministers and administrators concerned were still recalcitrant to the voice of reason when their resistance was finally overcome by another factor which took them entirely by surprise. Their own incompetence in managing the national economy led at this moment to the sudden devaluation of the pound sterling, in circumstances which demanded a large loan and the acceptance of a program of financial cuts. In the light of these the Aldabra extravagance and the East of Suez fantasies of which it formed part could no longer be persisted in. While the right answer had been forthcoming in the end, and Aldabra had been saved, the incident left a bad taste. It served warning on conservationists that where such a project has been taken to the heart of the System in Britain no amount of fact-finding and no weight of contrary reasons can avail to secure a change of mind, while a change of heart is entirely out of the question. Nothing short of a massive national calamity such as devaluation, or a resistance campaign of almost Czecho-Slovak dimensions, as over the Stansted Airport project, will in these conditions secure a stay of execution. Even then the slipperiness and secretiveness of the authorities make it dangerous to relax vigilance for a moment. These hard-learnt lessons have been well digested, and future games of this kind will be played according to different rules, less favorable and less congenial to the secretive manipulators of public policy and public funds. In the present worldwide revulsion among men and women at being pushed around and kept in the dark by bureaucracy and its Ministerial slaves the challenges posed by the conservation movement have had a significant share in stimulating critical objection, and in demonstrating that it can prove effective. In reflecting upon the problems of harmonising the wants and needs of mankind with the care of the natural environment and of its living creatures it is worth bearing in mind that in such matters as resisting ill-considered and disingenuous projects hatched for "Reasons of State" people and nature often share a common interest. "Conquests of Nature" are frequently also conquests by special interests of resources which could have been better used to fulfil more basic and urgent human needs in less spectacular ways.

10

WHERE WE STAND NOW

HAVING now reviewed what has so far been thought and done concerning conservation and its role in applying ecology to the environment, the time has come to appraise progress so far. The word "*conservation*" is itself sometimes a stumbling-block, through no fault of its own. Although it has undergone several changes of meaning, or at least of emphasis, it has related throughout to a clearly differentiated approach to a definable range of problems. This approach, however, cuts across the preconceived narrow and materialist set of values and idea-systems inculcated by dominant existing cultures both of East and West. Largely for that reason the word itself has been widely shunned up to very recently in conventional circles, until unmistakeable developments have forced it upon the notice of all serious people.

Difficulties raised about defining it sometimes thinly cloak a wish that it and all that it signifies would simply go away. It contains revolutionary potentialities, indirectly inimical to many comfortable habits of mind. Semantically, the real difficulties probably stem mainly from the fact that until lately the various subsidiary approaches and activities which as a group add up to *conservation* in the broad sense were not properly distinguished or placed in any meaningful relation to it.

A narrower and better understood approach to some of the same problems is expressed in the term *preservation*, implying an effort so far as possible to keep in existence *unchanged* things or situations which have been inherited from the past. Another, familiar approach is to stress defence against interference, damage or destruction as the relevant aspect and principal aim; the key-word for that approach is *protection*. Another line of thought concentrates upon *withholding* from exploitation or use areas and resources which it is felt ought to be held back either against future needs or because they are best kept as they are, or because currently available resource managers cannot be trusted to use them with discretion; here the key-word is *reservation* and the areas so treated are *reserves*, such as forest or game reserves. Yet another approach, especially applicable to threatened animals, is more pre-occupied with taking advantage of and reinforcing a geographically or otherwise isolated and undisturbed area by conferring on it the status of a guarded *refuge* or sanctuary. At the other extreme emphasis may be put either on enforcement of restraints and technical practices on measures of *resource management*, to safeguard the future of renewable resources through giving paramountcy to the principle of *sustained yield*, or on securing a balanced blend of several distinct types of economic and social "crop" through insistence on *multi-purpose use*. If the method of enabling a number of diverse uses to be reconciled is by assigning a separate subdivision to each within the total area, the approach is better called *zoning* or *segregation* of users.

Conservation in its modern sense is a broader concept, comprehending all of these limited approaches and more. Originating with the work of such scientifically-minded and forest-conscious pioneers as George Perkins Marsh a century ago it became caught up in controversial campaigns of economics, politics and developing technology. Somewhat distorted by these experiences it was redefined sixty years ago by the forester Gifford Pinchot as a *comprehensive and well-planned management of natural resources of every character, based on sound ethical and economic grounds*. His associate W. J. McGee defined it as *the use of the natural resources for the greatest good of the greatest number for the longest time*. The briefest definition runs: *Conservation is wise use*, but this implies acceptance of the sophisticated assumption that non-use may be an acceptable type of use.

Do such earlier definitions adequately convey what conservation has now come to mean? To meet present needs we might be nearer the mark in using some such formula as this; *Conservation means all that man thinks and does to soften his impact upon his natural environment and to satisfy all his own true needs while enabling that environment to continue in healthy working order.*

While still far from perfect, such wording imports the necessary elements of universality and permanence, of conscious collective self-restraint, of the overriding significance, as a limiting factor, of the natural environment and its health, and of the problem of satisfying human needs, both immediate and long term, as one to be solved within this context. All that has gone before can, without straining, be comprehended within such an approach. This is why conservation touches the heart of public affairs, and of ethics, economics and the application of science. It registers the proper limits of human interference with the environment, and shows how to ensure their observance.

Reference to *"environment"* calls for comment on that word also. Until quite recently its common use was largely topographical; it signified the surroundings, loosely indicated of some point or area such as a city.

Recently popular usage has taken over what was earlier almost a restricted biological sense, denoting everything affecting the way an organism lives or grows. When I was taking part in early official discussions in 1964 concerning the naming of the Natural Environment Research Council the choice of this word was still regarded by some as rather strange and far-fetched. Now it has attracted such a following that it might make things easier for many to explain to them that conservation is care for the natural environment, or that environmental policies are virtually indistinguishable from conservation policies wrapped up with a currently more fashionable label.

Conservation is a late-comer—still virtually a newcomer—to the hierarchy of human thoughts and motives. As soon as primitive man began to hunt, or to domesticate livestock, or to sow seed he was engaging in a definable activity, which would qualify in due course for description among cultures, even of a low order. When he later went on to create organised societies, and urban settlements, or to develop warlike pursuits, or external trade, the evolution became more subtle and indirect, and its identification involved a higher degree of abstraction, observation and generalisation. Our modern society has now moved to a plane of much greater abstraction, when such fluid and indefinite activities as tourism, recreation and conservation have to be assessed and measured in relation to their effects upon that other fashionable imponderable, the environment.

One of the pitfalls of such third-order abstractions and generalisations is the tendency to confuse the adoption of new terms or labels for things already existing and well known with the emergence of new factors or situations. We may thus both fail to appreciate new developments or important changes which remain unidentified, and delude ourselves into supposing that other factors, actually unaltered, are new merely because it has suddenly become fashionable to stick new labels upon them. In no field of discussion is it more important, and in none should it be simpler, to insist always on keeping our feet on the ground. The "site" of the civil engineer, the "zone" of the regional or town and country planner, the "landscape" of the landscape architect, the "ecosystem" of the ecologist, the "stand" of the forester, the "land" of the farmer or developer, the "countryside" of the preservationist and the "natural area" of the conservationist exist side by side on this same earth, even when they do not actually overlap or coincide. Only the jargon, the mental compartments, and the artificially segregated professions and intellectual disciplines which we create as obstacles to our own understanding prevent the rather simple truth from becoming plain to us.

While we are discussing definitions it may be convenient here to add a few sub-divisions which will be helpful in later discussion. Conservation issues cannot arise except where something affecting the natural environment, or the wild creatures included in it, is done or proposed to be done by human beings. But within that broad area conservation issues fall into a number of readily distinguishable classes. In part, conservation is concerned with works or practices directly aimed at improving the functioning of the environment, such as flood and erosion control, soil and water conservation, coast defence and land reclamation from the sea. This aspect may be called *structural conservation*. Its motive and nature may be *remedial*, to check damage already set in train, or *improving*, to take advantage of some unused potential.

For many, the most practical aspect of conservation is that which guides wise use and continuing productivity of renewable natural resources. This may conveniently be termed *sustained yield conservation*. Originating with forestry, it has been extended to other fields. For others, emphasis is strongest on the demarcation, study and continued existence of the natural heritage in terms of ecosystems, sites and species of plants and animals. This is known as *nature conservation*, while a body which gives effect to it is a *nature conservancy*.

Fully as important to many is the safeguarding for public enjoyment of scenery or landscape, and of opportunities for outdoor recreation, field sports, tourism and kindred activities. The pursuit of such objects may be termed *landscape or amenity conservation*. This includes not only *preservation* of what has been inherited but the making of new landscapes, amenities and facilities. Bodies pursuing such objects may be National Parks Services, Countryside or Regional Planning Commissions, Sports Councils or Bureaus of Recreation.

No doubt certain other categories might usefully be added; the point has however been sufficiently made that there are large and active movements, tending sometimes to regard themselves as the whole of conservation, which are really only parts of it, and would do well to bear that in mind.

Conservation, however, is not only more comprehensive but more teleological, more dynamic and more positive in its approach than its parts. Not content with desiring to see the continuance of essential features in the natural environment and of its full and healthy functioning, conservation persists in delving more deeply into the reasons for its own and conflicting attitudes, the methods by which its aims can be achieved, and the changes of outlook and practice implied on the part of all the interests concerned.

Conservation demands a positive, interventionist, self-conscious, participating approach. It demands openmindedness, energy, effort, leadership, unity of aim, and the ability to resolve discord and sectional conflicts. While history shows that these qualities have not infrequently been forthcoming when they were most needed, it also provides many instances of conservationists failing to live up to such standards. How far has the progress of conservation been checked by such shortcoming? How far does the rate of advance depend upon the contribution of declared conservationists, or how far is it demanded and brought about by the interplay of broader social and economic trends? Such issues are complex, and not to be readily answered.

The specific traceable contributions of many groups and individuals are clearly written on the record, as is the cost of certain schisms and bouts of inertia. Yet the sum of conservation activity and development appears to be something greater, elicited and shaped partly by tacit and hidden forces generated in other parts of human societies and economies. There is some reason to suppose that this more cryptic element is playing a role of increasing importance as compared with the overt movement.

Because the theater of action for conservation is the natural environment, however modified it may be, we are easily misled into regarding it as something belonging to and shaped by that environment. On the contrary, the consciousness of a need for conservation, the formulation of its pattern and its nature, and the significance socially and politically attached to taking any action about it are inseparably linked with specific types and evolutionary stages of human society. In a primitive food-gathering and hunting culture the idea of conservation occurs to no one and the problem itself hardly exists. Hunting has to become sufficiently effective to cause dramatic reductions in game before the problem arises, and even then a number of psychological conditions will determine whether it is recognised, and if so whether the need is acted upon. Where the danger signals are plain to powerful rulers, and point to a trend which they are unwilling to accept and have the resources to rectify, measures of conservation have been known to emerge very early in history, particularly in connection with hunting of large game by the privileged.

A second favorable case for the early emergence of conservation measures is when men permanently settled on an area are compelled to recognise the appearance of some new unfavorable factor which they believe to be capable of control, such as drought or flood, or certain kinds of erosion, bringing consequences which they are under some compulsion to mitigate as an alternative to abandoning their settlement.

A much less favorable case is that where mobile pastoralists, or shifting cultivators, or miners cause damage which their way of life readily permits them to move away from and forget, and which they feel no inducement to repair. Less favorable still is the situation in which decisions relating to conservation requirements rest with politicians, administrators, managers or technicians ignorant of any such background and preoccupied solely with other objects. Even an illiterate nomad has more awareness of the limits of tolerable land use and of the penalties for ignoring them than have such literate ignoramuses. Lacking first-hand experience of the environment and its responses, and lacking also any education and training to inform them of what is scientifically known on the subject, they use modern technological resources to inflict vast and enduring injuries, often on lands to which they are strangers sent in the sacred name of technical assistance.

We are living at a moment of history when specialisation and division of labor may have reached their most destructive stage in this respect. In earlier years no men knowing so little of the land would have acquired such great power over it; in later years there is reason to hope that human knowledge will be so mobilised and disseminated that it will serve effectively to guide and restrain human impacts on the environment. Indeed, the record shows that there is already a fairly strong trend in that direction.

It is a great mistake to believe, as many still do, that the need for conservation is a minor matter and that the capacity technically to meet it and politically to ensure that it is met may safely be despised. The handicap for conservationists has been that their effectiveness must await a certain stage in cultural evolution, but precisely the same was true of the rule of law. Considering the relatively poor level of leadership until recently of the world conservation movement, its minute resources and the amount of inertia and opposition with which it has had to contend, its inexorable advance on so many fronts is all the more impressive. It has not finished yet.

Conservation was inherently disqualified from maturing at a much earlier stage of civilisation than the present. The necessary basis of knowledge and understanding, the bitter experience required to educate public opinion, and the evolution of institutions, habits of mind, and techniques essential to enable it to function could not have come much earlier.

That is sad, in view of the serious damage which has been inflicted meanwhile, and it adds to the urgency of making conservation effective everywhere without further delay. In order to succeed in this task a clear understanding of the difficulties and limitations, and of the true potential of conservation and the means of realising it is indispensable. Although knowledge of past mistakes and achievements cannot by itself provide such an understanding it can contribute greatly towards it.

As the urge towards conservation is provided mainly by failures to prevent injury to the environment it tends to originate in some painful and often controversial situation which makes for a bad start. To convert such a negative drive into positive and balanced policies and programs is all the harder because to a large extent the two phases appeal to and demand the energies of incompatible human personalities. It is therefore not surprising that the history of conservation abounds in controversies, schisms and rifts, and in periods of anachronistic rigidity alternating with rapid transformations. It follows also that conservationists frequently make themselves unpopular through what may seem to others a tendency to arbitrary and inconvenient interferences or objections.

One of the main recent trends in conservation has been to supersede impulsive half-baked reactions by the careful choice of major test cases to be fought according to a much broader strategy. That strategy employs each selected contest to press home the full significance of the conservation issues and to show all concerned that they have more to gain by recognising these issues and seeking a common meeting-ground than by seeking to ignore and override them at the cost of antagonising world public opinion and meeting unexpected difficulties and delays. Merely emotional reactions on parochial, sectional or sentimental grounds to projects which are essentially reasonable and necessary have been successfully discouraged in many cases. To choose which ones to fight, to win a substantial proportion, and for the rest to leave only a Pyrrhic victory to opponents has been the line.

In such ways a new climate of opinion has been formed, and new ground-rules have been gradually accepted, enabling much new development to go forward uncontested because the objections which conservationists would have had to press have been intelligently anticipated and their contribution to a more balanced project has been perceived and embodied from an early stage, before open conflict could arise. This profound and rapid evolution has demanded not only new strategy and tactics, but new patterns of conservation body manned by new types of conservationists.

Although the driving influence has been to improve conservation's capability for successful struggle, the effect has been to open quite new perspectives, to win a new and much enhanced status, and to trigger off new thinking which in turn leads to new and expanded programs and more complex interrelations. For example, conservationists are less and less exclusively preoccupied with "saving" particular national parks and reserves (although the absolute importance of these is greater than ever) but with monitoring, protecting and improving the total environment, whether natural or man-moulded. The focal area for this interest is landscape, its deterioration and decline, and the means by which it can be revived. An important ancillary interest is the creeping pollution of the total environment and the means of identifying, checking and reversing the processes responsible.

Until very recently there were bewildering contrasts between the goals, methods, affiliations and performance of different national or regional groups of conservationists. Even among English-speaking peoples the Americans, British, New Zealanders, Australians and East and South Africans all went about the business in entirely different ways, which were scarcely comprehensible to one another. Conferences, visits and other exchanges have lately ironed some of these difficulties out among the leaders, but down the line they still tend to persist, until suddenly some major incident leads to an abrupt change.

Given the present leadership and organisation on the world plane, this is no longer a serious handicap to co-operation on important issues. It does, however, mean that many conservationists still find themselves in a considerable muddle over their basic values and aims, and may have to look far afield for skilled help in sorting themselves out. Clearly we are in the midst of the most rapid transition ever known during the long story of relations between men and nature. Clearly also the age-old predominance of contact arising from everyday labor and activity by a large part of mankind in the open air is rapidly ending. Men so occupied are becoming, in all but the least developed countries, a minority, and in places a small minority, of the working population. On the other hand, in most advanced countries the number of hours spent in some form of open-air leisure, often at a distance from home and in environments hitherto largely left alone by mankind, is rapidly increasing, with a resulting periodic mass experience of nature totally different from the previous continuous experience of countrymen.

Being voluntary and spontaneous, and aided by high mobility, this new mass experience is highly selective and responsive to encouragement and guidance. As a result of all this enthusiasm for leisure spent out of doors, new activities and employments more or less directly concerned with the natural environment are springing up. There are rangers or wardens of national parks, game reserves or nature reserves, teachers and students engaged in field study courses, biologists such as ecologists working on research projects in the field, catchers and keepers of animals maintained for research, for education or for spectacular purposes in free-range conditions, nature photographers and film-makers, operators of tourist facilities based upon nature such as safari parties, and plenty more.

This growing band of mediators or bridging agents between man and nature is clearly destined to play a role immensely more important in the future than the already significant one which it is already performing. On the quality and vision of this picked band, and on its success in keeping close to nature and firmly tuned to the influences and needs of the natural environment, much will depend. On the one hand it will use its skills and resources to pre-select the kinds of natural experience which are sought or will be appreciated by different types of people or for different purposes, and to facilitate access to the right places in the right conditions. At the same time it will function, on a sustained yield basis, to conserve and if possible extend and improve the natural assets in face of the risks and pressures to which they are exposed. It will thus have to realise on a much expanded scale the concept of conservation as the practical application of ecology.

Differences and confusion among ecologists themselves add to the problems of those who seek to apply ecology through conservation, or to utilise it as raw material for education and training. Such differences also give rise to an often critical attitude towards ecology among other scientists.

The impact of ecology upon the attitudes and practices of mankind has hitherto been disappointingly limited, and far below the obvious potential of the contribution which it could and should make. Convinced adherents of the cause often put this down to the resistant mass of age-old prejudices embedded in human folklore and tradition, to the self-regarding hostility or coldness of great interests who see their brash exploitation of natural resources being threatened or reined back by adoption of ecological principles, and to the blindness and ignorance of so many educationists, editors and other masters of the media of communication, whose townbred outlook leads them to misunderstand and hamper free expression and informed discussion of ecological issues and contributions. All these are genuine and important factors in the conspicuous drag which has so badly retarded the conservation revolution, but they are not the whole story.

Reflecting on the modern history of science it appears that three main conditions must be satisfied before one of its branches can exert a revolutionary influence on the course of civilisation. First, it must have the potential, in terms of opportunities for new discoveries of great and dynamic significance both for other branches of science and for human practice. Second, it must enlist enough scientists of adequate caliber to make a convincing start in developing that scientific potential through research and experiment, and in creating a vigorous, self-conscious, confident grouping within the world scientific community. And third, it must build the right bridges, both within the sciences and across to the user and other related interests, to make itself a practical as well as an academic force in the world. Ecology has been perhaps too prone to preen itself over its good fortune in being born so well endowed with the first of these conditions that it has neglected to get on briskly enough with fulfilling the second and third.

In seeking reasons for the difficulties and weaknesses of the conservation movement, and an understanding of the means of surmounting them, it is essential to look searchingly into the condition of ecological science. Its long expected spectacular growth as a means of dynamic and synoptic interpretation of the functions and relationships of living creatures within their natural environment has not yet occurred. At a time when new studies such as molecular biology have rocketed to fame and leadership within a mere decade, ecology can point only to a below-average rate of expansion during now over half a century of organised effort.

The unfolding of such a science, some believed, would bring with it wisdom, refreshment and a balanced understanding, and would correct the inhuman distortions imposed by the runaway expansion of physics and chemistry, and by the brazen materialist greed of an exploiting civilization. Unhappily, as yet, things have not worked out like that. Far from breeding a race of benevolent superminds modern ecology has either been content or been compelled to accept a lowly role on the sidelines of biology, which has itself undergone a sad depression of relative status since the great days of Darwin and Huxley.

Ecology has bred only a handful of outstanding pathfinders and has tended to settle for a somewhat ineffective existence dispersed in small institutions and schools each convinced that the others fall below first-rate scientific standards, in which they are often right.

Are these, the question poses itself, really the men and women who are destined to restore unity and coherence to science in its quest for a key to the workings of nature? Do they look like inspiring and enlightening mankind to throw off the perversions of outlook which mar our relations with the natural environment?

If we are compelled sadly to give "No" as our answer that does not mean that we can write off ecology and ecologists. On the contrary, it means that redoubled efforts must promptly be made to secure for them the status which the world stituation demands, and to ensure that they live up to it.

To look down upon ecologists, and consequently to deny them resources, opportunities and collaboration is an attitude which has partly been responsible for the pitiably small current role and contribution of ecology in science and in public affairs. On the other hand ecologists must face the fact that they have largely failed to justify and to turn to advantage the immense goodwill which ecology in the abstract commands among thinking people. They have failed to establish effective and fruitful links with many neighboring branches of science and the professsions, which could help and stimulate them if such links had been created.

Their scientific standards and methods, and above all their sectarian divisions into conflicting or standoffish groupings, have been not unjustly criticised elsewhere in the scientific community. They have been slow to learn biometrics, slow to clarify the definition of terms and the methods of analysis or measurement, and slow to develop the possibilities of controlled experiment in the field. While some ecologists have seemed addicted to dubious generalisations devoid of experimental or even observational backing, others have retreated into elaborations of particular techniques or the pursuit of highly specialised studies remote from the main stream.

No evidence has been given of a vigorously expanding science making a series of successive breakthroughs on a basis of imaginative but down-to-earth teamwork. The more highly the potential value of the role of ecology is rated the more disappointment must be felt at its actual record.

It is now a quarter of a century since a retiring President of the Ecological Society of America aptly wrote in *Ecology*:

> "I am dissatisfied with the present professional position of ecology ... ecologists have 'missed the boat' so many times that the process is becoming habitual ... a scrum develops at the gang-plank and the boat leaves without them. . . . This is the picture as I see it. If it is a true image it is an unfortunate one as I know of no other group of biologists who have more to offer mankind in the practical economic sense and few disciplines, I think, have more to offer biology in the realm of pure science."

Distasteful as it may seem to some, most sciences which have made rapid strides have done so because of the keen interest and stimulating pressure of groups who wanted the answer to some problems and would not rest content until the scientists gave it to them. Ecologists on the whole have neither cultivated nor appreciated such a type of consumer demand for ecology, but have given an impression of preferring to be left to their own devices even at the price of being relegated nearly to the back of the queue for resources to expand their activities.

Such an attitude could only have been justified if ecology had been confidently pursuing definite lines which could be counted upon to yield first-class scientific results, and if the pursuit of such lines was either incompatible with, or removed all need for entering into, close relations with other interested scientific or technical workers. The record shows that neither of these justifications has existed, and that the fragmentation and isolation of ecology has not been in its own best interests.

At a world level, all previous efforts by the International Union of Biological Sciences and the Internationl Union for the Conservation of Nature to interest ecologists in giving the necessary minimum support for sustaining an international working group of their own have come to nothing. Whether the newest unit, modishly named INTECOL, will fare any better it is too early to say. Outside Britain, Japan appears to be the only nation in which ecologists of different types and institutional affiliations show some positive interest in actively co-operating.

As I said in my Horace Albright Lecture to the University of California in 1964;

"If ecology is not studied well enough, and if conservationists are not keenly enough interested in its development, people cannot be blamed for failing to understand its relevance or to appreciate its importance. Unfortunately, it is difficult to deny that this has been the case. Ecologists have failed on at least three major issues. First, unlike better disciplined sciences, ecology still uses different terms and standards for the same things, depending on whether the ecologist was trained in, say, Berkeley, Montpellier or Oslo, and there has been a serious lack in creating a firm experimental basis for many of its hypotheses. Secondly, there has been a failure to attract and to train adequately enough good men for the necessary effort in teaching, study and practice. Thirdly, ecology has so far signally failed to demonstrate its essentiality to such key potential users as the National Park Service, in the way that the agricultural sciences have to agriculture, or the physical sciences to defense and industry, or the medical sciences to doctors. Thus, while other sciences forge ahead to a higher and more secure status, ecology remains at once the Cinderella and the Peter Pan of the family, always poverty-stricken, and apparently resolved never to grow up."

In Britain luckily the Huxley-Tansley Special Committee in 1947 recommended, and the Government was persuaded to accept, that ecological research and conservation of nature should be united under a single body, with the status of an official research council, for which was coined, early in 1949, the original name The Nature Conservancy.

From time to time stupid or misguided men questioned the rightness of this choice and sought a separation between the functions of research and those of nature conservation. Such a separation exists in most cases in other countries, but comparison of their progress on both aspects with that achieved by the Nature Conservancy points strongly to the conclusion that integration of the two is the better approach. Once the need for scientific research into conservation was given shape in a body responsible for managing and advising on the management of natural areas there proved to be little difficulty in designing and fulfilling the necessary program of scientific work and in building up a varied and balanced scientific staff for the purpose, which soon became the strongest single ecological team in the world. Had no such practical and urgent demand existed it would have been impossible to attain such a result by any number of vague assertions of the value of ecology and the need for developing it.

The similar although modest impetus generated by the specific and timetabled task of the International Biological Program confirms this conclusion, and by inference indicates how much ecology has lost for lack of vigorous and far-sighted leadership on an international plane. The dedicated efforts of a few have not been equal to the need. During the past five years, since these failures began to be realised, intensified efforts have been made to remedy them, although still by too few people equipped with far too small resources. In time, there is now reason to hope, all of them will be remedied, but too late to save much irreparable damage being inflicted meanwhile.

It is especially sad that so much of the inadequate amount of energy available for the task among ecologists is still absorbed in neutralising counter-productive attitudes within ecological circles. Some of ecology's worst enemies are ecologists, who do not understand how a science advances and who exercise a veto wherever possible on steps leading to its advance, in order that they may comfortably play out time in the more or less cosy ecological niches which they have created for themselves and their intimates.

Perhaps the most essential step is to bring into close two-way communication groups of picked research workers in different countries, tackling a series of closely related problems where each discovery or new technique can quickly stimulate fresh advances at other points, and can assist and encourage growth of common standards and free interchange of ideas and data. It is in this sphere that the International Biological

Program can be helpful, with its emphasis on ecological approaches and its capacity to bring together so many institutions and specialists both in advanced and developing countries.

Once the scale of the potentialities has been unmistakeably demonstrated, and the capacity of ecologists to produce results able to withstand the most sceptical scientific scrutiny and their ability to interest and enlighten users of land has been vindicated, the way will be open for an expansion comparable to that of the most glamorous branches of science. With good fortune that stage should be reached by the early 'seventies. From then the difficulties of attracting and training the right recruits in the right strength may be expected to diminish. There must, however, still be a longish timelag before the now growing deficiency of fully trained and widely experienced senior ecologists begin to be made good.

Equally important is the growth in scope and in depth of the generally digested fund of ecological knowledge and understanding. The world at large has hardly begun to know what ecologists do and what it means to people. Even those most passionately convinced of the necessity for mankind to listen with close attention to the message of ecology still do not grasp thoroughly and completely what that message is. The slow and spasmodic advance of the science, and the atmosphere of emotion and impending doom which so often surround practical efforts to impose its findings on governments, industries or other land users, have emphasised and aggravated the distortion both in the internal growth of ecology and in its public image. Too much of ecology is concerned with consequences of the abuse of natural processes, and too little with the elucidation of these natural processes themselves. In public affairs ecology is oversold as an instrument for frightening and checking powerful interests from pushing through misconceived projects, and is underrated as a positive and immensely valuable addition to mankind's general mental equipment for the type of problem-solving and decision-making of which modern life at higher levels of responsibility so largely consists.

Ecology should focus and give new significance to an immense fund of educational material, information, radio talks, books, films, newspaper articles and television programs, which, being perpetually communicated to an insatiably curious public through media with a high degree of realistic immediacy, will progressively influence entire populations towards enhanced appreciation and fuller understanding of the natural environment. Indeed it is questionable whether any other single subject will be able to match appreciation of nature in universality of public acceptance and in sustained pulling power.

One particularly encouraging aspect, in contrast to much earlier experience, has been the displacement of sentimental, didactic or crudely popularising approaches by straight presentation of wild life and of natural processes and scenes, closely linked with the latest scientific interpretations. The new mediators are on the whole meticulously careful not to interpose their own sentiments theories or flippancies about nature to the detriment of straight presentation. But professional ecologists have contributed little towards this great advance.

Such developments may be expected progressively to remove much of the drag which has been operating in society to hold ecology and conservation back. The forces demanding them, quite apart from conservation, are fortunately gathering irresistible strength. The problem for conservationists will increasingly be one of turning to best advantage a favorable tide which is running strongly. They will less and less have to overcome rigidity and inertia. The need for diversity, for the imaginative interweaving of different types of urbanism and natural landscape, for research in abating nuisances and pollution, for the monitoring and enforcement of environmental standards and for a more satisfying and complete modern style of urbanised environment are among the world-wide requirements which are emerging.

Conservation is far from being the only factor vital to a new approach, but it is one of the critical elements for combining and synthesising the others in a satisfying whole. Probably the greatest and most effective single contribution hitherto towards informing public opinion on the true nature and significance of ecology has been the late Rachel Carson's *Silent Spring*. But if that had been its overt aim it would never have attained one-tenth of the influence which it won as a spirited and devastating attack on the thoughtless misuse of toxic chemicals on the land. The public does not similarly depend for its knowledge of nuclear physics upon denunciations of atomic bombs, nor for its knowledge of therapeutic drugs upon revelations about thalidomide or LSD.

There is something discreditable and unhealthy about a society which pays attention to a branch of knowledge vital to its survival only when some catastrophe or imminent threat of trouble frightens it into doing so. It is significant that while the International Geophysical Year gave rise to massive worldwide news and publicity the International Biological Program, involving many more countries on problems more fundamental to human welfare, has been so little written about in its five years of preparation that even among biologists the mere fact of its existence is still not universally known.

Modern world problems such as the plight of the underfed countries, the human population explosion, the great social stresses of civilisation, and the new impacts of medicine on standards and ways of living are inexorably compelling mankind towards a drastic revaluation of the sciences, in which biology must receive greater recognition and enlarged resources. But are contemporary biologists capable of rising to these opportunities?

The massive replacement of muscle power by mechanical and electrical applications of energy, and the fast increasing demand for brain as against brawn in industry are forcing upon the diehards of the educational world a revolution in educational methods and curricula. Weak and divided as it has until recently been, the conservation movement can nevertheless claim some share in stimulating and smoothing the path for these new approaches, which are so essential to its own future.

A more integrated, better led and more imaginative group of biological sciences, viewing problems on a world scale, will for the first time provide conservation with an adequate scientific base. A transformed education, replacing traditional pedagogy and over-reliance upon the written word by fresh ways of learning, and by contact with living and functioning systems, could gradually create a public capable of understanding what ecology and conservation are about. This may help to correct another evil legacy from the past, the nineteenth-century educational snobbery, widely disseminated not only in Britain but overseas, that no gentleman would wish to be educated in science, and least of all in biology.

The decisive error in preferring to give a dominant place to studies based on "general ideas of a literary kind" (as Michael Faraday called them) rather than admitting to parity those based on observation, experiment and measurement has produced the new extreme and unworkable maladjustments between a technological civilisation and a scientifically illiterate leadership, which always asks the wrong questions, always follows the same fallacious methods of decision-making and always therefore pursues the wrong courses to the wrong ends. The demonstrable fact that existing types of scientist and technologist would with a few exceptions themselves not be qualified to correct such errors is itself a further example of the fundamental mischief caused by the arbitrary decision of nineteenth-century educationists in favor of splitting British culture in half. Although the resulting injuries were so widespread perhaps none was more crippling than that imposed on ecology and conservation. The much-needed studies in ecology and conservation which Charles Darwin himself had developed and relied upon in his great formative work were left to languish for a further century, neglected equally by science and by society.

In order to improve our total environment it is vital to look clearly at the world we have created and ask ourselves, what have we got? Do we like what we have? What shall we do about it? What do we want?

Modern man has improvised without foresight a steel-and-cement wilderness about him which is in many ways more frightening and uncongenial to him than the natural wilderness from which he sprang. Do people really want this great urban sprawl, or does it alienate and unsettle them? A disturbing minority seem to take refuge in a mental wilderness accessible only to addicts of drugs. Much larger numbers seek on every holiday to find somewhere away from it all, only to spread the evil from which they are fleeing.

Despite the immense investment in megalopolitan steel-and-cement remarkably little research has been undertaken to see if it does indeed provide man with the sort of home he wants and needs. There are few long term studies which have tried to analyse its potential, its trends, its future possibilities. Most of the intelligent discussion of the problem has reached pessimistic conclusions, and the megalopolitans of the world are an increasingly depressed and frustrated human group. The only wise assumption now is that the course to which current civilisation has become overwhelmingly committed is simply not viable. Unfortunately the great foundations, universities and other bodies holding the necessary resources have until very recently been laggard and timid in encouraging studies of viable alternatives. *Prima facie* there seem to be two:

(*a*) persistence with the megalopolitan steel-and-cement approach beyond a point of no return, followed by its catastrophic collapse under its own stresses, e.g. in nuclear warfare, or its more gradual degeneration through racial and other internal conflicts, and through drug addiction, to a stagnant or retrogressive state or

(*b*) the finding of a new healthy and positive dynamic pattern for society through a fresh equilibrium between development and conservation for human fulfilment.

Many people today feel deeply disillusioned and disenchanted with the wonders of technology and the space age. Particularly where these new inventions affect the way they live, they have created much frustration and discomfort and have led to intense cravings for space, peace, beauty, and many more things that advertisers cannot sell. As the affluent society expands leisure and saturates consumers with consumable goods it eventually compels its addicts to seek other outlets, and to question the nature of human fulfilment. Being

INTRODUCTION

In contrast to every other human approach to the land and its uses the conservation approach begins by asking some key long-term questions. What is the character, the potential and the status of this land? Is any given proposed use consistent with the answers to that? Is it in fact the most desirable use having regard to alternative uses for the site and to alternative sites for the use? Will its biological productivity and any unique qualities which it has survive the use unimpaired? Is it any way so unique that it ought to be withheld from any active use whatever, or restricted to one which conforms to that unique quality? Given that a certain use is acceptable are there practices or incidental accompaniments which ought to be ruled out for the good of the land or of its animal and plant life? If there are right and wrong ways of fulfilling a certain use how do we determine what they are and how do we ensure that they are known and observed?

By starting from such a responsible and thoughtful standpoint, and by refraining from the common hasty, slipshod, inconsiderate and greedy attitudes of man towards land, conservationists start with the possibility at least of getting the right answers. Unhappily this possibility is easily lost sight of through righteous indignation at selfish or short-sighted projects, or through lack of capacity to probe deeply enough and to obtain valid answers, or because the necessary time, resources and public understanding do not exist. Much that we know as conservation is therefore still crude, fragmentary, biased, ill-informed or simply ineffective. Its improvement depends upon a wider and fuller appreciation in informed circles of the problems and what might be done to solve them.

Some excellent conservation has been achieved in an almost somnambulist fashion by people who so far as we know sensed and largely resolved the problem in practice without discussion or formulation of it in theory. Only very lately has modern anti-erosion practice, for example, through contour ploughing, managed to match the effectiveness of traditional methods of terracing long practiced in countries as far apart as Japan and Peru. National Parks and game reserves, which withhold land from use, or limit killing seasons and numbers, have close counterparts far back in history. The modern concept of a nature reserve set aside for scientific experiment and for recording and comparing effects of different management methods is perhaps the newest thing in this field.

In our blinkered modern way we tend to think of nature conservation and of the care of man's own environment in different compartments. Such a distinction is false. Without understanding how to ensure the health of nature we have no hope of ensuring the health of mankind. The more research is done in both contexts the more they converge. Until very recently nature conservationists have lacked the will or the means for such research, while many who could have commissioned it for environmental health and welfare have been bone-headed or hostile. At last such work is well under way, and in this theme its natural and human aspects are purposely blended to indicate their common means and ends. Hydro-electric installations, oil refineries and motorways begin to be tailored to the landscape into which they are to fit. Nature reserves are provided with their own powerhouses of knowledge in the form of research stations or field experiments. Parks are managed with increasing recourse to devices for making them more rewarding but at the same time less vulnerable to their visitors. The will to conserve must be matched by knowing how to do it.

In several parts of the world early farmers on sloping land discovered independently that they could do much to avoid loss of topsoil through erosion and to build up fertility by applying plenty of labor to making series of terraces. Picture D.1 near Kyoto, Japan is interesting in showing how forest has been clearfelled to extend the agricultural area, with terraces dovetailed in among the trees. This conflicts with the landscape principle observed in C.7, but the conformity of the scale and siting of building to the landform is again evident. Here is a conservation-minded community.

In the National Parks of East Africa, where great herds of large mammals are the main attraction, the lesson had to be learnt that there must be some management and it must be based on research into the ecological needs of the fauna and flora. Picture D.2 shows the sorry state of Tsavo National Park, Kenya after well intentioned but, as it proved, unsustainable policies of allowing elephants to multiply unchecked had led to their literally tearing down a great part of the tree cover. In Britain, from 1950 on, the Nature Conservancy took the logical step of acquiring Nature Reserves not as exhibiting anything unique but to facilitate drastic controlled scientific experiments. Here in Yarner Wood, Devon (D.3) we see the world's first attempt to reconvert a long-exploited scrub woodland into as nearly as possible the state it was probably in when man first interfered with it. Whether or not this aim succeeds Yarner will certainly be productive, but of knowledge rather than timber.

With the dawn of intellectual and emotional appreciation of the extent of injury by man to the natural environment the first reaction was to revert to the primitive feeling that the most awe-inspiring and impressive natural features, such as great waterfalls, tall crags and great ancient trees should formally be accorded a quasi-sacred status. and that interference with them should be made *tabu*. The modern device invented for such withdrawal from the land use arena was designation as a National Park. It was in this (D.4) Californian Valley of Yosemite, and in face of this noble waterfall that the concept first broke through to acceptance by the United States Congress in 1864. But as Yosemite's own subsequent record has plainly shown, *tabu* must be matched by management, as its creator Olmsted recognised from the outset.

Picture D.5 from Monroe County, Wisconsin, USA is the modern counterpart of D.1 with contour-planted cropland and grass enlivening a rolling landscape reminiscent of the Scandinavian ancestors of many farmers in this state. Wisconsin is a world leader in surveying landscape qualities and in educating the public about them.

North of 60 degrees, in Shetland, cold strong winds and bleak hillsides give constant reminders of the value of cover and shelter. No Shetlander has solved the problem so successfully by natural means as the owners of this snug little mansion at Kergord (D.6), but even in this inland valley the shearing force of prevailing winds is clearly indicated by the drastic trimming of the outer plantation to the south-west, as well as the outer belts of the main defensive system. Once breached it would be hard to repair or re-establish, and the benign micro-climate within would suffer.

On a more massive scale the Hiwassee Dam (D.7) of the Tennessee Valley Authority has modified local climate by creating a lake with a 180-mile shoreline. When not generating electricity the pump-turbine can lift water back into the reservoir, incidentally reducing the unsightly "draw-down" bands visible in this view. Other engineering scars are gradually being healed by tree growth, vigilantly guarded by a fire-tower, a useful device of conservation.

At Milford Haven, Wales admirable co-operation over the siting and design of the Esso Refinery (D.8) has minimised its conspicuousness from across the water by the lifeboat station so skilfully that its large scale (D.9) would hardly be suspected by a ground observer. Milford Haven displays many features of a model regard for conservation and amenity.

D.6

D.7

D.8 (top)
D.9 (bottom)

Monks Wood Experimental Station, England (D.10) seen from the air in August 1963 shortly before its completion is one of the world's most important centers for research on the natural environment, using Monks Wood National Nature Reserve (background) as one of its study areas. (It has had to be much expanded already since this picture). Thailand's Khao-Yai National Park makes full use of national excellence in design for its entrance, an agreeable form of welcome (D.11).

If, as we must expect, all surviving herds of large animals in the wild have to

D.11

D.12

D.13

be conserved within National Parks and Reserves grave problems must be faced in maintaining ample and workable boundaries, especially for such migratory herds as these Wildebeeste in the Serengeti, E. Africa (D.12).

No comment is needed on the view of Waikiki Beach, Honolulu (D.13). While the many can have fun, of a kind, at a price, the few must ceaselessly watch over the helpless environment, as at this Technical Meeting of conservationists at the Hague in 1951 (D.14). (At extreme right is the pioneer P. G. Van Tienhoven).

D.14

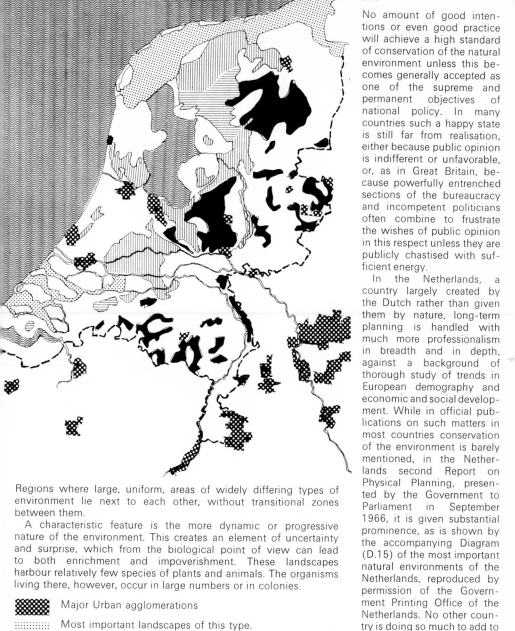

No amount of good intentions or even good practice will achieve a high standard of conservation of the natural environment unless this becomes generally accepted as one of the supreme and permanent objectives of national policy. In many countries such a happy state is still far from realisation, either because public opinion is indifferent or unfavorable, or, as in Great Britain, because powerfully entrenched sections of the bureaucracy and incompetent politicians often combine to frustrate the wishes of public opinion in this respect unless they are publicly chastised with sufficient energy.

In the Netherlands, a country largely created by the Dutch rather than given them by nature, long-term planning is handled with much more professionalism in breadth and in depth, against a background of thorough study of trends in European demography and economic and social development. While in official publications on such matters in most countries conservation of the environment is barely mentioned, in the Netherlands second Report on Physical Planning, presented by the Government to Parliament in September 1966, it is given substantial prominence, as is shown by the accompanying Diagram (D.15) of the most important natural environments of the Netherlands, reproduced by permission of the Government Printing Office of the Netherlands. No other country is doing so much to add to its land surface and to reshape its natural environment by civil engineering. Countries more backward environmentally would do well to study carefully the Dutch studies and plans looking forward to AD 2000, and available in English.

Regions where large, uniform, areas of widely differing types of environment lie next to each other, without transitional zones between them.

A characteristic feature is the more dynamic or progressive nature of the environment. This creates an element of uncertainty and surprise, which from the biological point of view can lead to both enrichment and impoverishment. These landscapes harbour relatively few species of plants and animals. The organisms living there, however, occur in large numbers or in colonies.

Major Urban agglomerations

Most important landscapes of this type. The entire Wadden Sea, including the adjoining coastal strips and the complex East Scheldt—Grevelingen—Haringvliet—Biesbosch, including the adjoining coastal areas.

The most important areas with geese and waterfowl outside the landscapes mentioned above.

The most important meadow-bird areas.

The areas where there are still extensive moorlands, remnants of peat moors, sand dunes and uniform stretches of woods, which are important, inter alia, for birds of prey, curlew, grouse and crane.

D.16

Problems also have to be faced on the ground, putting together local and world experience. Here are (D.16) Sir Julian Huxley, Chief Edward of the Masai and Dr Bernard Grzimek of Frankfurt at Ngorongoro Crater, Tanzania, after the Arusha Conference of 1961. Following these talks the Crater was successfully managed as a Conservation Area under African administration, with international specialist advice.

· · ·

So ends the display of this work's four visual themes—the emergence of man as a dominant species making ever greater and faster impacts on his natural environment; the evolution and character of that natural environment itself; the dawning human awareness that satisfaction can be won through ordering man-made changes in the environment by means of landscaping and rational land use; and finally the acceptance of measures of self-restraint and of working with nature to mitigate or avert loss of environmental values through the practice of conservation.

Thus the twin basic themes of nature's and man's stewardship of the earth, and their respective performances, are matched by the twin applied themes of man's still fumbling and half-awake efforts to fulfil a constructive role through disciplining his own activities by the positive rational and aesthetic guidance of landscape and land use, and the intelligent acceptance of withdrawal from use or limitation of use with the aid of the methods and devices of conservation.

This is the present state of play. Possibly some future reviewer may be able to reduce the themes to three—how nature evolved the biosphere, bringing life to a dead planet, how man evolved Man and absent-mindedly came close to destroying the biosphere and himself with it, and how, awakening just in time, he learnt, accepted and applied the right means of adjusting his way of life to living happily ever after in and with his natural environment. Such a success story remains to be written. Many in this generation are making promising steps towards writing it.

inherently incapable of itself giving any satisfactory answer to such yearnings such a society is not unnaturally faced with a remarkable number of people whose first impulse is to smash it up, especially where social tensions provide a suitable occasion. This raises the question whether such alarming and destructive outbursts may be connected with the barrier which this same society has recently erected between many millions of town-dwellers and their heritage in the natural environment. Society as presently organised may well contrive by its blindness to environmental influences to provide quite avoidable opportunities for internal conflicts and outbreaks which might spontaneously be safeguarded against by a more environmentally sensitive and aware social outlook. Unfortunately there is no means at present of testing this proposition experimentally, but we can at least gain more insight into it by a critical look at the past record of man's relation with his environment.

The dawn of human consciousness and the beginnings of thought and imagination must have been dominated by a confrontation with the challenge of entering new types of natural environment. Bent as they have subsequently been to many other ends, man's higher faculties are still basically and most naturally faculties for contemplating and for coping with changing natural environment. The more our civilised cultures forget and repudiate these original springs of human nature, and the more drastically other incompatible artificial and abstract patterns are substituted for them, the more we risk developing a fundamental conflict affecting the deepest drives and instincts of modern man.

Recent ethological studies on birds, apes and other animals have unmistakeably demonstrated how much there is in common between the behavior of the young animal and of the human infant. They have exposed the crude unwisdom of sudden arbitrary subordination of young human beings to an insensitive and shallowly rationalised type of pedagogy from the outset of formal education. Intelligence and capabilities cannot usefully be considered or fostered in a vacuum. They have evolved in the context of an age-old struggle of mankind to win security, prosperity and self-respect within narrow limits set by the natural environment. The range of intelligence which has built and maintains our current civilisation must undoubtedly have developed in man long before the attitudes, techniques, social institutions and information to utilise it effectively arose.

Even now, it is evident that fuller and better use of readily available human intelligence and social capabilities could create and sustain a far less stupid, sordid and impoverished civilisation that that in which

I

we are currently doomed to exist. The repudiation by modern scholasticism and philosophy of this immense and still pervasive unwritten inheritance, stamped deeply upon human psychology by a love-hate relationship with nature, has induced a deep traumatic injury. It is comparable to the cutting of the tap-root of a tree, which henceforth has to rely on a diffuse superficial ancillary root system in its stead.

Growing up in and from nature, man has found it in all past times the main and most enduring element in his age-old search for self-fulfilment. His efforts to penetrate, explore and exploit nature, and to bend to his will its resources and processes have had all-pervading effects on his attitudes and responses, both individually and socially. The process is recapitulated in the behavior of any baby getting the feel of its immediate environment. Gradually nature's capricious gifts, its sudden savage chastisements and its dimly perceived patterns and processes have evoked in man religious responses, in which propitiatory gestures and approved rituals could overshadow the pursuit of more practical methods for obtaining benefits. Sacred mountains, groves and springs have lately lost the powers attributed to them, and fertility rites have been transformed into religious festivals or secular relaxations. But the awe, wonder and reverence for outstanding natural scenes and occurrences is by no means extinct, as great waterfalls, storms on seacoasts and the rush out of towns to the countryside at fine weekends bear witness.

Such feelings, however, have grown increasingly divorced, even among countrymen, from the common use, management and exploitation of land and water. Advanced technology creates an economy and eventually a society, apt to treat nature as merely an expendable factor. Those who continue to value it most highly tend to be found rather in the towns rather than in the countryside. The resulting problems are only now becoming widely recognised.

Human civilisation has a double root in nature. The challenge to understand it, to tame it and to exploit it, has moulded the character of the hunter, the fisherman, the herdsman, the farmer and the miner. Carried on from father to son the stubbornly developed attitudes and drives of such men eventually spread to more modern and less picturesque vocations, where they continue to form a main part of the productive capital embodied in the manpower of industry. Men may already use computers and synthesise food and clothing, but it will be a long time yet before any are born who are fully bred and adapted to such a sophisticated environment.

Today's managers and rank-and-file workers are essentially displaced persons carried over from a much more primitive society. They are doubly displaced, because in advanced countries the old tradition which shaped them is also fast disappearing on the land itself. Thus the ancient source of wisdom and sifted experience, and the sense of living roots brought to the cities by successive generations of country-bred recruits is drying up, not only in quantity but in quality.

The new makeshift uprooted civilisation, urban, innovating and technological, lacks a base to guide its relationships with its wider environment, and equally with its inner most intimate psychology. Now recruited predominantly from town-bred young people, brought up in low-grade and even chaotic surroundings, and conditioned by an education still mainly traditional and pre-technological in spirit and pedagogic method, it is and feels itself rudderless, confused, cheap and sterile. It has not yet managed to dispense with, or braced itself finally to reject the leadership of traditional priestly and soldierly hierarchies working through timid and conventional political and administrative acolytes, whose unease and incapacity for giving effective leadership in a world which has moved beyond their field of vision are chronically and ludicrously exposed by each week's events. Innocent of scientific background and of technological and economic competence they can no longer preserve the respect and maintain the illusions of the managers and technicians on whose backs they ride.

No creeds, old loyalties, proverbs, myths or dominant institutions bind the increasingly restless and restive masses of mankind any longer with any firmness to the conventional hierarchies which have lost the magic of exerting effortless leadership, and with it their own faith in themselves. In this partial vacuum Victorian materialism proliferates in strange shapes, freed from the inhibiting forces which used partly to restrain or balance it, and strongly encouraged by great commercial interests both private and public, whose well-being and impetus is essential to the justification by works of an ever-expanding affluent society. In immediate terms that society has no use for environmental values, either measurable or imponderable. The wide spectrum of political regimes now extant nearly all agree in practice at any rate on this one point, that the environment merits little, if any, serious consideration.

Society as well as nature has become distorted. The frustration and dismay of naturalists and lovers of landscape at the damage inflicted upon nature by bigger and better technology is belatedly becoming shared by millions of ordinary men and women who feel robbed, hungry and malnourished through the lack of a satisfying and healthy environment. Noise, overcrowding, assault on the senses, pollution of air and water induce a sense of claustrophobia which people blindly try to relieve by refugee-like mass movements, from the areas which their presence has blighted to others which they are destined quickly to blight by it in turn. For nature is more than material natural resources. Its womblike role for man, and its infinite capacity to inspire, refresh and recreate, are no less important. The feelings so eloquently expressed or so vividly documented by so many naturalists probably differ in degree rather than in kind from those of many millions of others, inarticulate and ignorant but ready to respond with enthusiasm, for example, to nature films leading even fleetingly and indirectly to the outdoors.

The brutal and loutish treatment to which natural areas and great landscapes are now exposed, even in advanced countries enjoying widespread higher education, is merely an outward indication of this deeper injury and distortion. Consciousness or subconsciousness of it can be seen at work in many of the irrationalities and outbursts of conflict to which our ostensibly reason-directed cultures in the west are so embarrassingly prone. Unless civilisation honestly faces and learns to harness and benefit from these hitherto neglected aspects of man's nature they will continue to make nonsense of the well-meant aspirations and conclusions of cosily literate minds.

Wild nature has until recently been man's great sparring partner and moulder of character in his struggles for development. The proper study of mankind must therefore include man's past and present environment, as well as man. Art, religion and folklore, like science, technology and working practice have been hewn, synthesised or dreamed up from man's exploitation or contemplation of nature. To regard human nature as something immutably fixed and handed down, or as being derived from origins of which we know nothing is a pre-evolutionary error. It is simply the product of an age-old and still unfinished dialogue between man and nature, on which our modern culture has abruptly and unwisely turned its back.

Reconstruction of past struggles and perception of their psychological results for modern man are of key importance to understanding and resolving some of the central problems of modern society. It is no less important to review the surviving natural environment and to discover how best to manage and conserve it, not only for the material but for the psychic needs of future generations of men. We may be at fault today in assuming that our social values and psychological drives are already in harmony with contemporary civilised needs, rather than with the primitive conditions from which they sprang. Are we at the same time neglecting and destroying sources of help which existing natural environments might give us in our formidable task of adaptation?

Surprise and disgust at outbreaks of individual or group violence in ostensibly civilised communities are gradually giving way to a reluctant recognition that such outbreaks on the part of the alienated are inherent in our current pattern of civilisation. They raise in a disturbing form the question whether any true and enduring civilisation can be built upon such an unstable and primitive human base.

Ours is not the noble and mature polity we so lately supposed it to be. It represents merely the improvised achievement, impressive but fragmentary and precarious, of a rather small minority of partially civilised men during their more constructive moments.

The vast majority have originated little or nothing. They go along, dragging their feet, wherever they are led. All that they have contributed would have left mankind still in the Stone Age. They change their fashions of dress, they learn to operate machines and to apply techniques which are handed out to them, and they preen themselves on a spurious sophistication and an unearned affluence to which they are only superficially attuned.

At the deeper levels of emotional energy, violence derives mainly from forces moulded during a much earlier, far from civilised human past. Crude manifestations of these forces can be seen daily, for example in the behavior of drivers on any highway. Command of the tools and toys of modern technology vastly multiplies the impact and power of such primitive forces, and confers a glamour and prestige which are less and less able to disguise from thinking people their genuine and unredeemed barbarism. We delude ourselves if we assume that the rationality is more real, more fundamental or stronger than the barbarism.

So long as all social and economic faults and failures could be ascribed to misery, poverty and neglect it was reasonable to look for rapid improvement in the types of progress now actually enjoyed by advanced societies, and to attribute to ignorance such misconduct as their maltreatment of the natural environment. Now that a measure of affluence has arrived, and that nature is so largely subdued, we can see that such an explanation will not do. We can no longer find any excuse for failing to regard man himself as a major and menacing delinquent element in nature, and giving urgent priority to the task of reshaping his role to permit him in future to work in harmony with it and to purge himself of the alarming tendencies to destructive violence which threaten his environment as well as himself.

This perennially upwelling barbarism, bursting out as fiercely in the streets of Detroit or Los Angeles as in the forests of the Congo or on the banks of the Mekong, is only the most extreme and incontrovertible of many proofs that the building of a true civilisation is not just a matter of technology, affluence, hygiene and fashionable ways of life, but a problem of fundamentally adapting primitive psychology inherited from the distant past to the totally changed requirements of sophisticated living. The road ahead from technologically advanced barbarism to any civilisation deserving of the name is still long and hard.

11

THE WAY AHEAD

R OUGHLY speaking, the first third of this century can be regarded as the infancy of the conservation movement, when it first began to learn its place in the world and to develop muscles, briefly exhibited under the skilled tutelage of Theodore Roosevelt as President of the United States.

During the middle third its growth was rapid but very uneven, and its limited energies were taxed by the need for efforts and development in many diverse ways. Only during the final decade of this period could clear signs of approaching maturity be seen.

What now are the problems and tasks which must be tackled, with at least equal resolution and success during the final third of the century, in order that mankind may not be wholly defeated in the struggle to fulfil its environmental responsibilities?

Some of these problems are cosmic and abstract, and can be outlined only in general terms. Others are specific and concrete, and can be focussed in relation to particular areas or situations. It seems best to look mainly at the more general ones, since they also frame the perspective for the coming three decades, the 'seventies, 'eighties and 'nineties.

In the long run the only way for man to adjust to his natural environment is by resolving collectively to do so, and by making the necessary effort. This, however, can occur only as the culmination of a long succession of earlier steps. In preparing the way a great deal can be achieved by missionary efforts of persuasion, pilot projects and demonstration of the needs and the potential. Here much has already been done, but much more must be. Until an advanced stage has been reached in this process and an adequate impact has been attained it would be futile to go directly for a wider and deeper transformation. On the other hand every year's delay in initiating such a transformation results in irreparable losses.

A preliminary softening-up campaign got under way some twenty years ago, but its effects were inevitably confined mainly to the more forward-looking and public-spirited, leaving even the ranks of scientists, educationists and professionals almost unaffected, while other great interests such as the churches and industry could hardly have cared or helped less. A second wave, in the 'sixties, has adopted the more pene-trating line of a direct attack on the pretensions and complacency of man himself, relying on the recent findings of biology and psychology, as discussed in Desmond Morris's *The Naked Ape* and Konrad Lorenz's *On Aggression*. It can at last be said that the champions of all the main intellectual and moral forces which have contributed to modern man's appalling disregard of his responsibilities to his environment have now been thrown back on the defensive. The Papal Encyclical *Humanae Vitae* and its dismayed reception even within Catholic circles is an outstanding illustration of this.

The way is thus becoming clear for a broad move forward. The first step must be plainly to reject and to scrub out the complacent image of Man the Conqueror of Nature, and of Man Licensed by God to conduct himself as the earth's worst pest. An intensive spell of environmental repentance is called for, coupled with frank recognition that mankind must finally and unequivocally renounce all claims to be above ecological laws.

It will no longer be sufficient to preach mainly to the converted and to the readily convertible, since it is not they who are in the main responsible for the current widespread misuse and mismanagement of land and of natural resources, nor for the persistence of stubborn prejudices and inhibitions against adopting a more objective and scientifically defensible view of nature and of man's place in it. Once the lines of a new approach have been established, and the moral and intellectual bases of outdated beliefs and practices have clearly been undermined, it will be necessary to challenge on their own ground institutions and interests which remain sluggish in getting the message.

Historically the core of the cultural complex disseminating and maintaining errors of attitude and practice on these matters, and obstructing the way to harmony between man and nature has been organised religion. The dogged and calamitous resistance of the churches against acceptance of the findings of Darwin is only one conspicuous example.

Inevitable though it may have been as a step towards progressive civilisation, it was a tragedy that of all the religions in the world it should have been one of the very few which preached man's un-qualified right of dominance over nature which became the most powerful and influential, through the agencies of ancient Judaism and modern Christianity. Although it is arguable that the Old Testament implies some limits to man's right ruthlessly to trample upon nature and recklessly to multiply his own numbers at its expense, any qualifications and restraints are feeble compared with its chronic and uninhibited incitement towards aggressive, exploitative and reproductively irresponsible behavior in the human species. So long as the harsh checks of war, famine and disease and the narrow limitations of earlier technology set bounds to these crude aspirations, some semblance of tolerable co-existence between man and nature could be maintained. The recent removal of these checks and limitations ought clearly to have been accompanied by a thorough theological rethinking and restatement of the appropriate standards of responsibility, but this the churches have abysmally failed to undertake. Their adherents have, with few exceptions, persisted in behaving as rampant Old Testament tribes, now terrifyingly endowed with modern technical knowledge and equipment, and making mischief for the world on a corresponding scale. The inherent dangers and distortions enshrined in their dominant myths of man's role on earth have been aggravated by increasing blindness and neglect to keep alive even those by no means negligible sympathetic contacts with nature which were part of the heritage of such earlier Christians as St Jerome, St Cuthbert and St Francis.

In the course of this century, under sustained literary, artistic and scientific criticism, the stranglehold of the churches in the West over human freedom in matters of private conduct has been largely, although by no means entirely broken. Except, however, in relation to the birth control controversy and the population explosion, little that has been said or done so far even begins to undo the injury inflicted by the churches on the natural environment through their condonation and encouragement of the most selfish, brutal and shortsighted attitudes towards its exploitation. In South America giant crucifixes stand proudly on summits overlooking deforested hillsides and dried-up stream beds. In Spain, Italy and in many other lands the extent of erosion and of wanton destruction of wild life is closely correlated with the proportion of regular churchgoers. Episcopalians and nonconformists in the English-speaking countries have also a shocking record in this respect.

Deriving its earliest inspiration from the wilderness, Christianity has signally failed to bear witness to its indebtedness, and to teach the need for respect and reverence towards what it professes to regard as the works of the Creator. Only during the past few years, under pressure from outside, have there been any signs within the churches of interest in evaluating and reviving vital elements in Christian tradition which have been increasingly neglected since the days of St Francis of Assisi. To develop a debate within the churches on the theological contribution to the problem of man's place in nature, and on the churches' obligations to speak up against violations of man's responsibilities in this field, must be listed high among the background requirements which are overdue to be met. Only when the churches reawaken to their positive duty to the environment will they be able to see in perspective their errors in working against the limitation of human numbers.

Education is the other great organised source of neglect, of misdirection and of obstruction in relation to the attainment of the needed harmony between man and nature. Perhaps the greatest tragedy now is the extent to which this long misrule of education has cut it off from so many creative sources within the human community, and has thrown so much of the task of reform into the hands of those most compromised and most professionally deformed by the errors of the past.

Only during the past decade have serious efforts begun towards comprehensive and fundamental revision of the role, methods and content of education in relation to science in general, and to the environmental sciences in particular. The laggard leadership and still impoverished and feeble status of the environmental sciences has proved a great obstacle to taking advantage of the opportunities, even when they belatedly arise. A start has however been made, and the thorough-going infusion of environmental elements at all levels must clearly be a main target for effort throughout the educational revolution which has at last begun.

Even on the most optimistic expectation it will take the rest of this century at least to bring the attitudes and activities of the churches and the educationists into some reasonable degree of harmony with modern knowledge about man and his appropriate role in relation to nature. Their mills grind too slowly, and the world cannot wait meanwhile. Fortunately modern mass media, if rightly used, can powerfully assist in re-educating adults as well as juveniles. Unhappily no sensible middle course has yet been found between the totalitarian subjection of, for example, television programs to political supervision and direction, as recently in the U.S.S.R. and its satellite states (and in Cuba, France, Spain and elsewhere), and reliance on the unaided efforts of practitioners in these media to select their own subjects and material wherever something of the desired degree of mass or group appeal happens to win the interest of a producer or program controller.

Conservationists, who were long the victims of neglect or distortion under this *laissez-faire* pattern, have created their own organisations in various countries for ensuring that the necessary news and feature material which has been generated by the movement is got across through the media to the public. This, however, is clearly less than satisfactory, and very recently efforts have been made with some success to broaden out to related fields the coverage of communications, through such events as the Countryside in 1970 Conference in Britain, the White House Conference on Natural Beauty in the United States and the planned European Conservation Year in 1970.

It may reasonably be anticipated that by the middle 1970's this broader approach to the publicising of environmental problems will have achieved an impact on public opinion in most advanced countries sufficient to create a firm base for sustained and realistic policies of care of the environment, so far as that is still possible in spite of all arrears of neglect and misuse, and in face of the growing population explosion, reinforced by much greater mobility. But this will not necessarily assist in handling the very difficult new problems of coming to terms with an ill-educated, impatient and self-indulgent wave of recruits to the affluent society, passing through a mood in which destruction of the environment, and even self-destruction, may be lightly regarded.

It seems clear that in order to live through this phase successfully it will be necessary to develop something fresh, parallel to the conservation movement in its recently broadened form. A kind of human conservation movement seems to be called for, which can study, analyse, devise remedies for, and tackle the self-defeating and self-destructive tendencies of mankind, in the light of modern science and independently of the dogmas and retrograde patterns of churches, political parties and other conservatively-minded and out-of-touch institutions. Urbanism, delinquency, racialism, commercialism, bureaucracy, dogmatic politics, pop culture and social satisfactions will be among the central preoccupations of such a new approach. If successful it may gradually supersede earlier patterns of well-meaning but ineffective reform and charitable effort, and provide some outlet for the growing demand for participation in coping with the problems by which so many people feel personally troubled.

It is no part of the job of the existing conservation movement, already stretched to the limit, and prospectively further burdened as fast as it can grow, to take on such entirely distinct and immense tasks. Yet the story of the conservation movement, as it has been here outlined, surely suggests that by absorbing the sum of what it has by now learnt about the highly practical art of reshaping human attitudes and activities, a parallel effort centered on mankind might well achieve much, if enough human conservationists of high caliber can be found to get it running.

Eventually a time must come when through fusion of ideas, through reappraisal and shaking out of values, and through the removal of obstacles to inter-communication between what are now separate worlds of discourse, it will become impossible in current practice to make the kinds of distinction which unfortunately still need making now

267

between ecology, conservation, and environmental aspects on the one hand and education, religion, prevailing cultural patterns and public affairs on the other. A new ecologically-oriented culture will find it hard to imagine how people of our times could ever have supposed that any other approach made sense, just as our own ecologically-illiterate culture, even at its highest educational levels, still has a struggle to conceive what it would be like to live in a culture liberated from ecological illiteracy.

Pending such a happy day the efforts of ecologists and conservationists must be directed to creating and channelling the necessary inputs of information and ideas to enable and assist the rejuvenation of civilisation, eastern as well as western, along such lines. In the first place this is a task for science, which is concerned with truth and advancing knowledge, and in the second it becomes largely a responsibility of the professions. It is not primarily a matter of propaganda but of fuller information and more advanced advice. Over-eager conservationists have not always learnt to appreciate and respect the principles which science must follow, and the limits which it cannot transgress. Partly through this, and partly through the obstruction by others of fundamental scientific studies of nature, an unfortunate gulf has developed between much of modern science and the conservation movement. There is reason to hope that within the next decade this gulf may be largely closed through such initiatives as the International Biological Program and its possible successors, but the task remains large and difficult.

A good deal has already been said about the problems of strengthening and integrating ecology, which must be accorded the highest priority as the key to effective advances in scientific conservation and also to the integration of biological science in support of human welfare. Integration with other sciences related to the natural environment, such as land research, climatology, pedology and hydrology is no less essential, as well as a much closer relationship with such allied arts and techniques as landscape design, land use and regional planning, and land management.

All else is, however, secondary to and dependent on the success of the environmental sciences in producing without much more delay a coherent and comprehensive picture of the basic workings of biological productivity, and of ecological and ethological processes, within the entire context of the natural environment. Given intense application and co-ordinated effort there is no reason why this should not be done to an adequate extent for practical purposes in the course of the early and middle 'seventies. A combination of fairly detailed extensive survey of all the main ecological factors and of thorough experimental research on processes and their results will make it possible, with the aid of computers, to assess the condition, trends, capabilities and limitations of any site on earth in relation to any past, present, or proposed future use, and to show in each case what the performance may be expected to be, and what effect it will have on conserving fertility and other aspects of the biological capital asset.

In this way scientists and technologists will enable the professions concerned to make a full running audit of all existing land use of both used and humanly unused areas. This will show what gains or losses would accrue from any changes in use, including withdrawal from use or putting to use for the first time, in given conditions of technology, economics of investment, operation and demand, and the state of ecological knowledge. Agriculture, forestry and other land uses can be monitored and evaluated, and where necessary corrected in much the same way that ground controllers already monitor the performance and program fulfilment of the personnel and equipment of a spaceship in orbit. Warning lights or the equivalent will indicate where existing use and management patterns carry risks of erosion, loss of water yield, soil impoverishment or exposure to crop or livestock losses. Trusteeship for the land will be able to become a reality, since it will be armed with the equipment and information to perform that function reliably and in good time. The necessary techniques, personnel and equipment to enable this to be done are already being developed within the International Biological Program.

There could, however, be a disastrously long time-lag, as has often happened elsewhere, between the winning of new knowledge with revolutionary implications and its thorough application in world-wide practice. If this is to be averted vigorous efforts must be made to modernise the outlook and methods and to integrate the thinking and basic principles of the numerous professions which are either directly linked with the land or which are responsible for impacts on the natural environment, through technology and what is called development. Among the first group are land managers, agronomes, farm managers, foresters, landscape architects, regional and country planners, and surveyors. In the second fall civil engineers, architects, industrial chemists, property and investment specialists, sanitary engineers, veterinarians and many miscellaneous types of administrator and manager whose activities impinge on the environment.

Not until the holding of the first Countryside in 1970 conference in London in 1963 was a start made in identifying and getting together these varied interests, and in arranging for them to consider some of the main environmental problems concretely and constructively in conjunction with conservationists, preservationists and others. A somewhat similar confrontation was organised in the United States in 1965, entitled the White House Conference on Natural Beauty, following President Johnson's Message to Congress on the subject at the outset of that year. As possibly the only person playing a part at both these great gatherings I was deeply impressed with their potential for superseding a crude dialogue between conflicting pressure groups by a serious new professional treatment of these vast problems, both comprehensively and in depth. The diverse requirements of development and conservation may thus be practically and technically reconciled.

So far no more than a start has been made in clearing the way for real progress in this direction. Much more impetus and hard thinking will be needed to bring about any real co-ordination of effort and mutual understanding of the respective languages, aims and technical requirements and limits of the different professions involved. Some of the impetus must come from public opinion, some from the gentle but firm insistence of organisations and persons acting as clients or project initiators, and much from enlightened leaders of all the professions themselves.

There is plenty of goodwill and there are some encouraging initiatives, but so far the pace of response is too tardy. The urgent need is not only for a re-orientation of outlook and methods within and between the professions, but for a much closer understanding between them and those who use or should use their services, not only within each nation but internationally. Several of these professions need in today's conditions to think and operate on a world basis. So far none does, with partial exceptions in a few cases such as civil engineering and forestry. It is essential that recruitment and training should be adapted to provide the world with a body of professional men equipped with sufficient breadth and depth of knowledge not only to function within narrowly demarcated fields, but to form effective flexible interprofessional and international teams, able to bring to bear the necessary diversity of knowledge and skills wherever and on whatever scale they may be needed. This is bound to come about eventually, because the nature of modern problems and of modern projects demands it, but special far-sighted and imaginative effort is called for to hasten the process.

While missionary campaigns, and demands for action to right wrongs and to make good neglects and omissions, may be essential at a certain stage, a moment comes when continued reliance upon them can only lead to frustration. The work of the world at this level of specialism and complexity rests at the end of the day on full-time

members of all the land-linked professions. It is upon the failure of the
professions concerned to get organised and equipped for the evident
requirements of caring for and using the natural environment in modern
conditions that attention now needs to be concentrated. It serves little
practical purpose to denounce the misdeeds of interests failing to fulfil
expectations and demands, to satisfy which no suitable professional
assistance is yet available. Admittedly there is as yet little expressed
demand for such assistance on the part of developers and others, but
it is unrealistic to blame managers for not demanding types of service
which can be obtained only in impossibly fragmented and inconvenient
forms, incapable of being fitted in with practical timetables and requirements.

Apart from professions already mentioned as being directly concerned with the land, or with impacts upon it, much the same applies to
such important background professions as economics, law, administration and those responsible for communications media, such as newspapers. With almost negligible exceptions these professions are still
virtually illiterate in respect of environmental knowledge. As a result
the presentation of issues to the public generally, and to Ministers and
heads of key organisations, is commonly handled with moderate to
extreme incompetence. The awakening of all these professions to their
responsibilities in this field is a neglected and overdue duty.

Turning to what may be called the ecological industries—agriculture
in its crop, livestock and horticultural aspects, forestry, fisheries and
those concerned with outdoor recreation and tourism—the problem is
somewhat different. The historical accident that man stumbled into
practising farming and fishing a few thousand years before developing
the research and scientific knowledge on which they should be based
will clearly need to be corrected and compensated for as soon as
possible. Equally clearly the necessary revolution to insert a comprehensive ecological underpinning will take time. Agricultural and
fisheries research have however during the past few decades gone far
to bring about a comparable revolution in methods of agricultural
production and of fishing practice. An expansion of the ecological
contribution already manifest in certain fields would represent simply
a logical follow-through of the existing scientific influences, often already
equally drastic in their impact on those who plough the fields or the
seas.

As usual, however, the pace and thoroughness of absorption of new
knowledge and methods is dependent upon the digestive capabilities
of those at the operational end, and on the effectiveness of channels for
bringing and interpreting the new material to them. Fisheries and

forestry are already inevitably somewhat exposed to ecological influences, although many foresters at least have proved singularly obtuse in adapting to the basic principles. The tourist and recreation industries, of recent mushroom growth, have hardly yet begun to consider their ecological interests and responsibilities.

The first necessity for all the industries in this group, which rely for their basic conditions and raw material on ecological processes, is to re-examine their functions and requirements in the light of a comprehensive grasp of the implications of harmonising them gradually with the emerging findings and principles of ecology. Such a re-examination should indicate where further research is needed, and how to fit the necessary ecological elements into the existing provision for training and advice.

A group of industries of peculiar significance and difficulty in relation to the care of the environment is that concerned with extraction from the earth of non-renewable natural resources such as minerals. Modern demands make it necessary, and modern technology makes it possible, to extract enormously greater amounts of such materials at much increased rates, from greater depths and from deposits of lower grade, or buried under deeper overburden. The distribution of many of the materials concerned, and considerations of production and market economics, often put a premium on working a particular deposit even if this causes much inconvenience or injury, sometimes to local residents, sometimes to other producers and often to conservation and amenity interests. The removal of an entire mountain or the destruction of some other major natural feature can be involved. Widespread disturbance of beaches or seacliffs, or sacrificing a semi-mature forest plantation can be a precondition or working.

Some industries, particularly British opencast coalmining, and iron ore and gravel extraction, have given much thought and taken much trouble to study such problems and to produce schemes of subsequent reinstatement or conversion to new uses which, it is fairly claimed, can result in an eventual improvement on the *status quo*. Although such developments are obviously to be encouraged in general they do not cover the cases where something existing which is of unique and irreplaceable importance, scientifically or to amenity, is involved. In some of these hidden extraction by working underground from a distance may be economically possible; this is in any case necessary for working certain types of undersea deposits. More research, experiment and costing is needed to widen the range of choice and to enable the comparative costs to be more fully assessed and taken into account, and where necessary by suitable government assistance to compensate for less economic working enforced for reasons of environmental policy.

Major utilities, notably reservoir construction for hydro-electric or water supply purposes, can be even more extensive in their demands. Some man-made lakes such as Kariba and Volta in Africa take a place among the world's largest inland waters. Consultative arrangements have already been made through UNESCO for reviewing their implications in a number of scientific and technical fields, including ecology and conservation. In Britain links have lately been established between the Natural Environment Research Council (which now includes the Nature Conservancy as well as the Institute of Geological Sciences and the Hydrological Research Unit), and the Water Resources Board, through which the environmental aspects of major reservoir and barrage projects can be comprehensively examined. More fully integrated arrangements have existed longer in the Netherlands, notably for the reclamation of the Ijsselmeer (the former Zuyder Zee), and the consequential creation of new landscapes.

A further first-rate challenge and opportunity is afforded by the project for duplicating the Panama Canal, with its far-reaching implications for man and nature.

Whether through special mixed teams under an integrated organisation, or through joint arrangements between two or more, it is already clear and is becoming recognised that really major new works of this kind must be planned *from the outset* with full knowledge of and regard for their total environmental repercussions. This point must be taken and acted upon in every appropriate case, and the appropriate trained personnel and supporting research and advisory channels must be developed so that the right expertise can be quickly and smoothly assembled to deal with the increasing number of such projects which must be expected to emerge.

A further class of industry, largely manufacturing, differs in that its needs for land are mainly or wholly as site, and make no serious demand upon local natural resources, other than water supply and air. Such self-contained industries nevertheless create a substantial environmental problem. The scale of units involved is rapidly increasing, and although some welcome tendencies towards miniaturisation are perceptible the main trend is still towards wider and wider sprawl on what is known in the trade as a "greenfield" basis. The correspondingly extensive demands on space for transport of personnel, materials and products, and for storage, together with special access facilities and provision of conveniently located housing, all add to the pressure on the environment, and to the need for a kind of concerted co-operative planning which as yet is only beginning to develop. At this end of the spectrum ecology and conservation are relatively less important in many cases, their place being taken by a more artificial kind of landscaping function which must embrace them so far as necessary in an inevitably more cosmetic treatment.

Planning teams should be formed of varying mixes of specialists at different stages of planning, preparation and execution, and on projects or problems differing in the relative significance of their environmental, technological, investment and administrative or managerial aspects. The lead should be assumed by whichever happens to be best placed to promote at that stage the integrated and economical realisation of the objective. No longer content or permitted merely to stand shouting on the sidelines, conservationists, through their kindred professions, must be ready to take off their jackets and come into such working parties, permeating the whole activity and its results with a respect for and understanding of the environment, which is no longer to be raped but to be sensitively seduced and cherished.

This environment is still basically to be regarded as natural and destined to remain capable of some degree of natural functioning, however much it may need to be transformed and blended with humanly injected elements in the interests of production or of requirements for human living. The illiterate concepts of "waste land" and of "conquered" or eradicated nature must be replaced by a new awareness that elements of nature will always and everywhere remain of critical importance, and that man must always and everywhere learn to understand and respect them in all his activities.

In the great tasks of making good past destruction and damage, and of adjusting all future human activities to the conservation and most beneficial use of the environment, it will be necessary for the increasingly strong and enlightened public demand to be matched by drastic structural changes in organisation of government at national, regional and local levels. These changes have been discussed in detail as they relate to Britain in my previous book *The System*; they are the changes necessary for good government in today's conditions, and they are just as necessary for the conservation and well-being of people as for the conservation and well-being of the environment. There is no conflict at that stage.

A new structure, backed by increasingly effective international co-operation through organisations which are already being adapted to this need, will provide the base, support and marshalling of effective demand to bring together the expertise for fulfilling the environmental requirements on which public opinion is already beginning to crystallise. Indeed, despite the sorely inadequate information and guidance yet available from science, public opinion in some respects has been remarkably quick to appreciate the necessity for effective and comprehensive environmental standards to be enforced. This is evident in respect for example of water and air pollution, noise, smells and visual nuisances or distractions, indolently or greedily permitted or antisocially devised by the more grossly exploitative or parasitic elements in a materialist society.

As this public opinion further strengthens and hardens, pushed as it will be by new and worse horrors and nuisances, the greatest problem is to ensure that the governmental servants of the citizens awaken from their widespread lethargy and ignorance on these matters and are redeployed and redirected so that the plain duties of government can in future be perceived in good time and fulfilled with efficiency, zeal, and not least, imagination.

At the most general level planning must provide for a strong geographically expert element including ecologists and other scientists and technologists, preparing surveys and submitting integrated plans for adequate advance public discussion and comment. At the more intimate regional and local levels the landscape designer and planner must assume an increasingly important role in reconciling all the requirements and existing ingredients with spatially and visually satisfying solutions on a sound ecological and economic basis, sensitively related to all expressed human needs.

Such landscapes must not only be created but regularly monitored to ensure that their health and quality is not imperceptibly impaired by misuse or neglect. Among the tasks which have recently appeared on this part of the agenda are the choice of factors to be monitored; the building up of a suitable network of monitoring stations and of centers for digesting and appraising their results with computer aid; the formulation, testing and revision of standards of environmental quality in relation to one another and to changing conditions; and the education of all concerned in the detailed means of converting polluted, neglected and slum landscapes into renewed landscapes expressive and worthy of the age.

It will be natural at this stage to expect a gradual meeting and even partial fusion of what in the past have been thought of in separate mental compartments as public health, town and country planning, landscape architecture, amenity preservation, leisure and recreation, nature conservation and so forth. This sectional blinkered approach was an inevitable stage historically, but it has outlived its usefulness.

In all human affairs the need is becoming recognised for integration, for harmonisation of varying interests, attitudes and conditions, for the linking of what is done and how it is done to what is thought and felt, for two-way communication and for the removal of unnecessary blocks of participation, and for the wider tolerance, understanding and instantly available information which make such an approach possible, with the aid of modern technology.

One of the most significant features of the conservation movement, closely linked with its main successes, has been a readiness to embrace and to initiate a wide diversity of policies, programs and projects all related loosely and flexibly to a coherent purpose and set of principles.

More and more people are becoming increasingly concerned about conserving their environment, and the mass media are spreading the message all the time with significant results. But history warns us that any such rapid and successful expansion as is now being achieved in conservation is likely to have to be paid for later in terms of an increasingly rigid structure and ideology, growing steadily less relevant to the future problems to be faced, and to the views and feelings of the next generation. Which are the neglected areas where such stresses may be foreseeable? Are there ways of guiding current development which can guard against rigidity and keep the doors open to the changes of direction which may be demanded by further challenges in the future? What is the secret of perpetuating the freshness and enthusiasm, and the creativeness of mind and spirit which has distinguished the conservation movement at its best?

My own experience leads me to emphasise the importance of cultivating a rich diversity of loosely related aims, methods, programs and institutions, rather than to concentrate too narrowly, to eliminate too many secondary but potentially significant lines of growth and to rate tidiness and rationalisation above other conditions possibly more essential to continuing creativeness and to a full sense of participation.

Having myself been heavily involved in the major rationalisation efforts of the past couple of decades, which have so well justified themselves by results, I have some fears that the impetus and fashion for such expedients may outrun the true need for them, and lead to diminishing returns, or even prove counter-productive. Such dangers are much increased by the expansion of the professional element which, with all its benefits, could only too easily degenerate into a stiff conventional bureaucracy, unless it is continually kept on its toes and prevented from rigidifying by a lively, watchful, imaginative amateur movement of the highest quality. The insistence, which has been so necessary, upon the scientific, factual, practical and co-ordinated approach during this chaotic and emotional phase of adaptation could also lead to too much subordination of the imaginative and psychological aspects to the practical and narrowly scientific. Somehow it is essential that ways should be found of enabling these potentially conflicting elements to continue to co-exist in the body politic, on a basis of mutual understanding and esteem. Relegated by society to the status of a residuary legatee, whose interests would be met only after all others had been first served, conservation has long been faced with the imperative need to win and work with allies in order to become effective and to get itself taken seriously. As nothing succeeds like success, and as the influence of conservationists is increasingly respected in widening circles, this aptitude for give-and-take working alliances may become blunted, or the drive behind it may be dissipated. These dangers must more than ever be watched and guarded against, now that the movement appears on the threshold of a decisive breakthrough in influencing some of the main lines of modern social evolution, as it is well fitted to.

With the growth of the affluent society, and of leisure and expanded communications, more and more people begin to feel unsatisfied aspirations and frustrations, ignored by government and private enterprise and by other institutions of society. These are somewhat comparable in their psychological aspect and in the kinds of action which they demand to the attitudes and practices here shown to have taken shape in the conservation movement, from which such people have much to learn. The ready response by so many non-naturalists to initiatives by conservationists in favor of safeguarding places, values and conditions such as freedom from air and water pollution amply indicate this affinity.

It is to be expected and hoped that long before AD 2000 many influential organised voluntary movements of troubled citizens for protest, vigilance and participation will arise. There is a good prospect of mutual advantage in alliances between many of these and the conservation movement, wherever they have any objects in common. In this way the current usurpations of bureaucracy can not only be checked, and in some cases reversed, but they can be continuously inhibited from renewal, thus creating a climate in which the tasks of all such upholders of long-term civilised values will become that much easier.

The tendency among supporters of good causes to narrowness and sectarianism, often aggravated by heresy-hunting and a cult of personalities, requires perpetual vigilance in order to ensure that they do not become counter-productive. It is therefore essential for the leadership, in addition to pursuing concrete objectives by practical means, always to have an eye on the climate of public opinion, the emergence of new threats and problems, and the degree to which the atmosphere and spirit of the movement is being kept attuned to the times.

With this in view even far-reaching excursions may be justified if they bring into existence some fresh source of strength, or convert or neutralise some source of obstruction or embarrassment. If the ultimate goal is to be full harmony between man and nature all those influences and vested interests which lead mankind into postures and situations inconsistent with that goal must in turn be converted or otherwise brought into line, or in extreme cases neutralised. This process cannot be left to chance. Being above all concerned with ends the conservation movement must be untiring in devising and applying the means to achieve them as fully and as swiftly as possible.

It begins to appear that the long pilgrimage of the dedicated band of conservationists has led them not only to the pursuit of truths and principles essential to man's well-being, but also to ways of learning and of conducting their quest which have immense significance for many other branches of human affairs. Long scorned by politicians and business men, ignored by the churches and most of the teachers, neglected by science and the professions, and fought by many narrow selfish interests, conservationists have themselves often behaved badly and stupidly. But under the continual threat of impotence in face of victorious opponents they have had to learn the hard way how to find the right objectives and the right means of attaining them. Some of their early efforts at alliances, as in America at the outset of this century, turned out somewhat poorly, but tenacity and single-mindedness gradually gave increasing returns, as the record plainly shows. The adoption of a similar approach by other great related movements and interests sharing a concern with the environment gives some promise of a breakthrough, if only the leadership can rise to this challenge to its wisdom and strength of character.

Most cruelly, however, all this progress is imminently threatened through the folly of those who have until this late hour obstructed and delayed the necessary effective measures to adapt human reproduction to altered human conditions, and to bring the population explosion under control. The problem will now be so well known to all who read these words that a brief treatment of it here would be superfluous and a comprehensive review in depth must await another occasion. While sheer animal pressure of growing numbers to be fed, housed and employed will inevitably strain man's environment to the uttermost in coming decades this prospect does not tell against, but merely renders more urgently necessary, all the steps towards environmental planning and conservation which have been discussed earlier. Miniaturisation, recycling and re-use of resources, provision for more compact living such as the space program is pioneering, and above all new methods of teaching and training to cut down abuses and waste can at least do something to mitigate the pressures to which our children have been so stupidly and wickedly condemned by ecclesiastical and political leaders.

Referring back to this book's third chapter, some scant comfort can be found in the tough and tenacious resistance which many of the earth's less benign habitats will continue to maintain against the encroachments of improvident and destructive mankind. But for all those regions which are best able to sustain vegetation and living animals the outlook is grim. Perhaps some day—might it be as soon as AD 2250?—a sadder and wiser human race will have re-adjusted its numbers not only to the capacity of the earth to bear them but to the levels which will permit and enable a high standard of life in every sense to be lived by all. For something like a minimum of three centuries, on that optimistic basis, we have therefore to look forward to a Great Siege of Nature by mankind, in which strongholds and refuges on the inspiration of Noah's Ark must be resolutely maintained in order that when the siege is over as much as possible of the wealth and diversity and beauty of the earth may be recreated, and regained by those not so unlucky as to be born meanwhile.

CONCLUSION

ABUSES, errors, crimes and distortions of growth have continually marked man's social evolution on earth, and nowhere are they more conspicuous than in his treatment of the earth itself and its living creatures. Man's obstinate stupidities, his character defects due to badly adjusted aggression, possessiveness and greed, and his passion for embracing myths strongly at variance both with objective circumstances and with manifest human needs, have gravely marred the great achievements inherent in his rapid self-induced promotion above the rest of the animals. What is most strange and disturbing is that the frequency, scale, and sheer folly of these errors and abuses, far from diminishing along the line from brutish savagery to ostensible civilisation, have actually gone on increasing, right up to our day.

How and why this discreditable trend has occurred, and the growth of efforts to identify and counter it, have been main topics of this book. In a sense the conclusions to be drawn are encouraging. Although hindsight fiercely illuminates innumerable mistakes and misdeeds, there were often in the context of the time built-in obstacles to recognising and averting them through the existing institutions operated in the light of existing beliefs and knowledge. Such obstacles have, at least potentially, now been neutralised or overcome to a considerable extent, and the process is rapidly continuing.

It can be said with some confidence that the 1970's will mark the first moment during man's tenure of this earth when the nature and conduct of his stewardship will be continously under critical scientific scrutiny, not too far separated from the seats of power and from the enforcement of accountability. Evidently the scale of the arrears to be made up and the continuing drag from so many environmentally illiterate citizens and organisations will continue to slow the progress of conservation. Many as yet unalterable trends of population growth and of wasteful use of land and natural resources will inflict further damage, perhaps far outweighing that which can now be made good from the past.

Basically, however, conservation is passing through the phase, critical and testing for all kinds of revolutions, of leaving behind the period of missionary exhortation and protest, and of assuming a responsible and constructive share in the management of the planet. It is on the wisdom, dedication, adaptability and not least the horse-sense of the movement that the successful harvesting of what has so long been dreamed of and striven for now rests. No longer can intense conviction of the righteousness of the cause, or splendid firework displays of self-generated psychodrama, stand in or atone for failure to achieve the tangible and intangible results which alone can justify the movement. The contribution of each part to the performance of the whole needs to be critically watched and measured. The performance of the whole must in turn be judged by its progress in leavening and converting all human society to the willing acceptance and full observance of the principles and practices of conservation in the widest sense.

This immense task would be quite impossible if it had to be tackled on the conventional model of simply struggling to convince a majority of the rightness of the cause within the context of a fairly rigid set of inherited values, prejudices and practices and a fixed social and economic pattern. It becomes possible only because so many of the inhibitions and resistances within society have been relaxed or neutralised in the general slide away from tradition and custom, and because the kind of aspirations and attitudes underlying the conservation movement largely correspond to the feelings of those who are most keenly critical of various dominant tendencies in modern materialist civilisation. The tide is thus favorable.

Even so, it would be optimistic to expect any sweeping success but for two other well-timed and powerfully helpful trends of the present day. The first of these is the emergence of the computer, and of its complex accompanying programming, data collection and data analysis in progressive replacement of the more disordered, fragmentary and ill-digested methods on which we have hitherto had to rely. Just as World War II thrust physics to the fore, especially through nuclear developments, the computer age will compel ecology, in spite of the ecologists, to assume a central role, because ecology and its applications in conservation, land use and other ways are fundamental to the management of the earth with computer aid.

The second great current trend is towards restraining and remedying man's threats and injuries to the natural environment. Starting in a piecemeal and defensive way, as a series of unrelated efforts to countering such obvious evils as oil pollution of the seas, chemical pollution of land and rivers, and smog in the air, this new extension and counterpart of the nature conservation movement is becoming locked in a full-scale confrontation with technological civilisation in its present distorted phase and form. So rapidly are things moving that new prospects and potentialities are emerging almost monthly, with ever broader and deeper implications.

Many people have long suspected that governments, bankers, economists and business leaders were flattering themselves in claiming to understand and to be able to guide or control the evolution and performance of modern technological economies. That such suspicions were well founded has been demonstrated to all by recent events. Technological civilisation has entered a phase in which it virtually acquires a will and a strength of its own, tending to dominate and bend to its necessities even the most powerful human rulers and groups. This is not an inevitable trend but, as in most cases of being thrown back strategically upon the defensive, is due to failure to appreciate the forces at work on the other side.

Those in charge of inherited institutions have assumed that they could avail themselves of science and technology to an ever-increasing extent without correspondingly reshaping their prescientific attitudes and patterns of organisation. Through this blindness and lack of adaptability they have drifted into a deadlock with the increasingly coherent and incompatible interests and elements comprising technological civilisation. The deadlock has resulted in loss of confidence in the established System, and in a feeling of alarm at man's helplessness, no longer in face of God and Nature but against the imperatives and demands of a new technological system which he has created but neither understands nor directs, and which seems to be acquiring a capacity for autonomous working in often undesirable ways.

From such a standpoint Man himself may wonder if he should not be added to the list of threatened species on the earth, belonging as he does in the last analysis to the ancient biosphere or realm of all living things rather than to the new impersonal "technosphere" of flows of energy through man-made structures, devices and economic or social channels. Through its corps of dedicated managerial and technical human acolytes the technosphere demands ever-increasing sacrifices of human values and cherished attitudes. At the same time it physically seizes, processes and releases into circulation not only unassimilable quantities of such products as vehicles and armaments but also innumerable pollutants and interferences for the environment. Functioning side by side with the biosphere on the same planet the technosphere leaks or deliberately injects or dumps within it so many, so vast, so pervasive and so deadly poisons and irritants as to threaten its capacity to continue functioning effectively, and its value as a source of support and a natural environment for mankind. The problem is no longer one of nature threatened by man but of both man and nature in the same boat, both equally threatened by the temporarily uncontrolled workings of the technosphere.

Conclusion

To recast human education, training and institutions in such a way as to restore man's authority over the technosphere thus emerges as the next item on the agenda, whether we approach these great problems from the standpoint of conservationists concerned to safeguard the future of the biosphere and of the earth as a total environment, or whether we are driven to tackle them by the universal evidence of the bankruptcy of inherited institutions and ideas, and the need for finding a new basis on which the march of civilisation can be successfully resumed. The fact that there is no tolerable alternative to such a vast readjustment is the best reason for a measure of optimism that it will gain the necessary support.

Chance, and lack of leadership elsewhere, has led to the current situation that conservationists are temporarily more advanced, or at least less backward than others in moving towards recognition of this problem in terms of possible action. One might suppose that the fearful sufferings of so many human beings under existing trends would have led political, social and economic thinkers to an equally fundamental appraisal, but so far nearly all prefer to continue to wander around in the intellectual circuits, grooves and blind alleys to which they are conditioned, rather than to make the effort of looking at the end-twentieth-century predicament as it is.

Fortunately recent ecological studies, however imperfect, have opened a prospect of an intellectual break-through by surveying and analysing the technosphere itself as a kind of semi-autonomous ecological system. This indeed is a more immediately practical task than the vaguely fore-shadowed wider developments of "human ecology".

In a natural ecosystem solar radiation, moisture and nutrients from the soil are absorbed and processed to build plants which in turn serve to feed animals on which other animals then live. Similarly the techno-sphere picks up water, fossil fuels, minerals, biological products and so forth for processing through even more complex channels and treatments into the extremely diverse requirements of a technological civilisation. Physically and chemically the resemblances between these two worlds are obvious, and they can be studied, measured and evaluated in much the same way. The striking difference is that while the biosphere is a complete, self-contained permanently balanced system organised to provide all its own needs and to break down, disseminate and re-use its waste materials through subtle processes of dissolution and decay, the technosphere is dependent on the biosphere not only for much of its input but also for important outlets at the far end of the production chain. Many of its demands are made on the biosphere in crude and reckless disregard of the requirements of sustained yield, while many of its unutilised or discarded elements are irresponsibly tossed out into a biosphere entirely unequipped to deal with them, at any rate in such quantities and at such a pace.

As the most experienced of applied ecologists, and as the only group concerned with human affairs who seem to have troubled so far to try and grasp fundamentally what is going on, conservationists accordingly face the challenge of helping to construct and evaluate the necessary true models of the workings of the modern technosphere, viewed as a giant bastard ecosystem, with its inputs and outputs, its growth in "standing crop" of capital equipment and its efficiencies and wastes. Once such models are constructed, functionally evaluated and sufficiently understood to form a basis for computerised programs the way will be opened to managing and correcting the performance of the economy in harmony with the rival or complementary world of the biosphere, and, no less importantly, in harmony with the genuine needs and desires of mankind.

Only by thus developing computer methods harnessed to ecological principles and insights can the rival world of the technosphere be mastered in the interests both of man and of nature. The start which is now being made towards assessing, predicting and regulating the ill-effects upon the biosphere of current impacts and leakages from the technosphere is also a start towards the goal of an eventually integrated ecological-technological civilisation. By applying to our runaway world economy principles already tested in ecology, and computer-born opportunities of measuring the total performance of modern technology in relation to all kinds of costs and to human needs, we may not only save the natural environment, but redeem the disastrous failures of those to whom the development of higher standards of living and of growing human happiness were supposed to be securely entrusted.

The implications for scientific study, the educational requirements, the necessary professional and institutional adaptations, the practical politics, the international and national programs and many other previously obscure parts of the picture are now becoming fairly clear. Although the tasks for the foreseeable next stage are immense there is no reason to be pessimistic over the future, so far as the great task of securing a *rapprochement* between human aims and nature is concerned. The big question is whether this *rapprochement* will be gained in time, or whether it will arrive too late to save a tolerable inheritance for posterity. We can only work and hope.

As workers we must be practical, and fortunately the effect of recent advances in technology, as also in science, has been to establish an unanswerable and increasingly conceded practical case for virtually the

entire program of the conservation movement. For purposes of persuasion and controversy it is now hardly necessary to adduce or rely upon
arguments in the aesthetic, moral or spiritual realm; the practical
arguments alone are strong enough, and they are much less debatable or
dangerous. Nevertheless, it may well be that if ever we can find our way
about the intangibles and imponderables as confidently as we are now
beginning to see where we stand on the more tangible aspects of man's
relations to his environment, the gains involved may be even more
impressive and exciting.

Plainly it is far beyond the bounds of possibility for the vast majority
of people ever in their lives to enter into anything that can rightly be
called wilderness. Most of them would neither wish to do so, nor be
willing to submit to the necessary sacrifices of convenience, nor be
capable of throwing themselves open enough to the experience offered
them to absorb its rewards and to come away renewed. We need not,
however, be unduly daunted on this account. After all, much the same
applies to every great spiritual, aesthetic or intellectual experience, and
also in such physical realms as the Olympic Games. For every man who
must attempt to climb Everest "because it is there", millions can somehow share in the Alpine challenge and response, either on some lesser
mountain or through the vivid interpretive media which are among the
greatest gifts bestowed on this generation.

A third channel of access to a sufficient part of the full experience can
be through a well-designed and well-managed system of parks and
outdoor reserves, within which small human sanctuaries kept free from
noise, disturbance and jarring influences might be maintained to yield
at least the more basic and essential elements of tranquility and withdrawal needed in order to return refreshed. Immunity from sonic
booms of aircraft, from inflow of polluted waters and drift of polluted
air, would be indispensable to such a concept, and would imply that
such pocket wildernesses would need to be set within extensive zones
of environmental conservation, during the interim period until such
standards could be made a universal minimum throughout national
jurisdictions.

It is in North America that most recent and practical thought has
been given to the significance and the safeguarding of wilderness. In
the U.S. National Park Service brochure on Wilderness (1957) the
central point was well put in these words:

"Wilderness is a physical condition. Wilderness is also a state of
mind. Both concepts are important—the *former* in matters of protection and management, the *latter* in evaluating the benefits of

wilderness, *both* in planning for the intelligent and beneficial use of this important cultural and recreational heritage."

The types of experience which maintenance of wilderness can perpetuate were identified as including

"A scene or vista of unusual interest or beauty.

An area secluded or removed from the sight, sounds and odors of mechanization and man-made intrusions.

A spot where one can feel personally removed from modern civilization.

A place where one can experience a feeling of adventure such as the pioneer might have felt in conquering the frontiers.

A condition where full enjoyment depends upon one's own perception, physical skill and self-reliance."

In some ways it may be tedious and even unpalatable to have to discuss what used to be felt as an uncommunicable heaven-sent ecstasy in terms of its conscious provision and arrangement, but that is the price of achieving so much power to injure or destroy natural environment. In principle, a similar reaction might be expressed against keeping great paintings in an art gallery, or assembling music-lovers in the highly artificial confines of a concert hall, or expecting the faithful to commune with God in a crowded church.

In relation to wilderness values mankind's existing creative centers and channels of participation are still almost as primitive as wilderness itself. The means of distilling, expressing and propagating even fragments of the essential experience are no more advanced than was the early church in the days when the ordinary man might see a Christian only on the occasion of his being thrown to the lions. It must be possible to devise some more satisfying, continuous and two-way pattern than this, capable of at least enabling the majority to gain an understanding of the fundamentals of nature no less than that which they will have of science, art and politics.

While many may dream at times of being provided with instant wilderness, into which they may be comfortably jet-propelled, ready to alight and immediately drink in its essence at a gulp, the truth is not like that. Those who cannot through long preparation and through contributing a satisfying personal effort come to wilderness in the right frame of mind to appreciate it would mostly do better to stay away and see it by means of films, or through good and well illustrated books, or alternatively through getting to know well some substitute wilderness near enough home to be visited often enough and long enough for some degree of familiarity to be achieved with it.

It is futile to buy expensive binoculars with an exit pupil much greater than that of one's own eyes, since it is the eyes which dictate the limits of the performance obtainable. Equally, it is unrewarding to seek experiences and visual impressions far beyond the capability, training and readiness of the mind and senses to resolve and absorb them.

Modern man, often corralled in narrow corridor streets, or conditioned to fitting into streams of noisy and smelly vehicles, cannot hope without some serious preparation and training to be other than a misfit and a blot on the wilderness scene. He can, however, fairly hope to be enabled to benefit considerably from that part of wilderness values which he can quite readily absorb if they are brought to him in the right way. For the rest he can identify, as men and boys have so often done, with the fortunate few for whom the adventure and revelations of true wilderness have become an essential part of living.

Among gifts which can be acquired by patient effort under good guidance in the field is the ecological eye—the eye able to see and interpret every scene in terms of what nature has done there in the past, and of what is going on now. Endowed with this scientific variant of second sight it becomes possible to find new meaning in everything out of doors, and even in pictures of scenery. A new interest, a new pleasure, a new source of refreshment and a new stimulus to the imagination is won, which can last as long as the power of sight itself. The eye of the ecologist, and the eye of the connoisseur of landscape can in themselves pull out of even everyday scenes many of the values of wilderness. They can help to make good the deformities imposed upon man by exchanging an healthy natural open-air environment for such an unhealthy artificial indoor container as an apartment or an office.

Before straying away to other planets let us first learn the facts of life and discover who we are by what we do on this one. Here in brief is the tale of man's earth. Here, if we dare face what we see, is the mirror image of earth's man.

ANNEX I

THE VEGETATION COVER OF THE EARTH

Of all the elements composing the natural environment in its infinite variety the total plant cover which we call *vegetation* is at once the most conspicuous to even a casual eye and the most significant for all forms of life. Men at all cultural levels distinguish woods and grasslands, swamps and deserts, but such commonly used distinctions are vague and inexact, and afford no sound basis of analysis or comparison.

Botanists were at first much preoccupied with collecting, identifying, classifying and plotting the occurrence of species, genera and families of plants composing the *flora* of an area. Only on this basis was it found possible to study *communities* of plants often forming a mosaic of neighbors habitually occurring together. The fact that these communities consist of members of certain species is for many purposes less important than the fact that some are woody and grow tall while others are herbaceous and short, and that in different parts of the world communities can be found which look alike and occupy a similar ecological niche or role even though they may be composed of different species in each region.

A requirement has thus arisen for a scientific basis of classification based entirely upon the features of plants themselves, regardless of considerations of climate, soil or topography, and capable of enabling ecologically similar types of vegetation from different parts of the earth to be inventoried, mapped, and analysed with reasonable accuracy on the basis of information readily obtainable from a large number of recorded points or areas. Given such a tool, and a world-wide network of recorders, the existing sketchy kind of material used in the first endpaper of this book could be superseded by something immensely more reliable and informative both for scientific and practical purposes.

Such a classification has been contributed for use in world-wide surveys for the International Biological Program by my colleague Dr F. R. Fosberg of the Smithsonian Institution, Washington D.C. and with his permission is reproduced here. (It is discussed in the text on pps. 57–59.) While the named examples of each type are selected because Dr Fosberg is personally familiar with them or has found them adequately described and illustrated they also serve to indicate the extent of the possible range of vegetation types and to help us to imagine at least a number of them. The list is not yet exhaustive and is currently being expanded, but the ascertained gaps are not particularly significant for our present purpose, which is to provide a broadly comprehensible scientific statement of the types which go to form the vegetation cover of the earth, and to indicate the approach which is now being energetically pursued for enabling us to compare any site on earth with any other.

Computers and other advanced aids to data processing and retrieval will before long enable the personal impressions and descriptions of a few to be superseded by vast inputs of information on a more objective basis, which will transform our knowledge and understanding of the living organisms on the earth and their biological productivity. It will become possible to specify required characteristics of land for any purpose and to locate the position of sites meeting these requirements. Whether these sites are also specially suitable for other purposes, such as nature conservation will emerge at the outset. Wasteful trial and error will be practically eliminated in favor of scientific choice in land use.

288

Classification

1 CLOSED VEGETATION
(Crowns or peripheries of plants touching or overlapping)

1A *Forest*
(Closed woody vegetation 5 meters or more tall)

1A1 Evergreen forest (at least the canopy layer with no significant leafless period)

1 Multistratal evergreen forest (rainforest) — (Tall, multistratal, orthophyllous or top of canopy sclerophyllous; epiphytes and lianas usually common) example, Dipterocarp forest (Malaya, Borneo)

2 Evergreen swamp forest — (Bases of trees or root systems adapted to lengthy or permanent submergence; multistratal or unistratal; peat development often notable)

(a) Evergreen orthophyll swamp forest — (Leaves of ordinary thickness) e. *Barringtonia racemosa* swamp (Guam) Most freshwater swamp types

(b) Evergreen broad-schlerophyll swamp forest (Mangrove swamp) — (Sclerophyllous; usually unistratal; trees commonly provided with pneumatophores or prop roots) e. *Rhizophora* swamp *Avicennia* swamp Mixed mangrove swamps Most salt or strongly brackish water swamps, if trees over 5 meters tall

(c) Evergreen megaphyllous swamp forest — (Usually composed of palms, more rarely *Pandanus*) e. *Mauritia* swamp (Colombia) Sago (*Metroxylon*) swamps, if over 5 meters tall *Nypa* swamps, if over 5 meters tall

3 Gnarled evergreen forest — (Low, trunks and branches tending to be twisted or gnarled, usually with one tree, usually more or less sclerophyllous)

(a). Gnarled evergreen mossy forest — (Bryophytes and other epiphytes abundant; generally mixed sclerophyllous and orthophyllous)

(b) Gnarled evergreen sclerophyll forest

    e. *Metrosideros-Eugenia-Cheirodendron* forest (Hawaiian Islands)
    Most "cloud forest" types
    (Moss and epiphytes not abundant; strongly sclerophyllous)
    e. Montane forest (Ceylon)

4 Evergreen hard-wood orthophyll forest

    (One or two woody layers, irregular canopy, medium to low stature, much-branched trees)
    e. Dry evergreen forest (Northern Thailand)
    Dry oak forest (Ishigaki Island)
    Guava (*Psidium* forest (Hawaii)
    Intermediate evergreen forest (Ceylon)

5 Evergreen soft-wood orthophyll forest

    (Usually unistratal, of fast-growing trees, tangled with lianas)
    e. Belukar (Malaya)
    Most secondary forests in the humid tropics

6 Evergreen broad sclerophyll forest

    (Leaves hard, stiff or coriaceous)

  (a) Mesophyllous evergreen broad sclerophyll forest

    (Leaves medium in size)
    e. Dry evergreen forest (Ceylon)
    Dispyros-Osmanthus forest (Hawaiian Islands)
    Arbutus-Umbellularia forest (California)
    Laurus forest (Canary Islands)

  (b) Megaphyllous evergreen broad sclerophyll forest

    (Leaves very large)
    e. Coconut (*Cocos*) groves
    Palm forest (Peruvian Amazonian drainage)

7 Evergreen narrow sclerophyll forest (needle leafed forest)

    (Leaves (or equivalent) linear or scale-like, hard)

  (a) Resinous evergreen narrow sclerophyll forest

    (Dominantly coniferous)
    e. *Pinus* forest
    Picea forest

  (b) Non-resinous evergreen narrow sclerophyll forest

    (Dominantly non-coniferous)
    e. *Casuarina equisetifolia* forest

8 Evergreen bamboo forest

    (Dominant layer of large bamboo or giant reed)
    e. *Schizostachyum* forest (Tahiti)
    Gynerium brake (Amazon)

9 Microphyllous evergreen forest — (Frequently but not always of compound-leafed trees, sometimes thorny)
    e. *Leucaena leucocephala* forest (Palau Islands)
    Prosopis forest (Hawaiian Islands)
    Leptospermum (*Manuka*) forest, taller aspects (New Zealand)
    Pemphis acidula forest (Pacific Islands)

1A2 Deciduous forest
(at least canopy layer bare of leaves for a period during cold or dry season)

1 Winter-deciduous orthophyll forest (hardwood forest)
    e. Beech-Maple (*Fagus-Acer*) (Eastern North America)
    Oak-Hickory (*Quercus-Carya*) (Eastern North America)
    Beech (*Fagus*) forest (Europe)
    Oak (*Quercus*) forest (Europe)

2 Deciduous swamp forest
    e. *Larix* swamp (Northern North America)
    Taxodium swamp (South-eastern U.S.)
    Nyssa swamp (South-eastern U.S.)
    Acer rubrum swamp (Eastern U.S.)

3 Dry-season deciduous forest — (Orthophyllous; thick herb or shrub layer)
    e. Deciduous dipterocarp forest
    Most monsoon forest

4 Microphyllous unarmed deciduous forest — (Trees mostly thornless or spineless)
    e. *Albizia lebbek* forest (Saipan)

5 Deciduous thorn forest — (Trees mostly armed with thorns, spines or prickles, usually microphyllous)
    e. Caatinga (Ceara, Brazil)

1B Scrub
(Closed woody vegetation 5 meters or less tall)

1B1 Evergreen scrub

1 Evergreen orthophyll scrub
  (a) Broad-leaf evergreen orthophyll scrub
    e. *Scaevola* scrub (dry coral islands)
    Coastal sagebrush when dominated by *Salvia* (California)
  (b) Evergreen orthophyll vine scrub — (Shrubby vegetation tangled with climbers)

2 Evergreen bamboo or reed brake — (Early stages of secondary vegetation in humid tropics) (Dominant layer of dwarf bamboo, cane or woody reeds, may be strictly erect or tangled)

3 Evergreen swamp scrub

(a) Evergreen orthophyll swamp scrub
(b) Evergreen reed swamp

(c) Evergreen broad sclerophyll swamp scrub

(d) Evergreen narrow sclerophyll swamp

4 Evergreen broad sclerophyll scrub
(a) Mesophyllous evergreen broad sclerophyll scrub

(b) Megaphyllous evergreen broad sclerophyll scrub

5 Mossy evergreen sclerophyll scrub

6 Gnarled evergreen narrow sclerophyll scrub (krummholz)

7 Straight evergreen narrow sclerophyll scrub

8 Microphyllous evergreen scrub
(a) Green microphyllous evergreen scrub

e. *Chusquea* brake (Andes)
Pleioblastus brake (Ryukyu Islands)

(Composed of shrubs with adaptations to stand lengthy or permanent submergence of root systems; peat development may be notable)

e. *Hibiscus tiliaceus* swamp (Pacific Islands)
(Composed of canes or reeds)
e. *Phragmites karka* swamp (Pacific Islands)
e. Low phase of mangrove swamp
Avicennia swamp (New Zealand, Australia)
Rhododendron swamp (Eastern North America)
e. *Picea mariana* swamp or bog, low phases (Canada)

(Stiff shrubs, leaves generally rather small)
e. Secondary scrub (Colombian Andes)
Maquis (Mediterranean)
Ceanothus chaparral (California)
Quercus dumosa chaparral (California)
Rhododendron maximum scrub (Eastern U.S.)
e. Low palmetto scrub (Florida)

(Stiff shrubs, leaves generally rather small; with abundant epiphytes—scrub equivalent of mossy forest)
e. Stiff scrub of wet mountain crests (Pacific Islands)

e. *Pinus flexilis* krummholz (Rocky Mountains)

(Not especially gnarled)
e. *Pinus pumila* scrub (Japan)
Pinus mugo scrub (Tyrol)?
Adenostemma chaparral (California)

(Often thorny)
e. *Acacia farnesiana* scrub (Tropics)
Lucaena leucocephala scrub (Pacific Islands)
African heaths?

(b) Evergreen thorn scrub

    Ilex vomitoria scrub, or yaupon (South-eastern U.S.)
    Some phases of *Ceanothus* chaparral (South-western U.S.)

(c) Gray microphyllous evergreen scrub

    e. *Acacia farnesiana* scrub (Tropics)
    e. Sage brush (*Artemisia tridentata*) (Western U.S.)
    California sage when dominantly of *Artemisia california* (California)

1B2 Deciduous scrub
(shrubs periodically bare of leaves, usually in dry season or winter)

1 Deciduous orthophyll scrub

  (a) Mesophyllous deciduous orthophyll scrub

    e. *Salix* scrub, taller phases (Arctic and Subarctic)
    Spiraea scrub (Eastern U.S.)
    Crataegus thicket (Eastern U.S., Europe)

  (b) Microphyllous deciduous orthophyll scrub

    e. *Leucaena leucocephala* scrub (E. Java)

2 Deciduous swamp scrub

  (a) Mesophyllous deciduous orthophyll swamp scrub

    (Root systems adapted to prolonged submergence)
    e. Alder (*Alnus*) swamp (Eastern U.S.)

  (b) Microphyllous deciduous swamp scrub

    e. *Larix* swamp low phases (North-eastern North America)

  (c) Deciduous broad sclerophyll swamp scrub

    e. Mangrove swamps (Guajira Peninsula, Colombia)
    Excoecaria swamps (Malaysia and S.E. Asia)

3 [Deciduous sclerophyll scrub]

4 Deciduous thorn scrub (Thornbush)

    (Usually microphyllous, cacti often abundant. Rare in this closed form)
    e. Caatinga, low phases (North-eastern Brazil)

1C *Dwarf scrub*

(Closed predominantly woody vegetation less than 0·5 meters tall)

1C1 Evergreen dwarf scrub

1 Evergreen orthophyll dwarf scrub

    e. *Rhododendron* mat (Eastern Himalaya)?

2 Evergreen broad sclerophyll dwarf scrub

  (a) Mesophyllous broad sclerophyll dwarf scrub

    e. *Arctostaphylos uva-ursi* mat (Northern temperate region)

  (b) Microphyllous evergreen dwarf scrub

    (Without significant peat accumulation)
    e. Coastal *Osteomeles* scrub (Miyako Island)
    Calluna heath without peat (Western Europe)

(c) Microphyllous evergreen dwarf heath

(With peat accumulation)
e. *Empetrum* heath (Arctic and Subarctic)
  Loiseleuria heath (Arctic)

3 Evergreen dwarf shrub bog

(Dwarf shrub with significant peat accumulation, root systems of plants adapted to constant immersion)
e. Mountain bogs, more closed phases (Hawaii)
  Chamaedaphne bog (Eastern North America)

1C2 Deciduous dwarf scrub

1 Deciduous orthophyll dwarf scrub
(a) Deciduous orthophyll dwarf scrub

(Without significant peat accumulation)
e. Low bush *Vaccinium* scrub (North temperate and sub-arctic regions)

(b) Deciduous orthophyll dwarf heath

(With peat accumulation)
e. *Vaccinium myrtillus* heath (Subarctic regions)

1D *Open forest with closed lower layers*

Trees with crowns not touching, crowns mostly not separated by more than their diameters)

1D1 Evergreen open forest with closed lower layers

1 Open evergreen orthophyll forest

e. Denser phases of niaouli (*Melaleuca*) vegetation New Caledonia
  Foret-claire (Indo China)

2 Open evergreen swamp
(a) Open narrow sclerophyll swamp
(b) Open orthophyll swamp

e. Open spruce muskeg
e. Peat swamp (North Borneo)
  Barringtonia racemosa swamp (Micronesia)

(c) Open broad sclerophyll swamp

e. Open phases of mangrove swamp with closed shrub layer (Tropics)

3 Open evergreen broad sclerophyll forest
(a) Megaphyllous open evergreen broad sclerophyll forest

(Open palm or pandan forests)
e. *Mauritia* groves (Colombian Ilanos)
  Sabal forest (Central Eastern Mexico)

(b) Mesophyllous open evergreen broad sclerophyll forest

e. Denser phases of Orinocoan "savanna"
  Open oak forest (Northern Thailand)
  Live oak (*Quercus*) woodland (California)

4 Open evergreen narrow sclerophyll forest
  (a) Resinous open evergreen narrow sclerophyll forest

    e. Open *Pinus* forests (Philippines, Mexico, Ryukyu Islands)
    Open aspects of pine barrens (New Jersey)
    Denser aspects of pinyon and pinyon-juniper (*Pinus-Juniperus*) with herbaceous or shrubby lower layers (Rocky Mountains and east slope of Sierra Nevada, Western U.S.)

  (b) Non-resinous open evergreen narrow sclerophyll forest

    e. Some open phases of *Casuarina* forests (Mariana Islands)

5 Open microphyllous evergreen forest

    [May be somewhat thorny]
    e. Open phases of *Prosopis* forest (Hawaii)

1D2 Open deciduous forest with closed lower layers

1 Open deciduous orthophyll forest

    e. Deciduous dipterocarp forest (Thailand).

2 Open deciduous swamp
  (a) Open broad orthophyll swamp

    e. Tupelo (*Nyssa*) swamp, open phases (South-eastern U.S.)

  (b) Open broad sclerophyll swamp

    e. Mangrove swamp, open phases where deciduous (Ryukyu Islands)

  (c) Open narrow sclerophyll swamp

    e. Open *Larix* muskeg (Central Canada)
    Open *Taxodium* swamp (South-eastern U.S.)

3 Open deciduous narrow sclerophyll forest

    e. Open *Larix* forest (Central Canada)

4 [Open deciduous broad sclerophyll forest]

    [Possibly does not exist]

5 Open microphyllous deciduous forest

    e. Miombo forest (South Central Africa)

1E   *Closed scrub with scattered trees*

1E1 Closed evergreen scrub with scattered trees (at least shrub layer evergreen)

1 Evergreen orthophyll scrub with trees

    e. *Scaevola* scrub with scattered trees (Pacific coral islands)

2 Evergreen sclerophyll scrub with trees

    e. Scrub oak with scattered live oaks (*Quercus*) (California)
    Larger leafed phases of chaparral with scattered *Pinus* (California)
    Maquis with scattered *Pinus* (Mediterranean)
    Kalmia latifolia with scattered *Quercus* and *Pinus* (Virginia mountains)

3 Microphyllous evergreen scrub with trees

    e. *Purshia tridentata* with *Pinus* (Western U.S.)
    Artemisia tridentata with *Pinus* (Western U.S.)
    Artemisia californica with *Quercus* (California)

4 Megaphyllous evergreen broad sclerophyll scrub with trees — e. Saw palmetto scrub with *Pinus* (Florida)

1E2 Closed deciduous scrub with scattered trees

1 Deciduous orthophyll scrub with trees — e. *Quercus ilicifolia* with *Pinus rigada* (Appalachians)
2 [Deciduous sclerophyll scrub with trees] — (Perhaps does not exist)
3 [Microphyllous deciduous scrub with trees] — (Perhaps does not exist)

1F Dwarf scrub with scattered trees

1F1 Evergreen dwarf scrub with scattered trees

1 Microphyllous evergreen dwarf scrub with trees — e. *Calluna* heath with *Pinus* (England)
  - (Without significant peat formation)
  - (With peat accumulation)
2 Microphyllous evergreen heath with trees — e. *Empetrum* phase of heath birch *Betula* forest (Lappland)

1F2 Deciduous dwarf scrub with trees

1 Deciduous heath with trees — e. *Vaccinium* phases of heath birch (Betula) forest (Lappland)
  - (With significant peat accumulation)

1G Open scrub with closed ground cover

1G1 Open evergreen scrub with closed ground cover

1 Open evergreen orthophyll scrub — e. Low phases of campo cerrado (Brazil)
2 Open evergreen broad sclerophyll scrub
   (a) Megaphyllous open evergreen broad sclerophyll scrub — e. Saw palmetto (*Serenoa*) prairie (Florida) / *Eugeissonia* scrub (Malaya) / *Chamaerops humilis* scrub (Algeria)
   (b) Mesophyllous open evergreen broad sclerophyll scrub — e. Low phases of *Diospyros-Osmanthus* forest (Lanai, Hawaiian Islands)
3 Open gnarled evergreen narrow sclerophyll scrub or open krummholz — e. Open *Pinus flexilis* krummholz (Rocky Mountains) / Open *Picea* krummholz (White Mountains N.H.)
4 Open microphyllous evergreen scrub — e. Open phases of *Sarothamnus* scrub (N.W. Europe)

1G2 Open deciduous scrub with closed ground cover

1 Open deciduous orthophyll scrub with closed ground cover — e. Open phases of *Salix* scrub and *Betula* scrub (Subarctic)

1H Open dwarf scrub with closed ground cover

1H1 Open evergreen dwarf scrub with closed ground cover

1 Open evergreen orthophyll dwarf scrub — e. *Sida-Heliotropium* dwarf scrub (Christmas Island, Pacific)
2 Open evergreen shrub bog — e. Open phases of mountain bogs (Hawaii)
3 Open evergreen microphyllous dwarf scrub — e. Open *Calluna* and *Erica* heath lower phases (Western Europe)

K* 1H2 Open deciduous dwarf scrub with closed ground cover

1 Open deciduous orthophyll dwarf scrub (Without significant peat accumulation)
e. Open phases of low-bush *Vaccinium* scrub (Eastern U.S.)

2 Open deciduous orthophyll heath (With significant accumulation of peat)
e. Open phases of *Vaccinium myrtillus* heath (Sub-arctic)

1I Tall savanna
(Closed grass or other herbaceous vegetation 1 meter tall or more with scattered trees)

1I1 Evergreen savanna (trees evergreen)

1 Evergreen orthophyll savanna
e. Fern savanna (Palau Islands)

2 Evergreen broad sclerophyll savanna
(a) Mesophyllous evergreen sclerophyll savanna
e. *Curatella-Byrosonima* savanna (northern South America)
(b) Megaphyllous evergreen sclerophyll savanna
e. Various palm savannas (tropical America and Africa)
Pandanus savanna (Guam)

3 Evergreen sclerophyll swamp savanna
(a) Evergreen narrow leaf swamp savanna
e. Saw-grass everglades with pines (Florida)
(b) Evergreen broad sclerophyll swamp savanna
e. Coastal swamp savanna (West Africa)

4 Evergreen narrow sclerophyll savanna
e. *Pinus* savanna (Luzon)
Casuarina equisetifolia savanna (Guam)

5 Microphyllous evergreen savanna
e. Closed erosion scar community with ferns, grasses and *Myrtella* (Guam)

1I2 Deciduous tall savanna (trees deciduous)

1 Deciduous orthophyll savanna
e. *Adansonia* savanna (Sudan)

2 Deciduous microphyll savanna
e. Less thorny phases of *Acacia* tall grass savanna (Africa)

3 Deciduous thorn savanna
e. Thorny phases of *Acacia* tall grass savanna (Africa)

1J Low savanna
(Herbaceous vegetation less than 1 meter tall, with scattered trees)

1J1 Evergreen low savanna (trees evergreen)

1 Evergreen orthophyll low savanna
e. Fern savanna (Palau Islands)
Live-oak savanna (California)

2 Evergreen broad-sclerophyll low savanna
e. Heavily grazed phases of evergreen broad-sclerophyll tall savannas

3 Evergreen narrow-sclerophyll low savanna
e. California foothill savanna where *Pinus sabiniana* predominates
More open phases of pinelands of South-eastern U.S.
Juniperus virginiana savanna (Eastern U.S.)

4 Evergreen narrow sclerophyll lichen savanna

   e. Lichen muskeg with *Picea* dominant

5 Evergreen narrow sclerophyll swamp savanna

   e. *Sphagnum* muskeg with *Picea* dominant

1J2 Deciduous low savanna

1 Deciduous orthophyll savanna

   e. *Quercus lobata* and *Q. douglasii* savanna (California) *Crataegus* pastures where trees are well developed (Eastern U.S.)

2 [Deciduous broad sclerophyll low savanna]

3 Deciduous lichen savanna

   e. Lichen muskeg with *Larix* dominant (most open phases)

4 Deciduous swamp savanna

   e. *Sphagnum* muskeg with *Larix* dominant (most open phases)

1K Shrub savanna

(Closed grass or other herbaceous vegetation with scattered shrubs)

1K1 Evergreen shrub savanna

1 Evergreen orthophyll shrub savanna

   e. *Sida-Lepturus* savanna (Pacific coral islands)

2 Evergreen broad sclerophyll shrub savanna

   e. Lower phases of *Curatella-Byrsonima* savanna (South America)

3 Evergreen narrow sclerophyll shrub savanna

   e. *Juniperus communis* savanna (North temperate zone)

  (a) Resinous evergreen narrow sclerophyll shrub savanna

  (b) Non-resinous evergreen narrow sclerophyll shrub savanna

   e. *Casuarina* savanna, early stages (Guam)

4 Evergreen microphyll scrub savanna

  (a) Green evergreen microphyll shrub savanna

   e. Sparse, grassy phases of subalpine scrub (Hawaiian volcanoes)

  (b) Gray evergreen microphyll shrub savanna

   e. Grass with scattered sagebrush (*Artemisia tridentata*) (Western U.S.)

1K2 Deciduous shrub savanna

1 Deciduous orthophyll shrub savanna

   e. Early stages of forest succession in old fields (Eastern U.S.)

2 [Deciduous broad sclerophyll shrub savanna]

3 Microphyllous deciduous shrub savanna

4 Mesophyllous deciduous thorn shrub savanna — e. Pastures with *Crataegus* (Eastern U.S.)

5 Microphyllous deciduous thorn shrub savanna — e. *Acacia* savanna (Caribbean)

1L Tall grass

(Closed herbaceous vegetation exceeding 1 meter in height, predominantly graminoid)

1L1 Evergreen tall grass
(Shoots remaining green the year round)

1 Evergreen orthophyll tall grass — e. Stands of *Panicum purpurascens* and of *Panicum maximum* in Pacific Islands

2 Tall evergreen graminoid marsh — e. *Scirpus* marsh
Typha marsh
Papyrus (Tropics)

3 Evergreen orthophyll tall tussock grass — e. Snow-tussock (*Danthonia*), closed phases (New Zealand)

4 Evergreen sclerophyll tall grass — e. *Saccharum spontaneum* stands (Western Pacific)
Miscanthus floridulus stands, where these are not seasonally brown (Western Pacific)
Imperata savanna, taller phases (Western Pacific)

1L2 Seasonal tall grass
(Turning brown in dry season or winter, often burned)

1 Seasonal orthophyll tall grass — e. Tall grass prairie (Mississippi Valley)
High veld (*Themeda*) (Transvaal)
Patna, taller aspects (Ceylon)

2 Seasonal sclerophyll grass — e. *Miscanthus floridulus* or sword grass, in areas with dry season (Western Pacific)
Themeda stands (Western Pacific)

1M Short grass

(Closed herbaceous vegetation, less than 1 meter tall, predominantly graminoid)

1M1 Evergreen short grass

1 Evergreen orthophyll short grass — e. Lalang, *Imperata cylindrica*, shorter phases (Western Pacific)

2 Evergreen orthophyll graminoid marsh — e. *Paspalum* marsh; *Cyperus* marsh (Guam)

3 Evergreen orthophyll short tussock grass — e. *Festuca* tussock (New Zealand)

4 Evergreen short grass and sedge bog — (Growing from a mass of grass- and sedge-peat)
e. *Oreobolus* bog

1M2 Seasonal short grass
1 Seasonal orthophyll meadows (short grass)
  e. Patna shorter aspects (Ceylon)
    Short grass prairie (western Mississippi Valley)
    Grass and sedge tundras (Arctic)
    Most temperate zone pastures
2 Seasonal orthophyll marsh
  e. Marshes of Granges Delta
    Rice field
    Salt marsh (temperate Atlantic coasts)
3 Seasonal sclerophyll short grass meadow
  e. Closed aspects of puna (Andes)
4 Seasonal sclerophyll marsh
  e. Saw grass everglades (Florida)

1N *Broad-leafed herb vegetation*

(Closed vegetation, predominantly of broad-leafed herbaceous plants)

1N1 Evergreen broad-leafed herb vegetation
1 Evergreen broad-leafed weedy vegetation
  e. Pioneer weedy vegetation after clearing (Tropics)
2 Evergreen broad-leafed marsh
  e. Cultivated taro pits (Polynesia)
3 Evergreen fern meadow
  e. *Gleichenia* sward (Tropics)
    Nephrolepis meadow (Western Pacific)
4 Evergreen giant herb thicket
  e. Banana plantations and wild banana stands

1N2 Seasonal broad-leafed herb vegetation
1 Seasonal broad-leafed meadow
  e. Early stages in old-field vegetation (Humid Temperate areas)
    Trollius meadow (Lappland)
2 Seasonal fern meadow
  e. *Pteridium aquilinum* brake

1O *Closed bryoid vegetation*

1O1 Closed bryophyte vegetation
1 *Sphagnum* bog
  e. Raised bog
    Muskeg
2 Moss meadow
  e. *Rhacomitrium* meadow (Hawaii)

1O2 Closed lichen vegetation
1 Lichen bog
  e. *Cladonia* muskeg
2 Lichen meadow
  e. *Cladonia* meadow (Subarctic)

1P *Submerged meadows*

(Vegetation of rooted aquatic herbs, adapted for permanent complete submersion except in some cases for floating leaves)

1P1 Evergreen submerged meadows
1 Evergreen watergrass
  e. Turtle grass
2 Macrophyllous evergreen submerged meadows
  e. Canal vegetation (Thailand)

300

3 Megaphyllous evergreen submerged meadows

    e. *Victoria* meadows (South America)

1P2 Seasonal submerged meadows (plants disappearing, at least their shoots, in winter)

1 Seasonal watergrass

    e. Eelgrass (*Zostera marina*) (Temperate coasts)
    Closed *Potamogeton* meadows (North-eastern U.S.)
    (Leaves of ordinary size, not narrowly linear of grasslike)

2 Broad-leafed seasonal submerged meadows

    e. Broad-leafed *Potamogeton* stands (eastern North America)
    (Water lilies and similar plants dominant)

3 Macrophyllous seasonal submerged meadows

    e. *Nymphaea-Nuphar* meadows (eastern North America)

1Q Floating meadows

(Closed vegetation of aquatic herbs, adapted to floating conditions, not rooted in bottom)

1Q1 Evergreen floating meadows

1 Broad-leafed evergreen floating meadows

    e. Water hyacinth (*Eichhornia*) (Tropics and Sub-tropics) *Salvinia, Pistia*

2 Evergreen floating grass

    e. Gramalote (Amazonia)

3 Thalliform evergreen floating vegetation

    e. Duckweed (*Lemna*, etc.) (Tropics)

4 Microphyllous evergreen floating meadows

    e. *Azolla* (Tropics)

1Q2 Seasonal floating meadow

1 Thalliform seasonal floating meadow

    e. Duckweed (*Lemna*, etc.) (Temperate Zone)

2 Microphyllous seasonal floating meadow

    e. *Azolla* (Temperate Zone)

2 OPEN VEGETATION

(Plants or tufts of plants not touching but crowns not separated by more than their diameters; plants, not substratum, dominating landscape)

2A Steppe Forest

(Often called woodland or woodland-savanna) (Tree layer and lower layers may be open or sparse)

2A1 Evergreen steppe forest (Tree layers, at least, evergreen)

1 [Evergreen orthophyll steppe forest]

    (Possibly does not exist with open lower layers)

2 Evergreen broad sclerophyll steppe forest

(a) Megaphyllous evergreen sclerophyll steppe forest

    e. *Borassus* forest (Northwest India, North Ceylon)
    Phoenix groves in oases (Arabia, North Africa)

(b) Mesophyllous evergreen sclerophyll steppe forest

    e. Mallee (*Eucalyptus*) bush (Australia)?

3 Open evergreen sclerophyll swamp

    e. Open phases of mangrove swamps (tropical coasts)

301

4 Evergreen narrow sclerophyll steppe forest
   (a) Resinous evergreen narrow sclerophyll forest — e. Some open *Pinus* forests (Western U.S.)

   (b) Non-resinous evergreen narrow sclerophyll forest — e. Some open *Casuarina* forests (Saipan, Guam)

5 Microphyllous evergreen steppe forest — e. Some *Prosopis* forests (Hawaii, Caribbean)

2A2 Deciduous steppe forest

1 Deciduous orthophyll steppe forest — e. Drier phases of deciduous dipterocarp forests (Thailand)
At least some phases of "foret-claire" (Indo-China)
Open oak (*Quercus*) forest (sandhills of south-eastern U.S.)

2 Microphyllous deciduous steppe forest — e. Denser aspects of Atlantic coastal forest (Colombia)

3 Deciduous bamboo steppe forest — e. *Bambusa arundinacea* forest (near Bombay, India)

4 Open dedicuous thorn (steppe) forest — e. Open thorn forest (Caribbean lowlands)

2B Steppe scrub

(Like steppe forest, but with shrubs (over 0·5 meters tall) instead of trees)

2B1 Evergreen steppe scrub

1 Evergreen orthophyll steppe scrub — e. *Sida fallax* scrub (Northern Marshall Islands)

2 Evergreen broad sclerophyll steppe scrub — e. Scrub of serpentine areas (New Caledonia)
Scrub of Mineral Belt (Near Nelson, New Zealand)

3 Gnarled evergreen narrow sclerophyll steppe scrub (open krummholz) — e. Open *Pinus flexilis* krummholz (Rocky Mountains)
Picea-Abies krummholz, open aspects (Northern Appalachians, Adirondack Mountains Eastern U S)

4 Microphyllous evergreen steppe scrub

   (a) [Green evergreen microphyllous steppe scrub] — e. Open aspects of *Calluna-Erica* heath (Western Europe)
Tola (*Lepidophyllum*) heath (Peru, Bolivia)
(Perhaps does not exist)

   (b) Gray evergreen microphyllous steppe scrub — e. Open sagebrush (*Artemisia tridentata*) (Great Basin, U.S.)
Krameria or *Coleogyne* scrub (Western U.S.)

5 Evergreen succulent steppe scrub — e. *Sarcobatus* flats (Great Basin, U.S.)
Tamarix scrub (Arid areas, Mediterranean, Central Asia, Asia, South-western U.S.)
(Shrubs with gray scurfy leaves)

6 Evergreen saltbush steppe scrub — e. *Atriplex* flats (Great Basin, U.S.)

2B2 Deciduous steppe scrub

1 Deciduous orthophyll steppe scrub
  e. Deciduous scrub-oak and shin-oak (*Quercus* spp.) (South-west U.S.)
  Denser phases of *Ulmus pumila* scrub (Central Asia)

2 [Deciduous sclerophyll steppe scrub]

3 Microphyllous deciduous steppe scrub
  e. Grassy phases of *Pentzia-Rhigozum* scrub (South Africa)

4 Deciduous thorn steppe scrub (thorn-bush)
  e. Open thornbush (Caribbean lowlands)

2C *Dwarf steppe scrub*

(Open predominantly woody vegetation less than 0·5 meters tall)

2C1 Evergreen dwarf steppe scrub

1 Evergreen orthophyll dwarf steppe scrub
  e. Early stages of evergreen steppe forest and steppe scrub

2 Evergreen broad sclerophyll dwarf steppe scrub
  e. Dwarf phases of garrigue (Mediterranean)
  Low woody aspects of puna (Southern Andes)

3 Evergreen narrow sclerophyll dwarf steppe scrub
  e. Low denser phases of tola (*Lepidophyllum*) heath (Peru, Bolivia)

4 Microphyllous evergreen dwarf steppe scrub
  e. Low open sand heath (Western Europe)

2C2 [Deciduous dwarf steppe scrub]
(Perhaps does not exist)

2D *Steppe savanna*

(Steppe with scattered trees)

2S1 Evergreen steppe savanna (trees evergreen)

1 Evergreen orthophyll steppe savanna
  e. *Guazuma* savanna (Northern South America)

2 Evergreen sclerophyll steppe savanna
  e. Sparse phases of *Curatella-Byrsonima* savanna (Colombia)

3 [Evergreen microphyll steppe savanna]
(Perhaps does not exist)

2D2 Deciduous steppe savanna

1 Deciduous orthophyll steppe savanna
  e. Sparser aspects of *Quercus lobata-Q. douglasii* savanna (California foothills)

2 [Deciduous broad sclerophyll steppe savanna]
(Perhaps does not exist)

3 Microphyllous deciduous steppe savanna
  e. Deciduous savannas of northern Colombia

4 Deciduous thorn steppe savanna
  e. Low phases of *Acacia*-desert grass savanna (Africa)

2E *Shrub steppe savanna*

2E1 Evergreen shrub steppe savanna

1 Evergreen orthophyll shrub steppe savanna
  e. *Polylepis* puna (Bolivia)
  Sophora-Myoporum savanna (High altitudes, Hawaii)

303

2 Evergreen sclerophyll shrub steppe savanna
 e. Desert grassland with *Yucca elata* (South-western U.S.)
  Desert grassland with scattered *Chamaerops* (North Africa)

3 Evergreen microphyll shrub steppe savanna
 e. Llareta (*Azorella*) puna (Bolivia, Chile)

4 Evergreen succulent shrub steppe savanna
 e. Desert grassland with *Opuntia* (South-western U.S.)

2E2 Deciduous shrub steppe savanna

1 Deciduous orthophyll shrub steppe savanna
 e. *Ulmus pumila* scrub, open phases (Central Asia)

2 [Deciduous sclerophyll shrub steppe savanna]
 (Possibly does not exist)

3 Microphyllous deciduous shrub steppe savanna
 e. Mesquite (*Prosopis*) grassland (Texas–New Mexico)

4 Deciduous thorn shrub steppe savanna
 e. *Acacia maracantha* savanna (Andes)

2F   *Dwarf shrub steppe savanna*

2F1 Evergreen dwarf shrub steppe savanna

1 [Evergreen orthophyll dwarf shrub steppe savanna]
 (Possibly does not exist)

2 Evergreen narrow sclerophyll dwarf shrub steppe savanna
 e. Low phases of tola (*Lepidophyllum*) heath (Peru, Bolivia)

3 Succulent dwarf shrub steppe savanna
 e. Desert grassland with low *Opuntia* (South-western U.S.)

2F2 Seasonal dwarf shrub steppe savanna

1 Seasonal sclerophyll dwarf shrub steppe savanna
 e. *Tetraglochin* puna (Andes)

2G   *Steppe*

(Open herbaceous vegetation, tufts or plants discrete, yet close enough to dominate the landscape)

2G1 Evergreen steppe

1 Evergreen saltbush steppe
 e. Herbaceous *Atriplex* steppe (Australia, Hawaii)

2 Evergreen succulent steppe
 e. *Suaeda* flats (Coastal or alkaline sand flats, (Africa, Thailand, New Mexico, etc.)
  Portulaca steppe (Marshall Islands)

3 Evergreen cushion plant steppe
 e. *Pycnophyllum* puna (Bolivia)
  Raoulia steppe (New Zealand)

2G2 Seasonal steppe

1 Seasonal grass steppe
 e. *Stipa* puna (Peru and Bolivia)
  Desert grassland (South-western U.S.)

2 Annual herb steppe — Cenchrus-Lepturus grassland (Canton Island and other dry coral islands)

e. Denser aspects of *Abronia*, *Eschscholizia*, *Astragalus* and other ephemeral types on sandy areas (South-western U.S.)

2H   *Bryoid steppe*

2H1 [Open bryophyte vegetation]   (Perhaps does not exist)

2H2 Open lichen vegetation
    1 Lichen tundra   e. *Cladonia* heath (Lappland)

2I   *Open submerged meadows*

2I1 [Evergreen open submerged meadows]   (Perhaps does not exist)

2I2 Seasonal open submerged meadows
    1 Seasonal watergrass   e. *Zostera* (open phases)
    2 Broad-leafed seasonal submerged meadows   c. *Potamogeton* communities (Open phases)
                                                       Lobelia dortmanna-Littorella communities (Scotland)
    3 Macrophyllous seasonal submerged meadows   e. *Nuphar lutea* community (open phases)

2J   *Open floating meadows*

2J1 [Evergreen open floating meadows]   (Possibly does not exist)

2J2 Seasonal open floating meadows
    1 Thalliform seasonal open floating meadows   e. *Lemna* communities (open phases)
    2 Microphyllous seasonal open floating meadows   e. *Azolla* (open phases)

3   SPARSE VEGETATION OR DESERT
    (Plants so scattered that substratum dominates landscape)

3A   *Desert forest*
    (Scattered trees, subordinate shrub or herb layers very sparse, or absent)

3A1 Evergreen desert forest (may be evergreen because of persistent leaves or because of green stems)
    1 Evergreen non-succulent desert forest   e. *Parkinsonia* desert (Arizona, Peru)
                                                      Olneya desert (Arizona (May be deciduous in coldest winters)
    2 Evergreen succulent desert forest   e. *Cereus giganteus* desert (Arizona)

305

3A2 Deciduous desert forest

  1 Microphyllous deciduous desert forest
    e. *Prosopis* desert (Arizona, Peru)
       Idria desert (Baja, California)

3B *Desert scrub*

(Scattered shrubs in an otherwise bare or only ephemerally vegetated landscape, not here differentiated into shrub and dwarf shrub classes.)

3B1 Evergreen desert scrub

  1 Evergreen sclerophyll desert scrub
    e. *Capparis* desert (Peru)
       Welwitschia desert (South-west Africa)
       Phoenix arabica desert (Arabia)

  2 Microphyllous evergreen desert scrub
    e. *Larrea-Franseria* desert (South-western U.S.)
       Cologyne desert (Arizona)

  3 Saltbush desert
    e. *Atriplex* flats (South-western U.S.)
       (Dominated by rigid green-stemmed, spinose, leafless or ephemerally leafy plants)

  4 Evergreen desert thorn-scrub
    e. *Koeberlinia* desert (New Mexico)

  5 Evergreen succulent desert scrub
    e. *Opuntia fulgida* desert (Arizona)
       Suaeda-Zygophyllum desert (Arizona)
       Tamarix desert (Arabia)

3B2 Deciduous desert scrub

  1 Microphyllous deciduous desert scrub
    e. Sparse phases of *Pentzia Rhigozum* scrub (South Africa)

  2 Deciduous desert thorn-scrub
    e. *Fouquieria-Acacia gregii* desert (South-western U.S.)
       Acacia constricta desert (New Mexico)

3C *Desert herb vegetation*

(Scattered herbaceous plants only)

3C1 Evergreen desert herb vegetation

  1 Evergreen succulent herb desert
    e. Karroo succulent desert (South Africa)
       (Plants with special adaptations enabling them to survive in shifting sand)

  2 Evergreen psammophyte desert
    e. *Cyperus conglomeratus* desert (Arabia)

  3 Lichen tundra sparse phases
    e. Sparse *Cladonia* tundra (Arctic)

3C2 Seasonal desert herb vegetation

  1 Seasonal desert grass
    e. *Aristida* desert, where shrubs are lacking (South Africa)
       (Vegetation principally of ephemeral annuals and geophytes, appearing only for short periods after infrequent rains)

  2 Ephemeral herb desert
    e. *Loma* vegetation (Peru)

3D Sparse submerged meadows

3D1 [Evergreen sparse submerged meadows]

3D2 Seasonal sparse submerged meadows

1 Seasonal watergrass   (Possibly does not exist)

2 [Broad leaves seasonal submerged meadows]

3 [Macrophyllous seasonal submerged meadows]

e. *Zostera* (sparse phases)
(Possibly does not exist)

(Possibly does not exist)

(Possibly does not exist)

CHART OF HUMAN IMPACTS ON THE COUNTRYSIDE

In addition to written descriptions and analysis of the varied and complex human impacts on the countryside it is convenient for many purposes to have a chart setting them out schematically so that each can readily be identified and compared with others. For this purpose four points are critical in enabling us to answer key questions. *What particular human activities make an impact on the countryside? What kinds of land or geographic regions are affected by each? What is the nature of the effects of each, direct and indirect, deliberate or unintended? And finally; What is the incidence of each in space, time, intensity, trend and so forth?*

From the answers to the first point we can readily trace the industries, occupations, interests or sports involved in each impact, and thus define the problems of reconciliation or adjustment to be faced, and the parties to be consulted.

Answers to the second enable us to plot the relative vulnerability either of particular provinces, districts or localities or of particular types of terrain such as coasts, limestone outcrops or forest. Combining the first and the second we can find which particular interests are in competition for specific types of site, or conversely which sites are of interest to a number of either conflicting or of potentially complementary interests.

Answers to the third enable us to distinguish between activities making a once-and-for-all impact, usually at an early stage such as construction or excavation; activities which inevitably if not intentionally involve continuing disturbance or damage; activities causing damage through lack of forethought, neglect or not caring, as in avoidable pollution; activities leading cumulatively to damage such as erosion unless early and continuing preventive measures are taken; and activities normally innocuous but liable to cause catastrophic damage by accidents such as fire or collisions of oil tankers. On this basis we can appraise the scale and nature of the hazards to which any particular site is vulnerable. Answers to the fourth point assist in tracing the times, seasons, or stages at which maximum risk occurs. We can also determine whether it is widespread or concentrated, gradual or abrupt, and how closely it is bound up with the satisfaction of some socially or economically important objective.

In collaboration with A. W. Colling I prepared such a chart for the first Countryside in 1970 Study Conference in 1963, and had the benefit of several hundred corrections and suggestions from many authorities on special aspects in producing the final drafts. Although this Chart relates only to Great Britain, and clearly could not be extended to cover the whole earth without making it intolerably complicated, it is reproduced in part here both in order to demonstrate the applicability of the technique to other areas (as has already been done in a number of cases) and to serve as a tool of analysis for those who wish to probe some particular problem more deeply than the text alone would permit. In the original additional details were provided on actual parties interested, examples of problems and possible solutions, and bibliographic references. These are omitted here in the interests of compactness; they are to be found in Papers No. 2 and No. 3 in the Proceedings of the Study Conference published in 1964 by H.M.S.O., price 25s.

The sequence of treatment begins with activities which actually reshape the land and continues through cropping and mining to construction and to what may be termed free-range activities on the surface of the land, finishing with those which aim to leave the land alone. Water, except insofar as it touches emerging land is not covered, nor does the Chart cover land which has once lost any semblance of rural character through becoming entirely engulfed in urban or other fully developed areas. Some of the activities listed are very small, others very large; some rapidly expanding, others dying out. Sometimes however even small activities can be illuminating in recognising points of principle or trends. Some effects are so intangible or indirect that they are not caught by the Chart, although they may be factors to be reckoned with in the background, since the Chart is concerned with what can be identified, located and analysed.

It is thought that by following up such an approach valuable assistance can be gained both in the study and the handling of problems of the care of the environment. For this the Chart represents merely a first step. Being prepared for a conservation conference it is drawn up primarily from that standpoint, although it seeks fairly to recognise other interests and attitudes. It should, however, be regarded as an aid and stimulus to further effort, rather than as a definitive or dogmatic statement.

1. Activity or Operation	2. Area or Land-type Affected	3. Nature of Effects Arising	4. Incidence (Time, Space, Degree)
I LAND RECLAMATION, DRAINAGE AND IMPROVEMENT			
1.1 Sea Defence works	Low-lying parts of coastline or unstable sea cliffs	Often linked with reclamation of marshy hinterland (see below). Sea walls provide butts for shooting wildfowl. May cause obliteration of geological features directly or by causing beach to aggrade	All year round
1.2 Winning new land from sea or estuary	Low-lying coasts and estuaries	Lowering of water table resulting in alteration of flora, fauna and habitats	All year round
1.3 Drainage of fresh water marshes	Lowland wetlands	Destruction of wetland habitats sometimes of scientifically very important sites	All year round
1.4 Making of new drainage channels	Lowland bogs, fens, marshes and rivers	Lowering of water table and alteration or destruction of water habitats.	All year round
1.5 Straightening and deepening of existing channels and of "main" rivers	Rivers	Destruction of bank and marginal aquatic vegetation by dragline machines, and by dredged spoil. Increased run-off sometimes leading to sudden and more drastic spates; rivers rise and fall more rapidly and annual average flow decreased, so that pollution concentrations raised and abstraction potential lowered (See also Sections 3.14 and 3.15)	

309

	1. Activity or Operation	2. Area or Land-type Affected	3. Nature of Effects Arising	4. Incidence (Time, Space, Degree)
1.6	Improvement of mountain and hill land	Uplands in S.W. England, Pennines, Wales and Scotland	Alteration of habitat, flora and fauna, and character of landscape. Limitation of access	All year round
1.7 1.71	Peat extraction (mechanised commercial)	Peaty areas in W. and N.	Destruction of raised bog ecology; serious damage to wetland habitats in some cases; creation of new habitats in others; and may enable agricultural reclamation	Local; intense
1.72	(traditional for fuel, e.g. crofters)	Scottish Highlands and Islands	Damage to ecology not serious, and may preserve wet and marshy habitats	local; limited
1.8	Rehabilitation of derelict land	Deposits of mining and industrial waste, e.g. spoil heaps; and reclamation of "unproductive" land, derelict factory sites, buildings, etc. Midlands and North; S. Wales	Some sites rehabilitated as recreation grounds, etc. Increase of vegetation, including planted trees. Reduction of bare surfaces and exposed toxic deposits	All year round
2	FORESTRY AND SILVICULTURE:			
2.1	Planting of Timber	Some lowlands and most uplands	Much open heathland and dune habitat lost. Well mixed F.C. forests occur, but proportion small. Reduction of ecological diversity and alteration of scenery by even-aged stands largely of one or two exotic species. Cutting off of hill-grazings from lower-lying farms. Possible reduction of water yield from catchments. Increased acreage of forests may be partly responsible for increase in Woodpigeon populations. Commercial forestry requires control of deer, and afforestation may force deer to become pests on farm crops and	All year round; one of the major land users; increasing in recent years under Forestry Commission.

2.2	Exploitation of natural or semi-natural stands	Mainly isolated areas in uplands	pastures. Introduction of alien seeds in brash. Planting sometimes obscures geological interest. Felling and replanting bring about drastic alteration of habitat, and wildlife is destroyed or driven elsewhere	Very localised: small areas
2.3	*Establishment and maintenance of:*			
2.31	Amenity Woodlands	General; National Parks, NT, FC and local authority land; private estates	Provide cover for fauna, where not disturbed by woodland operations, but ground flora damaged by trampling. Owners often under economic pressure to fell and replant with conifers	Local: Limited
2.32	Shelter Belts and Windbreaks	Hill country and exposed lowlands	Beneficial, providing increased cover for animals, reducing soil erosion by wind, which restarts when windbreaks felled	Local: Limited
2.33	Coverts for Game	Lowlands mainly	Ground flora often destroyed, but beneficial as cover for wildlife. Introduction of alien plants	Local: Limited
2.34	Roadside and hedgerow trees and shrubs	Most lowland areas	Cutting in breeding season, and especially permanent removal of hedgerows and verges reduces available wildlife shelter	Hedgerows still widespread, but much reduced in some areas
3	AGRICULTURE:			
3.1	*General:*			
3.11	Farm improvement and Mechanisation	General, especially lowlands and richer farming areas	Trend towards elimination of hedgerows, headlands and farm ponds, and more complete utilisation of land and produce results in loss of habitats, shelter and food supplies for wildlife. Trend towards bigger farm units. Horses replaced by tractors; fewer pastures and fodder crops than formerly	General in arable areas; increasing

311

	1. Activity or Operation	2. Area or Land-type Affected	3. Nature of Effects Arising	4. Incidence (Time, Space, Degree)
3.12	Use of fertilisers, and of sprays, and other chemical controls	Arable areas	Waterborne fertiliser residues modify biological conditions on NR's, etc. Toxic chemicals tend towards elimination not only of pests and weeds but of other harmless fauna associated with human food crops. Persistent chemicals entering into food chains create complex long-term problems. (See above)	Predominantly in E. and S. Britain; all seasons
3.13	Control of land pests	General	Misguided destruction of Badgers still common. Reduction of rabbits by myxomatosis from 1954 aided palatable herbage and flowering plants but led to growth of scrub (hitherto checked by rabbit grazing), which alters ecology of downlands, sand-dunes and heathlands. Some control measures, e.g. in breeding season, involve risks to other wildlife, some (e.g. Coypu destruction in E. Anglia) may be beneficial	All seasons; widespread but patchy
3.14	Farm drainage	General	Drainage sometimes over-improved, and this gives quicker run-off, lowers the general water table and aggravates water deficit and its effects during drought. Also causes lower average levels and volumes of water contained and held by soil and by rivers, reducing latters' abstraction potential (See also section 1.4)	General in farming areas
3.15	Farm irrigation	Progressive farming areas especially in drier regions	Increases crop yields but uses much water, often at expense of local river flows	Local but rapidly increasing on farms, market gardens and fruit growing areas

3.16	Farm fencing practice	Farming areas, especially arable land	In rich highly arable areas hedgerows and permanent fencing become redundant except on farm periphery. Portable or electric fences used when necessary (see also sections 2.34 and 3.11); fences replacing hedgerows and walls (as those too expensive to replant or rebuild) in livestock farming areas	General
3.17	Siting and Use of Farm Buildings	General	Activities may involve uncontrolled effluents while lack of control of siting of farm buildings can cause detriment to landscape	General
3.2	*Cultivation:*			
3.21	Cereals	Most arable areas	Ever increasing intensification means trend towards more rigid monoculture for each crop, and this tends towards elimination of some other forms of life. Use of certain chlorinated hydro-carbon insecticides on cereal seeds has been shown to have serious effects on birds. Some of these insecticides may also be having an undesirable effect on soil and aquatic fauna and related food-chain organisms	General in arable areas, increasing
3.22	Other Field Crops			
3.23	Fruit and vegetables		Chemical spraying of orchards and market gardens. Destruction of finches, tits, etc. which damage fruit and fruit buds	
3.24	Watercress	Especially lowland areas of S. & E. England, e.g. Hants., Cambs., etc. chalk streams and others	Excavation of watercress beds provides extension of wetland habitat but persecution of wildfowl and use of DDT and similar insecticides often follows. Insecticides liable to cause serious damage to fish stocks	Increasing but still local, on rivers and streams which are rich in calcium and other minerals

313

1. Activity or Operation	2. Area or Land-type Affected	3. Nature of Effects Arising	4. Incidence (Time, Space, Degree)
3.25 Grassland Management	All farming areas including hill land	Seeds mixtures reduced to few species, and weeds eliminated; so variety of pasture and meadow wildlife much reduced. Silage effluents and other crop residues add to pollution	Widespread and general
3.26 Cutting and Removal of Turf for Lawns	Coastal and inland marsh-edge grassland	Not harmful generally as regeneration fairly rapid and ecology only temporarily altered. May increase erosion in some coastal areas	Local
3.27 Reed, "Sedge" and Rush cutting	E. Anglia	Regular cropping perpetuates reed habitat in drier fens where it would otherwise give place to scrub. Also increases tillering of young green reeds and reduces fire risk	Local
3.28 Moss gathering	Woodlands and moors in areas of very high rainfall; also downlands	Destruction of ground flora and possible erosion of woodland and moorland soil	Local: limited
3.3 Livestock and Animal Rearing:			
3.311 Sheep rearing on mountains and rough pastures and commons	Uplands in Wales, Scotland, Pennines and S.W. England	Grazing of unfenced woodlands prevents regeneration. Over-grazing can occur, leading to reduction of diversity of flora, spread of bracken and erosion on higher slopes. Destruction of potential predators of lambs. Toxic chemicals (sheep dips) dangerous to predators, e.g. Eagles, Buzzards and other carrion feeders. Burning by shepherds	Low level winter shelter; intense concentration in valleys. On mountains April to October
3.312 Sheep-rearing on lowlands	Especially downlands, salt-marshes coastal grassland and to a decreasing extent mixed farms	Effluents from sheep dips dangerous to wildlife. Sheep grazing essential to maintain downland habitat in open condition	Localised: limited; much reduced over past 50 years

314

3.32	Cattle rearing	Grasslands and heaths generally	Introduction of Galloway cattle on moorlands (especially wintering of cattle on the hill), altering vegetation pattern created by previous traditional grazing; waterways polluted by effluent from byres and rearing pens	Recent locally increasing trend towards cattle ranching linked with improvements of hill pasture
3.33	Pony and horse rearing	Certain upland rough grazings and large open heathlands	Selective grazing with coarser grasses thriving. Problem of ponies concentrating on verges of unfenced roads	Very local and small scale
3.34	Pig keeping	Mixed grasslands and heath and areas of felled or devastated woodland	Rooting; erosion; possibly beneficial to regeneration in woodlands, but destructive effects on ground flora	Local: limited
3.35	Poultry keeping	Largely on agricultural land. Change to battery rearing and other intensive methods rapidly reducing open range flocks	Some destruction of predators, e.g. hawks, owls, corvids, stoats, weasels, foxes and badgers	Widespread
3.361	Game Preservation: Pheasants and Partridges	Lowland Britain	There is still appreciable persecution of predators by poison, shooting, snares, gin and pole traps. Preservation of game and wildfowl habitats on big estates has helped to conserve other species	General, lowland rural areas
3.362	Game preservation: Deer and Grouse	Northern Britain	Indiscriminate heather burning damages soil and vegetation	General and intense in moorland areas
3.37	Fur farming	Coypu farms have declined and Mink is now main type	Escape of mink, and coypu; damage to river banks, fishery and game interests, and to agriculture	Escaped Coypu recently widespread in E. Anglia. Mink farming widespread but limited; escapes destructive
3.38	Pets especially cats and dogs	General, rural areas	Disturbance and destruction of wildlife and game by feral domestic cats and dogs. Latter also nuisance to farm livestock	Massive and widespread

	1. Activity or Operation	2. Area or Land-type Affected	3. Nature of Effects Arising	4. Incidence (Time, Space, Degree)
3.39	Private Zoos, Waterfowl collections etc.		Risks of escapes involving damage or interference with scientific studies; possible spread of disease	Very local
4	FISHERIES:			
4.1	Offshore fishing	All seas around Britain	Modern trawlers, by cleaning catch at sea and throwing offal overboard thought to have contributed largely to the considerable increases, during the last 20 years, of populations of some species of gulls, which are now becoming a nuisance. (See also Sections 22.13 and 22.18)	All year round: limited numbers
4.2	Inshore fishing (including Shellfish)	Foreshores, Oyster, Cockle and Mussel beds	Demands for control of Oystercatchers	Local; very few
4.3	Salmon netting	Estuaries and neighboring coastal waters	Destruction of and demands for elimination of seals	Limited to tidal waters and estuaries of certain rivers; season Feb.–Oct.
4.4	Fish hatcheries	Upper reaches of tributary streams	Useful in restoring depleted gamefish populations. Some destruction of Herons and Kingfishers	All year round; local; very few
5	WATER			
5.1	Supply undertakings and similar developments	Upland catchment areas of relatively high rainfall	Pumping of ground water lowers water tables, visible in dying back of larger trees, and ultimately affects agriculture and landscape	Widespread: demands increasing rapidly
5.2	Abstraction	Upper or lower reaches of rivers, and underground sources	Abstraction from upper and middle reaches results in reduced river flow, both in average volume and current rate, increased silting up, and drastic changes in ecology. Restriction of public access to gathering grounds	

5.3	Reservoir construction	Immediate surroundings of large consumer centres, and suitable valleys near upland catchment sources	Lowland or valley reservoirs take in bottom land from agriculture. Raising levels of existing lakes may destroy zonation of marginal vegetation. Detriment to landscape. Drowning of river valleys may destroy one habitat and provide a valuable new one for resident and overwintering wildfowl	Local, but increasing as water demand grows
5.4	Recharging of ground water supplies	Not yet a significant factor		Very local: few cases so far
5.5	Industrial re-use of water		Effects important savings in demands for water, especially of higher grades, and aids conservation	
6	EXTRACTION OF MINERALS OTHER THAN COAL:			
6.1	Sand and gravel	Many coastal and river valley sites and areas of glacial deposits	Beneficial to wildlife in some cases by providing gravel pit water habitats. Mining and quarrying generally have supplied vast amount of geological information. Beach and bank erosion; pollution of rivers by gravel washing; disturbance and destruction of surface ecology, physiography and archaeology	Suitable areas intensively worked for a period of years. When worked out and operations abandoned new problems of use or restoration arise
6.2	*Clay extraction:*			
6.21	Brick clay and brick making	Superficial clay deposits mainly in E. England	(Similar to sand and gravel)	(As above)
6.22	Ball clay	Dorset and S. Devon	Workings very untidy and spoil heathland, but result eventually in valuable and more varied habitats	Localised in S.W. England; similar to sand and gravel
6.23	China clay	Devon and Cornwall	River and sea beach pollution; detriment to landscape. Creates large spoil heaps	Localised in Devon and Cornwall. Duration of workings relatively long-term before abandonment
6.3	Opencast ron ore working	Northamptonshire; S.W. Lincs.	Marred landscape pending restoration; severance; tree and hedge destruction	Locally intense, confined to very few areas

	1. *Activity or Operation*	2. *Area or Land-type Affected*	3. *Nature of Effects Arising*	4. *Incidence (Time, Space, Degree)*
6.4	Road metal quarrying	Areas geologically suitable with bed-rock near surface	Destruction of surface ecology; detriment to landscape. Worked out quarries create artificial cliff faces and pools which often become interesting habitats for wild life	Fairly general
6.5	Quarrying for masonry and building materials, e.g. slate	Areas geologically suitable	Destruction of surface habitats; detriment to landscape	Localised; limited
6.6	Limestone quarrying and cement making	Limestone areas: Devon, Somerset, Pennines, S. Wales, Denbigh, Flints, etc.	Destruction of surface ecology and of cave systems; atmospheric pollution; quarrying sometimes beneficial to geological interest, sometimes the reverse; pollution and diversion of underground water supplies. Detriment to landscape; downland vegetation covered with dust	Localised in a number of widely scattered areas
6.7	Underground mining for salt	Cheshire	Creation of flashes and inland saline habitats of interest for wildlife	Localised
6.8	Underground mining for lead	Wales, Pennines, Lake District, Mendips	River pollution by lead residues leaching out of disturbed spoil heaps around old lead mines may destroy all fish and most other aquatic wildlife	Localised
7	COAL EXTRACTION:			
7.1	Opencast coalmining	Areas especially of mid and N. England and Scotland where coal deposits close to surface	Disruption of drainage; damage to amenity and conservation interests but subsequent restoration effective	Locally intense in limited areas for limited periods
7.2	Underground coalmining	Areas mainly of E. and W. Midlands, Kent, Northumberland, Durham, Yorks, Lancs., S. Wales, Fife, W. Lothian and Forth-	(See below)	Limited but dominant where it occurs

318

7.3	Subsidence	Clyde, underlain by major coal deposits (As above)	Subsidence sometimes gives rise to wetland habitats beneficial to wildlife, but generally harmful to farming	Local
7.4	Coal pithead installations	(As above)	Detriment to landscape. Air pollution	Local
7.5	Spoil disposal, bings, tips, etc.	(As above)	Cover up all natural features and potentialities of land; destroy scientific interest of marshes, ponds or lakes; beach pollution, damage to coastline, amenity, wildlife; geological features often buried when quarries used for spoil disposal. Air pollution from burning tips	Widespread and serious in most coalfields
7.6	Other processing plant, depots and stocks	(As above)	Creation of blighted areas covered by fluctuating masses of stored coal with incidental pollution and pest problems. Effluents from carbonisation plant containing carbolic acid, cyanides, etc, polluting rivers	Local
8	OIL INDUSTRY:			
8.1	Oil drilling	Sussex; Notts. and adjoining counties, and underwater in North Sea	Risks of local pollution. Oil prospecting underwater involving explosives can damage fish life	Local
8.2	Shale Working	West Lothian	Large areas of ground blanketed by spoil heaps	Locally intense
8.3	Oil: Shipping	Coastal waters and beaches generally; some estuaries and harbours; navigable rivers	Pollution by oil-spillage destroys sea-birds, seals, etc. Even slight oiling may poison birds and also render them more susceptible to predators (e.g. Shearwaters on Skomer)	Besides accidental spillage there is still considerable cleaning of tanks and emptying of bilges while tankers are at sea
8.4	Oil refining	Flat sites of at least 500 acres adjoining deep water estuaries or bays	Air pollution by refinery fumes. Detriment to landscape	Sources few and localised but may affect large areas downwind

	1. Activity or Operation	2. Area or Land-type Affected	3. Nature of Effects Arising	4. Incidence (Time, Space, Degree)
8.5	Waste Disposal and Pollution		(See above) Slight pollution occurs all the time in most harbours, but major sources of gross pollution are emptying of oil residues and tank washings into open seas, and accidental spillage resulting from "human error". Use of emulsifiers for dispersing oil and cleaning beaches also damaging to littoral fauna	Widespread contamination of beaches, usually on a a minor scale; increasing
8.6	Installation and maintenance of Pipelines	Connecting refinery sites to main distribution areas	Damage to drainage and disturbance to land and vegetation along route during installation, maintenance and inspection	Limited but rapidly increasing
8.7	Distribution depots and roadside filling stations	Harbours; Roadside land; scattered in areas of demand	Pollution (of harbours and neighboring coastal and estuarine waters). Filling stations often detrimental to landscape	Limited; widespread
9	ELECTRICITY SUPPLY:			
9.1	Generation: nuclear	Fairly level sites able to bear heavy structural loadings and adjacent to large supplies of cooling water, either sea, estuaries or large inland waters	Destruction of habitat and of scientific interest on building site. Warming of very large quantities of cooling water may be biologically interesting. Improvement of access roads for heavy vehicles, and network of associated power lines enlarge effects of power stations. Disposal of radio-active waste. Detriment to landscape	Few stations up to present, but transmission lines widespread
9.2	Generation: coal	Level land usually by the sea, a river or an estuary, often in or near a coalfield	Air pollution, notably with sulphur oxides; detriment to landscape; warming of water. Fly-ash disposal in quarries, gravel holes and surface hollows, and in spoil heaps above	New larger power-stations will produce greatly increasing amounts of fly ash

			Effects	Extent
			ground level may obliterate scientific interest, but beneficial where surface restored for agriculture	
9.3	Generation: oil	As above but more confined to coastal areas, accessible to tankers	Air pollution; warming of water; detriment to landscape	Localised: few sites
9.41	Generation: hydro (A)	Upland rivers and catchment areas, especially high rainfall areas, e.g. N.W. Highlands	Dams alter scenery, river flow and ecology and affect movements of salmon; leets divert run-off and drain adjacent land	Installations few and localised, but each affects whole river system
9.42	Generation: hydro (B)	Upland Lakes and Reservoirs	Problems of draw-down and alteration of levels which is damaging to marginal zonation of aquatic flora and fauna and to landscape	Few schemes; effects localised. Draw-down daily in case of pumped storage schemes and seasonally in other cases
9.5	Transmission and distribution	General	Makes power available in rural areas. Erection of overhead power lines may require destruction of trees and other vegetation and interfere with cultivation and with flight lines of wildfowl, causing for example, "Swan faults". Also general effects on scenery	Widespread
9.6	Switchgear and substations	Important grid junctions and junction points of H.V. and L.V. systems	Detriment to landscape	Limited but widespread
10	GAS			
10.1	Manufacture and storage	Mostly in or on edges of urban areas	Detriment to landscape; atmospheric pollution	Limited but widespread
10.2	Installation and maintenance of Pipelines	Between major producing units and points of demand	Destruction of flora; alteration of drainage pattern	Local but increasing
10.3	Underground storage	Areas where geological features permit storage without loss	Damage to ground flora etc. by installations; alteration of water tables; accidental seepage of methane destroys flora	Local

1. Activity or Operation	2. Area or Land-type Affected	3. Nature of Effects Arising	4. Incidence (Time, Space, Degree)
MANUFACTURING INDUSTRY:			
11 Factories and sites	Countryside generally but especially near important communications or where transport facilities exist	Possible detriment to landscape (for special aspects see below) by choice of unsuitable or unsatisfactory design, layout or handling of access, noise, effluent or other problems outside factory gate	Fairly widespread
11.11 Disturbance and degradation of soil	(As above)	Excavation and local dumping of spoil (e.g. in making alkalis). Destructive use of sites, e.g. in vehicle testing	
11.12 Pollution and misuse of Water	Most rivers, lakes and tidal waters close to industrial areas	(See also sections 1.4; 5.2; 5.5; 14.3). Waterways polluted by hot water, chemicals or organic wastes which use up oxygen, destroying aquatic fauna and flora. Wasteful demands for excessive amounts or for unnecessarily high qualities of water indirectly cause repercussions by requirement for larger reservoirs and increased abstraction	Widespread; increasing
11.13 Pollution: Air	Most industrial and large urban areas and their leeward environs	Livestock fluorosis: Damage to vegetation by factory smoke, dust, refinery fumes containing sulphur oxides, etc.: effects measurable up to 30 miles down-wind. Smog in winter affects fauna	Increasing: localised, but air pollution may affect vulnerable plants to a considerable distance
12 DISTRIBUTION			
12.1 Depots: bulky, dangerous or nuisance items	Near points of discharge from ships, railway stations or markets, and accessible to efficient bulk transport	Stock piles and storage dumps of large industrial merchandise, munitions, toxic chemicals, timber, prefabricated concrete, piping and building materials take up much land and may present special risks of fire, pollution, etc.	Local
12.2 Wharfage	Ports accessible to road and rail transport and to ships of adequate size		Local

			General
12.3	Packing and packaging	(a) Points of manufacture where much handling of goods; (b) Areas of retail consumption out of doors, e.g. resorts, racecourses, picnic sites; (c) Disposal sites where litter inefficiently dealt with	Use of unnecessarily large amounts of packaging material and especially of relatively indestructible polythene containers, aggravates litter problem	
12.4	Mobile selling points, e.g. ice-cream cars, refreshment vans, etc.	Recreation areas, beauty spots and open access. Reserves near towns, NP's, NT sites and seaside and inland waters	Litter; severe damage to ground flora and other vegetation by trampling, unless selling point in car park or on concrete	Increasing pressure in recent years. Limited but widespread
13	BUILDING AND HOUSING:			
13.1	Housing estates and other grouped housing	Sheltered or less exposed sites, as level as possible, near existing centres of population or near large projects, e.g. power stations	Absorption of rural land; landscaping problems, especially with trend to increased height of buildings; erosion and disturbance of surroundings by children; predation and disturbance by cats, dogs, etc.; pollution and litter; requirements for overhead wires, sewers, etc.; pest problems	Permanent and continuous
13.2	Individual dwellings	Similar but may also be perched on steep slopes or in other extreme situations		Dwellings permanent, but occupancy may be seasonal
13.3	Institutions and other large buildings in the countryside, e.g. Educational institutions, Prisons, Hospitals	Tuberculosis hospitals on high sites now becoming outdated, but modern mobility gives increasing scope for breakaway moves from congested to isolated sites, especially in attractive surroundings	Similar, but often involve creation of relatively undisturbed surroundings, usually however planted with non-native and often unsuitable trees and shrubs	Occupancy often permanent but sometimes restricted (e.g. on term-times)
14	SEWAGE AND RUBBISH DISPOSAL:			
14.1	Piped transport and underground sewers	Rivers down-stream of centres of population		Limited

1. Activity or Operation	2. Area or Land-type Affected	3. Nature of Effects Arising	4. Incidence (Time, Space, Degree) Local
14.2 Open sewers			
14.3 Industrial and sewage effluents	Rivers and other inland and coastal waters where factories and other sources of effluent occur	Higher forms of animal and plant life killed off by warm de-oxygenated or poisonous effluents. Adjacent land wild life also affected	Serious and intense over long periods of time, and effects increasingly aggravated by water abstraction
14.4 Sewage farms	Generally in low-lying areas near centres of population	Extensive irrigation system prevalent over last 50 years was highly attractive to birds, but has now largely given place to sprinkler filtration plant. Sewage works not harmful *per se* but effluents enter rivers and streams. Detergents inhibit breakdown of sewage and reduce oxygenation of water	Local: overall area affected decreasing
14.5 Incinerators, etc.	Sites near larger communities	Beneficial, as they reduce refuse to small volume of inert uniform material which is more easily disposable, thereby reducing spoliation of the land by dumps	All too rare
14.6 Rubbish dumps	General near centres of population	Smaller communities cause most damage to amenity and wild life, by using wetlands, quarries, sea coves and ravines. Dumps provide extra food and may thus be responsible not only for making possible increase in populations of rats, crows, rooks, jackdaws, sparrows, gulls. Problems increasing where disposal facilities lacking. Effluents pollute streams, ponds and ground water. Special problem of bulky and heavy refuse, e.g. old vehicles and other	Serious, massive and universal problem, increasing rapidly in all populated areas

14.7	Waste metals, iron, etc.	Widespread, but mainly near towns	large metallic consumer goods, disposal of which is difficult. Scrap iron dealers and car breakers take up and ruin large areas of land. In addition much illegal dumping of old car bodies takes place in lanes and woodland edges, on foreshores, uncultivated ground and in rivers, ponds and lakes	(As Rubbish Dumps) (see above)
15	TRANSPORT:			
15.1	New roads, e.g. motorways	Mainly linking large centres of population to each other and to resorts, etc.	Encroachment on S.S.S.I.'s. can usually be avoided by careful choice of alignment, but destruction of habitats often occurs, though may be compensated for by good landscaping. Opening-up of countryside increases all impacts of tourism. Land marginal to motorways isolated (no stopping) and may form useful conservation areas. Petrol and diesel fumes	Increasing
15.2	Road widening or straightening	General	As above; sometimes results in improved demonstration of geologically interesting features. Damage to rare flora occasionally	Increasing
15.3	Road maintenance: highway verges	General	Use of chemical sprays to kill vegetation on verges is very destructive to flora and associated fauna. Cutting of grass verges affects some birds in nesting season	Most serious 1950–59; still presents frequent problems
15.4	Use of Road Vehicles	General	Heavy mortality of birds, hedgehogs, etc. on roads. Petrol and diesel fumes. Problems incidental to parking, e.g. litter, compacting of soil, injury to vegetation, fire risks etc.	General all year round but especially in summer

1. Activity or Operation	2. Area or Land-type Affected	3. Nature of Effects Arising	4. Incidence (Time, Space, Degree)
15.5 Railway modernisation, reconstruction and maintenance	Railway lines of continuing high traffic potential	Unwise siting of new marshalling yard on edge of dune system has caused local instability of sand. Electrification eliminates smoke nuisance	Very local
15.6 Abandonment of lines, stations, etc.	Areas of low traffic levels	Extension of undisturbed wildlife habitat beneficial. Reduction of pollution by smoke. Demands for improved roads and bus services in areas where railways closed down. Increased traffic on existing roads to holiday areas	May become widespread in rural areas
15.7 Canals and waterways	Location determined by historical conditions during canal-building phase which ceased in mid-19th century	Valuable aquatic habitats in danger of being lost if no longer economically maintainable. Destruction of canal vegetation by herbicides detrimental to scientific interest	Local
15.8 Ports and Harbours	Increasing size of ships and need for mechanisation dictates concentration in fewer larger ports with modern facilities. Implies decay of many smaller ports and harbours	Destruction of habitats through extension of port facilities over formerly wild areas	Local
16 DEFENCE			
16.1 Permanent training areas		Sometimes preserves land from other developments and disturbances, but often also detrimental to landscape. Damage to soil and vegetation by	Mostly weekdays

16.2	Temporary or occasional training areas	Mountain, upland, moorland, heathland, and coastal areas	tracked vehicles missiles, etc., leading to erosion. Damage to beaches and coastal dunes by amphibious vehicles, and to other areas by vehicles and missile testing. Firing on ranges and activities of troops on training schemes constitute serious disturbance. Litter	
16.3	Artillery, vehicle and missile testing areas	(As above)	(As above)	(As above)
16.4	Former training and testing areas	(As above)	Unexploded missile hazard to visitors	Danger lasts for many years
16.5	Former Defence Installations	(As above)	Left derelict for others to clear	
16.6	Sites for secret or dangerous defence installations	Remote localities	Detriment to landscape (unsightly (fencing) and public access; quiet isolated areas under strict security occasionally provide useful refuges for wildlife	
16.7	Ancillary facilities, e.g. housing		Disturbance to wildlife by Services communities and their pets in otherwise unpopulated areas	
17	TELECOMMUNICATIONS:			
17.1	Masts for telecommunications, TV, Radar towers, etc.	Hilltop sites commanding uninterrupted horizon	Detriment to landscape and damage to vegetation. Sites chosen are often hills of high scientific interest	Widespread and growing competition for prominent hill tops
18	AVIATION:			
18.1	Military Airfield operations	Level areas with unimpeded approaches; grasslands and heath	Military airfields, where public access denied, may provide valuable refuges for wildlife away from runways and buildings. Wildlife near airports accustomed to noise, but low flying is a serious disturbance elsewhere, especially to colonial nesting birds and winter flocks of wildfowl, and to farm animals and poultry	Localised; all year round, but more activity in Summer. Increasing trend to use of high speed and high altitude jet aircraft

1. Activity or Operation	2. Area or Land-type Affected	3. Nature of Effects Arising	4. Incidence (Time, Space, Degree)
18.2 Commercial passenger and freight air-line services	Grasslands on or around commercial airports, and neighboring approach runs	Birds on runways or airfield approaches dangerous to planes landing and taking off, and vice-versa	All year round. Largely jet or turbo-jet aircraft
18.3 Private flying	Grasslands or other suitable open areas	Disturbance, low flying noise	Small slow low-flying planes often operating continuously over relatively restricted circuit
18.4 Helicopters	Arable areas and coastal and mountain areas and along routes of local helicopter services, powers lines and pipelines, highways and other transport routes	Spray drift from agricultural use now known to be carried long distances and widely spread, contaminating soil and water in unsprayed areas. Disturbance from low flying particularly serious where dense breeding colonies of seabirds occur, and in areas where farm livestock numerous	Increasing use for crop-spraying and other contract services, postal transport, air-sea and mountain rescue, inspection of pipelines, etc., often in areas where mechanical disturbance is otherwise exceptional
18.5 Hovercraft	Estuaries, lakes and inshore coastal waters	Damage to marshes and water habitats. Noise disturbance, especially to birds	In early stages; very localised but may increase
18.6 Gliding	Upland areas with suitable escarpments for updraughts	Attraction of crowds of visitors; traffic congestion; litter; trampling; noise of power launching. Camping by participants near launching sites	All year round; local; limited following
19 TOURISM:			
19.1 Motoring and sight-seeing from vehicles or stopping places	Mountains, "beauty spots", hill tracks and summits, beaches, margins of inland water, etc. accessible to vehicles	Organised coach tours result in severe trampling around stopping places; litter, especially cans, milk bottles and cleaning tissues; pollution at laybyes; soil erosion by vehicles; traffic congestion and damage to verges, roadside land and approaches to beaches and other attractions; cars	Large scale massive impact with peak in summer; locally intense; including large numbers of overseas visitors

	Activity	Areas	Impact	Timing/Intensity
19.2	Sightseeing on foot	Rivers, mountains, "beauty spots", hill tracks and summits, beaches, and margins of inland waters	Trampling, erosion, fires, litter; driven into dunes and on fore-shore Portable radio noise. (See also Caravanning)	Summer mainly; locally intense
19.3	Sightseeing on horseback			Localised; limited
19.4	Chair lifts, viewing towers, observation posts, etc.	Mountains and hill country; forests; flat country without natural vantage points	Disturbance (see above) where ski-lifts operate in summer, taking large numbers of visitors to hitherto quiet, isolated areas. Litter, trampling etc.	All seasons: local
19.5	Information and Education services for visitors	Rural areas, especially NP's and attractive land accessible to the public		
19.6	Fixed accommodation for tourists (e.g., motels, caravans, youth hostels, climbing huts, etc.)		Good siting and design minimise impact of accommodation on landscape, which can otherwise be severe. Local pest problems from waste or feeding by visitors may affect rare vulnerable species	
20	CAMPING AND CARAVANNING:			
20.1	Private, unorganised (temporary) sites	Especially coastal, mountain areas and National Parks, margins of inland water and woodlands	Cluttering of coasts and landscape unless most carefully sited. Disturbance; litter; sewage pollution of land and water; broken glass, gates left open; fires; radio noise	Summer: increasing; locally intense; fair numbers
20.2	Commercially organised (permanent sites)	Mainly coastal and mountain areas as above	(See above)	All year round; locally intense; limited
20.3	Gypsy Encampments (Tinkers in Scotland)	General lowland rural areas, lanes, commons, and un-cultivated areas, especially peripheral to race courses	Disturbance, damage, trespass, poaching, rubbish dumping, flower and moss gathering. Verges spoilt; ditches filled with refuse; fences and gates broken; burnt areas	All year round; locally limited

1. Activity or Operation	2. Area or Land-type Affected	3. Nature of Effects Arising	4. Incidence (Time, Space, Degree)
21 EDUCATION AND FIELD STUDIES:			
21.1 Organised youth activities out of doors, e.g. School games, field studies, "Outward Bound", voluntary conservation and rehabilitation schemes; Combined Cadet Forces	General (see appropriate sections)	(See sections on: Games on Playing Fields; Field natural history; Field Scientific work; Bird watching, etc.; walking; climbing; caving; canoeing; camping; swimming)	(See appropriate sections)
21.2 Field Natural History	Particularly in areas of rich flora and fauna, e.g. coasts, inland waters, limestone areas, mountains and woodlands	Collecting, both private and commercial (e.g. of geological, plant or insect specimens) may damage scientific interest or ecology of area (Mercury vapour lamps for insects)	Summer and autumn; widespread
21.3 Field Scientific Work	(As above)	Where access unrestricted, disturbance and interference by visitors to research sites, equipment and wildlife, and removal of notice boards and marker posts occur frequently. Difficulties are minimised where such studies are conducted on areas where there is no public access.	All year round; limited; localised
21.4 Archaeology	Areas of ancient human habitation	Interference and excavation by unskilled person destroys features. Intensive archaeological work may disturb rare species	Limited; localised
21.5 Bird watching and Bird photography	Mainly wilder areas with high ornithological interest	Disturbance; "gardening" and trampling near nests may lead to failure through desertion, or attract other visitors or predators	Especially in summer; widespread limited, but intense locally
22 RECREATION:			

Aquatic Sports:

22.1	Swimming and bathing	Sea-coast, rivers, canals and other inland waters	Disturbance, litter, erosion of banks, sand dunes, etc.; trespass on adjacent private land	Summer; weekends; massive; social activity; localised
22.12	Diving and Sub-aqua	(As above)	Aids studies of lake and marine biology and off-shore geology. Disturbance, destruction of aquatic life. Cars on beaches (heavy gear)	Mainly summer; weekends; small numbers; very local
22.13	Spear-gun fishing	(As above)	Introduces to underwater habitats new conservation problems similar to those created by killing wildlife on land; alleged driving away of fish from inshore waters	(As above)
22.14	Canoeing and rowing	Rivers, canals, other inland waters and sea-coast	Disturbance by landing on islands and by penetration into small waterways	Mainly spring to autumn; weekends; limited following; fairly widespread
22.15	Sailing	Rivers, canals, other inland waters and sea-coast, and estuaries and reservoirs	Disturbance of birds; erosion and destruction of aquatic vegetation; Dredging of shallows. Cluttering of coastal landscape by unsightly shore-facilities, but sailing itself can greatly enhance landscape beauty	Mainly summer; some in winter; increasing; widespread
22.16	Motor-boating and cruising	Rivers and canals, other inland waters and sea-coast	Noise and mechanical disturbance especially to nesting birds; erosion and destruction of aquatic vegetation, pollution by oil, petrol and sewage. Sometimes conflicts with sailing, canoeing and angling interests	Mainly summer; small numbers; localised; increasing
22.17	Speed-boating and racing and water ski-ing	Rivers and canals, other inland waters and sea-coast	Disturbance, erosion, noise; penetration to shallow waters not otherwise affected by deeper draught boats. Cars on foreshore	Mainly summer; very small numbers; localised; increasing

1. Activity or Operation	2. Area or Land-type Affected	3. Nature of Effects Arising	4. Incidence (Time, Space, Degree)
22.18 Angling	Rivers, canals, other inland waters and sea-coast	Angling interests have preserved unspoilt many stretches of river and other aquatic habitats and have often successfully combatted water pollution. Relatively minor factors are:—Disturbance of birds; litter; damage to vegetation; injury through discarded nylon lines. Use of Motor boats by anglers may bring disturbance and oil pollution to otherwise unaffected lakes. Destruction of Mergansers, Herons, Kingfishers, Otters. Alteration of ecology by stocking and/or removal of other fish species. Poachers in fisheries who use cyanide, explosives, etc. kill other fish besides salmon. (See also Section 4)	Weekends all year round, but mainly summer—increasing; intense—massive; widespread; certain exclusive sites
22.2 Land sports:			
22.211 Games on playing fields, commons and parks	Heaths, commons and open ground near towns	Destruction of original natural vegetation; but may preserve rural and wildlife features against urbanisation	More in winter than summer; especially in school term-time; massive; widespread; many exclusive sites
22.212 Model aircraft flying	Heaths, commons and open ground near towns	Disturbance to wildlife and amenities. Interference with other users	Spring to autumn; local; small numbers
22.213 Golf	Grasslands, especially sand dunes, heathland, downland	Weed Spraying, levelling, and mowing of vegetation inimical to variety, but golf courses may be beneficial as buffer zones, limiting trampling and reducing dune erosion; golf course roughs beneficial as reservoirs of dune-land, heath, etc.	Local; all seasons; limited. Mainly on exclusive sites

332

22.221	Shooting; Game	Rural areas	Destruction of predators; poaching; burning of moors for grouse. Restriction of public access. (See also Section 3.36)	General—August–February; widespread; limited following
22.222	Shooting: Wildfowl	Foreshores, estuaries and inland waters	Properly conducted with restraint can increase local care for wildfowl habitats and discourage excessive concentrations. Irresponsible practices include indiscriminate shooting of protected species and disturbance to wildfowl roosting areas. Artificial stocking (e.g. with Canada Geese, Mallard), may create local problems	September–February localised; moderate following; fairly widespread
22.23	Hunting: Fox	Many rural areas	Maintenance of fox population; damage to rides, culverts; disturbance; trampling; earth-stopping; killing of badgers; cutting fences. Some elimination of wire fences. Damage to experimental plots and equipment by hounds and followers	Winter; widespread; limited, but foot followers increasing
22.241	Horse racing	Open grasslands, heaths and downs	Exercise and practice areas may provide and preserve valuable wildlife habitat; some race meetings occasion heavy traffic damage and litter on open courses and attract undesirables who despoil neighboring areas	Intense; massive local effect during meetings, but of short duration (only a few days each year)
22.242	Gallops	Downs, etc.	Mowing; trampling and puddling of soil and vegetation	All year round; local; limited
22.243	Riding and Pony Trekking	Rural areas, some coastal areas and hill country	Erosion of sand dunes and slopes; trampling, especially of verges, woodland rides and ground flora. Damage to experimental areas	All year round; widespread; limited following

333

	1. Activity or Operation	2. Area or Land-type Affected	3. Nature of Effects Arising	4. (Incidence Time, Space, Degree)
22.25	Motor rallies and motor cycle scrambles	Upland heathlands and other rough ground	Noise, disturbance, erosion (severe in scrambling), damage to vegetation; gates left open; spectators add to vegetation damage. Illegal use of footpaths and bridleways	All year round; local; limited
22.261	Ski-ing and effects of Ski-lift	Mountains	Disturbance and damage to flora where ski-lift open in summer; bulldozing of banks to encourage snow accumulation may accelerate erosion	Summer—local, very small numbers, but likely to increase
22.262	Sand-ski-ing	Sand dunes	Destruction of fixing vegetation, increasing instability and danger of blow-outs	Summer; local; extremely small numbers
22.27	Climbing and Ancillary Camping	Mountains and Cliffs	Mountaineering at high standards encourages appreciation of wilderness and vigilance over remote unspoilt places. Irresponsible practices may involve disturbance, erosion; removal of vegetation, fires, litter	All year round; especially weekends; local but intense; limited
22.28	Caving (Potholing)	Limestone areas	Responsible cavers take initiative for subterranean conservation but damage caused by unskilled excavators and specimen collectors to scientific interest of caves; litter; pollution of subterranean waterways. Camping outside cave entrances also leads to litter and damage to vegetation	All year round; especially weekends; local; limited
22.29	Walking	Especially in upland, wooded and coastal areas; often in NP's and on NT land	Keen walkers keep footpaths open and provide essential vigilance for conservation of wild country. Irresponsible conduct involves disturbance to wildlife and game,	Summer mainly; widespread; large numbers in a few favored regions

334

			trampling, fires, erosion, litter, gates left open, and may give rise to arguments about access restrictions	
22.3	Picknicking	Attractive uncultivated areas, e.g. woodlands, coastal areas, and sites of high viewpoints, especially near roads	Disturbance, litter, trampling, pollution, fires, polythene bags and wrappers. Car parking and sanitation problems; radio noise; damage to country tracks and verges	Summer; widespread; massive; especially weekends
23	Conservation: (Nature, Landscape and Natural Resources)	Wild and uncultivated areas and open land. Conservation vigilance extends to other types of area as occasion arises	Concentration of use by scientific workers, naturalists, geologists, etc. and often by educational and recreational users; use of sites for experiments and new treatments for management of vegetation and animal populations; attempts to revive or restore damaged habitats	All year round but field work particularly active during spring and summer

ANNEX III

FLOW CHART OF CONSERVATION PROCESSES

In view of the somewhat complex blend of subjects, problems and activities comprehended in conservation, and the difficulty of bearing in mind the structural relations of these to one another it may prove helpful to the reader to reproduce here a diagram prepared in 1959 to illustrate my report to the Nature Conservancy on education for conservation, which led to the establishment of the post-graduate course at University College London, and indirectly to a series of other advances. The report itself was never published.

This diagram is arranged to indicate the physical resources with which conservation is mainly concerned and to show the sequence of extracting relevant knowledge through the various sciences; communicating that knowledge through information, education and training services; storing and refining it ready for use in the organised professions and technologies; and applying it in the course of the full range of land-linked and environmental activities.

The result is a flow chart stemming from the raw material provided by the natural environment of the planet, and showing how human resources are applied to harvesting, disseminating and applying the knowledge which derives from and is called for by man's relationships with the environment. Those items which are most closely connected with the central tasks of conservation and resource management are italicised to distinguish them from numerous peripheral or shared items. The chart is simply indicative, not exhaustive.

It would be possible to construct a number of alternative charts dissecting the processes of conservation, but the present form has appeared to be most appropriate for demonstrating how modern practical activities in conservation are or should be based upon a firm scientific, educational and professional foundation, and how the necessary two-way communications should be developed to ensure that what is done is scientifically sound and what is scientifically sound is done. Complementary charts are in preparation to demonstrate the repercussions upon the biosphere of the technosphere (see p. 282).

FLOW CHART OF CONSERVATION PROCESSES

FUNDAMENTALS

Minerals

Soils

Water

Land Surface

Vegetation

Animal Life

Air

Outer Space

HUMAN INFLUENCES AND RECIPROCAL EFFECTS RESEARCH

Geophysics
Geology
Glaciology
Pedology
Geography
Physiography
Hydrology
Limnology
Oceanography
Botany
Zoology
Physiology
Genetics
Biometrics
Ecology
Meteorology
Astronomy
Astrophysics
Statistics
Economics
Cybernetics
Resource studies
Environmental Medicine
Social studies
History
Law

INFORMATION AND EDUCATION

Informal contacts
Research Teams
Conferences
Scientific publications
Other journals and books
Library and information Services
Scientific films
Museums
Administration and management process
University Postgraduate Training
University Undergraduate Teaching
Technical education
School education
Post-school education
Out-of-school education
Adult education
Radio and television
Press
Reports, leaflets, etc.
Other information to interested groups
Other information to general public
Interpretation, lecturing and discussion
Integration with other subjects
Surveys and reviews
Training of educators
Training of information Officers
Training of others incidentally engaged in education or information
Hybrid activities including an element of education or information

PROFESSIONS AND TECHNOLOGIES

University Researchers and teachers
School Teachers
Librarians
Museum Keepers
Radio, television and film staff
Naturalists
Parks and nature research staffs
Foresters
Soil Conservationists
Agricultural advisers and control staffs
Fishing staff
Farmers
Fishermen
Land managers
Wildlife managers
Bankers
Timber exploiters
Real Estate
Developers
Administrators
Publishers
Press
Voluntary associations
Mining engineers
Civil engineers
Regional planners
Economists
Medical Officers
Historians
Lawyers

FIELDS OF APPLICATION

Learning and research
Education
Information
Entertainment
Professional training
Land Use Planning
Land Management
Landscaping
Investment Policy
Water Conservation and supply
Extractive industries
Agriculture
Forestry
Fisheries
Game management
Wildlife management
Recreational management
Civil engineering
Site development
Government
Leisure activities

337

NOTES ON SOURCES

As it seeks to knit together the long and varied personal experience outlined in Chapter I with the contributions of countless others who have contributed to the literature this wide-ranging book can only be selectively documented. The aim has been to give as much help as possible to readers wishing to follow up particular aspects by giving preference to reasonably comprehensive works, wherever possible in English, which are up-to-date and accessible, and which themselves lead back to more detailed documentation on a primary or specialist level. Where however new advances are treated in papers too recent to have been digested in broader reviews, or where such works are only available in a form irrelevant to the aspects considered here, more specialist references are given, most frequently in the main text. In that case they are included in the Index and do not need to be listed again.

As the last three chapters (including the Conclusion) consist of discussion and forecasts it has not been found appropriate to provide material on sources for them.

Because conservation of nature and natural resources and the care of the natural environment are only now taking shape as a well-defined and generally recognised field of study, training and action the necessary specialist information and documentation services to assist the student are only gradually developing. Although more than a hundred relevant abstracting services could now be listed few of them are so designed as to prove more than incidentally helpful over much of the field of this book. (It is hoped shortly to develop a selective but comprehensive series of Environmental Science Abstracts in English.)

Certain libraries already provide a valuable specialised coverage, including the Van Tienhoven Library of the International Union for the Conservation of Nature at Morges, Vaud, Switzerland, the group library of the Nature Conservancy at London, Edinburgh, Bangor, Monks Wood and elsewhere, the Pacific Science Information Center at the Bishop Museum Honolulu, and the Library of the Bundesanstalt fur Vegetationskunde, Naturschutz und Landschaftspflege in Bad Godesberg near Bonn, West Germany.

Despite its many obvious deficiencies the following digest of sources by chapters will it is hoped enable the reader to make contact, if only at one or two removes, with much of the more important available material.

CHAPTER ONE   THE APPROACH STATED

The references here are necessarily to my own publications, mostly already cited in the text, but in incomplete form.

Birds in England. An Account of the State of our Bird Life and a Criticism of Bird Protection. London 1926.

How Birds Live. Bird Life in the light of modern observation. London 1927.
  Report on the "British Birds" Census of Heronries, 1928. London 1929.
The Study of Birds, an introduction to ornithology. London 1929.
Gilbert White. *The Natural History of Selborne*. (Edited) London 1929.
The Art of Bird-watching. London 1931.
Birds and Men. London 1951. *Britain's Nature Reserves*. London 1957.

CHAPTER 2   MAN'S USE OF THE EARTH

A clear and compact introduction from a biological standpoint is given by
Sir Gavin de Beer in his chapters on "the evolution of man" and "the
emergence of modern man" in *A Handbook on Evolution* published by the
British Museum (Natural History) London (1964 ed.) The Museum also
publish another invaluable low-priced illustrated handbook with maps
entitled *The Neolithic Revolution* by Sonia Cole (4th ed, 1967).

Much more detailed authoritative reviews of the latest advances are
provided in the Library of Early Civilizations edited by Professor Stuart
Pigott. Particular use has been made of *The Stone Age Hunters* by Professor
Grahame Clark (London 1969) in final revision, but others such as *Earliest
Civilizations of the Near East* by James Mellaert are highly relevant. Many
excellent large illustrations with an authoritative commentary are provided
in *The Art of Prehistoric Man in Western Europe*, by Andre Leroi-Gourhan,
London 1968. Another valuable treatment of art aspects is provided by
Karl Jeltmar's *Art of the Steppes; The Eurasian Animal Style*, London 1967.

A highly condensed and cartographically well presented outline of cultural
evolution is cheaply available in the German *Atlas zur Weltgeschichte*, Vol I.
Von den Anfängen bis zur Franzosichen Revolution, Munich 1964, to be
translated as a Penguin.

An Atlas of World History by S.De Vries, T. Luykx and W.O. Henderson,
originally published as Elsevier's Historische Atlas but republished in
English by Nelson's in 1965 is much less informative on the earlier periods.

The weighty compendium of the memorable *Wenner-Gren Symposium on
Man's Role in Changing the Face of the Earth*, Edited by W. L. Thomas, Chicago
1956, still provides possibly the most comprehensive factual review of its
subject, although unfortunately its bibliographic information and certain
aspects of the treatment are no longer up-to-date.

From the North American angle an important contribution also providing
valuable critical analysis for interpretation of evolutionary stages in early
cultures has just become available in Peter Farb's *Man's Rise to Civilization*
as shown by the Indians of North America from Primeval times to the coming
of the Industrial State. The agricultural background is stimulatingly
discussed by A.N. Duckham in *The Farming Year*, London 1963, and for the
tropics by John Phillips in *The Development of Agriculture and Forestry in the
Tropics: Patterns, Problems and Promise*, London 1961.

In relation to urbanism Lewis Mumford has made the most profound
and comprehensive contribution, especially with *The City in History, Its*

Origins, Its Transformations and its Prospects, London 1961, and most recently with *The Myth of the Machine*, London 1967.

CHAPTER 3   THE EARTH AND ITS LIVING PATTERNS

One of the clearest and most accessible introductions to modern physical geography in relation to the evolution of land-forms is a Pelican Book *The Face of the Earth* by G.H. Dury (London 1959). Another useful conspectus from the standpoint of the disciplines contributing to geographical know-ledge is *Allgemeine Geographie* edited by G. Fochler-Hauke (Frankfurt 1959).

From a climatic angle most useful conspectus is afforded by the Proceedings of the 1966 International Symposium in London published as *World Climate from 8000 to 0 B.C.* by the Royal Meteorological Society, London. This includes not only atmospheric circulation, glaciology and climatic and sealevel changes but also reviews of vegetation changes.

A well-written and well-presented popular illustrated review is given in *Nature; Earth Plants Animals*, edited by James Fisher and Sir Julian Huxley, London 1960, which can be strongly recommended to those seeking a simple but comprehensive guide on encyclopaedic lines to the facts, figures, mechanisms and outstanding research findings in this broad field. A some-what similar factual treatment of strictly marine aspects will be found in *Oceans: An Atlas-History of Man's Exploration of the Deep*, edited by G. E. R. Deacon, London 1962. Rachel Carson's *The Sea Around Us*, London 1951, is still a classic here.

Land Use statistics are summarised in the Food and Agriculture Organization's Production Yearbooks (Rome) and in less up-to-date but still valuable context in the Woytinsky's magnum opus *World Population and Production: Trends and Outlook*, New York 1953.

Although predominantly from a North American standpoint *Animal Ecology* by S. Charles Kendeigh (London 1961) gives a remarkably well arranged factual and visual analysis and explanation of the approach, processes and findings of ecology in all its aspects, with a commendable freedom of bias.

Another leading American ecologist Marston Bates has in *Animal Worlds* (London 1963) very readably reviewed the main ecological types of the earth, terrestrial and marine, with 242 excellent illustrations which are most helpful in visualising the worldwide diversity of habitats, and some of their principal animal and plant species. The same author's *The Forest and The Sea* (New York 1960) is a compact series of stimulating and informative essays on ecology, ending with a most engaging and candid few pages on Notes and Sources, the confessions in which would be equally applicable in the present case.

Among the highly formative contributions of Charles Elton special mention must be made of his *Animal Ecology* (London 1927), *The Ecology of Invasions by Animals and Plants* (London 1958), and *The Pattern of Animal Communities* (London 1966).

The world-wide role of water is simply analysed and presented with many illustrations and diagrams by P. H. Kuenen in *Realms of Water:* Some aspects of its cycle in Nature (London 1955).

Methods of measuring, describing and interpreting the land surface are given up-to-date treatment in the results of the C.S.I.R.O. Symposium in Canberra, Australia in 1968 published as *Land Evaluation*, Melbourne 1968.

(Reference should be particularly made to J. A. Mabbutt's paper on Concepts of Land Classification.) The present author's *Handbook to the Conservation Section of the International Biological Programme*, and its more detailed companion *Guide to the Check Sheet for IBP areas* by G. F. Peterken (IBP Handbooks 5 & 4, London 1968 & 1967) review methods now in international use for survey, analysis and data processing.

CHAPTER 4   SEVEN CIRCUITS ROUND THE EARTH.

Since this chapter was first drafted Gerhard Bischoff of the Universities of Berlin and La Paz has published an entire work, *Die Welt Unter Uns; Wel und Länderkunde aus der Vogelperspektive*, based on a similar idea, but following the arbitrary pattern of a selection of existing airline routes and written from a mainly geological standpoint. (Berlin 1968). This is an interesting complementary account.

Among works presenting specific regions in terms of aerial or ground photography must be mentioned *Europe from the Air* (London), and the large superbly illustrated series entitled *The Continents We Live On*, including *Europe: A Natural History* by Kai Curry-Lindahl (London 1964); *The Natural Wonders of North America* by Ivan T. Sanderson (London 1962); *South America and Central America: A Natural History*, by Jean Dorst (London 1967); *Australia and the Pacific Islands; A Natural History*, by Allen Keast (London 1966); *Africa: A Natural History* by Leslie Brown (London 1965) and *Asia: A Natural History* by Pierre Pfeffer (London 1968). For those who wish to extend their visual appreciation and their information of the earth's natural environments this series is of exceptional value.

For more localised reading reference should be made to such works as Guy Montfort's *Portrait of a Wilderness: The Story of the ornithological expeditions to the Coto Donana* (London 1958) and *Portrait of a Desert: The Story of an expedition to Jordan* (London 1965), both with contributions by the present author and many excellent illustrations by Eric Hosking and others. *Britain's Green Mantle* by A. G. Tansley (Second Edition, revised by M. C. F. Proctor, London 1968) is valuable, not only for its area, as a stimulating and readable presentation of ecological processes and their effects on vegetation. A similar role in respect of central Europe is filled by H. Ellenberg's *Vegetation Mitteleuropas mit den Alpen* (Stuttgart 1963). The vegetation types of the United States are mapped, described and illustrated by A.W. Kuchler in *Potential Natural Vegetation of the conterminous United States*, New York 1964. Ecological maps on the Holdridge system are available for Peru, Colombia and certain other Latin American countries. H. Ellenberg and D. Mueller-

Dombois have published a tentative physiognomic-ecological classification of plant formations of the earth (Zurich, 1967) which is in some respects complementary to F.R. Fosberg's strictly botanical model used in the *Check-sheet Survey of the International Biological Programme*. (See Annex 1).

Methods of survey and progress in mapping vegetation were reviewed in 1968 in the IBP Technical Meeting on Nature Conservation and Ecology of the West Mediterranean, North Africa and the Sahara (Report in the press). An approach to a comprehensive treatment of oceanic islands in the Pacific was begun at the IBP Technical Meeting in 1968 on the Conservation of Pacific Islands, including a *Checklist of Pacific Oceanic Islands* (Micronesica, Guam, 1969). These reports are indicative of the latest comprehensive and systematic approach to the comparative study and monitoring of ecological conditions area by area, in order to build up by stages a comparative worldwide picture.

The concept and distribution of the *refugia* referred to in this chapter are discussed in *The Suborder Charadrii in Arctic and Boreal Areas during the Tertiary and Pleistocene*. A Zoogeographic Study, by Sten Larson in *Acta Vertebratica;* Vol 1. No 1. (Stockholm 1957).

It is impossible to cite here numerous detailed sources other than those which help in addition to illustrate and amplify the particular approach to an interpretation of regional and local environmental and land use patterns developed in this chapter.

CHAPTER 5   THE MARKS OF MAN

Much of the subject matter of this chapter is incidentally covered by works cited more particularly for others. Among more specialised sources are the Proceedings and Papers of successive Technical Meetings from 1949 of the IUPN/IUCN, particularly the 5th (Copenhagen 1954), the 6th (Edinburgh 1956), especially Theme III the Rehabilitation of Areas Biologically Devastated by Human Disturbance), the 7th, Athens 1958 which focussed upon the disastrous effects of unsuitable types of land use in Mediterreanean and Near-East countries, and the 8th, Warsaw 1960 which produced an international review of Ecology and Management of Wild Grazing Animals in Temperate Zones. Among further specialised reviews promoted by IUCN special mention must be made of the important contributions of Project Mar from its first meeting at Les Saintes-Maries-de-la-Mer, France in November 1962 (Morges 1964). It dealt broadly and deeply with problems of the conservation and management of temperate marshes, bogs and other wetlands, and was quickly complemented by a series of partly governmental meetings on wildfowl conservation, the first of which took place at St Andrews, Scotland in October 1963. (Proceedings published London 1964.)

Subsequently the International Biological Programme further enlarged the range of these investigations, for example through its Herbivore Group publication (Handbook No 7) entitled *A Practical Guide to the Study of the Productivity of Large Herbivores*.

Much additional material is summarised in such regular reports as those already cited of the Nature Conservancy (London 1953.)

Although it is over a century since George Perkins Marsh first published his considered analysis of *Man and Nature; or, Physical Geography as Modified by Human Action* it is only now that works entirely focussed upon tracing, describing and assessing the varied results on the natural environment of human impacts and interferences are beginning to appear. The story still has largely to be disentangled from material primarily concerned with other aspects. Such material is fortunately plentiful, although not always easily traced.

The state of international development and conditions in National Parks and Equivalent Reserves is now summarised for 136 countries in the IUCN's *Liste des Nations Unies des Parcs Nationaux et Reserves Analogues*, Brussels 1967. (A considerably revised and up-dated English text is now in the press).

A good example of the tracing of human impacts within one county is *Cornwall; An illustrated essay on the history of the landscape* by W. G. V. Balchin, London 1954.

CHAPTER 6 THE ROAD TO CONSERVATION

By comparison with intense recent studies of prehistoric and early historic tools, cultures, art and agriculture the first emergence of gardening and of other leisure activities appears still to be a relatively neglected field, awaiting critical and comprehensive treatment. This book has had to be based upon scrappy references discovered here and there. Sylvia Crowe, however, in Part One of her *Garden Design* (London 1958) has given a succinct summary of the Oasis garden, the Sino-Japanese garden, the Hispano-Arabic Garden and the Italian Garden which provides some valuable guidelines for tracing back the evolution of gardening traditions, and relating them to primitive patterns of pleasure park or hunting reserve. It is to be hoped that this fascinating field will be better studied in the near future.

The estimated population densities for early farming systems are taken from R. F. F. Smith's *Origins of Farming in Russia* (not the original source).

CHAPTER 7 THE BRITISH STORY

Much has lately been done towards tracing and coherently describing the very important developments in English landscape design and land use during the 17th and 18th centuries. The picture, however, is still in parts confused and obscure, and no doubt it will appear somewhat differently after another decade or so of investigation and review.

Among sources on which most reliance has been placed here are *The English Garden* by Edward Hyams (London 1964), one of the most rewarding of books, with its magnificent pictures complementing the written word, and *English Gardens and Landscape 1700-1750* by Christopher Hussey (London 1967), another impressive new contribution emphasising how little we understood earlier of the background of these grand designs which so wonderfully changed our environment. As an arboriculturist Miles Hadfield complements these in his *Landscape with Trees* (London 1967) as successfully as Sylvia Crowe from the designer's standpoint in her *Garden Design*, already cited. In an earlier treatment, more preoccupied with different streams of inspiration, and more visually presented as a Vista Pictureback entitled *The Art of the Garden*, Miles Hadfield (London 1965) provides an uncommon link between various styles of garden and modern attitudes towards nature.

Writings by and about John Evelyn have been brought into relation to the early history of iron-founding, especially by the Darby family in Shropshire, to develop the industrial repercussions of early conservation legislation – another promising field for further study.

Among sources for the 19th century transformation of land use in the Scottish Highlands considerable reliance has been placed upon F. Fraser Darling's findings in his *West Highland Survey* (1952) and his *Natural History of the Highlands and Islands* (2nd Ed London 1965) These have however been supplemented for example by more detailed accounts of particular areas such as Rothiemurchus Forest and Rhum, by Arthur Hugh Clough's fascinating long contemporary poem, *The Bothy of Tobar-na-Vorlich*, and by *Plant communities of the Scottish Highlands* by D. N. McVean and D. A. Ratcliffe (London 1962).

Darwin's long delay in publishing his ideas on mutability of species and on natural selection, and its implications, are acutely analysed in Sir Gavin de Beer's Foreword to the centenary commemorative volume *Evolution by Natural Selection: Darwin and Wallace*, Cambridge 1958, published for the 15th International Congress of Zoology.

Among many significant works on 19th century pioneers mention can be made only of the story of Sir J. Paxton's Birkenhead Park opened in 1847 and its influence upon Frederick Law Olmsted, in *The Park and the Town – Public Landscape in 19th and 20th century*, by G. F. Chadwick, London 1966: Robin Fedden's account in *The Continuing Purpose* (London 1968) of the origins of the National Trust and the stimulus given to its eventual legal formation in 1859 by the constitution in 1891 of the Trustees of the Reservations of Massachusetts; and Philip Boardman's appraisal of Patrick Geddes, *Master of the Future*, published in 1944 by the University of North Carolina.

The story of the growth of the natural history and conservation movement in Britain is so voluminous that it is possible to give only a selection of outlines and appraisals which will put the reader on the right track for further detail. One of the most compact and comprehensive is Richard Fitter's Pelican Original entitled *Wildlife in Britain*, summarising the growth of the natural history movement and of conservation with many references. (London 1963). The most useful, accessible and compact conspectus in British terms of the entire range of problems involved in modern care of the environment is to be found in a more recent Pelican Original, *Man and Environment: Crisis and the Strategy of Choice*, by 'Robert Arvill' which has

345

recently been publicly disclosed as a pen-name for Robert Boote, Deputy Director of the Nature Conservancy, and for long my indefatigable colleague in countless not unavailing struggles.

Another first-class treatment from the angle of a dedicated countryman is *Tomorrow's Countryside; The Road to the Seventies*, by Garth Christian (London 1966) whose early death soon afterwards took away the most gifted, scholarly and informed of professional writers on conservation.

Two briefer summaries of my own should be added: *Advances in British Nature Conservation*, included in the Handbook for 1965 of the Society for the Promotion of Nature Reserves, and "The Countryside in 1970", which appeared in *Nature* for December 25, 1965.

British ornithology has been well reviewed on several occasions, the latest in James Fisher's *Shell Bird Book* (London 1966).

A Directory of Natural History and other Field Study Societies in Britain, compiled by A. Lysaght (London 1959) is now unfortunately badly out-of-date.

Among works which had much practical influence mention must be made of two by J. A. Steers, *The Coastline of England and Wales* (1948) and *The Sea Coast* (London 1962), and H. E. Bracey's *Industry and the Countryside* (London, 1963). Many more of importance are inevitably omitted. The field has grown too rich.

CHAPTER 8   THE AMERICAN STORY

Condensing into a few lines a select bibliography for each chapter is in several cases extremely difficult, but in this one virtually impossible. Fortunately a number of recent secondary sources of wide coverage help to bridge the gap, and several of them such as Hans Huth's excellent *Nature and the American* (Berkeley, 1957), and Peter Matthiessen's *Wildlife in America* (New York 1959) contain useful bibliographies. *The Quiet Crisis* by Stewart L. Udall (New York, 1963) "is primarily a work of synthesis and interpretation, the transference of old wine into new historical bottles" but is unique in being the work of a highly successful Secretary of the Interior, steeped in experience of the conflicting pressures inseparable from conservation. A useful complement is provided by David Cushman Coyle's *Conservation: An American Story of Conflict and Accomplishment* (Rutgers, 1957) which is however somewhat sketchy on sources. From an economic angle the work which has proved most useful here is *Scarcity and Growth: The Economics of Natural Resource Availability*, by Harold J. Barnett and Chandler Morse (Baltimore, 1963) one of the many excellent and scholarly products of Joseph Fisher's Resources for the Future Inc. in Washington D.C. Another worth citing is *Quality of the Environment: An Economic Approach to some Problems in using Land, Water and Air* by O. C. Herfindahl and A. V. Kneese (Baltimore 1965).

The best exposition of the enlightened American approach to land use is still Edward H. Graham's *Natural Principles of Land Use* (New York 1944), with its beautifully simplified and vividly illustrated pendant *The Land*

Renewed; The Story of Soil Conservation, by William R. Van Dersal (revised New York 1968).

On National Parks the most useful sources include *Our National Park Policy: A Critical History* by John Ise (Baltimore 1961), the official compilation of Administrative Policies for natural areas of the National Park System (Washington D.C. 1968 revise), and for particular descriptions *The National Parks* by Freeman Tilden (New York, 1968 revise) and *Seeing America's Wildlife in our National Refuges* by Devereux Butcher (New York 1955). *Man and Nature in the National Parks* by F. Fraser Darling & N. D. Eichhorn (Washington 1967) contains some stimulating reflections on policy.

In April-May 1965 two important conferences in or near Washington thoroughly surveyed the state and prospects of American conservation. Although I participated in both, the task of fully digesting their immense contributions has defeated me. They are recorded in *Beauty for America: Proceedings of the White House Conference on Natural Beauty* (Washington, D.C., 1965) and in *Future Environments of North America: Transformation of a Continent,* edited by F. Fraser Darling and John P. Milton, New York 1966. A useful official follow-up to the White House Conference is *From Sea to Shining Sea; A Report on the American Environment by the President's Council on Recreation and Natural Beauty* (Washington D.C. 1968.) As a progress report and guide for action it is supplemented by practical annotated lists of *Publications and Films Which Can Help,* and *Agencies and Organizations Which Can Help,* including voluntary as well as official bodies. A fuller official summary of the work of more than two dozen agencies within the Department of the Interior is given in its attractively illustrated Conservation Yearbook No. 3 (Washington, 1966) entitled *The Third Wave.*

As examples of countless interesting specialist documents may be mentioned *A proposed Program for Roads and Parkways,* prepared for the President's Council on Recreation and Natural Beauty by the U.S. Department of Commerce, Washington D.C. 1966, and *Surface Mining and Our Environment,* by the Department of the Interior, Washington D.C. 1967.

CHAPTER 9   TOWARDS WORLDWIDE ACTION.

The quotation from the Bureau of Sport Fisheries and Wildlife and the background for the initial American developments are based on papers by Walter F. Crissey and Gustav A. Swanson in the *Proceedings of the First European Meeting on Wildfowl Conservation* (London 1964). *The First World Conference on National Parks, volume of proceedings,* appeared in Washington D.C. 1964, edited by Alexander B. Adams.

The general lines of the Netherlands approach are perhaps best indicated in contributions to the Technical Meeting of IUPN (later IUCN) at the Hague in September 1951. The up-to-date state of integration of conservation of natural areas in general development policies is well demonstrated in the two parts of the *Second Report on Physical Planning in the Netherlands* issued by the Government Printing Office, The Hague, 1966 (in English).

Notes on Sources

The events leading up to the formation of successive international organisations are derived from various sources available in the Van Tienhoven Library of the IUCN at Morges. The International bird protection story is largely based on an account in the VIth Bulletin of the International Council for Bird Protection (London, 1952), and from the records of International Ornithological Congresses.

In addition to much documentation produced or held by the IUCN a useful source for developments since 1961 is the World Wildlife Fund (also at Morges) whose first report, *The Launching of a New Ark*, covered up to 1964, while the second, *The Ark under Way*, covering 1965-67, has now been followed by *Yearbook 1968* to keep the record up to date.

Among numerous other authoritative and regular sources are the IUCN Bulletin, *Oryx*, the Journal of the Fauna Preservation Society, London and the German language publications *Natur und Landschaft* and *Mitteilungen zur Landschaftspflege* from the Bundesanstalt fur Vegetationskunde, Naturschutz und Landschaftspflege, Bad Godesberg. For American developments the CF Letter; a Report on Environmental Issues from the Conservation Foundation is a valuable source.

The First Seven Years of the Charles Darwin Foundation for the Galapagos Isles, 1959-66, by Jean Dorst and Jacques Laruelle, Brussels 1967 (in English) documents the history and progress of this international initiative.

Since this book went to press the documentation for marine conservation has been importantly strengthened by the appearance of *The Whale*, by L. Harrison Mathews (London 1969) and of an important FAO report on Management of Fishery Resources, in *Advances in Marine Biology, Vol 6* edited by Sir F. S. Russell and Sir M. Yonge (London 1968).

Another notable addition to publicly available sources is *The Red Book: Wildlife in Danger*, prepared by James Fisher on the basis of the IUCN/WNF looseleaf record, maintained by the Survival Service Commission.

The *Torrey Canyon* has given rise to a copious literature including the Report with that title of the Zuckerman committee of official scientists (London 1967) *The Wreck of the Torrey Canyon* by C. Gill, F. Booker and Tony Soper (Newton Abbot, 1967) the Report from the Select Committee on Science and Technology, London 1968, and *Pollution and Marine Life: A Report by the Plymouth Laboratory of the Marine Biological Association*, 1968.

Pesticides and Pollution by Kenneth Mellanby, London 1968, and *Pesticides and the Living Landscape* by R. C. Rudd, Madison 1964 are valuable reviews of an increasingly serious aspect of conservation.

THE SPELLING OF ENGLISH

In attempting to discuss on a world level a subject so largely based on British and American concepts and actions, and so much of mutual concern on both sides of the Atlantic it is peculiarly frustrating for an author to be faced with the problem of spelling his words differently, in insignificant ways and for insignificant reasons, according to the side of the Atlantic on which they are to be printed and read.

These pedantically upheld minor spelling differences between English and American usage are utter nonsense. The highly conservative Oxford English Dictionary states, for example under "Honour, honor," which it gives as alternatives. "Honor and honour were equally frequent down to the 17th century. In England honour is now generally accepted, honor in U.S.". But the English practice is so inconsistent and arbitrary that while one would be faulted for describing a man as honorable one would equally be wrong in describing an unpaid officer as honourary. The same applies to Labour, which OED recognises merely as "usual" in the British Isles while Labor is "preferred" in the U.S. Here again, while writers in England are expected to equate toil with "labour" they may not describe their toilsome lot as "labourious".

An even more absurd situation arises over such classically derived words as "Programme", where the OED actually prefers "Program" on good scholarly grounds. That was the original and correct English spelling at a time when the word was much more rarely used than now, but somehow it got supplanted in Britain, although not in America, by the Frenchified version "Programme" with its two extra pointless letters. In some analogous cases, however, such as catalog, there is no good English precedent for adopting the more practical shortened form.

A third group of variants centers upon such words as centre. As a verb the spelling "center" used in the previous sentence was standard in 17th and 18th century English, before it was replaced by "centre". The history of spelling the noun is slightly different, but if we who speak the tongue that Milton spake would also follow his spelling we would return to our Paradise Lost. "As from the Center thrice to th'utmost pole." And as Milton prefers center so does Spenser prefer "theater", along with the erudite critics of New York.

A fourth group is typified by the word for which modern English usage indefensibly insists upon "defence" as the sole spelling. Here again OED gives parity to defense. Difficulty arises with other words of this group which are used both as nouns and as verbs, such as license, which is correct as a verb on both sides of the Atlantic, but is rejected by OED as a noun in favor of "licence" (Cf. advice, practice).

A fifth group consists of words originally containing dipthongs, over which for example OED until recently stuck to "oecology" for "ecology" a form of linguistic anemia which is enough to give the reader diarrhea.

A sixth group is exemplified by "judgement/judgment" or "Acknowledgement/ Acknowledgment", where the insertion of a further silent "e" is redundant and there is good precedent in literature for dropping it.

As books in English come to be read by more and more people to whom it is not a native tongue, and who are unfamiliar with the quirks of the English and American peoples it seems indefensible avoidably to perpetuate spelling distinctions which are not demanded by good scholarship, are confusing to many readers, and add to costs by prejudicing the interchangeability of printed texts across national boundaries.

Being faced with this problem, and being blessed by the support of very reasonable and understanding publishers on both sides of the Atlantic I take this opportunity to strike a blow for liberty from the tyranny of arbitrary custom by adopting in this book every spelling which has respectable dictionary authority for use on both sides of the Atlantic in preference to that which is permissible only on one side or the other. The fact that this principle usually means adopting what modern English fashion has tended wrongly to regard as American spellings is in itself a commentary on the situation which has been permitted to grow up almost unchallenged. Not claiming any expertise in this orthographic field I can do no more than make what I regard as a long overdue step in the right direction, hoping that a serious attempt to deal more comprehensively and fundamentally with this problem may follow sooner rather than later.

It would be possible to make an even longer list of words the spelling of which cannot be reconciled by following the above principle, and for these pardon must be asked from those readers who may find the following of English rather than American practice somewhat strange to them. It is inherent in any step towards greater unity and rationality that some adaptability should be demanded and some inconvenience suffered, but I for one feel that this is a much lesser evil than continuing to shirk the problem. In seeking primarily to promote harmony between man and nature I therefore offer this incidental contribution towards harmony between the British and American branches of the English world language.

Mercifully, unlike French, the English language is not saddled with any officially entrenched Vatican of pedantry to fetter its natural growth and renewal. In its greatest days English literature showed a refreshing freedom of spelling. Milton, who was not only a poet of genius but a notable scholar and public servant preferred such forms as "iland" "perfet" "femal" and "facil", which would doubtless be dismissed as shocking Americanisms if any contemporary author should revive them.

Professor John W. Clark of the University of Minnesota, who contributed an erudite and urbane chapter on American Spelling to the contribution in the Language Library entitled Spelling by G. H. Vallins (London 1954), has pointed out that standard American spelling does not differ so widely or complexly from standard British spelling as many British readers suppose. Though the differences are not of many kinds however, three or four of them appear in very considerable numbers of quite common words, and rightly or wrongly many British readers react to the American variants as being ugly and illiterate, while American readers do not react the same way against the British practice. As Professor Clark shows, while the charge of illiteracy may lie against plenty of variants proposed for use in America, it definitely does not lie against those generally accepted there. Professor Clark concludes,

"there might be something to be said for Americans adopting British spelling. They are certainly not going to do so however, and at the conclusion of this study I am left with the wistful hope that all Britons, in the course of time, may come round to granting that spellings used by a very large fraction, if not the majority, of cultivated native writers of English might calmly be accepted as legitimate."

This enlightening essay puts the matter in such wise perspective that it is disappointing fifteen years later to find it so poorly followed up in Britain, whence the first move must clearly come.

As one who firmly rejects the recent British assumption that nineteenth-century practice and authority has any true claim to superiority over earlier and often better

English attitudes and traditions I welcome the opportunity, as elsewhere, to combine sensible modernisation with a renewal of close contacts with the wellsprings of our common English-speaking culture. If both these desirable aims converge in calling for adjustments in Victorian British practice, then so much the worse for Victorian British practice. In truth, however, the claims of adequate harmonisation, as opposed to rigid uniformity, can be met by a relatively trifling series of reversions to earlier English practice. It might be hoped that in return American writers would also make some gestures towards maintaining the position that where alternative spellings are kept in currency by living practice there is something to be said for maintaining them as variants in use on both sides of the Atlantic rather than permitting the emotions of linguistic nationalism to become encrusted with them.

In all such affairs it must never be forgotten that since English has adventitiously made itself also a world language the interests of its immense and growing band of users who do not speak it as a native tongue ought always to be respected by the writers of nations born to its use. Prejudices and divergences which unnecessarily complicate the task and confuse the minds of such users are increasingly difficult to justify.

INDEX

Aachen (Germany), 136
Abercrombie, Patrick, 156
Aberdeen University, 231
Abstracting Services, 339
Adare, Cape (Antarctica), 100
Adirondack Mountains (U.S.A.), 167, 302
Ægean Sea (Greece), 41
Africa, 35, 40, 50, 51, 52, 53, 66, 79, 84, 85, 86, 90, 91, 92–3, 96, 118–20, 124, 126, 128, 150, 190, 202, 203, 224, 303, 304, 306, *see also* North Africa and South Africa.
agriculture, primitive, 36 *et seq*; forest clearances made for, 63; rejection of ecological revolution by, 67–8; effects of erosion upon, 123–5; attitude of ancient civilisations towards, 132 *et seq*; use of chemicals in, 217–22; need for ecological approach by, 271
Ahaggar *see* Hoggar
Ajai's Game Sanctuary (Uganda), 228
Alabama (U.S.A.), 222
Alaska, 72, 79, 184
Alberta (Canada), 190
Alcuin of York, 136
Aldabra Island (Indian Ocean), 93, 153; conservation of, 234, 236–7
Aleutian Islands (Bering Sea), 72
Alexander the Great, 137
Algeria, 296
Alps (Europe), 58, 71, 72, 129
Altai Mountains (Central Asia), 40
Altamira cave paintings (Spain), 35
Amazon Forest and River (South America), 20, 49, 53, 77, 90, 92, 290, 301
Amenophis III, King of Egypt, 135
American Fisheries Society (1870), 188
Amsterdam (Netherlands), 191, 194, 214, 230
Anatolian Uplands (Turkey), 37
Anchorage (Alaska), 72

Ancient Monuments Act (1882), 154
Andaman Islands (Bay of Bengal), 87
Andes (South America), 72, 89, 90, 93, 97, 123, 292, 300, 304
Anne, Queen of England, 143, 145
Antarctica, 21, 52, 53, 55–6, 100–1, 105, 106, 107, 126, 171, 197, 229; Antarctic Treaty (1959), 100, 206–8
Antigua (Leeward Islands), 84
Antipodes Islands (Pacific), 200
Antiquities Act (U.S., 1906), 184
Appalachian Mountains (U.S.A.), 77, 296, 302
Apollo 8, 128
aquaria, 198
Arabia, 41, 87, 301, 306; Arabs, Conquests and civilisation of, 41, 42, 80, 86
Aragura Sea (Indonesia), 94
Arctic, 52, 53, 56, 58, 71, 72, 88, 293, 294, 297, 300, 306
Argentina, 51, 97–8, 115, 155, 194
Arizona (U.S.A.), 305, 306
Arusha Declaration on Conservation of Wild Life (1961), 202–3
Asia, 37, 40, 42, 49, 50, 52, 53, 72, 76, 86–8, 90, 99, 117, 124, 126, 150, 193, 204, 302, 303
Asia Minor, 80–1, 115
Assam (India), 82
Assuan High Dam (Egypt), 86
Assyria, 136
Atacama Desert (Chile), 94
Athens, IUCN meeting at (1958), 201
Atlantic, 23, 52, 72, 73, 79, 83, 84, 85, 87, 90, 96, 97, 98, 100, 128, 159, 222, 230
Atlas Mountains (North Africa), 72
Attingham, TELMA meeting at (1967), 204
Australia, 49, 50, 52, 94, 96–7, 100, 115, 191, 224, 292, 301, 304
Austria, 194, 196, 197
avalanches, 48, 53

Azores (Atlantic), 78, 79
Azraq Oasis (Jordan), 55
Aztec civilisation, 89

Babylon, 136, 137
Baffin Island (Canada), 73
Bagehot, Walter, 169
Baldwin, Stanley, 157
Bali Island (Indonesia), 94
Balleny Islands (Antarctica), 100
Ballinger, Richard Achilles, 176
Balmoral, 152
Baltic (Europe), 71
Baluchistan (Pakistan), 87, 116
Banff National Park (Canada), 118
Bangkok, IUCN meeting at (1965), 204
Bangor, University College, 231
Banks, Sir Joseph, 153
Barbados (West Indies), 66
Barnack (Huntingdonshire), 122
Barnett, Harold J. (*Scarcity and Growth*), 170, 172
Bartram, John, 162
Basel (Switzerland), 193; Conference for Protection of Nature at (1913), 194
Bass Strait (Australia), 100
Basutoland (South Africa), 119
Bath, 151
Beardmore Glacier (Antarctica), 101
Bedford, Duke of, 155
Belgium, 191, 194, 195
Bengal, Bay of, 87
Bennett, Dr Hugh, 123, 180-1
Bergen (Norway), 71
Bering Sea (Asia-America), 72
Berlin, Fifth International Ornithological Congress at (1910), 197
Bernard, Dr Charles, 195
Bernhard, Prince of the Netherlands, 227
Berkeley (California), 250
Bigelow, Dr Jacob, 165
birds, *see* ornithology
Birkenhead Park, 166
Bischoff, Gerhard, *Die Welt Unter Uns*, 342
bison, U.S. action to protect, 182
Blakeney Point (Norfolk), 156
Bligh, Captain William, 100
Bloomsbury (London), 151

Blue Nile (Africa), 86
Bois de la Haye (Netherlands), 142
Bolivia, 95, 303
Bombay (India), 81, 302
Boone and Crockett Club, 124
Boote, Robert, 'Robert Arvill', 345-6
Borneo, 57 88, 289, 294
Boston (U.S.A.), 165
Bournemouth, 151
Bowles, Samuel, 167
Brahmaputra River (India), 49, 81
Brasilia (Brazil), 95
Brazil, 57, 90, 91, 95, 97, 291, 293, 296
Bridgeman, Charles, 144, 145
Brindley, James, 149
Bristol, 75
Britain, 35, 42, 51, 52, 58, 62, 65, 66, 70, 75, 80, 83, 98, 108, 109, 110, 113-4, 115, 121, 122, 127, 136, 138, 139-40, 296; efforts on behalf of Conservation, 141-61, 162, 166, 169, 177, 178, 181, 182, 188, 194, 195, 197, 199, 200, 201, 204, 205, 206, 208, 210-6, 217, 218, 219, 220, 221-2, 224-5, 229, 231, 232, 235, 236-7, 246, 266, 272, 273, 274
Britain's Nature Reserves, 26
British Birds, 24
British Ecological Society, 155, 158
British Museum, 153
British Trust for Entomology, 157
British Trust for Ornithology, 22, 24, 157
British Vegetation Committee, 155
Brown, Lancelot ('Capability'), 145
Brunel, I. K., 149
Brunnen (Switzerland), Conference at (1947), 195
Brussels, international conservation foundations at, 194, 195, 204, 226
Bryant, William Cullen, 166
Budapest, Second Ornithological Congress at (1891), 196-7
Buenos Aires (Argentina), 98
buffalo, mass slaughter of, 168
Bukavu (Congo), 93
Bundesanstalt für Vegetationskunde &c., 339, 348
Bureau of Reclamation (U.S.A.), 186
Bureau of Recreation (U.S.A.), 177, 186, 242

Burlington, Richard Boyle, 3rd Earl of, 145
Burma, 87, 106
Burnet, Thomas (*The Sacred Theory of the Earth*), 143, 144
Burnham Beeches, 154
Burroughs, John, 164, 165
Byron, George Gordon, 6th Lord, 44
Byzantine Empire, 42

Cadiz, Gulf of (Spain), 80
Cairngorms (Scotland), 112, 192
Cairo (Egypt), 23
California (U.S.A.), 58, 76, 83, 90, 99, 131, 166, 167, 174, 183, 184, 250, 290, 291, 292, 293, 294, 295, 297, 298, 303
Callaghan, James, 214
Cambodia, 87
Campeche, Gulf of (Mexico), 84
Canada, 52, 72–3, 126, 291, 292, 295, 297, 298; conservation activities in, 168, 188–9, 199
canals, 45, 75, 146, 149
Canary Islands (Atlantic), 57, 290
Canberra (Australia), Commonwealth Scientific and Industrial Research Organisation at, 201, 342
Canton Island (Phoenix Islands), 305
Cape of Good Hope (South Africa), 99
Cape Verde Islands (Atlantic), 84
Capel, Sir William, 153
Caracas (Venezuela), 199
Caribbean (Central America), 84, 85, 299, 302, 303
Caroline, Queen of England, 144
Caroline Islands (Pacific), 88
Carolina Parakeet, extinction of, 174
Carson, Rachel (*Silent Spring*), 222–3, 253
Carthage, 80
Caspian Sea (Russia), 76
Catlin, George, 164
Caucasus Mountains (Asia), 72
Ceara (Brazil), 291
Celebes Islands (Indonesia), 94
Central African Republic, 202
Central America, 37, 42, 50, 84, 126 *see also* Mexico and Panama
Central Park (New York), 170

Ceram (Indonesia), 94
Cerro Aconcagua (Argentina), 97
Ceylon, 290, 299, 300, 301
Chad, 202
Chagos Islands (Indian Ocean), 93
chamois, threat to, 105
Charlemagne, 136
Charles I, King of England, 144
Charles II, King of England, 142, 145
Charles Darwin Foundation (Brussels), 204, 348
Charles Darwin Research Station (Galapagos), 88, 204
Chelsea Physic Garden, 153, 162
chemicals, use of in agriculture, 45, 67, 171, 183, 217–22, 253, 281; chemical warfare, 82; *see also* insecticides, pesticides
chestnut, fate of American, 106
Chile, 94, 97, 100, 123
Chimborazo (Ecuador), 89
China, 38, 41, 42, 49, 76, 81, 82, 132; influence over landscaping, 135–6
Chiswick Garden, 145
Christmas Island (Pacific), 296
Clark, Prof. John W., 350
Claude (Lorraine), 145
climate, 53 *et seq*, 70 *passim*, 102, 115–6, 179–80, 341
Coalbrookdale (Shropshire), 113
Coleridge, Samuel Taylor, 150
Colfax, Schuyler, 167
collection of specimens, effects of, 108–10, 112
Collin, Dr. Nicholas, 163
Colombia, 58, 89, 97, 123, 289, 292, 293, 294, 302, 303
Colorado (U.S.A.), 178
Columbus, Christopher, 84
commercialism, 109, 129, 151
Congo (Brazzaville), 202; (Kinshasa), 201, 202, 203, 261; River, 92
conservation of nature, problems involved in, 16 *et seq*, 104–31; early efforts on behalf of, 132 *et seq*; Britain's approach to, 141–61; American efforts on behalf of, 162–87; international concern for, 188–238; present position, 239–62; future tasks, 263–79; conclusion and outlook, 280–

conservation of nature—*cont.*
7; Flow Chart of conservation processes, 336–7
Conservation Foundation, U.S.A., 348
Cook, Captain James, 153
Coolidge, Calvin (U.S. President), 180
Coolidge, H. J., 201
Cooper, James Fenimore, 163
Cooper, William, 163–4, 171
Copenhagen (Denmark), 210; international conservation meetings at, 200, 218
Coral Sea, 94
Cordillera (South America), 89, 95
Cornwall, 146, 148, 213
Coshocton (Ohio), Soil and Water Conservation Research Station at, 178, 179
Coto Donana (Spain), Wild Life Preserve at, 228
Cottam, Dr Clarence, *quoted*, 218–9
Council of Europe, 205–6
Council for Nature, 158
Council for the Preservation of Rural England, 156–7
Countryside Commission, 181
Countryside, human impact on (Chart), 308–35, *see also* Council for the Preservation of Rural England
Coweeta Laboratory (North Carolina), 178
Crete, 80
Crozier, Cape (Antartica), 101
Cuba, 84, 266
cultivation, methods of, 123–5
Cuthbert, St, 140, 265
Czechoslovakia, 201, 205, 238

Dahomey, 202
Daiches, David, 143
Damodar Valley Project (India), 180
dams, 45, 65, 86, 134, 178–80, 181, 186
Danube (Central Europe), 40, 97, 117
Darby, Abraham, 113, 114
Darius I, King of Persia, 137
Darling, Frank Fraser, 178, 345, 347
Darling River (Australia), 97
Darwin, Charles, 67, 93, 153, 173, 203, 229, 236, 248, 254, 264, 345
Dead Sea (Palestine), 78

deer, threatened extinction of, 155, 193
Definitions of terms, 239–42
Defoe, Daniel, 97
defoliation, 82; *see also* chemical war
deforestation, by primitive man, 37, 38, 39, 43, 70, 80, 138; in modern times, 63, 71, 110, 112–3, 114, 116, 123–4, 141, 168
Denmark, 194, 201
Derbyshire, 148
Desolacion Island (Chile), 100
Detroit (U.S.A.), 261
Devon, 146
Dinosaur National Monument (U.S.A.), 186
Doane, Lieut. Gustavus, 173
dodo, extinction of, 236
Dohrn, Anton, 198
Downing, Andrew Jackson, 165–6
drainage (and reclamation), 45, 61–2, 70, 75, 124, 146, 177–8, 179; *see also* dams, irrigation and land reclamation
Drury, Newton B., 186
duck shooting, 189, 190
dumping, 113–4, 130–1, 191; *see also* pollution
Dungeness (Kent), 55
Durham, 113, 148
Dutch overseas empire, 42, 94
Dzungarian Gate (Sinkiang), 76

Earth, living patterns of, 48–68; geography of, 69–102, 340–3
earthquakes, 36, 39, 48, 53, 72, 80, 82, 97, 100, 102
Eastbourne, 151
Easter Island (Pacific), 39, 97
ecology, science of, 16, 22 *passim*, 32, 55, 61, 66, 67, 158–9, 173, 201, 228 *et seq*, 239 *et seq*, 247–54, 268 *et seq*, 341–2
Ecuador, 89, 123, 203
Edinburgh, Philip, Duke of, 161, 225, 227
Edinburgh (city), 151; (university), 231; conservation meetings at, 200, 230
Edward Grey Institute of Field Ornithology, 22, 157
Egypt (ancient), 40, 42, 80, 134, 135; (modern), 86
Elburz Mountains (Iran), 81

Ellesmere Island (Canada), 73
Elton, Charles, 341
Emerson, Ralph Waldo, 164, 167
England, *see* Britain
English, The Spelling of, 349–51
entomology, 24, 156, 157, 198
Epping Forest, 154
Equator, 87, 88, 89, 102
Erik the Red, 20
erosion, 37, 39, 45, 48, 53, 66, 77, 80, 105,
  119–20, 122–4, 172, 175 *et seq*, 180–1,
  201
Eskimos, 43
Ethiopia, 86, 87
Euphrates (Iraq), 38
Europe, 40, 43, 49, 50, 52, 58, 62, 70, 71,
  72, 76, 78, 79, 80, 83, 84, 92, 98, 100,
  114, 117, 118, 122, 150, 168, 261, 291,
  293, 296, 303
Evelyn, John, 141–2, 162
Everest, Mount, 285
evolution, *see* man

Fairbanks (Alaska), 72
falconry, 140
Falkland Islands (Atlantic), 197
Faraday, Michael, 254
Farne Islands (Northumberland), 140
Fatio, Professor V., 195–6
Fauna Preservation Society, 155, 235, 348
Fernando Noronha Island, 90
Fertile Crescent (Mesopotamia), 37, 81
Fiji Islands (Pacific), 94, 200
Finland, 71
Fiordland National Park (New Zealand),
  54–5, 100
Fish and Wildlife Service (U.S.A.), 170,
  177, 183
Fisher, James, 225
fishing, 34, 73, 107, 198, 200, 209–10,
  271
Fitter, Richard S. R., 345
Flamborough Head (Yorks.), 155
flooding, 36, 38, 39, 49, 62, 72, 77, 86,
  102, 116, 124, 177–80
Flores, Island and Sea (Indonesia), 94
Florida, 58, 182, 292, 296, 297, 300
Fontainebleau, conservation meeting at,
  195

Forel, A., 193
Forest Service, 170, 175–8, 183, 185
Forest Reserve Act (1891–U.S.), 183
Forestry, 33, 36, 38, 39, 49, 53, 62–6, 72,
  73, 76, 79, 89–90, 106, 110, 112–3, 118,
  123–4, 138, 139–40, 141, 147, 149–50,
  162, 163, 176–7, 178, 183 *et seq*, 191–3,
  241, 242
Formosa (Taiwan), 82
Fosberg, Dr F. R., 59, 198, 343
France, 58, 60, 115, 134, 194, 200, 204,
  214, 266
Francis of Assisi, St, 140
Franklin, Benjamin, 163
Fraser (Colorado), Forest research at,
  178–9

Gabon, 91, 202
Gabrielson, Dr Ira, 183
Galapagos Islands (Pacific), 88–9, 203–4,
  236
Gan Island (Maldive Islands), 236
Ganges (India), 49, 81, 300
gardens, construction of, 21; (in ancient
  times), 133, 134, 135–7; (in modern
  times), 141–5
Gary, Romain (*The Roots of Heaven*), 200,
  223
Gaulle, General Charles de, 94
Geddes, Patrick, 157
General Grant National Park (U.S.A.),
  174, 183
Geneva (Lake), 193; (U.N. Conference
  on Trade and Development), 234
Germany, 60, 75, 115, 140, 194, 196, 200
Gezira Project, 86
Ghana, 91
Ghats (Western-India), 87
Gilbert Islands (Pacific), 88
Glacier-Waterton International Peace
  Park (Canada), 189
Glasgow, 16
Glass, Dr Bentley, 232
Gobi Desert (Asia), 76
Gosse, Philip Henry, 198
Graham, Edward H., 346
Grand Canyon (U.S.A.), 114
Grant, General Ulysses S. (U.S. Presi-
  dent), 182

Graz, 8th International Zoological Congress at (1910), 193, 197
Great Barrier Reef (Australia), 94
Great Exhibition (1851), 154
Great Lakes (Canada and U.S.A.), 73
Great Slave Lake (North Western territories), 73
Greece (ancient), 41, 80; (modern), 51, 120
Greeley, Horace, 166
Greenland, 20, 23, 52, 70, 73
Grey, Sir Edward, 155–6, 182
Grobman, Dr Arnold B., 232
Grzimek, Bernard (*Serengeti Must Not Die*), 223, 235–6
Guadeloupe (Leeward Islands), 84
Guam (Pacific), 289, 297, 298, 299, 302
Guaira Falls (Brazil), 95
Guayaquil (Ecuador), 89
Guinea, Gulf of (Africa), 91
Gulf Stream, 70
Guyana, 20

Hague, The (Netherlands), 188, 199
Hall, Sir Daniel, 118, 119, 120, 123–4
Halmahera Island (Pacific), 94
Hamilton, William, 162
Hamilton, Lieut.-Colonel Stevenson, 191
Hannibal, 85
Harroy, Jean-Paul, 195, 201
Harvard Forest (U.S.A.), 62–3
Hawaii-Hawaiian Islands (Pacific), 57, 78, 82–3, 88, 105, 290, 291, 294, 295, 296, 298, 300, 302, 303, 304
Heim, Dr Roger, 200
Helsinki (Finland), 71
Henry VIII, King of England, 141, 144
Henry the Navigator, Prince of Portugal, 80
Highlands (Scottish), 70, 118, 151–2, 192
Himalayas (India), 58, 72, 81, 293
Hindu Empire, 42
Hispaniola (West Indies), 84
Hittites, 42
Hluhluwe Game Reserve (South Africa), 191
Hoggar Mountains (Africa), 86
Hokkaido Island (Japan), 76
Holmes, Oliver Wendell, 166

Hong Kong, 82, 88
Hoover, Herbert (U.S. President), 180
Horace Albright Lecture (1964), 250
Hot Springs National Reservation (U.S.), 188
Howard, Ebenezer, 157
Huang Ho River (China), 81
Hudson, W. H., 20, 22, 155, 157
Hudson Bay (Canada), 73
Humboldt current, 89
Hungary, 194, 195, 196
hunting, by primitive man, 34, 35, 40, 43, 46, 136, 137; in ancient and medieval times, 139–40; effects of, 112; as a sport, 127, 150, 152, 168, 243
Hurcomb, Cyril, Lord, 220
hurricanes (and typhoons), 63–5, 82, 84, 102, 182
Huth, Hans, 164
Huxley, Sir Julian, 159, 194, 195, 226, 229, 341
Huxley, Thomas H., 248
Huxley-Tansley Special Committee, 250

Ijsselmeer, reclamation of, 75, 191, 273
Inca civilisation, 89, 132
India, 41, 49, 81–2, 84, 87, 120, 180, 200, 302
Indian Ocean, 52, 87, 93, 96, 100, 236, 237
Indians (American), 43, 83, 89, 90, 164, 166
Indo-China, 294, 302
Indonesia, 93–4, 204
Indus (Pakistan), 38, 81, 97, 118, 134
Industrial Revolution (industrialisation), 65, 74–5, 77, 81, 83, 86, 104, 113–4, 122, 130, 142, 147–9
Inland Waterway Commission (U.S.A.), 179
insecticides, 110, 217
International Biological Program, 28, 56, 61, 198, 230, 251, 268, 269, 342, 343
International Botanical Congress, 204
International Commission on National Parks, 201
International Committee for Bird Preservation (1922), 197
International Conference for the Protection of Nature, 194–5

International Convention for the Protection of Birds Useful to Agriculture (1902), 197
International Council for Bird Preservation, 196, 348
International Council of Scientific Unions (I.C.S.U.), 229–30
International Date Line, 88, 94, 97
International Geophysical Year (1957–8), 28, 206, 229, 253
International Office for the Protection of Nature, 194
International Ornithological Congress, 196–7
International Technical Conference on the Protection of Nature, 217, 218
International Union for the Conservation of Nature (I.U.C.N.), 201, 203, 204, 205, 208–9, 226–7, 250, 343, 348
International Union of Biological Services, 194, 250
International Whaling Commission, 208–9
International Wildfowl Research Bureau, 197, 204
International Zoological Congress (1958) 203
Inter-Departmental Advisory Committee on Poisonous Substances used in Agriculture and Food Storages, 220
Inter-Governmental Maritime Consultative Committee (I.M.C.C.), 212, 215
Inverness (Scotland), 70, 79
Iowa (U.S.A.), 184
Iquique (Chile), 94
Iran, 40, 81, 87, 115, 136, 138, 139
Iraq, 40, 81, 137
Ireland, 74, 75, 181
Irrawaddy River (Burma), 81
irrigation, 37, 38, 42, 89, 97, 124–33, 135, 177–9
Ishigaki Island, 290
Izaak Walton League of America, 182
Ivory Coast, 202
Italy, 167, 194, 200, 265

Jacks, G. V. (*The Rape of the Earth; A World Survey of Soil Erosion*), 223
Jamaica, 84, 94

James I, King of England and Scotland, 142
Japan, 52, 58, 76, 99, 136, 192, 194, 250, 256, 292
Java, 52, 93, 94, 293
Jefferson, Thomas, 162
Jericho, 64, 122, 135
Jerome, St., 265
Johnson, Lyndon B. (U.S. President), 270
Jordan, 55
Juan Fernandez Island (Pacific), 97
Jugoslavia, 105

Kalahari Desert (South Africa), 96
Kamba Reserve (Kenya), 119
Kamchatka (Russia), 72
Kariba Dam (Rhodesia), 273
Katmai, Mount (Alaska), 72, 184
Kauai Island (Hawaiian Islands), 82
Keele, University of, 232
Kennedy, John F. (U.S. President), 182
Kennedy, Robert, 182
Kensington Gardens, 144
Kent, William, 135, 136, 145
Kenya, 203, 235; Kenya Land Commission, 119
Kermadec Islands (Pacific), 97
Kermanshah (Iran), 139
Kew, Royal Botanic Gardens at, 90, 153
Keynes, Maynard, 169
Khartoum (Sudan), 86
Kilimanjaro, Mount (Kenya), 93
Kinabalu National Park (Borneo), 88
King, Martin Luther, 182
King, Thomas Starr, 165
Kivu (Congo), 92–3
Klondike River (Yukon), 73
Kordofan, 86
Korea (South), 99
Kruger, Paul (Kruger National Park), 191
Kublai Khan, 140
Kyoto (Japan), 256

Labrador, 23, 73
Lacey, John, 182, 184
Lake Eyre (Australia), 96

Lake Success (New York), World Conference on Natural Resources at (1949), 196
Lambarene (Gabon), 92
land reclamation, 61–2, 75, 76, 89, 191–3, 273
Land and Water Conservation Fund (U.S.A. 1965), 186
landscaping, 21, 77, 95, 135 *et seq*, 142–51, 165, 174, 192 *et seq*, 201, 241, 275, 344–5
Landseer, Sir Edwin, 152
landslides, 39, 48, 53
Lane, Franklin K., 185
Lappland (Europe), 58, 296, 300, 305
Lascaux (France), cave paintings of, 35
Leakey, Dr L. S. B., 35
Lebanon, 99
Leeward Islands (West Indies), 84
Leningrad (Russia), 71, 205
Leopold, Aldo (*Sand County Almanac*), 223
Les Saintes-Maries-de-la-Mer (France), IUCN Conference at (1962), 204
Liberia, 91, 212
Libraries, specialised, 339
limnology, 198
Limpopo River (Mozambique), 96
Lincoln, Abraham (U.S. President), 167
Lincolnshire, 157
Lindbergh, General Charles A., 208–9
Line Islands (Pacific), 88
Linnaeus, Carl, 145, 153; Linnean Society, 154
Lisbon (Portugal), 230
litter, 106, 107
Lomond, Loch, 192
London, 75, 123, 142, 151, 154, 162, 195; Nature Protection meetings at, 190, 191, 194, 197, 203, 230, 269
Longfellow, Henry Wadsworth, 20, 223
Lord Howe Island (Pacific), 97
Lorenz, Konrad (*On Aggression*), 264
Los Angeles (U.S.A.), 261
Louis XIV, King of France, 143, 145
Lowell, James Russell, 166
Luzon Island (Philippines), 82, 297

McGee, W. J., 240
Mackenzie River (Canada), 73
McKinley, Mount (Alaska), 72

Madagascar, 52, 96, 202
Madras (India), 81, 87
Madura Island (Indonesia), 94
Magellan, Strait of, 100
Mahomet, 86, 117
Maine (U.S.A.), 167
Malaya 57, 87, 289, 290, 293, 296
Mali, 202
Mammal Society of the British Isles, 157
Man, evolution of and impact on environment, 33–47, 64 *et seq*, 104–31, 340
Manaus (Brazil), 90
Manitoba (Canada), 190
MAR Project, 204, 343
Mariana Islands (Pacific), 295
Mariposa Grove of Big Trees (California), 166–7
Marsh, George Perkins (*Man and Nature*), 153, 167, 240
Mas Atierra (Pacific), 97
Mas Afuera (Pacific), 97
Marshall Islands (Pacific), 302, 304
Masai tribe, 93, 118, 235; Masai Mara Game Reserve, 235
Massachusetts (U.S.A.), 62, 63, 154
Mather, Stephen T., 185
Mauritania (Africa), 84
Mayan civilisation, 84, 89
Mediterranean, 58, 79, 80, 84, 86, 116, 117, 120, 201, 292, 295, 303
Mekong River (Indo-China), 81, 88, 261
Melbourne (Australia), 100
Meru, Mount (Tanzania), 93
Mesopotamia (Asia Minor), 38, 136, 139
Mexico, 82, 83, 163, 188, 190, 294, 295
Michigan (U.S.A.), 222
Micronesia (Pacific), 82, 88, 294
Milford Haven, 74, 213; Milford Haven Conservancy Act (1958), 210–12
Milford Sound (New Zealand), 100
Millais, Sir John, 152
Milton, John, spellings, 350
Mindanao (Philippines), 88
Mississipi (U.S.A.), 59, 77, 88, 90, 179, 223, 299, 300; Mississipi Valley Improvement Association, 179
Missouri River (U.S.A.), 77, 88, 90, 164
mobility of modern man, 41, 44, 45, 69, 83, 88, 105–6, 129, 151
Mozambique (Portuguese Africa), 96

Mongolia, 71, 76; Mongols, 42
Montana (U.S.A.), 181
Montevideo (Uruguay), 98
Monticello (U.S.A.), 162
Montpellier (France), 250
Montreal (Canada), Expo '67 at, 225
Moore, Dr N. W., 220
Morges (Switzerland), International Union for Conservation headquarters at, 227, 230
Morocco, 80, 99
Morris, Desmond, (*The Naked Ape*), 264
Morrison, Herbert, 159
Moore, Chandler (*Scarcity and Growth*), quoted, 170, 172
Mount Auburn Cemetery (Boston), 165, 170
Mount Vernon (Virginia), 162
Mountfort, Guy, 227, 342
Muir, John, 165, 167, 174, 175
Mumford, Lewis, 340-1
Murray River (Australia), 97
Muscle Shoals nitrate plant, 179-80
Muskingum Conservancy District (Ohio), 178

Naardermeer Nature Reserve (Netherlands), 191
Nairobi, IUCN General Assembly at (1963), 203
Naples, Stazione Zoologica at, 198
Nasser, Lake (Egypt), 86
Natal (South Africa), 191, 200
National Audubon Society (1885), 174, 182, 225
National Nature Weeks, 225
National Parks, 110, 125-7; African, 118, 191, 202-3, 228, 235; American and Canadian, 167-8, 174, 183 *et seq*, 188-9, 225; Australian, 191; Dutch, 191; New Zealand, 190-1; Spanish 228; Swiss, 193-4; Conferences on, 190, 201; U.N. List, 344
National Parks Service (U.S. 1916), 174, 177, 185, 242, 285
National Parks Commission, 160-1, 212
National Trust (for Places of Historic Interest or Natural Beauty), creation of, 154, 156

National Trust for Scotland, 157
National Wildlife Federation (U.S.), 182
Natural History Museum, 18
Nature Conservancy, creation of, 159-61; *see also* 24, 26-7, 199 *et seq*, 215 *et seq*, 251
Nature Reserves, *see* National Parks
Nature Reserves Investigation Committee (NRIC), 158-9
Nauru (Gilbert Islands), 88
Netherlands, 75, 142, 188, 191, 192, 194, 199, 200, 205, 273, 347
Neuchatel (Switzerland), 230
New Amsterdam, 100
New Caledonia, 194, 302
New England (U.S.A.), 63, 65
New Forest, 154, 156
New Guinea, 52, 88, 94
New Hebrides (Pacific), 94
New Jersey (U.S.A.), 295
New Mexico (U.S.A.), 304, 306
New South Wales (Australia), 96
New York, 164, 165, 166, 167, 170, 190, 196; New York state, 51, 65
New Zealand, 55, 57, 58, 97, 100, 107, 120-1, 126, 190, 291, 292, 299, 302, 304
Newfoundland (Canada), 23, 188
Newport (Monmouthshire), 75
Ngorongoro Crater (Kenya), 235
Niagara Falls, 167, 168, 170
Niger, 202
Nigeria, 91, 202
Nile (Egypt), 37, 38, 41, 86, 90, 115
Nineveh (Iraq), 137
noise, effects of, 45, 105, 112, 207-8, 259
Noordwijk (Netherlands), Wildfowl Conservation meeting at (1966), 205
Norfolk, 156, 157; Broads, 122
Norris, Senator George, 180
North America, 40, 50, 52, 53, 57, 58, 65, 72, 76, 84, 88, 89, 106, 126, 162 *et seq*, 188-90, 224, 291, 292, 294, 301
North American Wildlife Institute, 182
North Carolina (U.S.A.), 99, 178
North Pole, 70, 100, 101
North Sea, 71, 75
North of Scotland Hydro-Electricity Board, 180
Northumberland, 113, 140, 148
Norway, 70, 194

Nottinghamshire, 148
nuclear explosions, 45, 82, 94, 105, 216–7
    253
Nyerere, Dr Julius, 202

Oates, David, 137
Oceanic, 50, 52, 88, 126
oceanography, 198
Ohio River (U.S.A.), 77; flooding of,
    177–8; Ohio Conservancy Act (1913),
    178
Oklahoma (U.S.A.), 181, 183
Olmsted, Frederic Law, 166, 167, 345
Olmsted, Frederic Law, Jr., 184
Olympic Games, 285
Open Spaces and Footpaths Preserva-
    tion Society (1865), 154
Orinoco River (Venezuela), 58, 294
Ornithology, interest in, 18–9, 22–4, 55–
    6, 173; threat to bird life, 107–8, 110,
    139, 140, 141, 150, 152; preservation
    activities of, 155, 157, 182, 189, 196–7,
    208, 220, 221; *see also* International
    Ornithological Congresses.
Osborn, Fairfield (*Our Plundered Planet*),
    223
Oslo (Norway), 71, 250
Oxford, Ashmolean Museum at, 140;
    botanic garden at, 153, 162; Edward
    Grey Institute at, 157; University, 20,
    231
Oxford Bird Census, 22, 24
Oxford English Dictionary, 349
Oxford University Expeditions, 20
Oxus River (Asia), 81

Pacific Islands, 106, 291, 292, 295, 298,
    299
Pacific Ocean, 42, 51, 52, 58, 72, 76, 78,
    82, 83, 87, 88, 89, 90, 94, 97, 166
Palau Islands (Pacific), 88, 291, 297
Panama, 89; Panama Canal, 273
Papua, 94
Paraguay, 95
Parana River (Argentina), 95, 98
Parc National Albert (Congo), 191
Paris, conservation conference at, 194,
    197, 200

pastoralism, effects of, 36, 39, 93, 115–22,
    138
Patagonia (South America), 72, 100
Paxton, Sir Joseph, 166
Pearsall, Professor W. H., 23, 198, 235
Pearson, Dr Gilbert, 197
Pelican Island (Florida), 182
Pembrokeshire, 107, 210
penguins, 56, 100
Penn, William, 162, 163
Pennsylvania, 162
Père David, 155
Persepolis (Iran), 137
Persians (ancient), 42, 80, 137, 139
Persian Gulf, 87, 212
Peru, 132, 302, 303, 304, 305, 306
pesticides, effects of, 105, 217–8
Peterborough, 122
Peters, Sir Rudolph, 230
Philadelphia (U.S.A.), 162, 163, 165
Philippines, 52, 82, 88, 204, 295
Phillips, Professor John, *quoted*, 124
Phoenicia, 80
Phoenix Islands (Pacific), 88
Picturesque America (1872), 223
pigeon (passenger), extinction of, 174
Pinchot, Gifford, 175, 176–7, 240
Pitcairn Island (Pacific), 97
Plate River (Argentina), 98, 99
Platt (Oklahoma), sulphur springs at,
    183
Plunkett, Sir Horace, 181
Poland, 75, 194
Polanyi, Karl, 171
pollution (air, land, water), 37, 45, 75,
    104–5, 130–1, 142, 193, 197, 209–16,
    275, 281; *see also Torrey Canyon*
Polynesia, 94, 97, 300
Pondoland (South Africa), 118
Poore, Dr M. E. D., 160
Pope, Alexander, 150
population, 37, 38–9, 40, 41, 51, 76, 81,
    82, 83, 87, 93–4, 95, 98, 100, 101, 124,
    125, 136, 137–8, 152
Portugal, 79, 194; Portuguese Empire,
    42
Potosi (Bolivia), 95
Potsdam (Germany), 23
Potter, C., 219
Poussin, Nicholas, 145

preservation (as distinct from conservation), 239
protection (as distinct from conservation) 239
Prudhoe (Alaska), 72
Puerto Rico, 84
Puntas Arenas (Chile), 100
Purple Heron, threat to, 191
Purus River (Brazil), 90
pyramids, 39

Quebec (Canada), 23
Quito (Ecuador), 102

Raup, Hugh M., 63, 65
Ray, John, 145, 153
recreation, 43–4, 95, 111–2, 127–9, 142,
recreation and sport, 43–4, 95, 111–2,
    127–9, 142, 145, 161, 186, 189, 236–8,
    271–2; *see also* Bureau of Recreation
    and Tourism
Red Sea, 87
Reed, Charles A., 139
reservation (as distinct from conservation), 239
Resources for the Future, Inc., 346
Rhine (Europe), 75
rhinoceros, threatened extinction of, 93,
    228
Rio de Janeiro (Brazil), 95
Rio Grande (U.S.A.), 126
river valley civilisations, 37, 38 *et seq*
Rocas Reef, 90
Rockefeller, Laurence, 186
Rocky Mountains (U.S.A.), 58, 72, 77,
    78, 292, 295, 296, 302
Rome (ancient), 41, 42, 80, 85, 138, 167;
    (modern), 230
Roosevelt, Franklin D. (U.S. President),
    179, 180
Roosevelt, Theodore (U.S. President),
    his work for conservation, 156, 167,
    174–5, 176, 179, 180, 181, 182, 184,
    188, 263
Rosa, Salvator, 145
Ross Ice Shelf, 101
Rothamsted Experimental Station, 219
Rothschild, Charles, 156

Rothschild, Walter, 197
Rotterdam (Netherlands), 75
Royal Parks, 142, 154
Royal Society for the Protection of Birds,
    155
Rudolf, Crown Prince of Austria, 196
Rugiati, Captain, 212–3
Ruhr Industrial Area (Germany), 75
Rumania, 194
Russia, 71, 75–6, 112, 117, 126, 194, 200,
    202, 205, 229, 266
Ryukyu Islands (Japan), 292, 295

Sabie Game Reserve *see* Kruger National
    Park
Sahara (Africa), 40, 49, 50, 84, 85–6, 96
Saharan crags, cave paintings of, 35
St Andrews (Scotland), Wildfowl Conservation meeting at (1963), 204
St George's Channel, 74
St James's Park, 142
St Lawrence River (Canada), 73
St Louis (U.S.A.), 77
St Lucia Game Reserve (South Africa),
    191
St Vincent, Cape (Portugal), 78
Saipan Island (Manana Islands), 291,
    302
Sakhalin (Russia), 52
Salar de Uyuni (South America), 95
Samoa Island (Pacific), 94
San Francisco (U.S.A.), 76, 204
San Joaquin Valley (California), 77
Santa Elena Peninsula, 89
Santiago (Chile), 97
Sao Paulo (Brazil), 95
Sarasin, Dr Paul, 193, 197
Sardinia (Mediterranean), 80
Sargasso Sea (Central America) 78,
Saskatchewan (Canada), 190
Scandinavia, 70–1
Scientific Committee for Antarctic
    Research (SCAR), 206–7
Schweitzer, Albert, 92
Scilly, Isles of, 212–3
Scotland, 49, 70, 112, 118, 141, 148, 151–
    2, 157, 159, 180, 200, 204, 305
Scott, Peter, 119, 225, 227
Scottish Wildlife Trust, 157

Scythians, 42
Selkirk, Alexander, 97
Senegal, 202
Sennacherib, King of Assyria, 137
Sequoia National Park (California), 174, 183, 184, 185
Serengeti National Park (Tanzania), 93, 223, 234, 235
Setubal (Portugal), 79
Severn, River, 75, 211
Seychelles Islands (Indian Ocean), 93
Shackleton, Edward, Lord, 221
Shaftesbury, Anthony Ashley Cooper, 3rd Earl of, 143
Shannon River (Ireland), 74
Shark Bay (Australia), 96
Shelley, Percy Bysshe, 44
Shenandoah National Park (Virginia), 77
Shetland, 156
Siberia, 71, 72
Sicily, 80
Sidmouth, 151
Sierra Club, 174, 185
Sierra Nevada (California), 77, 295
Sinai (Egypt), 87
Singapore, 102
Smithson, James, 165, 169
Society for the Promotion of Nature Reserves, 62
soil *see* erosion
Soil Conservation Service (U.S.A.), 177, 181
Solomon, King of Israel, 136
Somalia, 202
South Africa, 99–100, 118, 197, 202, 303, 306
South America, 23, 37, 42, 50, 52, 53, 84, 89–91, 92, 94–5, 97–8, 113, 126, 190, 224, 265, 301, 303
South Georgia (Antarctica), 100
South Pole, 53, 100, 101
South Sandwich Islands (Pacific), 100
Spain, 80, 194, 228, 265, 266; Spanish Empire, 42, 89
Spoonbill, threat to, 191
Sport *see* Recreation
Stamp, Dudley, 140
Stockholm (Sweden), 71
Stolan, Victor, 226

Stonehenge, 39
Strasbourg (France), 205
Sudan, 86, 200, 297
Suez (Egypt), 236, 237
Sumatra (Indonesia), 52, 93
Sunda Strait, 93
Sussex Weald, 113
Swansea, 75
Sweden, 70, 194, 196
Switzerland, 115, 129, 193–4, 195, 226, 230
Sydney, Royal National Park near, 191
Syria, 81, 135

Tabiteuea (Gilbert Islands), 88
Taft, William Howard (U.S. President), 176, 184, 188
Tagus River, 79
Tahiti Island (Pacific), 94, 290
Taiwan (Formosa), 82
Talbot, Dr Lee M., 201
Tampico oilfield (Mexico), 83
Tanganyika, 202, 235, 236
Tanganyika, Lake (Congo/Tanzania), 93
Tansley, Sir Arthur G., 23, 25, 155, 158, 159, 198, 229, 231, 342
Tasman Sea, 97, 100
Tasmania, 100
Taurus Mountains (Asia Minor), 72, 81
Te Anau, Lake, 100
Te Heuheu Tukino (Maori chief), 190
Telford, Thomas, 149
Tennessee Valley Authority (TVA), 77, 177, 179, 180, 181
Tierra del Fuego, 100
Texas (U.S.A.), 304
Thailand, 87, 290, 294, 295, 300, 302, 304
Thomson, James, 150
Thoreau, Henry David, 164
Thornthwaite, Dr C. W., 53
Thotmes (Thutmosis) III, King of Egypt, 135
Tibesti Mountains, 86
Tibetan Plateau, 81
Tiglath Pileser I, King of Assyria, 136
Tigris River (Iraq), 38
Timber Culture Act (U.S., 1873), 168
Timor (Indonesia), 94

Tongariro National Park (New Zealand), 190

Torres Strait, 94

Torrey Canyon, 212–5, 348

tourism, effects of, 44, 83, 93, 105–6, 107, 110–1, 129, 151–2, 184, 202, 271–2

Trafalgar, battle of, 80

Transvaal (South Africa), 299

trapping, 71, 112, 118

Tristan da Cunha (Atlantic), 98, 213

Tropic of Cancer, 82, 87; of Capricorn, 94

Tsavo National Park (East Africa), 93

Tuamoto-Gambier Group (Pacific atolls) 94

Tunisia, 99

Turkey, 40, 134

Uccello, Paolo, 140

Udall, Stewart L., 175, 346

Udjun Kulong Nature Reserve (Java), 93

Uganda, 200, 203, 228

Ukraine, 75

Umfolozi Game Reserve (South Africa), 191

Unesco, 195, 199, 200, 217, 273

United Nations, 190, 195, 199, 201, 217, 231, 234

United States (U.S.A.), 52, 57, 58, 60, 76–8, 80, 83, 99, 110, 115, 120, 126, 151, 154, 155, 156, 160, 161, 291, 292, 293, 295, 297, 298, 299, 301, 302, 304, 305, 306; contribution to conservation, 162–87, 188, 189, 193, 194, 196, 197, 199, 200, 201, 202, 217, 218, 222, 223, 225, 229, 232, 237, 246, 249, 263, 267, 270, 285

U.S. Biological Survey, 169

Upper Volta, 202

Uppsala, International Council for Bird Preservation meeting at, 196

Uruguay, 98

Ural Mountains (Russia), 71

U.S.S.R. *see* Russia

Vallins, G. H., Spelling, 350

Vaux-le-Vicomte (France), gardens of, 192

Valparaiso (Chile), 97

van Straelen, Professor Victor, 191, 204

van Tienhoven, P. G., 194, 195

vegetation, types of, 49, 50–1, 53, 56–60, 288–307, 341–3

Venezuela, 123

Versailles (France), gardens of, 143, 192

Victoria, Queen, 190

Victoria (Australia), 100

Victoria Nyanza, Lake, 93, 235

Vienna, First Ornithological Congress at (1884), 196; ICSU meeting in (1963), 230

Vietnam, 82, 87, 183, 187

Virginia (U.S.A.), 150, 295

Vogt, William (*Road to Survival*), 223

volcanic activity, 36, 39, 48, 72, 78, 80, 82, 93, 94, 98, 102

Volta Dam, 273

Waialeale, Mount (Hawaiian Islands), 82

Wakamba tribe (Africa), 119

Wake Island (Pacific), 82

Wales, 74–5, 113, 127, 137, 139, 140, 148, 157, 159, 161, 194

Wallace, Alfred Russell, 153; Wallace Line, 94, 153

Walpole, Horace, 136

Walton Hall (Yorks), 156

Walvis Bay (South West Africa), 96

Warder, John A., 168

warfare, effects on nature, 43, 82, 93, 101, 105, 106

Warsaw (Poland), IUCN meeting at (1960), 201

Washburn, General C. C., 167

Washington (D.C.), 77, 78, 82, 163, 167, 168, 180, 183, 214, 237

Washington, George (U.S. President), 162

Waterloo, battle of, 44

Waterton, Charles, 156

Waterton Lakes (Canada), 188

West Indies, 52, 84

White, Gilbert (*Natural History of Selborne*), 18, 20

White House Conference on Natural Beauty (1965), 267, 270, 347

Whyte, R. O. (*The Rape of the Earth; A World Survey of Soil Erosion*), 223

Wild flowers, destruction of, 108–9
Wild Life Conservation General Committee, 24, 26
Wilderness Act (U.S. 1964), 186
Wildfowl Conservation, Meetings on, 204–5, 347
Williams-Ellis, Clough, 156
Willis, J. C. (*Agriculture in the Tropics*), quoted, 124
Willughby, Francis, 153
Windward Islands (West Indies), 84
Wirth, Conrad, 186
Wise, Henry, 144
Woburn Park, 155
Woodwalton Nature Reserve (Huntingdonshire), 61–2, 156
Wordsworth, William, 18, 44, 150
World War I, 156, 176, 179, 194
World War II, 23, 24, 62, 93, 106, 157, 203, 229, 281
World Wildlife Fund, 226–8, 348
Worthington, E. B., 202
Wye Agricultural College, 231

Yalta (Russia), 23
Yangtse River (China), 81
Yellow River (China), 38
Yellowstone National Park (Wyoming), 167, 168, 170, 173, 174, 183
Yemen, 86
Yenesei River (Russia), 71
York, Cape, 94
Yorkshire, 148, 153, 156
Yosemite National Park (California), 77, 166, 167, 170, 183, 184, 223
Yucatan (Mexico), 84
Yukon River (Alaska), 72

Zambia, 203
Zanzibar, 93
Zoo (London), 198
Zoological Society of London, 154, 155
Zuckerman, Sir Solly, 220
Zululand (South Africa), 118
Zuyder Zee, 191, 273

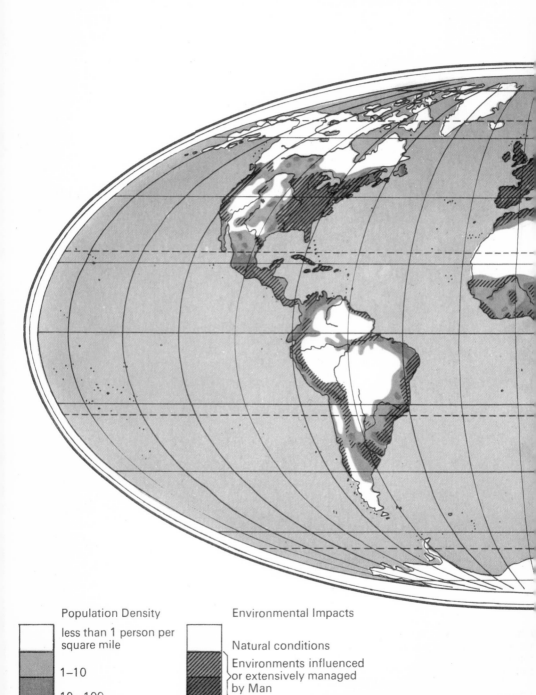

Population Density

less than 1 person per
square mile

1–10

10–100

100+

Environmental Impacts

Natural conditions

Environments influenced
or extensively managed
by Man

Artificial or modified environments:
urbanised or intensively cultivated areas